THEOLOGY TODAY

VOLUME I

Renewal in Dogma

EDITED BY JOHANNES FEINER, JOSEF TRÜTSCH,
AND FRANZ BÖCKLE WITH ESSAYS BY KARL
RAHNER, JOHANNES FEINER, ALOYS GRILLMEIER,
ALOIS MÜLLER, OTTO SEMMELROTH, THOMAS
SARTORY, EDWARD H. SCHILLEBEECKX, HANS
URS VON BALTHASAR

Translated by
PETER WHITE and RAYMOND H. KELLY

The Bruce Publishing Company
Milwaukee

Nihil obstat:

JOHN A. SCHULIEN, S.T.D.
Censor librorum

Imprimatur:

✠ WILLIAM E. COUSINS
Archbishop of Milwaukee

May 28, 1964

The *Nihil obstat* and *Imprimatur* are a declaration that a book
or pamphlet is considered to be free from doctrinal or moral
error. It is not implied that those who have granted the *Nihil
obstat* and *Imprimatur* agree with the contents, opinions or statements expressed.

Library of Congress Catalog Card Number: 64–24337

© 1965 THE BRUCE PUBLISHING COMPANY
MADE IN THE UNITED STATES OF AMERICA

INTRODUCTION

THE essays included in this volume reflect the dynamic, probing quality characteristic of leading Catholic theologians in Switzerland, Germany, and Holland. They are taken from the second part of *Fragen der Theologie Heute,** a work originally published in Switzerland in 1957 and now in its third edition. As the reader will discover, one of the outstanding features is the complete grasp these men have of contemporary Protestant thought and their appreciation of this thought as far as it bears relevance to the Catholic theologian's task of making the teaching revealed in Christ and proposed by the Church meaningful to twentieth-century man.

It is worth noting that these essays originally appeared before the Second Vatican Council was convened, for the reader will quickly realize that many of the positions taken by the authors of these essays foreshadowed the conciliar debates and that, indeed, the theology offered here has proved to be one of the most vigorous elements in promoting the *aggiornamento* so close to the heart of Pope John. Of special importance here are Alois Müller's essay on Mariology, Otto Semmelroth's probing inquiry into the meaning of the Church, and Thomas Sartory's illuminating and provocative study of the Church and the Churches. These significant and stimulating essays shed much light on the debates that have taken place at Vatican II over such questions as the relation between Mary and the Church, the juridical vs. the organic approach to ecclesiology, the challenge of ecumenism. The essays by Karl Rahner (on nature and grace), by Aloys Grillmeier (on Christology) and by Hans Urs von Balthasar (on eschatology) give readers a genuine insight into the work of speculative theology and its meaning for the Christian, for these essays show us some of the greatest living theologians in their task of seeking an understanding of what faith reveals. They show us that Anselm's description of theology as "faith seeking understanding" (*fides quaerens intellectum*) is as meaningful today

---

* The essays from the remaining two parts of this volume, on fundamental theology and moral theology respectively, will appear in English in the fall of 1965.

as it was in the eleventh century. Father Schillebeeckx, the brilliant young Dutch theologian, opens new horizons in sacramental theology in his essay "The Sacraments: An Encounter with God," and the reader will see immediately how successfully he has welded into a meaningful context the thought of Aquinas and the fresh insights provided by existential phenomenology. Finally, Father Feiner, in his study of man's origin, shows how Christian theologians should view the work of modern science — with open minds and fearless courage.

The bibliographies at the end of the volume have been specially prepared for this American edition of an important contemporary theological work by Father Gerald van Ackeren, S.J., and his staff on *Theology Digest* at St. Mary's College, Kansas. We are grateful to him and, to his associates: W. J. Weiler, S.J., B. Biever, S.J., A. R. Marlow, S.J., T. J. Shanahan, S.J., L. A. McKeown, S.J., T. A. Duggan, S.J., J. Wambach, S.J., and M. J. Garland, S.J. Finally, we are grateful to the translators, Messrs. Peter White and Raymond Kelly, for their part in bringing this important study to the English-speaking public.

CONTENTS

NATURE AND GRACE[1]

THE question of "Nature and Grace" is discussed today largely only in highly specialized professional circles. However, the subject is being discussed again at least there and not merely adverted to in manuals of the schools. Serious theologians are today discussing this question with impassioned commitment. Men realize that complete agreement on every aspect of the question is nonexistent, and that, furthermore, the controversy which began and continues is no mere academic quarrel. That is precisely what should give us true cause for rejoicing. For since the attenuation of the controversy between Catholic and Protestant theologians in the eighteenth century and since the thin-blooded theology of the enlightenment gave place to the reevaluation and restoration of scholastic theology in the nineteenth century, the opinion ruled more or less generally that the files were closed on the question of "nature and grace," that theologians were in general agreement on the subject, and furthermore, that the authorities already knew practically everything worth knowing about it.

In attempting to describe the common, ordinary understanding of nature and grace which has prevailed in post-Tridentine and neo-scholastic theology particularly, one must stress that this understanding has truly been *ordinary*. Naturally, contemporary theology embraces the entire wealth of yesterday, indeed of all the past. Nothing is ever wholly forgotten in the Church. And a truth that has been formally defined in theology always contains countless implications which are really part of it, although unexpressed. Thus it is not difficult to accuse the image issuing from the ordinary comprehension

---

[1] This essay of Father Rahner is also found in another translation in the Sheed & Ward book, *Nature and Grace*, by Karl Rahner (New York, 1964).

of a question in the regular seminary theology of distortion and in-
justice. Such common, everyday understanding does exist. And it
often has more relevance to life in the Church than the more
sublime kinds of knowledge, the exclusive property of the few.

Precisely what was the ordinary conception of the relationship
between nature and supernatural grace which was peculiar to neo-
scholasticism? In order to see this conception for what it was (though
never consciously held as such), we must set out from an aspect of
the doctrine of grace that seems to concern only a peripheral problem
of theology. It is the notion that supernatural grace, through which
man is justified and through which he can perform meritorious works,
is something in itself utterly beyond consciousness. But this is only an
opinion, and one that has always been disputed. For Thomistic
theology always contended that a supernatural act must have a
formal object which can never be attained by a merely natural
act. Still the opposing opinion prevailed and shaped the standard,
everyday outlook dominant in the schools. According to this
opinion supernatural grace is a reality which is known at least
partially through the teaching of faith, but which is in itself fundamentally inaccessible and cannot be detected in the conscious,
personal life of men. Men must be taught of its existence through
faith, they must align themselves to it, take care (through moral
acts and reception of the sacraments) to possess it, and treasure
it as the divinization of their being, as the token and guarantee of
eternal life. But that sphere of personal being where a person lives
with himself and experiences life in his own way is not marked by
this grace; and this is, of course, the sphere of life of which a man
is immediately conscious. What a person experiences of the spirituality and morality of his acts (in distinction to their intentional
purposes), is exactly the same as it would be if (though theoretically
it might be otherwise) there simply were no supernatural "elevation" in these acts. Grace, therefore, according to this widely held
view is a superstructure beyond consciousness, beyond the conscious
existence of the spiritual and moral man. And this is so even
though it is a known object of his faith, even though it is acknowledged as the highest, as something divine, as the *sine qua non* of
salvation.

It even seems as though this notion is the correct one, something to be taken for granted. For a person cannot really know

whether he is in the state of grace or not (one can only assume indirectly, from certain indicative circumstances, something about it with a certain degree of probability). A person does not "notice" anything about grace (at best, it is possible to observe something of those essentially natural helps conferred by "saving" grace as an aid to keeping the natural law). The most elementary personal experience as well as the teaching of the Council of Trent[2] (Denz. 802, 805, 825, 826) seem to substantiate this opinion as practically self-evident. Provided one has grace, then the area within which we suppose ourselves to be acting spiritually and morally seems immediately identical with the dimensions of "nature" in the theological sense. This state of things actually becomes one's working definition of what is meant by the term "nature," or that which we experience of ourselves without need for verbal clarification. For that alone is nature and *only* nature. To look at the matter from the other end, nature alone and its acts make up that life which we experience as our own. Our natural intelligence and natural behavior, etc., are the elements from which alone we build up those acts in which we relate ourselves intentionally to the realities of the mysteries revealed by God. We know that these natural acts are ontologically raised (but only in this way) to a supernatural level. Supernatural "illumination," ethical "impulses" and "inspirations" to perform good acts, "light" of faith, "pains of the Holy Spirit," etc., these and similar expressions of Scripture and Tradition (pathos, or groaning of the spirit, etc.) are reduced either to this entitative elevation of our natural moral acts, or else to influences of a psychological order, purely natural in themselves (yet regarded as providentially directed to supernatural salvation).

---

[2] On this, cf. A. Stakemeier, *Das Konzil von Trient über die Heilsgewissheit* (Heidelberg, 1947); V. Heynck, "Das Votum des Generals der Konventualen Bonaventura Costacciaro vom 26 Nov. 1546 über die Gnadengewissheit," *Franz. Studien*, 31 (1949), pp. 274–304, 350–395; Fr. Buuck, "Zum Rechtfertigungsdekret. Die Unterscheidung zwischen fehlbarem und unfehlbarem Glauben in den vorbereitenden Verhandlungen," and Fr. J. Schierse, "Das Trienter Konzil und die Frage nach der christlichen Gewissheit," both in Georg Schreiber, *Das Weltkonzil von Trient* (Freiburg, 1951), Vol. I, pp. 117–167; G. M. Lachance, "L'Homme peut-il savoir qu'il a la grâce?" *Revue de l'Université Ottawa*, 24 (1954), pp. 65–92; M. Guérard des Lauriers, "St. Augustin et la question de la certitude de la grâce au Concile de Trente," in *Augustinus Magister* (Congrès International, Aug. 1954), Communications, Vol. 2, pp. 1057–1067; L. M. Poliseno, "I Carmelitani et la certezza dello stato di grazia nel Concilio Tridentino," *Carmelus*, I (1954), pp. 111–145.

In short, the relationship between nature and grace is so understood that they appear as two superincumbent levels, each entirely
provident for its own needs, which interfere with one another as
little as possible. Accordingly, the orientation of nature toward grace
is conceived in the most negative sense possible. Grace is, in fact,
an unsurpassable perfecting of nature. Indeed, as the Lord of this
nature, God can demand that men comply with His undeniably
existing will for their supernatural life and purpose, and that they
open themselves to grace. Of itself, however, nature possesses to
that end only an "obediential potency" which is to be understood
in its most negative possible sense: the mere noncontradiction of
such an elevation of nature. Left to itself, nature would perfect
itself contentedly and harmoniously in its own province, in merely
natural ends, independent of a direct and unmediated encounter
with God in the Beatific Vision. Where nature is found in immediate
possession of itself (which is proper to the essence of spirit: *reditio
completa in seipsum*), it may be regarded as "pure nature." There
is a well-known axiom — which is nonetheless only an opinion —
which distinguishes real or concrete nature from "mere nature,"
sicut spoliatus a nudo. Here the "deprivation" is tacitly conceived
as a purely extrinsic aspect of the absence of saving grace, relating
this absence to a decree of God "requiring" its presence and to
an historical cause in the past, Adam's sin. There is here no thought
given to the possibility that the lack or absence might be essentially
different in the case of "mere" nature from what it is in the case
of "fallen" nature.

We cannot exonerate this ordinary conception from the charge
of "extrinsicism" (as it has been called) — granted, it can be shown
that all the aspects of the magisterium's concept of the relationship between nature and grace can be kept intact when one takes
this relationship in a more narrow sense than is commonly expressed in this widely held notion. Nor need we object (though
it is sometimes painful to be reminded of it) that such a stand
contains some dangers in its practical implications. For if this
stand is right, then the life experienced by the spiritual man is
enacted within the limits of his mere nature. The latter has two
sectors. First is the realm of "pure nature," which (prescinding
from its "elevation" beyond pure consciousness) is enacted entirely
within the dimension of mere nature. Second is the level of knowl-

edge, where subjectivity arises by purely natural means (insofar as it is concerned with the spiritual or immaterial order as such) and is related to the supernatural order only objectively, formally (in faith, in good intentions, etc.). If this is actually the case, there is no need to be surprised when we find that an individual is hardly interested in this mysterious superstructure of his existence, since grace is in fact not *there* where *he* is, i.e., in the immediate survey of his spiritual existence. The impression can be drawn (albeit unjustly) that what was originally called grace, in the course of the medieval history of dogma, came to be considered as a work of nature, an actualization of a potential proper to nature (e.g., the power to love God above all things), and that in order to cast a veil over that change grace was placed above nature as a "supernature." Thus grace came to be considered as an unconscious mode of the spiritual, ethical part of nature and was then relegated beyond consciousness, so that one could not say clearly any more just what role it played in the life of man.

Let us take for example the distinction between a natural and a supernatural "love of God above all else." Surely this distinction is in a reasonable sense just. But how are we to distinguish these two loves from one another as *love,* i.e., as *spiritual,* if the supernaturality of the supernatural love consists *solely* in an entitative "elevation"? Is modern naturalism entirely wrong when it *too* takes its departure from this theory? Can we deny that modern disinterest in the supernatural order could develop only on the basis of this notion of grace, a notion unmistakably nominalistic in some ways?

Theological controversy over the correctness or adequacy of this notion has opened up again. The causes occasioning it were numerous.

Philosophically, an important role must be given to the kind of scholastic philosophy connected with the work of J. Maréchal.[3] In his intellectual, transcendental dynamism, Maréchal conceives man's fundamental essence (to the extent that he is spirit by nature) as *desiderium naturale visionis beatificae* (to render Maréchal

---

[3] In this brief theological essay no bibliography will be given of this philosophical movement, so important in the meeting of scholastic and modern philosophy. Many Catholic philosophers today are indebted to a greater or less extent to the teaching of Maréchal, e.g., Hayen, A. Gregoire, Siewerth, Max Müller, K. Lotz, and others.

directly in a Thomistic formula). This desire actually remains conditioned and consequently does not annul the freedom of the real calling through grace to the direct vision of God. Yet it is a reason for every spiritual act, a real and existing longing for absolute being — although not explicitly and conceptually formulated — and is the a priori condition of all affirmative knowledge of the finite object. We can see in Maréchal's return to the doctrine of the *desiderium naturale* of the direct vision of God how a by-product of Thomas' thought became the central notion for understanding a spiritual nature. Quite naturally, then, theologians of a quarter of a century ago carried on a long discussion of how this *desiderium naturale* of Maréchal and his school was to be understood and how it could be shown to be compatible with the Church's teaching concerning the supernaturality and completely unmerited character of the direct vision of God.[4] At any rate, the notion developed that the ordering of man as spirit to God is not something simply "added" to him and that an ordering of this kind, even if it is only an implicit and a priori transcendental, literally makes man to be the self he experiences and the self he can keep down and suppress only through sin — even then his self is affirmed (also as an implicit and transcendental a priori) in every act of his spiritual existence.

Look at the matter now from the point of view of the history of theology.[5] Here we find that various investigations into the history

---

[4] Cf., for example, E. Brisbois, "Désir naturel et vision de Dieu," *Nouvelle Revue Théologique*, 54 (1927), pp. 81–97; H. Lennerz, "Kann die Vernunft die Möglichkeit der beseligenden Anschauung Gottes beweisen?" *Scholastik*, 5 (1930), pp. 102–108; H. Lennerz, "Ist die Anschauung Gottes ein Geheimnis?" *Scholastik*, 7 (1932), pp. 208–232; M. Corvez, "Est-il possible de démontrer l'existence en Dieu d'un ordre de mystères strictement surnaturels?" *Revue Thomiste*, 37 (1932), pp. 660–667; R. Garrigou-Lagrange, "La possibilité de la vision béatifique peut-elle se démontrer?" *Revue Thomiste*, 38 (1933), pp. 669–688; further literature is found in the *Bulletin Thomiste*, 1932, pp. 745–769; 1935, pp. 896–907; 1937, pp. 632–643, 728; P. Descoqs, *Le Mystère de notre élévation surnaturelle* (Paris, 1938); further literature in Z. Alszeghy, *Gregorianum*, 31 (1950), pp. 444–446. Connected with this whole question is the problem whether or not man's ordering to God, as proposed by Maréchal, can demonstrate at least the possibility of the Beatific Vision. It is impossible to enter into this subject here.

[5] Only a small sampling of the literature of the past twenty-five years can be given here. Biblical theology will be omitted, because on the whole it has, unfortunately, had little influence on the dogmatic theology of the schools during this period. First we must mention the survey of the whole history

of the theological reflective knowledge of the supernatural and its distinction from nature also began to shake the structure. We learned to appreciate that the prevailing theological notion of the supernatural (and of nature as its opposite) has developed only very slowly and

of the theology of grace by Rondet, then a few works on patrology, then medieval and modern histories of the theology of grace: H. Rondet, *Gratia Christi: Essai d'histoire du dogme et de théologie dogmatique* (Paris, 1948); H. Rahner, "Die Gottesgeburt. Die Lehre der Kirchenväter von der Geburt Christi im Herzen der Gläubigen," *Zeitschrift für katholische Theologie,* 59 (1935), pp. 333–418; E. Mersch, *The Whole Christ* (Milwaukee, 1942), Chaps. 1–2; A. Lieske, *Die Theologie der Logomystik bei Origines* (Münster, 1938); J. Gross, *La Divinisation du chrétien d'après les pères grecs* (Paris, 1938); A. Lieske, "Zur Theologie der Christusmystik Gregors von Nyssa," *Scholastik,* 14 (1939), pp. 408–514; J. Loosen, *Logos und Pneuma in begnadeten Menschen bei Maximus Confessor* (Münster, 1941); A. Mayer, *Das Bild Gottes im Menschen nach Clemens von Alexandrien* (Rome, 1942); H. Urs von Balthasar, *Présence et pensée. Essai sur la philosophie religieuse de Grégoire de Nysse* (Paris, 1942); J. B. Schoemann, "Gregors von Nyssa theologische Anthropologie als Bildtheologie," *Scholastik,* 18 (1943), pp. 31, 53, 175–200; J. Daniélou, *Platonisme et théologie mystique. Essai sur la doctrine spirituelle de saint Grégoire de Nysse* (Paris, 1944); H. du Manoir, *Dogme et spiritualité chez saint Cyrille d'Alexandrie* (Paris, 1945); P. Galtier, *Le Saint-Esprit en nous d'après les pères grecs* (Rome, 1946); A. Lieske, "Die Theologie der Christusmystik Gregors von Nyssa," *Zeitschrift für katholische Theologie,* 70 (1948), pp. 49–93, 129–168, 315–340; J. Grabowski, "St. Augustine and the Presence of God," *Theological Studies,* 13 (1952), pp. 336–348; E. Braem, "Augustinus' leer over de heiligmakende genade," *Augustiniana,* I (1951), pp. 7–20, 77–90; II (1952), pp. 201–204; III (1953), pp. 328–340; IV (1954), pp. 196–204; H. Merki, *Homoiosis Theo. Von der platonischen Angleichung an Gott zur Gottähnlichkeit bei Gregor von Nyssa* (Freiburg, Switzerland, 1952); H. Doms, *Die Gnadenlehre des seligen Albertus Magnus* (Breslau, 1929); J. Schupp, *Die Gnadenlehre des Petrus Lombardus* (Freiburg, 1932); F. Stegmüller, *Zur Gnadenlehre des jungen Suarez* (Freiburg, 1933); F. Stegmüller, *Francisco de Vitoria y la doctrina de la gracia en la escuela salmantina* (Barcelona, 1934); F. Stegmüller, *Geschichte des Molinismus I: Neue Molinaschriften* (Münster, 1935); E. Köster, *Die Heilslehre des Hugo von St. Viktor* (Emsdetten, 1940); H. Bouillard, *Conversion et grâce chez saint Thomas d'Aquin* (Paris, 1944); R. C. Dhont, *Le Problème de la préparation à la grâce. Débuts de l'école franciscaine* (Paris, 1946); M. Flick, *L'Attimo della giustificazione secondo S. Tommaso* (Rome, 1947); Z. Alzeghy, "La teologia dell'ordine soprannaturale nella scolastica antica," *Gregorianum,* 31 (1950), pp. 414–450 (survey of recent literature); S. Gonzalez Rivas, "Suarez frente al misterio de la inhabitacion," *Estudios Eclesiasticos,* 24 (1950), pp. 341–366; J. Auer, *Entwicklung der Gnadenlehre in der Hochscholastik mit besonderer Berücksichtigung des Kardinals Matteo d'Aquasparta,* I (Freiburg, 1942), II (Freiburg, 1951); A. M. Landgraf, *Dogmengeschichte der Frühscholastik,* Part I, Vols. 1–2: *Die Gnadenlehre* (Regensburg, 1951–1952); H. Lais, *Die Gnadenlehre des hl. Thomas in der Summa contra Gentiles und der Kommentar des Franziskus Sylvestris von Ferrara* (Munich,

that the elaboration and application of these notions to individual theological problems has been gradual. (Among these problems are: the necessity of distinctly supernatural and interior grace for every meritorious act; the possibility of distinguishing between natural and supernatural morality; the distinction between supernatural actual grace and habitual grace; the exclusion of any positive preparation for justification through moral acts which are not begun by the specific grace of salvation; the conceivability of a purely natural end for man beyond the grave; etc.) On the whole one can say that this development was carried out legitimately and was no more than the unfolding of those dogmas explicitly set forth in the data of revelation. Thus one cannot say that this development has been erratic. One might say that the teaching on grace and nature reached a point of development in St. Thomas where future developments were clearly visible in him. This does not mean to the point reached in theology with Cajetan and with the post-Tridentine period in general. From our vantage point, it is possible to see this development more clearly. It is now possible to see the fallacy of reading all subsequent insights and criticism into earlier theology. And because we see that, we are in a better position than ever to ask whether some valuable insights of earlier times have not been lost during such progress, whether our gains have not been bought with heavy losses, and whether in fact it is not imperative to regain, to possess anew, much that was possessed by theologians before. It may be that some studies of the history of dogma exaggerate the difference between the medieval (especially the Thomistic) and the post-Tridentine theology of grace. It may very well be that even the "Augustinian" theology of grace in the seventeenth and eighteenth centuries contains certain elements which may not be considered valid today, even though a pope, Benedict XIV, defended them against the accusation of a secret Jansenism. But it is necessary for us to acknowledge the complexity of spiritual history, to see that it cannot be oversimplified. Such oversimplification occurs, for example, when we view the

---

1951); J. Alfaro, *Lo natural y lo sobrenatural. Estudio historico desde santo Thomas hasta Cayetano (1274–1534)* (Madrid, 1952); O. Lottin, *Psychologie et morale aux XII° et XIII° siècles* (Louvain, 1942–1954), I, II, III, 1–2, IV, 1–2; W. A. van Roo, *Grace and Original Justice according to St. Thomas* (Rome, 1955); Z. Alzeghy, *Nova creatura. La nozione della grazia nei commentari medievali di S. Paolo* (Rome, 1956).

history of dogma as the struggle between the unchangeable truths presented clearly and serenely by genuinely orthodox theologians and the erroneous teachings of heretics. Only by looking back into history can we catch sight of the doctrine at stake and see how we have come to the definitive, indestructible achievement of contemporary theology; only in this way can we discover truths which were seen in earlier ages, but which may be forgotten in a classroom theology that always courts dangerously close to considering the handy and simplified form of a doctrine as the criterion of truth and sacred Tradition. In this way we discover that in St. Thomas, for instance, the notion of the "natural desire for the Beatific Vision" is perhaps not merely an "historically" explicable bit of atavism coming from a period of theology which was not yet so aware of the supernaturality and indefectibility of the direct vision of God (as it is with St. Thomas). We discover that behind our hesitation to see a truly supernatural actual grace (alongside the habitual grace) lies not simply a suspicion which is overcome only with time and effort, a suspicion which fails to see how the redemptive acts which precede justification and which could not take place without grace necessarily demand the existence of such a grace.[6] We discover that even today we can learn something from Aquinas about the interplay of sacraments and personal acts, which came to be more or less forgotten or diluted in subsequent theology. We discover that medieval theology had deeper and greater thoughts about "uncreated grace" than did the post-Tridentine theology, which deduced the "indwelling of the Holy Spirit" more or less exclusively from the "created grace" which the Counterreformation regarded only too frequently as grace pure and simple.

A third impetus for a theological reexamination of the relationship between nature and grace comes from the newly revived dialogue with Protestant theology.[7] As a matter of necessity, Protestant

---

[6] St. Thomas considered the genuine acts of "preparation" for justification as acts of justification "taking over," as acts done with the grace of justification already present; hence he did not need to be concerned very much with the acts of preparation which precede justification in time; he has thus something new to tell *us,* not only we him.

[7] Among Catholic works we can mention here only the following: H. Urs von Balthasar, "Deux Notes sur Karl Barth," *Récherches de science religieuse* (1948), pp. 92–111; J. Hamer, *Karl Barth. Essay on the method of dogma* (Eng. tr.) (Westminster, Md., 1962); H. Volk, *Emil Brunners Lehre von dem Sünder* (Münster, 1950); H. Urs von Balthasar, *Karl Barth, Darstellung*

theology must also inquire into the relationship between nature and grace (even if from other points of view); and it has faced this problem from fresh points of view: as related to the Bible, as related to Luther, as related to Protestant theology's conflict with modern humanism and with Anglo-Saxon, American optimism. Protestant theology was forced to ask just what is left of man's being when he is a sinner, and to what extent he remains a sinner when he is justified. It holds fast to the classical Lutheran doctrine that there is absolutely nothing good (nothing profitable to *salvation*) in man without grace. But with this assertion (which, correctly understood, must be affirmed by a Catholic too) the question only begins, and it is at this point that new possibilities for discussion with Catholic theology are opened up. And they have not been left unexploited. Catholic theologians (admittedly only a few to begin with) have felt it their duty to ask again just what is right in the Protestant assertions and how they might be made more clearly applicable for us. Many topics come up for discussion here. Among them are the Christocentric value of all creation and salvation; the worth of evidence which suggests that the supernaturality of grace does not mean reducing man to a closed, self-contained, and finished system in his "natural" existence, for whom grace is simply a superstructure leaving utterly unchanged his underlying being. Then, too, it is necessary to ask whether and in what sense a Catholic understanding of the axiom *"simul iustus et peccator"* is feasible. Here it is possible to bring out those existentialist, actualist, and personalist elements which are encountered even in the traditional Catholic notion of grace, and which are particularly appropriate for clarifying any misconceptions of "traditional" theology, for determining whether infused ontological grace necessarily involves an unjustifiable distortion of the biblical notion of grace.

We need not insist at length that the spirit and mentality of our day have, of necessity, a stimulating effect upon theology. Contemporary thought is seeking a unified idea of man, a synthetic view of his reality in all its diversity. Today we are thinking "existentially." And hence we attempt, to the utmost of our abilities, to "live" the reality of grace where we are ourselves in our existence.

und Deutung seiner Theologie (Cologne, 1951); A. Ebneter, *Der Mensch in der Theologie Karl Barths* (Zürich, 1952); H. Küng, *Justification. The Teaching of Karl Barth and a Catholic Reflection* (Eng. tr.) (New York, 1964).

We strive to see supernatural grace (not only healing grace!) as the entelechy, the power of concretely *alive* existence. In line with other trends in the modern consciousness, we are not content to see grace merely as the premise and substance of individual salvation, and we turn our consideration more expressly than ever before to the ecclesial aspects of the doctrine of grace, to grace in the history of salvation outside organized Christianity, to the possibility of grace and of holiness in the world of non-Christian religions.

We turn now to mention several "outcomes" of these theological movements, but it is naturally not a question of results which have already been accepted officially or become simply *sententia communis*. Church doctrine develops only with extreme circumspection. This is especially the case today, when the immediate questions of the moment (above all, questions of morals) and of Mariology exact even more attention than much more profound theological issues, since these inevitably require a long time in maturing. Hence we shall touch on our question only very vaguely because of space limitations, purposing only to set our reader's sights on the essential directions in which these theological efforts are moving.

We can very well expect the question of "uncreated grace" to be pushed further.[8] Pius XII pointed out in his encyclical *Mystici*

---

[8] Some recent works on the problems connected with the question of uncreated grace and the appropriated or unappropriated indwelling of the divine Persons include: H. Kuhaupt, *Die Formalursache der Gotteskindschaft* (Münster, 1940); H. Schauf, *Die Einwohnung des Heiligen Geistes. Die Lehre von der nichtappropriierten Einwohnung des Heiligen Geistes als Beitrag zur Theologiegeschichte des neunzehnten Jahrhunderts unter besonderer Berücksichtigung der beiden Theologen Carl Passaglia und Clemens Schrader* (Freiburg, 1941); Philip J. Donnelly, "The Inhabitation of the Holy Spirit: A Solution According to de la Taille," *Theological Studies,* 8 (1947), pp. 445–470; J. Trütsch, *SS. Trinitatis inhabitatio apud theologos recentiores* (Trent, 1949); S. J. Dockx, *Fils de Dieu par grâce* (Paris, 1948); C. Sträter, "Het begrip 'appropriatie' bij S. Thomas," *Bijdragen,* 9 (1948), pp. 1–41, 144–186; J. H. Nicolas, "Présence trinitaire et présence de la Trinité," *Revue Thomiste,* 50 (1950), pp. 183–191; J. Fitzgerald, *De Inhabitatione Spiritus Sancti Doctrina Sancti Thomae Aquinatis* (Mundelein, 1950); R. Morency, *L'Union de grâce selon saint Thomas d'Aquin* (Montreal, 1950); P. Galtier, *L'habitation en nous des trois personnes* (Rome, 1950); H. P. C. Lyons, "The Grace of Sonship," *Ephemerides Theologicae Lovaniensis,* 27 (1951), pp. 438–466; C. Kaliba, *Die Welt als Gleichnis des dreieinigen Gottes. Entwurf zu einer trinitärischen Ontologie* (Salzburg, 1952); P. de Letter, "Sanctifying Grace and Our Union With the Holy Trinity," *Theological Studies,* 13 (1952), pp. 35–58; P. J. Donnelly, "Sanctifying Grace and Our

Corporis that certain questions are open here, and are being kept open consciously by the teaching office of the Church. As Pius XII makes clear, grace and glory are two stages of one and the same divinization of man. Furthermore, classical theology has always stressed that in glory God communicates Himself to the created spirit possessing grace and that this self-communication is not the *efficient*-causal creation of a created quality or entity distinct from God, but the (quasi formal-causal) sharing of God Himself with man. If this is the case, then this thought can be applied to the theology of grace much more expressly than ever before. "Uncreated grace" then appears no longer as the mere consequence of the creation of "infused" static grace, as the accompaniment of a "physical accident," but rather as the true center in grace. (This also accounts much more effectively for the strict character of mystery in grace, since a purely created entity can never, as such, be an absolute mystery.) God shares Himself with man in His own reality. This is, in fact, the very mystery and fullness of grace. By giving full weight to this consideration, we can more easily cross over to the mystery of the Incarnation and to that of the Most Holy Trinity.

The opinion (advanced earlier by Petavius, Scheeben, and others, each in his own way) seems to be gaining ground that in grace a relationship is established between man and each of the three divine Persons, and that this relationship is not an appropriation, but a *proprium* of each divine Person. If one accepts that the immediate vision of God can rest only upon a quasi-formal self-communication of the God whom one thereby sees, and not (at least not adequately) upon a created quality in the spirit of man, and if one then considers (as is indeed self-evident) that the three divine Persons are each in their personal character the object of this immediate vision, then that entitative quasi-formal communication of God, which is, instead of a *species impressa,* the ontological reason in man for his knowing possession of God, must also contain a nonappropriated relationship to each of the divine Persons. From

Union With the Holy Trinity: A Reply," *Theological Studies;* 13 (1952), pp. 309–335; P. de Letter, "Current Theology, Sanctifying Grace and the Divine Indwelling," *Theological Studies,* 14 (1953), pp. 242–272; F. Bourassa, "Présence de Dieu et union aux divines personnes." *Sciences Ecclesiastiques,* 6 (1954), pp. 3–23; K. Rahner, "Concerning the Relationship Between Nature and Grace," *Theological Investigations* (Eng. tr.), Vol. I (Baltimore, 1962), pp. 297–318.

here it is possible to rethink the theology of the Trinity: to achieve a better understanding of the Trinity both in the inner life of the Triune God and in the economy of salvation (where various works are appropriated to Father, Son, and Holy Spirit). In this way the highest mystery of the Christian faith would appear more clearly as a reality which man encounters not only notionally (and through the Incarnation of the Logos) but also in the actual living of his life of grace. One could see not only that God is triune in Himself but also that He even communicates Himself as the Triune God (namely, in grace, which does not mean only an efficient causality of God outside Himself as a *creatio ex nihilo*). It still remains true that where God operates as efficient cause, the effect is that of the whole Trinity as of one cause.

One might, and perhaps should, go still further. It is customary to regard the connection between the Incarnation and the order of grace as a simple fact.[9] God wished, as a matter of fact, that the order of grace should depend upon the *Verbum incarnatum*. There is the tacit presupposition that it might have been otherwise. Is this presupposition unequivocally and certainly valid? The order of grace and the Incarnation are indeed both founded upon a free grace of God. But does it follow that these two objects of the free grace of God, in each of which He communicates Himself, differently in either case to be sure, are *two* distinct works of His loving freedom? God's primordial deed includes everything that follows, and for Scotus this deed is the self-divesting of the God who is self-giving love. Is there any Catholic principle which forbids us to affirm that this primordial self-divesting, which is consummated in the Incarnation, established simultaneously the order of grace, which would, we may presume, be unthinkable without this decision of God for a personal self-alienation? Moreover, who can assail with unequivocal arguments a theologian who adopts the position that the *possibility* of creation is based upon the possibility of the Incarnation, even if the reality of creation (as nature) does not necessarily include the actual realization of God's self-alienation by way of the Incarnation? This position has much to recommend

---

[9] Cf. N. Sanders, "Een bovennatuurlijke orde mogelijk zonder Christus?" *Studia Catholica*, 29 (1954), pp. 152–158; K. Rahner, "Zur Theologie der Weihnachtsfeier," *Schriften zur Theologie* (Einsiedeln, 1956), Vol. III, pp. 35–46; K. Rahner, "Die ewige Bedeutung der Menschheit Jesu für unser Gottesverhältnis," *Schriften zur Theologie*, III, pp. 47–60.

it, above all its sublime simplicity; and in addition it is implicit
in the theology of the Logos as developed by the ante-Nicene and
pre-Augustinian Fathers. If it is adopted, it confers a radically
Christological character to the theology of grace; the Word-come-
into-the-world is not only the actual mediator of grace through His
merit (which is necessary only because Adam has forfeited this
grace), but it is He who creates, in His free act of becoming incarnate, the orders of nature and grace in the world, creating nature
as the prerequisite condition for His entering the world, and grace
as His environment. This position would lead us, as we have said,
to a deeper understanding of the Trinity in its immanent life. The
Word would not simply be one of three divine Persons any One of
whom could have become man if He willed, but He would be *the*
Person in whom God communicates Himself hypostatically to the
world: the Incarnation would reflect the personal character of the
second divine Person, the Word as such. As a result, the work
appropriated to the three divine Persons in the economy of salvation gives us an insight into the immanent life of the Trinity. An
insight of this kind must be possible, because the axiom which
affirms that God's action as the efficient cause of beings other than
Himself is a causality of the one God without distinction of Persons
cannot be applied to this quasi-formal causality. At this point, we
should rethink the speculation of ante-Nicene and Greek theology
in general. It almost seems that Augustine understood little of the
thought of older theology on the Word as He who appears, and
must appear, if God wills to show Himself to the world.

A better grasp of what is meant by "uncreated grace" helps lead
us to a clearer understanding of the fact that Catholic theology
of grace can go beyond the conception of grace as a *merely* entitative created state and consequently as a merely "ontological" and
nonexistential result of a "physical accident."[10] Catholic theology,
in making this advance, is true to its fundamental principle, which
views grace not only as pardon for poor sinners but also and more
significantly as the "sharing in divine nature." Grace is God Himself; it is the communication of Himself, the giving of Himself to
man as the benevolence which He is, and a giving which makes
man divine. Here His work is truly His own being, Himself, as the

---

[10] J. Auer, "Um den Begriff der Gnade," *Zeitschrift zur katholischen Theologie,* 70 (1948), pp. 341–368.

reality shared with man. Such grace cannot be conceived in any way as separable from the personal love of God and its response in man. This grace is not thought of "objectively"; it is not a question of something which would be at man's disposal save in the sense that God lets Himself be disposed of in a way proper to the most free grace, to the wonder of love. In pondering divine mysteries we nonetheless think in ontological, yes Catholic, categories, and indeed this is necessary for a Catholic philosophy. It is necessary because reality — and what could be more real and more telling than the love of God? — must be thought of as "real" and as "being," the highest things must be expressed in the most abstract language. So it is with the work of divine love toward us which precedes our work, precisely because it is God's and not ours, however much it frees us not only for suffering, but for works. This work of divine love must necessarily be conceived as lying behind our ethics and belief, making them possible and therefore it can be stated only in categories of being (state, accident, habit, infusion, etc.). These abstract modes of expressing things never confuse the person who understands them. Correctly understood, they do not obstruct one's view of the fact that grace always remains the free act of divine love, over which man has "disposal" only to the extent that he is "disposed" to do so by this divine love. Of course one should always bear in mind that God does not become smaller when we grow greater. And finally Christianity is not a religion whose fundamental motif would be the fear that it must necessarily go to our heads (rather than to our grateful heart) when one praises, with a view to praising God, the greatness to which God has exalted man. Such it is in Mariology. And so also it is in the theology of grace, of which Mariology is only the most beautiful part.

This grace also transforms our conscious life, and not only in its essence but also in its being, its existence. The Thomistic teaching[11] on the specific object of acts that have been raised to the

---

[11] This is not the place to cite textbooks which discuss this matter. Only in passing, we should note that this question is of great significance for the problem of the foundation of faith. Cf. A. Lang, *Die Wege der Glaubensbegründung bei den Theologen des 14. Jahrhunderts* (Münster, 1930); F. Schlagenhaufen, "Die Glaubensgewissheit und ihre Begründung in der Neuscholastik," *Zeitschrift zur katholische Theologie*, 56 (1932), pp. 313–374, 530–595; G. Engelhardt, *Die Entwicklung der dogmatischen Glaubenpsycho-*

level of supernatural being must be thought through afresh and
brought to the fore — and remember this object is one which can
be attained in its formal, specifying being by no natural act. "Object"
in the Thomistic sense does not in any way signify a "thing simply
given as something standing 'out there,' distinguishable from others
by reflection and seen *alongside* others." A formal object is neither
a "thing," an item of knowledge nor a supplementary, abstracting
summary of the elements common to many single objects, but the
conscious, a priori horizon against which everything is recognized
in our grasp of individual objects given a posteriori; that is, it is
the horizon conditioning and making possible our grasp of what
is genuinely an object-thing. Once the scholastic doctrine of the
formal object as the a priori "light" under and in which all objects
are considered, it is not possible to attack the Thomistic thesis of
the supernatural formal object by resorting to "experience." For
experience clearly could note nothing of any formal object, of an
"object-thing" in its formality. It is necessary to add only that an
a priori formal object of an act is quite different from a formal
object unequivocally and conceptually *distinguishable* from another
formal object by subsequent reflection. For a metaphysics of knowledge there is no particular difficulty in seeing why reflective consciousness has difficulty in distinguishing clearly the overall transcendence of spirit in being — its natural openness to being in its
totality — from its supernatural transcendence, its transcendence as
spirit opened and borne by grace, particularly when there is at stake
each of its acts supernaturally exalted to the God of eternal life,
to the immediate experience of the triune divine Being. This difficulty of distinguishing these two modes of transcendence is present
to reflective consciousness even though both modes are given to
consciousness, one as the immediate formal object of the natural
spirit and the other as the formal object of the supernaturally
elevated spirit. When we view it from the standpoint of such considerations of a metaphysics of spirit, the Thomistic teaching is
thoroughly defensible. It presents itself as the translation, in meta-

---

*logie in der mittelalterlichen Scholastik vom Abälardsstreit bis zu Philip
dem Kanzler* (Münster, 1933); R. Aubert, *Le Problème de l'acte de foi,* 2 ed.
(Louvain, 1950); cf. also K. Rahner, "Über die Erfahrung der Gnade,"
Schriften zur Theologie, III, pp. 105–109,

physical and theological terms, of the conviction uttered in Scripture. What happens when we take the teaching of Scripture honestly and impartially, simply as it is uttered, and do not correct it in a silent a priori which denies it has said a certain thing because this thing cannot be? Must we not say that for Scripture the communication of the Spirit (the divine *pneuma*) is much more than an entitative "elevation" beyond consciousness of human acts, which of themselves remain on the level of conscious existence and are changed only from without by the faith that comes from hearing? Rather this communication of the Spirit is "life," "unction," "consolation," "light," ineffable supplication of the spirit, of the *pneuma* which is more than intelligence, an inner drawing and yearning, witness of the Spirit, etc. It would be of great benefit if one day the teaching of Scripture were examined in detail and made to confront this scholastic controversy. For we should gradually set ourselves free from the opinion, never articulated it is true, yet still deep-seated, that in a theologically serious and religiously important question it is a priori certain that no more clear knowledge remains to be gained from Scripture, because the question is still a controversy in the schools, and could not be if Scripture were decisive. If the opinions advanced by the theologians recognize that supernatural actual graces are to be qualified as "illuminations" and "inspirations," then this teaching of Tradition ought also to be taken seriously. It ought not to be dismissed by anti-Thomist polemicists as if it held nothing of substance. For an entitatively elevated act, which remains, as far as consciousness is concerned, a natural act cannot be designated as inner illumination and inspiration without doing violence to the words. The very fact that the Molinistic thesis claims it is anti-Thomistic, seeking to close the whole question on this claim, shows how thoroughly Tradition is convinced that the act borne supernaturally by grace is even spiritually different from every natural act. For Tradition, the supernatural act is existentially and thus in some measure consciously different from a natural act. The difference is *not* limited to a distinction in entitative modality.

Now we come to a point which should be made clear and remembered well. For it is not only in the order of justification that acts can be charged supernaturally by grace. Indeed there are stimulations of grace which precede the acceptance of love and justification in free belief. Furthermore, there is grace outside the Church and her Sacraments.

When God offers grace to a man who is advanced in his spiritual development to an existential possibility of decision, we need not necessarily conceive this offer of grace as an intermittent grace, as happening only on extremely apt occasions, as "actual" grace in a time-conditioned sense (indeed there is no compelling theological reason for positing this). On the other hand, "actual" means simply that grace is present antecedent to an existential decision as an "offer" and a "possibility" (of the free salutary act), and if we recall that in this sense man's moral freedom to dispose of himself rests permanently in the possibility that is his (through grace) of supernatural acts,[12] then we can justly say that supernatural transcendence is always present in every man who has grown up to the use of moral reason. He is not therefore necessarily justified; he can be a sinner and an infidel. But when and to the extent that the possibility of performing a morally good action is concretely present to him, then he actually and continually lives on a level of being that is open to the transcendence of God, of the God of supernatural life. And this is true whether he is or is not, by reason of his free act, at one with this openness of his spiritual being, now supernaturally elevated. If in each moral act he takes a positive or negative position toward the *totality* of his actual existence (a condition whose actual status we need not examine here), then one would have to say that every morally good act of a man is, in the actual order of salvation, also a supernaturally salutary act. This would bring us to the well-known position advanced by Ripalda. But this outcome need not frighten us. For to begin with, the thesis of Ripalda, though rarely held, has never been subjected to any theological censure; second, the condition just stated, by which one comes to Ripalda's thesis, could still be denied and one could thereby avoid Ripalda's position. However it may be, the train of thought sketched above shows how it is thoroughly admissible to hold that the entire spiritual life of man is constantly being shaped, formed, by grace. Hence grace is not, simply because it is *un-*

---

[12] The necessary condition of being able to believe at all. In Straub's theory everyone who has reached the use of reason can have this as *"fides stricte dicta sed virtualis."*

merited, a rare occurrence. (How long and how often has theology fallen into error by presupposing, more often tacitly, that grace ceases to be grace when it is granted too generously by God's love?) Our entire spiritual life is lived in the milieu of God's saving will, His antecedent grace, His efficacious call. All of this is an element of our conscious existence, a fact, even though unexpressed, of our being. Man lives consciously in the presence of the Triune God of eternal life even if he does not "know" and believe it (i.e., even though he cannot make it a specific object of his knowledge by merely reflecting interiorly). This is the inexpressible, but nonetheless real, why and wherefore pervading the dynamism of all spiritual and moral life throughout the realm of being established by God, that is, raised supernaturally for His spiritual creatures. It is a why and wherefore that is utterly a priori but nonetheless always real. It is not an objectively conscious why and wherefore, but it is, we repeat, nonetheless real.

This supernatural a priori, this condition for the realm of spiritual being makes itself felt as a hidden entelechy or perfection of spiritual life, both individual and collective, in a thousand expressions of this life which would be impossible if this hidden perfection and dynamism were not at work. (And this is true even if this supernatural a priori is capable of being expressed in thought in an unequivocal way only as an interpretation of the truths revealed through the Word Incarnate.) This requires no special explanation. Moreover, if it follows that the history of religion, even when we prescind from the history of revelation in the strict sense, is not merely the work of natural reason and sin, but (and precisely in its tangible effects upon the level of consciousness, in its objective spirit) is the work of natural spirit, grace, and sin. When the visible Church addresses man with its message of faith, this summons to faith is not the first encounter of man with the reality of faith (even on the conceptual level). Rather it is a summons which brings that person to reflect consciously and explicitly on a fact which previously confronted him, implicitly to be sure, but nevertheless in a real way; it is a summons to reflect consciously on the real fact that grace has already, as an element of his spiritual being, been an encompassing medium. Preaching is the explicit arousing, summoning to reflective consciousness, of what already lies at the root of man's essence, of what is there, not by nature, but by grace. But it is there as a grace which always encompasses man, even the sinner and the nonbeliever, as the unavoidable realm of his being. Only at this point are we really able to pose the question[13] of "nature and grace" in the strict sense. Clearly it is in "living out" his spiritual existence that man completely fulfills his "nature," even in the theological sense in which the notion of nature is the counter-notion to grace and to the supernatural. For man experiences himself in his inquiry concerning himself, in every judgment in which he confronts himself with an object and sees himself on the horizon

[13] We can give here only a somewhat arbitrary selection of the literature over this controversy, which centers mainly on the historical and theological works of H. de Lubac. We also mention several articles on the teaching of *Humani Generis,* for this encyclical, as is well known, took up a position on this question. Further articles on *Humani Generis* are given in, e.g., *Revista Española de Teologia,* 11 (1951), pp. 173–176, 311–339; H. de Lubac, "Remarques sur l'histoire du mot 'surnaturel,'" *Nouvelle Revue Theologique,* 61 (1934), pp. 225–249, 350–370; J. Martinez-Gomez, "Notas sobre unas notas para la historia de la palabra sobrenatural," *Archivo Teologico Granadino,* 1 (1938), pp. 57–85; H. de Lubac, *Surnaturel. Etudes historiques* (Paris, 1946); H. Rondet, "Nature et surnaturel dans la théologie de S. Thomas d'Aquin," *Recherches de Science Religieuse,* 33 (1947), pp. 379–395; C. Boyer, "Nature pure et surnaturel dans le 'Surnaturel' du Père de Lubac," *Gregorianum,* 28 (1947), pp. 379–395; G. de Broglie, *De Fine Ultimo Humanae Vitae. Pars prior, positiva* (Paris, 1948); H. Rondet, "Le Problème de la nature pure et la théologie du XVI siècle," *Recherches de Science Religieuse,* 36 (1949), pp. 80–121; P. J. Donnelly, "The Gratuity of the Beatific Vision and the Possibility of a Natural Destiny," *Theological Studies,* 11 (1950), pp. 374–404 (bibliography); W. Brugger, "Das Ziel des Menschen und das Verlangen nach der Gotteschau," *Scholastik,* 25 (1950), pp. 535–548; M. J. de Guillou, "Surnaturel," *Revue de Sciences Philosophiques et Théologiques,* 34 (1950), pp. 226–243; R. Paniker, *El concepto de naturaleza. Analisis historico y metafisico de un concepto* (Madrid, 1951); G. Weigel, "Historical Background of the Encyclical *Humani Generis,*" *Theological Studies,* 12 (1951), pp. 520–549; J. Simon, "Transcendance et immanence dans la doctrine de la grâce," *Revue de l'Université Ottawa,* 21 (1951), pp. 344–369; L. Renwart, "La 'Nature pure' à la lumière de l'encyclique *Humani Generis,*' *Nouvelle Revue Théologique,* 74 (1952), pp. 337–354; E. Gutwenger, "Natur and Übernatur," *Zeitschrift zur katholische Theologie,* 75 (1953), pp. 82–97; H. Urs von Balthasar-Gutwenger, "Der Begriff der Natur in der Theologie," *Zeitschrift zur katholische Theologie,* 75 (1953), pp. 452–464; J. Ternus, "Natur-Übernatur in der vortridentinischen Theologie seit Thomas von Aquin," *Scholastik,* 28 (1953), pp. 399–404; M. R. Gagnebet, "L'Enseignement du magistère et le problème du surnaturel," *Revue Thomiste,* 53 (1953), pp. 5–27; L. Malevez, "La Gratuité du Surnaturel," *Nouvelle Revue Théologique,* 75 (1953), pp. 561–586; K. Rahner, "Concerning the Relationship Between Nature and Grace," *Theological Investigations* (Eng. tr.) (Baltimore, 1962), Vol. I, pp. 297–318; R. Bruch, "Das Verhältnis von Natur und Gnade nach der Auffassung der neueren Theologie," *Theologie und Glaube,* 46 (1956), pp. 81–102.

of an unlimited transcendence. He experiences himself as something which he has to be, something which is a freedom and a fullness indivisible into parts, something which exists either as a whole or not at all. He grasps his metaphysical essence; he comprehends himself as spirit in transcendence and freedom. And from the standpoint of this assessment of what is implied about man in every human act, there is presumably still much more about man that is "essential" for him to come to, such things as his "being-in-the-world," his corporeity, his belonging to a community of his equals. In short, there is a metaphysical knowledge of man's essence and nature through the light of his reason. When we say "through reason," we mean, first of all, through a vision independent of any revealed word, but we also mean through the medium (reason) which is itself an element of the essence thus comprehended. But the theological facts already established here lead us also to the conclusion that the concrete human nature which experiences itself here (and all that it experiences by way of conditions) need not, and indeed cannot, be considered as the reflection of that "pure" nature which theology distinguishes from everything supernatural. Man's concrete nature is *never* a "pure" nature. It is a nature in a supernatural order out of which man (even as nonbeliever and sinner) cannot withdraw, and a nature which is constantly "shaped" (and this does not mean "justified") by the supernatural grace of salvation offered to man. And these "existential factors" of his concrete nature (his "historical" nature) are not pure states of being lying beyond man's consciousness, but enter into his experience. He cannot, through mere reflection about himself (with the light of natural reason) simply and unequivocally remove these factors from his natural spirituality, which is his nature. But if revelation once tells him that there is such an order of grace, one due neither to any merit of his own nor to his necessarily indissoluble essence, then he grows more careful. He must reckon with the possibility that perhaps many of the things which he experiences of himself and which he is almost involuntarily tempted to attribute to his "nature" are actually the effect of an unmerited grace, which he recognizes as such on theological grounds. This is not to say that he has now lost the notion of what was simply nature within him. The nature of a spiritual being and its supernatural elevation are not two "things," lying next to one another, which we must either separate or confuse.

The supernatural elevation of man is the absolute — albeit un-merited — fulfillment of a being which, by reason of its spirituality and transcendency to being as such, cannot be "defined" (i.e., de-limited) at all in the same way as subhuman beings. The latter are in fact "defined" in that it is proper to them to be limited to a certain realm of reality. (Hence it is impossible, for example, for them to be "elevated" to a supernatural fulfillment, since such an elevation would remove their being, their essential limits.) The "definition" of the created spirit is its "openness" to being in gen-eral. It is a creature because it is the openness to the fullness of reality; it is spirit because it is absolutely open to reality in general. Thus it should cause no surprise that we cannot recognize as "merited" or "unmerited" the measure, in itself variable, of the fulfillment of this openness. For it does not necessarily signify an absolute and insurpassable fulfillment — an absolute openness has, in fact, significance even if it is not fulfilled in *this* way, i.e., through grace. Nevertheless the basic essence of man, his "nature" con-sidered as such an openness (transcendence), remains basic. The beginning of such a fulfillment is indeed anticipated. It is manifest, for instance, in the experience of an infinite desire, of a radical optimism, of an unquenchable discontent; it is felt in the torment over the insufficiency of the tangible, in the radical protest against death, in the experience of standing face to face with an absolute love precisely where this love is intangible and speechless, in the experience of a deep-rooted guilt and of a nevertheless prevailing hope, etc. And this promise of fulfillment is actually supported by that divine power which inclines the created spirit — by grace — to an absolute fulfillment. It is here that grace *and* the natural being of man are experienced. For the natural being of man is such that it is experienced where grace is experienced since the latter is ex-perienced only where nature is spirit. But the opposite is also true. Where spirit is experienced in the actual order, it is elevated to the supernatural order. Provided that these considerations of the relationship between nature and grace are confined to the most uni-versal formalities, this question presents no particular difficulties. Still nature exists as spirit only in the supernatural order and spirit never can be encountered as "pure nature." Only when one chooses to look into the question in more detail does it become more trouble-some. What, concretely speaking, remains of nature in this elevated nature? What is real and proper to it when it is a question of a nature raised to the supernatural order? And what if one should ask, for example, whether the resurrection of the flesh belongs to any fulfillment of man as a spiritual person, or whether it is something which depends upon grace? And how would the fulfillment of a pure nature look *concretely?* These questions can be answered only if we could experience pure nature and could determine, on the experience of such a nature, a concrete doctrine of purposes.[14] But, in reality, such attempts come to a standstill; they lead to an essentially formal notion of "natural" ends, and, as might be expected in the light of what has already been said, a notion of this kind is only an abstract and formalized expression of the concrete supernatural doctrine of ends. Thus it would follow from these considerations that the great theology of the Middle Ages did well not to trouble too much in theorizing about natural happiness. This is true, first, because there actually is no such thing and, second, because such happiness is fundamentally a highly formalized and abstract image of the true supernatural end known to theology (and therefore the picture of natural happiness is not very useful), and finally because it necessarily borrows, whenever it voluntarily or involuntarily wants to become concrete, from theology what it neither can nor may dispose of in its own right.

In fact such a "pure" philosophy of the natural being of man is not even necessary. When we are called upon to speak with the nonbeliever we must only take care not to assume any premises from the historically revealed word, at least to the extent that he does not recognize its validity. When in the course of such a discussion an appeal is made to man's experience of himself, one will have to limit oneself to what the nonbeliever accepts as valid in that experience. If he refuses to accept a certain point, he does so either because he cannot concur in a legitimately "natural" experience because it is badly demonstrated to him or because he fails to grasp it (even though he also has the experience in question) in spite of proof of its authenticity; or it may be that his fellow disputant has actually invoked an experience of grace which does not exist in the other in such clarity that he understands this argumentative refer-

---

[14] If this nature's infinite openness *could have* a final destiny at all and not be, in the concrete, either the free limitation by God to a finite end, determined by Him but which could not have been deduced a priori from the nature itself, *or* absolute fulfillment.

ence to it (even though he also has it to some degree in the light of what has been said above). Since the case can be either the one or the other, since it is not easy even for the Christian to distinguish them clearly from one another, since a supernatural argumentation can be completely sensible and effective even for a nonbeliever (if and when an argumentation from revelation is not possible), then the question, as to whether a metaphysical (i.e., a preface to theology) argumentation has "pure" nature or historical nature as its tangible point of departure, is in the concrete not of any serious consequence.

The notion of pure nature is legitimate. When someone says: "I experience myself as a being unconditionally related to the immediate possession of God," he has not necessarily said anything false. Such a statement is false only if the person claims that this absolute inclination is an essential element of "pure" nature, or if he says that such a pure nature (which *does* not in fact exist) could simply not exist. Where man knows, through revelation, the *visio beatifica* as grace and, in his longing for it, experiences in himself a longing for it as a miracle of the free divine love, he must say that it is unmeritable to him (as nature), and indeed that as an existing person he has no claim on it (the unmeritedness of creation as an act of God's freedom, and grace as a free gift to the creature already existing, are not one and the same gift of the freedom of God). But the notion of "pure nature" is thereby implied. And indeed not only as the empty notion of leisurely theological speculation, but as a notion which constitutes the necessary background for considering the *visio beatifica* as an unmerited grace, unmerited not only by man as sinner, but also by man as a mere creature.

The endeavor to clarify the orientation of man's nature to grace (in the sense of a *potentia oboedientialis*) is also full of significance for human nature as such, and precisely in the recognition of grace as an unmerited gift. It is not necessary that the *potentia oboedientialis* for grace be conceived in the sense of a mere absence of contradiction, so that the extrinsicism mentioned earlier follows. An ordering to grace is not the same as an absolute relationship to grace of such a kind that this entire orientation to grace is meaningless without its actual communication. Even if spirit (in other words, openness to God, freedom, and a knowing, free possession of self) is essentially not possible without a transcendence which

has nothing less than grace as its absolute fulfillment, such a fulfillment is still not merited, provided that this knowing possession
of self in freedom before God has significance in itself (and is not
possessed merely as a pure means, as a mere stage on the way to
the *visio beata*). But this last provision can definitely be made. For
the absolute (not taken to mean endless) validity and authenticity
of every personal act in itself makes this provision. But if it is made,
then it must be true that there is no spirit without a transcendence
open to supernature; but spirit remains significant even without
supernatural grace. Its fulfillment by grace thus cannot be required
by its essence, even if it is essentially open to such a grace. But
if this is clear, then nothing stands in the way of elaborating clearly
and precisely this transcendence of the spirit open to the supernatural. Man is then completely recognized in his "indefinable"
essence only if he is conceived as *potentia oboedientialis* for divine
life, and if this is his *nature*. In fact his nature is such that it must
await grace as its *absolute* fulfillment and, because it is such,
it must reckon by itself with the *significant* possibility of the non-
arrival of an absolute fulfillment. The attempt can be even undertaken of seeing the *unio hypostatica* in the direction of this absolute
fulfillment of what man really is. Such considerations, endeavoring
to bring a metaphysical anthropology and the doctrine of grace as
near as possible to one another, and to show the higher to be the
unmerited fulfillment of the lower,[15] are no mere *jeux d'esprit*.
Without them it will prove impossible to awaken in man an existential
interest in that mysterious life which comes with supernatural grace.
Such an elaboration of the substantial notion of the *potentia
oboedientialis* must also look beyond man's *knowledge* (an effort
only too rarely attempted). If God in Scripture is Love and not the
noesis noeseos, then even an understanding of man and of the
absolute fulfillment of his being (by grace) comes to an end only
when man is conceived as freedom and love, and when this love
is understood not only as the consummation and attendant emotion
of knowledge. Given this analysis of man as *potentia oboedientialis*
it is, in view of the foregoing, no calamity if there is no such thing

---

[15] Everywhere in the hierarchically constructed universe of real differences
without "jumps" — with the many and different coming from the one —
"fulfillment" and "gratuitousness" both in one are the characteristic mark
of the relationship between two realities.

as a "chemically pure" example of pure nature, if traces of historical nature, of its ordering to grace are found mixed in our notion of man. Who can say that what is found in earthly philosophy, even in most para-Christian and pre-Christian philosophies, is only the voice of pure nature (and perhaps of its fault), and not also the longing of the creature which, already secretly moved by the Holy Spirit of grace, desires the glory of the children of God and which, unbeknownst, already conceives itself as such a child of God?

There is much more to say about the status of the doctrine of grace in contemporary theology and about its rightful position. One could speak, for example, of grace in its relationship to the Church,[16] about the social significance and orientation of grace as it is encountered in the usual theological treatises in a queer individualistic narrowing of horizons. One could stress the discussion, recently begun, of the relationship between grace and the personal acts of man. But space is wanting in this brief essay.

Small theoretical advances and realignments in any science are often of practically no noticeable significance. Such changes frequently seem to be diversions, the offshoots of a scholar's play. But if we remember that such new knowledge often becomes a matter of public information and becomes the self-evident premises of action, then we may realize that much, and often everything, depends upon these unfoldings of theory. This is true also in theology. It is strange that we Christians often seem, contrary to our Christian faith, to be less convinced than anyone of the power of thought, to believe less than any that "theory" can bring forth practical results. Hence our preference for matters of Church politics, social questions, propaganda, and similar things. Thus too we little appreciate living theology. Theology gives many people in the Church the impression that it is only superficially occupied with knowledge long since made clear, that it produces nothing but unrest, and neglects more important matters. Such people do not see that a living, investigating, questioning theology today is at work so that the message of tomorrow will find an echo in the spirits and hearts of men. This work of theology often appears complicated and fruitless. But it is nevertheless necessary, even if the heart and grace are the only things that cannot be replaced.

---

[16] H. de Lubac, *Catholicism: A Study of the Corporate Destiny of Mankind* (London, 1950).

JOHANNES FEINER

MAN'S ORIGIN AND CONTEMPORARY ANTHROPOLOGY

QUESTIONS relative to man's origin and prehistory and the responses made to these queries by the Church and theologians have been discussed in numerous books and articles, many of them intended for the general reader. Consequently, it might seem that an examination of these problems might be superfluous here. On the other hand, discussion of these matters has in no way been terminated, and thus a general review of the issues involved, since they belong to proto-logy, can very well be considered as pertinent to this collection as an examination of the end of history (eschatology). Many presentations of this subject deal with specific questions — the classic example is that of descent — in isolation from the whole problem area; and the direction of recent research, with which we are most vitally con-cerned here, is sometimes not given the attention it deserves. We shall attempt to survey, therefore, within a general framework, the major questions which cause the Church and theology to be con-cerned with the discoveries and assertions of the profane sciences during the past century. Our intention is to render intelligible the unquestioned development which — continued inquiry notwithstand-ing — has taken place in theology during the past century. It is easy to speak of the defensive action of theology under the pressure of the natural sciences, to accuse her of an ultraconservative attitude or of a tendency to settle for weak compromises, to praise those theologians who "move forward" as radically as possible and who sweep aside all the antiquated concepts of an "outmoded biblical *Weltanschauung*." Such criticism fails to recognize the seri-ous responsibility fundamental to theological effort; it also fails to grasp the fact that the profane sciences, engaged in constructing a new conception of the world, are in many ways incapable of sub-

27

stantiating their assertions, and that the Magisterium and theology, to which the revealed message has been entrusted, can arrive at a precise and articulate grasp of the substance of revelation only through patient and painstaking inquiry.

The question of human origins brings the natural scientist's conception of the world into contact with the world of supernatural revelation. We realize today that the divine revelation contained in Holy Scripture and in documents of Church tradition is intimately bound to a world picture which does not correspond to that of our contemporaries. It is a concept of the world which we can hold no longer. Under the impact of the Copernican revolution, and only after much pain and intellectual anguish, Christendom has learned to distinguish the binding, revealed truths expressed in Scripture and tradition from the old conception of the world in which they are embodied, from a notion of space and time which is not binding for us because it does not belong to the *content* of divine revelation, but rather to the *form* in which that revelation was presented. This process of differentiation is in no way terminated (if it will ever come to an end at all): on the one hand, the scientific conception of the world is always in a state of evolution; and on the other, the distinction between the substance meant to be communicated by revelation and the manner of expression used in the sources of revelation is no matter of simple arithmetic. As long as we keep in mind these necessarily obvious facts (obvious in view of both natural and supernatural knowledge), we will not be surprised to find that there are, precisely in the area under discussion here, no ready and final solutions, either in the profane sciences or in theology.

It is through the natural sciences that the modern conception of the world has been given its most definitive stamp. Since the nineteenth century these sciences have regarded as essential to this concept an element which pervades the whole with constantly mounting force. It is, of course, the notion of evolution.[1] It is the knowledge that the world did not come into existence a few days before man, as the Bible relates it, and that it did not come into existence in the form in which we find it today, but came to be what it is today through a development stretching over a period

---

[1] Cf. A. Mitterer, "Eigentümlichkeiten des naturwissenschaftlichen Weltbildes," *Gloria Dei*, 5 (1950–1951), pp. 119–136.

of billions of years. It is the knowledge that the earth developed through billions of years before it could sustain life, and that the forms of life evolved for millions of years until — approximately some 600,000 years ago — man finally appeared, or could appear, on earth. This knowledge was as revolutionary as the Copernican crisis in its day. There is no doubt that this notion of the evolving universe, backed up by an immense amount of research, is quite foreign to the biblical and, in general, traditional picture of the world. It surprised no one that man should also be drawn into the evolutionary view of the universe. Not only was his age increased from the presumed 6000 years to 60,000 and finally to 600,000 years or more, but the doctrine of evolution also began, soon after its ascendancy, to see man as genetically related to the animal kingdom and to define him as the final member of an evolved series of higher mammals. If evolution is a law of all life on the earth, why should the species *man* not have developed out of earlier living forms?

For centuries knowledge concerning the origin of man had been drawn from myths and from the revelation of the Bible, whereas now the natural sciences seized on the problem. Since the answer science provided differed from that of the Church, the encounter between profane science and Church doctrine led immediately to a conflict. If it was no longer possible, in view of the theory of evolution, to accept the biblical concept of the world, could one still hold the traditional doctrine that Adam was the first man, created immediately by God — without evolution from the animal kingdom — and the ancestor of all humanity? Could one still assent to the doctrine of his original paradisical state and to that of his Fall, disastrous for all mankind? Does this view not belong to those historically limited biblical conceptions which must be abandoned — considering the new world view so fatefully provided us — and which *can* be abandoned without sacrificing anything of the true content of revelation? If one accepts the Copernican and evolutionary views of the world and simultaneously affirms the historical existence of Adam, is it not true that he is making an impossible "juxtaposition"? As a consequence, "is it not necessary for us to abandon, on the basis of our acknowledging the Copernican principle, the world view of the ancients and to renounce that . . . intrinsically unacceptable juxtaposition"?[2] According to E. Brunner, those who today still wish to hold to the historical existence of Adam are trying to "put into the framework of their new conception of space and time a process which belongs to an entirely different concept of space and time, one which they are not even capable of reproducing. They are thus not simply 'conservatives,' but reactionaries of quixotic stamp. They are attempting the impossible: fitting two incompatible concepts of space and time into one another."[3]

Without doubt a difficult task has been imposed upon theology as a result of this encounter between a faith based on revelation and the modern concept of the world. Theology must ask itself whether it is at all possible, on the grounds of revelation, to attribute historical validity to the biblical affirmation, proclaimed by the Church, of a definite, unique ancestor of all humanity, of his original Eden-like state, and of his sinful Fall. And if theology must[4] unconditionally affirm these propositions, it must further ask *just what in particular* pertains to this historical validity. In view of the complexity of the problem it is easy to understand that a responsible answer requires much circumspection and patient attention to details. Nor is any thorough answer at all possible today.[5]

Many Protestant theologians have proposed radical solutions to the problem. Some deny that the creation of man and the Fall are historical events in the sense that they can be treated on the level of an historical relation. The creation of man (as mythologically depicted in the creation of Adam) related by revelation means, according to them, only that man is a creature of God. And the Fall, presented by revelation in the form of the myth of original sin, signifies only that man has ever been, through his own fault, a sinner. "We acknowledge sin as our constitution, as something irrevocably bound to our present being. But the question of the *when* and *how* of the Fall remains unanswerable, whether regarded in the

---

[2] E. Brunner, *Dogmatik,* Vol. II (Zürich, 1950), p. 58. "One cannot think in a Copernican manner without giving up the *history* of Adam." *Ibid.,* p. 59.

[3] *Ibid.,* p. 56.

[4] For the Church's doctrine concerning the historical validity of the accounts of Genesis, cf. Denz. 2123, 2302, 2329.

[5] Various theological conferences in different countries have taken up this whole problem, e.g., in Rome, 1948 (its report was printed as a special issue of *Gregorianum,* 29, 1948), in 1954 in Salamanca (its reports were published in book form, *El Evolucionismo en Filosofía y en Teología,* Barcelona, 1956).

individual or in the whole of historical humanity."[6] Thus an existential, radically unhistorical theology of creation and sin is proposed in place of the traditional theology which considers the biblical account a revealed, true, early history. With this neo-Protestant renunciation of the historical reality of Adam, it is necessary to change fundamentally the traditional Christian doctrine of original sin, and these theologians are clearly intent upon doing just this. Precisely at this point it becomes clear why Catholic theology cannot proceed in this direction. The teaching office of the Church and Catholic theology hold fast to the *historical existence* of Adam. They do not do this because they are of the opinion that one should look for a strictly historical content in every detail of the biblical story of creation, nor from a desire to save as much as possible of the biblical concept of the world. They do so because the historical reality of Adam as the sole ancestor of all men and the historicity of the original state and of the Fall are presupposed by the Church's teaching, received from the revelation of the New Testament, regarding original sin and redemption. The Church thus interprets the Old Testament story of Adam from the vantage point of the New Testament and its revealed vision of the man's disastrous situation and his delivery therefrom. Because the Church can not misinterpret, falsify, or in any way abandon the picture of salvation history given us in the New Testament, neither can she abandon the history of the fall and salvation revealed to us in the Old Testament, which is discernible in its whole significance only through the message of the New Testament.[7]

Thus to the question, "Has the Christian teaching concerning

---

[6] E. Brunner, *op. cit.*, p. 116.

[7] E. Brunner's solution of the problem is, incidentally, only apparently simpler than the Catholic. If, in the name of the contemporary conception of the world, the answer is sought by demythologizing the accounts of the Old Testament, then one could ask, in the name of the same modern notion of the cosmos, whether the events of salvation, considered until now to be historically real, might not also be mere mythological embodiments of metahistorical truths, for they do not fit into the modern conception of reality. It would be more consistent to demythologize not only the Old Testament, but also the New Testament, and to abandon, in the process, the historical validity of the events narrated in the New Testament, as R. Bultmann and his school do. To be sure, the two cases are not entirely similar, since the events of the New Testament contain historically verifiable aspects, whereas those of prehistory do not. But the divine witness bears testimony both in the prehistorical events and in those of the New Testament.

man's origin any meaning for us today?"[8] Catholic theology must
seek a different answer from that of the above-mentioned Protestant
theologians. It cannot accept the more comfortable "solution" to the
problem which declares the "story of Adam in paradise" to be a
naïve storyteller's way of presenting a truth lying beyond history,
a solution which casts the whole account overboard, as just so much
hindering ballast, in order to avoid uneasiness in an encounter with
the profane sciences. Catholic theology has the difficult but necessary
task of *determining what, within the picture of man's origin and
original state which has been handed down to us, is undeniably
revealed truth and what are historically limited ideas.* If Catholic
theology affirms the historical character of facts related in revelation (facts belonging, to be sure, to an area of history which remains
inaccessible to natural reason), deleting images tied by the ancients
to the *content* of revelation, and replacing these with others, the
"resultant picture of Adam in paradise" is by no means "totally
other than that of the ancients."[9] What is distinct is the *view,* conditioned by our contemporary conception of the world, which we
attach to the truth intended, and substantially stated, by revelation.
This is basically the same procedure as that used in exegesis of the
New Testament, where the men of New Testament times, even the
inspired writers themselves, attached to the events narrated a conception of things with which we today can no longer concur. Or
can it be said that the glorified Christ in whom we believe today
differs essentially from the Christ in whom the early Christians believed insofar as we no longer think of Christ's heavenly glory in
terms of a space overlying the firmament?[10] Our difficulty in recon-
ciling the story of Adam's original state with our Copernican conception of space and time should hardly surprise us. But this signifies
no objective contradiction between the doctrine of the Church and
our contemporary *Weltanschauung.* For not even in New Testament
Christology and eschatology do we attain to any true harmony.

In the conflict brought about with the evolutionary conception of
the world, three vital questions immediately came to the fore.

---

[8] E. Brunner, *op. cit.,* p. 55.

[9] *Ibid.,* p. 56.

[10] Even if the analogy is not valid, the two cases concur in that a traditional assertion intended by revelation is distinguished from the expression
used to communicate it. Our modern conception of the world does not exclude the existence of an area of history lying beyond natural investigation.

These questions could not have arisen or else had presented no particular problem before the advent of evolutionism. The *first question,* which from the very beginning was the subject of an impassioned discussion, today much less so, concerns the compatibility of anthropological evolutionism with the Church's teaching on man's origin (the problem of descent). The *second,* which came into the foreground only with the last phase of the conflict over the theory of descent, is that of the compatibility of polygenism with the Church's teaching regarding the original unity of humanity in Adam (the problem of monogenism). The *third question,* the exhaustive discussion of which has hardly begun, is the problem of the compatibility of the evolutionary thesis of man's primitive state prior to cultural development with the Church's teaching concerning the fullness and perfection of the original state of man in paradise (the problem of man's original state).

In the essay which follows, it will be impossible to examine all the various positions that have been advanced both pro and con in the conflict, and we shall necessarily restrict ourselves to surveying cursorily the present-day situation and then proceed to delineate whatever aspects of that situation may be of decisive importance for Catholic theology.

I. THE QUESTION OF THE ORIGIN OF MAN

With the rise of modern natural science, both theology and the profane sciences have taken up the problem of man's origin, considering the problem from essentially different viewpoints, of course. We shall first sketch briefly here the position taken today by natural science in the matter.[11]

A. *Natural Science and the Question of Origins*

During the first phase of evolutionism, there was a tendency to emphasize, almost exclusively, the numerous similarities between man and beasts, and as a result to reduce man to the most highly developed animal and to see him as having come up from the animal kingdom. This tendency itself sprang, as we well know, from a fateful

---

[11] For a thorough history of the doctrine of evolution, cf. W. Zimmermann, *Evolution, Die Geschichte ihrer Probleme und Erkenntnisse* (Series "Orbis Academicus") (Freiburg/Munich, 1953). Cf. also A. Mitterer, "Christliche Theologie und naturwissenschaftliche Entwicklungslehre in zwei Jahrtausenden," *Wissen und Weisheit* (1951), pp. 115–128.

union of two intellectual currents which are in themselves thoroughly different from each other: the doctrine of biological evolution and the philosophy of materialistic monism. It is history that the greater part of natural scientists professed a monistic dogmatism which left no room for revealed notions of man's origin and nature, and that this materialistic frame of mind made impossible a peaceful and fruitful debate between theology and the theory of descent. Today one still observes monistic thought on the part of many representatives of natural science; nevertheless, one encounters, with the majority of leading natural scientists today, an openness to knowledge derived from sources other than those of empirical natural science. This, of course, is the indispensable requisite for dialogue between theology and natural science. But the freeing of evolutionism from monistic thought did not lead to a general retreat from anthropological transformism. In fact, various hypotheses for a more exact explanation of descent from the animal kingdom were proposed, resulting in the well-known "crisis of transformism." But experts are largely agreed, in spite of vigorous attacks by some dissenters,[12] that there are genetic relationships between man and the animal kingdom.[13] Among

[12] Cf., e.g., O. Kuhn, *Die Deszendenztheorie. Grundlegung der Ganzheitsbiologie* (Munich, 1951).

[13] "It is clear that the application of evolutionary notions to man has become, within the area under study by the biologist, a fixed part of the scientific view of things. But thanks to a new and highly respected approach which tends to consider man in his totality, a notion of man is taking form today, even in the laboratories of biological research, which promises to do justice to both the spiritual and material aspects of man's nature." J. Kälin (Zoologist, Fribourg), "Die ältesten Menschenreste und ihre stammensgeschichtliche Deutung," in *Historia Mundi* (Bern, 1952), p. 34 f. — "We do not believe it is exaggerated to affirm that at present almost all paleontologists and anthropologists are evolutionists." V. Marcozzi, S.J. (professor in Biology and Anthropology at the Gregorian in Rome), "Poligenesi ed evoluzione nelle origini dell'uomo," *Gregorianum*, 29 (1948), p. 363. — "Let us not deceive ourselves that a biologist who is abreast of present knowledge has any right not to be evolutionist if he is unable to explain the facts in some other way." G. Vandenbroek (Anatomist and Anthropologist, Lyon), "Der Ursprung des Menschen und die jüngsten Entdeckungen der Naturwissenschaften," in J. de Bivort de la Saudée (ed.), *Gott, Mensch, Universum* (Graz, Vienna, Cologne, 1956²), p. 162 (Eng. tr.: Kenedy, 1960). — The most recent work, planned, in a number of volumes, as the collaboration of numerous research scientists of different countries, is based on the principle of evolution: *Primatologia. Handbuch der Primatenkunde*, ed. by H. Hofer, A. H. Schultz, G. Starck, first vol. (Basel-New York, 1956).

the many Catholic advocates of the evolutionary hypothesis are priests who have emerged as specialists doing research in various branches of natural science. Because of his far-reaching influence, and the fascinating elaboration of his "idea of a universe in evolution," particular mention should be made here of the renowned paleontologist Pierre Teilhard de Chardin, S.J., whose writings are now being published by two committees of learned authorities of different nations.[14]

One can rightly speak of an "evolution of the idea of evolution," for various significant changes have come about in evolutionary thinking. It is more clearly emphasized today than before, at least by many of those who are professionally acquainted with the methods of scientific research, that the theory of descent is a *hypothesis*. Man's emergence was a process which could not have been subject to direct observation. The assertion that there is a relationship of descent between man and beast is an interpretation of many established facts which point in this direction. To establish that man has descended from beasts evolutionists have been able to produce only an indirect proof, only circumstantial evidence.[15] But most specialists agree that this circumstantial evidence makes the origin of man from the animal kingdom at least highly probable.[16] The vast complexity

---

[14] *Oeuvres de Pierre Teilhard de Chardin*, Paris, in 5 vols. Four of Père Teilhard's books have appeared in English: *The Phenomenon of Man*, 1960; *The Divine Milieu*, 1962; *Letters from a Traveler*, 1963; and *The Future of Man*, 1964. Teilhard de Chardin's notions were often subjected to sharp criticism, even by authorities who do not reject the idea of evolution *per se*. Cf., eg., L. Malevez, "La méthode du P. Teilhard de Chardin et la Phénoménologie, *Nouvelle Revue Théologique*, 79 (1957), pp. 579–599. — A. Brunner, "Pierre Teilhard de Chardin," *Stimmen der Zeit*, 85 (1959–1960), pp. 210–222. — *Systema Teilhard de Chardin ad theologicam trutinam revocatum* (contributions of various authors). *Divinitas*, III (Rome, 1959), fasc. II.

[15] P. Overhage, S.J., refers repeatedly to this in his articles. Cf. "Um die Abstammung des Menschen," *Stimmen der Zeit*, 82 (1956–1957), pp. 103–121. Also his "Über die Frage nach der Abstammung des Menschen," in A. Hartmann (ed.), *Bindung und Freiheit des Katholischen Denkens* (Frankfurt, 1952), p. 181 ff. — The same point is emphasized by J. Kälin, A. Portmann, *et al.*

[16] "In its concrete application to definite findings, the theory of evolution has led to interpretations which are for the most part hypotheses, but which are frequently of such high probability that they merit the value of pragmatic (practical) certainty." J. Kälin, *loc. cit.*, p. 46. "Evolution is thus a hypothesis, but one which is of the highest degree of possibility." G. Vandenbroek, *loc. cit.*, p. 162.

of the problem is almost universally acknowledged today.[17] During
the early days of evolutionism, there was great confidence that the
problems involved, such as those over the causes and formative
forces of the evolutionary process and over the origin of diverse
genera, could be easily solved. These difficulties are still far from
being solved. Characteristic of science today is *an attempt to see
the total problem.* There is a realization that one does not do
justice to the appearance of a given form of life by isolating individual organs and processes for study.[18] There are other aspects
of this attitude, such as the stress laid upon the special character of
human nature. This emphasis further distinguishes contemporary
research from the earlier tendency to level man down to inferior
genera. Whatever appears as absolutely novel in man in any respect,
even in the purely biological area, and prescinding entirely from the
domain of the spiritual, is deemed a priori worth the effort required
to explain it. [19]

The profound change taking place in biological research has produced in many scientific authorities humility and an openness to
knowledge from other sources. There is a recognition that biology
cannot, with its methodology, comprehend man in his whole being
and essence, and it is generally agreed that the problem of the origin
of mankind defies final solution through biological research alone,
and that the problem is not fundamentally a biological problem at all.

---

[17] For an extraordinary presentation of the many-sidedness and difficulty
of the problem of origins, cf. the Swiss zoologist, A. Portmann, "Die werdende
Menscheit. Das Ursprungsproblem der Menschheit," in *Historia Mundi,* first
vol. (Berne, 1952), pp. 21–32.

[18] "The whole of each form of life is the reality waiting upon discovery!
This is the new, decisive approach. And we already sense this whole — even
before we are able to analyze it in detail — in its staggering foreignness and
autonomy." *Ibid.,* p. 29.

[19] "The biologists who put this question to the transformistic theories are
not 'anti-evolutionists.' They simply demand that a scientific theory should
remain a theory, genuinely open to discussion, and that it should not stiffen
into a new dogmatic system which attempts to sell verbal window dressings
as solutions for extremely serious and difficult problems." *Ibid.,* p. 31. — It is
characteristic of A. Portmann to lay stress on the peculiarity of the human
in man's evolution and essence. Cf. also *Biologie und Geist* (which also
contains an inquiry into the problem of man's origin) (Zürich, 1956).
Biologische Fragmente zu einer Lehre vom Menschen (Basel, 1951[2]) (which
also appeared in *Rowohlts Deutsche Enzyklopädie* under the title "Zoologie
und das neue Bild des Menschen," Hamburg, 1956); *Vom Ursprung des
Menschen,* Basel, 1944.

B. *Theology and the Question of Origins*

It is common knowledge that, with respect to the origins of the first man, theology has also undergone gradual, but basic, changes. The majority of theologians today do not, of course, consider that the theory of descent has been demonstratively proved; nevertheless the conviction continually gains ground that revelation intends to give us no real information concerning *how* the human body came into existence, so that there is room here for whatever knowledge the profane sciences are able to provide.[20] The position which must be maintained throughout all change, however, was most clearly stated in the famous decree of the Pontifical Biblical Commission of 1909; this has to do with the *historicity of the biblical accounts* concerning Adam as the unique ancestor of all men, his original state in Paradise, and his Fall from grace. The historicity of these accounts must be held as a fundamental truth of the revealed Christian religion.[21] The biblical account of "Adam in Paradise" may never be explained as a myth (in the sense of saga, legend, allegory, etc.). Even if everyone granted that the second creation account in Genesis describes the formation of the first man in an imaginative, concrete, anthropomorphic manner, many theologians still would be convinced that a theory of descent, however mitigated, would necessarily contradict Holy Scripture and the Magisterium relative to the question of man's origin. According to those theologians, the decree of the Biblical Commission implied that the body of the first man took its origin from inorganic matter through an immediate intervention of God (a

---

[20] Cf. E. C. Messenger (ed.), *Theology and Evolution* (London, 1950). In his book, *Evolution and Theology* (London, 1931), Messenger already declared his conviction that revelation does not necessarily exclude anthropological evolutionism.

[21] Denz. 2121 ff. Neuner-Roos, p. 198. Cf. the statements, by both Secretaries of the Biblical Commission, on occasion of the new edition of the *Enchiridion Biblicum* (Naples and Rome, 1954) in *Benediktinische Monatsschrift*, 31 (1955), p. 49 f., and *Antonianum*, 30 (1955), pp. 63–65. — When the Church emphasizes the historical veracity of the biblical statements concerning man's origin, his original state, and original sin, she does not mean that they must be regarded as historical in today's sense. Neither in the classical nor the modern sense are the biblical accounts historical but are (pictorial-symbolistic) representations of factual historical events which truly occurred at the inception of our humanity. — Cf. the letter of the Secretary of the Biblical Commission, J.-M. Vosté, O.P., to Cardinal Suhard, *AAS*, 40 (1948), 47.

literal interpretation of Gn 2:7). Only a few theologians dared to
hold differing opinions in the nineteenth century.

Many factors have led exegetes and theologians of the present
century to the opinion that the Bible and the Magisterium of the
Church do not exclude the possibility of a genetic relationship between man and the animal kingdom.[22] First of all there has been the
"pressure" of scientific research, which always assumed the more
probable relationship between man and the higher animal forms
to be one of definite descent. In addition, there has been a gradual
increase in the knowledge of the literary forms found in Holy Scripture, as well as a deeper knowledge of the special characteristics
of biblical history. But decades were to pass before the majority of
theologians would be persuaded that the second account in Genesis
(2:7) concerning the creation of man contains no more, from the
point of view of doctrine, than the first (Gen 1:26). As late as the
1930's and 1940's widely used theological textbooks maintained that
even a moderated theory of descent (which acknowledges both the
concept of the biological evolution of the body and a special intervention of God for the creation of the spiritual soul) is obviously
incompatible with the teaching of the Bible and the Church.[23] Today,
on the other hand, not a few Catholic philosophers and theologians
support the view that the assumption of a human body which evolves
from the animal kingdom is more appropriate to God's way of acting as known by reason and revelation than is the idea of an
immediate creation of man out of the lifeless matter of the earth.[24]

[22] J. Göttsberger: "It contradicts the patterned constancy of hermeneutics
to find the biblical (Gn 2:19) forming of man out of earth compatible with
a descent from the animal kingdom, and the same must be said regarding
Gn 2:7 and man's being formed out of inorganic matter. Hence more than
understandable is the increase of exegetes and theologians who hold a descent
of the human body from an animal body to be biblically acceptable," "Adam
und Eva," *Biblische Zeitfragen,* III (Munich, 1910), p. 18.

[23] J. Brinktrine, *Die Lehre von der Schöpfung* (Paderborn, 1956), p. 261,
says that most theologians believe that God formed the body of the first
man not from an animal body, but directly from nothing. — Should one not
rather say that the majority is of the opinion that the Bible and the Church
do not decide this question, and that the natural sciences have as yet brought
forward no convincing proof of the descent theory? — Even theologians of
the Pontifical Gregorian University hold the "more liberal" position here. Cf.
M. Flick, S.J., "L'origine del corpo del primo uomo alla luce della filosofia
e della teologia," *Gregorianum,* 29 (1948), pp. 392–416.

[24] Dr. H. Grenier (of Laval University, Canada) makes this proposition:
"Deus immediate et naturaliter disposuit materiam primam ad recipiendam

The change has come about because theologians are increasingly more convinced that the notion, as found in the biblical account of creation and in the whole of tradition, of the formation of the human body out of the inorganic matter of the earth is intended only as a descriptive illustration of a theological doctrine, and arises from the world view of the ancients, to whom the idea of evolution (in today's sense) was foreign. As long as this ancient world view prevailed, this description was never questioned by the man who believed in creation. But it is really only a description of an event which is itself indescribable, a helpful representation of a reality which cannot even be imagined. Thus it does not enter into the substance of the truth concerning man's origin, but is only the literary form for its communication. The second account of man's creation (Gn 2:7) is, no less than the first (Gn 1:26 f.), a thoroughly theological document which aims to communicate a doctrine of faith, but its author (the Yahwist) uses — and uses consciously — a concrete, imaginative, dramatic manner for teaching a revealed truth which had already been communicated in the first account.[25] If he chose to concretize the theological truth of the creation of Adam in a descriptive story, it is evident that this story should correspond to the conception of the world common to him and to his contemporaries, i.e., to a view to which the idea of a biological evolution was utterly foreign. And it was likewise to be expected that the tradition of the Church should make this view its own. Nor could it be recognized as historically

---

animam primi hominis *per evolutionem* specierum," *Cursus philosophicus*, I, 1944, p. 485; cited by E. C. Messenger, *Theology and Evolution* (London, 1950), p. 176 f. — It is remarkable how the philosophical arguments against the descent theory, of which theologians made use earlier, receive less and less attention as the dispute advances. "It is thoroughly inappropriate to drag in metaphysical notions against the theory of descent," J. Kälin, *loc. cit.*, p. 46. — Cf. also E. Brisbois, "Transformisme et Philosophie," *Nouvelle Revue Theologique*, 59 (1932), pp. 577–595.

[25] "It is a fact that, among the authors of the Pentateuch, the Yahwist goes farthest in anthropomorphic and anthropopathic assertions concerning Yahweh. He is aware that he can speak of Yahweh only in this way; and the strength of his portrayal rests as much upon this knowledge as upon the realism with which he views the empirical world and the man in it," L. Rost, "Theologische Grundgedanken der Urgeschichte," *Theologische Literaturzeitung*, 82 (1957), p. 323. — The Yahwist's account can be compared to a catechism. As the catechist portrays the truths of salvation in pictorial representations, so also does the Yahwist use for his people, culturally still children, not philosophical notions and definitions, but pictures and symbols.

conditioned until the new evolutionary conception of the world was proposed and accepted. Thus the Church and revelation do not bind us to the old view. On the contrary, the new transformistic conception of the world does not contradict the teaching of the Church on man's creation, nor does it impugn the historical existence of Adam (which will, however, be further discussed later). But we should realize that our idea of the process whereby "man came into being" loses much of the concrete plasticity of the thinking of the ancients, and that our thought here will never be devoid of some element of concretion.[26]

The carefully formulated statement of Pope Pius XII in the encyclical *Humani Generis* (1950) was intended neither as an irrevocable dogmatic decision nor even as a decision at all, either for or against the compatibility of anthropological transformism with the teaching of the Church. The Pontiff's statement fully expresses the fluid state of theological knowledge in the discussion between theology and the natural sciences over the theory of descent.[27] It declares — with those reservations which are perfectly obvious to a Catholic — that the discussion of the question of descent is officially open. One can easily understand that such a statement from the Magisterium was, until a few decades ago, hardly thinkable. It is clear from the words of the encyclical that, as far as contemporary theological knowledge is concerned, it is not possible to assert (at least not with certainty) that the formation of man out of inorganic matter is revealed truth; otherwise, the Pope would doubtless have referred to the sources of revelation, to Gn 2:7, and to the interpretation of this passage as handed down by tradition. If the encyclical asserts that the proofs previously brought forth in support of anthropological transformism are inadequate, it also leaves open the possibility that the proofs will one day be convincing. In view of

---

[26] As we generally can grasp a notion only insofar as we give it pictorial form, so also are dogmatic notions bound to concrete pictures (Christ sitting at the right hand of God, the Holy Spirit dwelling in our hearts, etc.).

[27] "For this reason, the Magisterium of the Church sees no objection to making the theory of evolution the object of research and scientific discussion by specialists of both the natural sciences and theology; the problem remains that of the coming forth of the human body and its development out of lower organic forms, while maintaining that the direct creation of the human soul by God is to be held as *de fide*," Denz. 3027. Pope Pius XII had already expressed similar ideas in 1941 (*AAS*, 33, 1941, 50 [Denz. 2285]), and then again in 1953 (*AAS*, 45, 1953, 603 f.).

the direction in which both the natural sciences and theology are moving one may well suppose that the Church will one day declare that a moderated theory of descent is not contrary to revelation.

As long as this question is not closed to discussion, it will remain the duty of theology to weigh all possible solutions. We shall list here some of the principal considerations which may contribute to a resolution of the problem.

1. With regard to the conflict over the compatibility of the doctrine of evolution with the teaching of the Church, the fundamental question is the following: Does the traditional assertion of the Church and of theology that man was formed out of inorganic matter belong to the dogmatic content of revelation or does it — in line with the preevolutionary conception of the world — offer a concrete view simply attached to, and not part of, the dogmatic assertions of revelation? There are two distinct possibilities. On the one hand, the biblical author and the tradition of the Church could have meant to include this element of the whole complex picture of Gn 2–3 as a binding declaration of the way in which the body of Adam was formed. On the other hand, this may not have been the intention. Consequently, a criterion must be sought which will permit us to determine how this part of the overall picture is to be taken. In any case it is not perfectly clear from Gn 2:7 that the Creator formed the body of Adam directly out of the earth. The six days for the formation of the world, the disklike shape of the earth, the vaulted firmament stretching over the earth, and many other images, particularly in the second account, are just as clearly expressed in Scripture and tradition. Still, no one today would think of considering these descriptions as the dogmatic content of revelation; they are ways, conditioned by the old conception of the world, of presenting the truths intended by revelation. In spite of the clear literal meaning of Gn 2:7 and of tradition, it is still true that statements concerning man's formation out of inorganic matter are merely human embodiments of divine statements.

2. A valid criterion for judging this matter can be gained only from an overall view of the whole body of revealed truths which was incomplete until the advent of the New Testament. It is clear that this criterion consists precisely in the fact that one revealed truth (in Holy Scripture or tradition) may be used to explain another, or even to cast light upon all the rest of revelation, upon the entire revealed

history of salvation. This means, on the one hand, that a statement may contradict the literal sense of the sources of revelation (for example, the formation of man from an animal body rather than from the soil of the earth), and still not deny any of the defined truths of revelation or lead to falsifications of the substantial content of dogma as explained by the teaching authority of the Church and known to us as part of the history of salvation. It means, on the other hand, that a literal interpretation of an assertion of Scripture or of tradition is not necessary for the preservation of doctrines which are clearly defined by the Church.[28]

3. When this criterion is applied to our question, the following points become clear. The assertion that the human body evolved from the animal world (moderate transformism) contradicts the literal meaning of Holy Scripture and tradition; nevertheless it denies no established and defined truth of revelation, and leads to no misinterpretation of any Church teaching whatsoever. Nor does it, in fact, even come into real contact with revealed, sacred history.

The theory of evolution, first of all, is in no way opposed to the *dogma* of creation. That alone can evolve which has already been created by God, which has received from the Creator the immanent capacity for change and self-development, and which is taken by Him into the service of His ends. The history of evolution is therefore also the history of creation. "Therefore we see in evolution no diminution of God's honor nor of the dependence of the creature upon Him."[29] One might assume that God gave subhuman life the capacity and energy to develop, over millions of years, to the state where God, by creating the spiritual soul (in a couple), could then work the miracle of bringing man into existence. This is to accept a modified evolutionary theory. Nevertheless this position recognizes the stamp of the Creator in the whole man no less than does the doctrine of creation which leaves no room for any evolutionary factor.[30]

---

[28] It is clear that only the Magisterium of the Church can give us full certainty concerning the significance of a statement of the Bible or tradition. But before the Church reaches a decision, it is the business of theology to weigh the pros and cons.

[29] H. Volk, *Schöpfungsglaube und Entwicklung* (Münster i. W., 1958[2]), p. 13. Cf. also A. Mitterer, "Schöpfung oder Entwicklung der Welt — eine Alternative?" *Wissenschaft und Weltbild*, 3 (1950), 289–297.

[30] "But it would be impertinent to see the history of creation as a merely natural (horizontally successive) history of evolution, excluding, with the

This moderate theory of descent does not contradict the distinction, taught by the Church, between the nature of man and that of beasts. This distinction holds that man alone, because he alone is personal, can participate in the divine exchange and covenant upon which revelation insists in its portrayal of human history. In opposition to monistic evolutionism, a theistic and moderate transformism recognizes the essential superiority of man over all subhuman life. Precisely because of this, it does not consider man as a mere product of the evolutionary drive. Not even the most highly developed beast is able by itself to cross the "critical point of hominization" (Teilhard). Even if there were certain evidence of a genetic connection between man and the animal kingdom in the area necessary for biological evolution, the inception of human life was in any case an original beginning anew, which could take place only through a strictly creative intervention of God, through the creation of the spiritual soul in the living substratum prepared to receive it.[31]

From what has been said, it is also clear that a modified doctrine of human descent in no way denies the historicity of the biblical account of the creation of man. Even the evolutionary conception of the world does not contradict the revealed truth that at a certain time and in a certain place on this earth the miracle of man's coming into existence took place through a free act of God, which Gn 2:7 portrays so concretely and descriptively. That this miracle should happen, and how often it should happen, depends directly upon the free and creative will of God Himself.

Furthermore, it is clear that evolutionary concepts force us in no way to deny the historical reality of Adam and his original state. The doctrine of evolution leaves untouched the premises and principles upon which depend theological prehistory, the Church's teaching concerning historical original sin, hereditary sin, and redemption.

4. In the light of the *principle of economy* (a metaphysical principle, which is also realized in revelation) we can take another step.

---

word natural, the (vertically simultaneous) creation by God, replacing it by a monistic interpretation of evolution," A. Mitterer, *Die Zeugung der Organismen, insbesondere des Menschen* (Vienna, 1947), p. 217.

[31] What A. Mitterer says of the origin of every man applies with particular force to that of the first man: "Should the history of evolution be understood as history of creation, as we have just proposed, then the creation of the spiritual soul fits perfectly, as the last act of creation, into the whole history of man's evolution," *loc. cit.,* 1217 f.

God, of course, is the primary efficient cause of all being, and secondary causes operate only insofar as they are sustained in being and operation by God. But in exercising His universal causality God makes use of real secondary causes, i.e., beings to which He has given real causal efficacy. According to the principle of economy, divine transcendental causality works into the course of nature in the most discreet and economical way. This means that it uses real secondary causes whenever possible, acting outside them only when something essentially new and irreducible to any previous creature comes into being for the first time. What creation itself can do, that it must do by itself in the most absolute possible way.[32] God does not give His creature a property, only then to do Himself what the creature was intended and able to do in virtue of this property. Thus if a subhuman creature is able, by reason of a potency conferred on it by the Creator, to prepare a biological substratum for the inception of human life, then it is to be assumed that it has in fact done just this. Whether or not the animal kingdom is capable of thus preparing the biological substratum is a question for the natural sciences to decide, not theology.

These reflections indicate that the assumption made by the moderated theory of descent is thoroughly acceptable to the overall picture of the relationship of God to the world provided by revelation. Thus if the profane sciences succeed in establishing valid biological evidence of an evolution from animal forms to a "hominization" (actually not too much in the way of strict evidence has as yet been brought forward), this conclusion would in no way require a change in the Church's teaching concerning the origin of humanity. It would only mean abandoning the old way of depicting man's origin, the frame in which the doctrinal content of Genesis was customarily set in the past.

What has been said here will serve as the foundation for establishing the truth of what we shall say in the two following sections. It will be seen that one can simultaneously accept the new con-

---

[32] K. Rahner, "Theological Reflections on Monogenism," *Theological Investigations* (Baltimore, 1962), Vol. I, pp. 229–296. — "God creates, it seems, as little or as seldom as possible; much more does He seem wont to tax the potency lent to His original creation, unfolding it to His own honor and to that of the creature . . . in line with this general notion of God's bearing toward His creatures it is possible, indeed probable, that God has not effected by creative acts what is possible by evolution," H. Volk, *loc. cit.*, p. 16 f.

ception of the world and the Church's teaching on Adam as our common ancestor and on his original state without forcing together two incompatible notions of the world.

5. There is one instance, however, where our proposed criterion on the compatibility of the theory of descent with the teaching of the Church seems inapplicable. Here I am referring to the formation of Eve out of Adam's side as portrayed in Gn 2:20–24. Tradition has taken this account almost universally in a literal way (i.e., in the sense that the first woman took her physical, material origin from the body of the first man). This concept does not fit into the picture of man's origin presented by the theory of descent.[33] To be sure, there would be no contradiction in assuming that the body of the first man derived directly from the animal kingdom, whereas that of the first woman stemmed from animals only indirectly (i.e., through Adam, from whose body hers was immediately formed). It must be admitted, however, that this assumption seems to be inconsistent and by nature an unsatisfying compromise; it certainly does not commend itself well to the scientific theory of descent. This difficulty has been advanced from the beginning as one of the principal arguments against admitting the theory of descent. But if one recalls that the second account of creation presents the doctrine of creation in a large, dramatic picture consisting of many individual elements, it seems just to ask whether this particular detail is to be taken "literally," or as a symbolic way of communicating theological meaning. "There is an increasing number of exegetes who take in all seriousness the literary character of the first chapters of Genesis and see in the formation of Eve out of the rib a dramatic symbol of her equality with man and of her orientation to him. See, for instance, Cajetan, Hoberg, Hummelauer, Nikel, Holzinger, Peters, Lagrange, Junker, Göttsberger, Schlögl, Lusseau, de Fraine, Hauret, Premm, Colunga, Chaine, Bartmann, Cordero, Remy."[34] This tendency in increasingly more Catholic theologians, who have not been impeded

---

[33] This question is treated in detail by E. C. Messenger in *Theology and Evolution*, pp. 199–211. One can with good reason be skeptical over his proposed solution.

[34] K. Rahner, *op. cit.*, p. 256, note 3 — "What Paul wishes to define (1 Cor 11:8–12; Eph 5:28–30; 1 Tim 2:13 f.) concerning the woman with this reference (to Gn 2:22 f.), still remains tangibly illustrated when one assumes a less 'literal' interpretation of Eve's coming into being 'out of Adam.'" *Ibid.*, p. 267.

in any way by the Magisterium, should indicate the direction in which theological thought is developing. It should also make evident the fact that this biblical and traditional assertion presents no insurmountable difficulty in integrating the teaching of the Church with the evolutionary ideas of the modern conception of the world.[35]

In order to shed light upon the whole question of the historicity of Adam and his original state, we must now consider several special questions.

II. Do All Men Have a Common Ancestor?

Suppose we grant that the contemporary scientific assumption of man's evolution from the animal kingdom does not contradict the Church's doctrine of man's origin. We must still prove that there are no elements entering into the modern scientific view which contradict the traditional teaching of the Church concerning Adam. Holy Scripture and the Church speak of a unique individual man as the ancestor of all humanity. Even if we affirm that there is a genetic connection between man and beast, we must remember that the origin of mankind (according to the teaching of the Church and Scripture) took place only once, and in a single couple, through a creative intervention of God. All other men descend by generation from this first couple and, by reason of this common origin, participate in the universal culpability of the human race which resulted from the historical fall of the first parents into sin (original sin). Holy Scripture and the Church do not conceive the unity of humanity simply in terms of a nature specifically the same in all men — a unity of this kind would be possible even if there were different first

---

[35] Occasionally, even by Christian thinkers, the idea is suggested that the first man may have been *androgynous* (bisexed), and that the division of man's original unity into man and woman came only as a consequence of the Fall. Cf. E. Benz, *Adam, der Mythos vom Urmenschen* (München — Planegg, 1955). This notion has been held by Leone Ebreo, Jacob Böhme, the English Böhmists, J. G. Gichtel, G. Arnold, the Berleburger Bible, E. Swedenborg, Fr. von Baader, J. J. Wirz, C. G. Carus, Wl. Soloviev, N. Berdyaev. E. Brunner is right when, speaking of Myth, he says, "Androgyny belongs to Platonic thought, polarity of the sexes to Christian thought," *Dogmatik*, Vol. 2, p. 77. The androgyne myth is not to be confused with the idea, advocated by Church Fathers (and by some today), that in spite of sexual polarity the generation of offspring in the marriage of our first parents was not to take place, as after the Fall, by sexual union of the two (in fact, according to some, it was not to take place at all). Whether Gnostic or Christian motifs underlie these views cannot be discussed here.

parents for various races (polygenism). Rather the Church conceives this as a unity of generation in the strictest sense of the word, as a unity which is rooted in the generation of all men from the same physical and sole ancestor, Adam (monogenism). Does not such a view contradict the position of current scientists relative to the theory of descent? Does it not become clear precisely at this point that the Church's teaching concerning Adam can be sustained no longer by anyone who makes the modern conception of the world his own, and that the traditional "story of Adam" must be abandoned? As noted already, the story of Adam's creation from the soil of the earth is an illustrative, colorful account of the revealed truth that man was created by God. Hence, is it not possible that the biblical view of man's unity of descent is also a picturesque rendering of a theological truth? This truth would be the existence in all men of a quality whereby all belong together, a quality accounted for by their origin from one Creator and by their community in essence. Even in admitting that the biblical author and all tradition envisaged Adam as one individual man and conceived the unity of the human race as a unity of descendency, one might nevertheless consider that this notion of a single ancestor, similar as it is to the notion of creation from lifeless matter, has a purely descriptive value. Moreover, should not the literary form of the account in Genesis be considered seriously, with the words concerning Adam interpreted in a nonliteral way? In this way a conflict with the assertions of the natural sciences would be avoided. Does not the attempt to integrate the scientific, evolutionary concept of man's origin with the old religious idea of an historical Adam lead to a mixing of heterogeneous views? If it is possible to forego the idea of man's creation out of lifeless matter, then it should very well follow that the old view of a single ancestor could be abandoned and serious consideration given to the possibility that the evolution from prehuman to human forms took place not only once, but on various occasions.

At this point the inquiry into Adam's historical existence and into the compatibility of the modern conception of the world with the Church's "story of Adam" becomes truly tense and impassioned. Naturally the need for a more precise understanding of mankind's unity of origin became acute only after the natural sciences developed the theory of evolution. Throughout the whole earlier tradition of the Church, there was no problem in holding to the doctrine of monogenism. It became a subject of exciting debate only as theologians came to realize that the Church's doctrine and the sources of revelation do not necessarily exclude the transformistic point of view. As late as 1932 Bartmann disposed of the question in his manual with the brief remark: "The unity of the human race is related to the universality of original sin and redemption. Special proof of this is unnecessary (Gn 2:5–7; 2:20; 10:1; Mt 19:4; Apoc 17:26)."[36]

Gradually, however, more and more theologians saw that they would have to recognize that the evolutionary theory of man's descent from subhuman forms could reach the stage of probability or even certainty. Some even attempted to make polygenism compatible with the teaching of the Church. Thus it became urgently necessary to reflect theologically on the question of monogenism.

If we are to be clear in relating the view of natural science to the teachings of Church and theology, we must distinguish two sets of notions from one another: the notions of monogenism and polygenism on the one hand, and those of monophyletism and polyphyletism on the other.

Monogenism holds that all men descend from a single ancestor or ancestral couple (whether the ancestral body was prepared through evolution or not); polygenism, on the contrary, assumes that humanity descends from a group of first progenitors whether these were corporally created by the Creator out of lifeless matter or not.

Monogenism and polygenism are unrelated to the question of man's descent from beast; they refer to the *number* of ancestors or ancestral couples, asserting respectively that there is one pair of ancestors, or more than one. Monophyletism and polyphyletism, however, generally presume that man has evolved from lower species; for them the question is: Has man derived from various animal forms, or only from one (*phylon*)?

According to evolutionary monophyletism, the human race is immediately related by descent to only one form of animal progenitor.

According to polyphyletism living or extinct races of humanity may descend from different animal forms.

It is clear that polyphyletism necessarily implies polygenism; if one predicates various prehuman forms as the progenitors of hu-

---

[36] Vol. I (Freiburg, 1932), p. 270.

manity, one must assume *eo ipso* various first parents of humanity at a secondary stage. Monophyletism, on the other hand, implies neither monogenism nor polygenism: the "transition" from the assumed single animal ancestor to man could have taken place in various individuals (or couples) or only in one.

A. *Natural Science and the Question of Man's Origin*

Here, too, fundamental changes have been taking place in recent scientific thought. In the eighteenth and nineteenth centuries there was almost universal agreement, on the part of evolutionist and antievolutionist alike, that the various races of human history could be traced back to a single parent (who had developed, according to the evolutionary thesis, from a single animal form). Darwin himself held this monophyletic position. The contrary position, poly-phyletism, or the multiplicity of ancestors for the various races, was held by only a few in the nineteenth century; but it found a larger number of proponents as the twentieth century opened. According to earlier polyphyletists, the various human races, whether living or extinct (e.g., the black, yellow, and white races) could be traced back to various primate groups (gorilla, chimpanzee, gibbon, orangutan). Today natural scientists are almost unanimous in supporting the monophyletic thesis. According to this view, all men, whether belonging to living or extinct races, have developed from a single prehuman form (today no longer extant) to which the extant anthropoids can also be traced. "There seems to be no scientific justification for dividing all humanity, whether living and extinct, into various families. In actual fact all men give evidence of being, by reason of their morphological, physiological, and psychological characteristics, one great family, which has had a very long history, undergone significant transformations, divided and sub-divided itself into many small and characteristic groups, some of which died out completely."[37]

This does not mean, however, that contemporary naturalists believe that the evolution from the assumed prehuman life-form took place in only one ancestral couple; and this is the question of most vital interest for theology. In recent decades, in fact, certain scientists

---

[37] V. Marcozzi, *L'uomo nello spazio e nel tempo* (Milano, 1953), p. 401. Cf. also H.–V. Vallois, "Les preuves anatomiques de l'origine monophylétique de l'homme," *Anthropologie*, 39 (1929), No. 1, p. 3.

have advocated polygenism. In the view of these men (among them Rosa, Colosi, Montandon and Coon), man (as well as other species) came into existence, more or less simultaneously in various parts of the earth, and the human race can be traced back to a large number of progenitors empirically known to us in the various extant human fossils. Nevertheless, most experts today hold that there was only one place of origin for all the species, from which they emigrated to other areas of the earth. This is believed to hold true of man. To be sure, the remains of the oldest human forms are found in various regions of the earth (Asia, Africa, Europe) which seem to belong to the same geological period. However, since geological periods cover time durations lasting many thousands of years, and since it cannot be said with certainty that these periods occurred simultaneously in the various continents, we can legitimately assume that man first appeared in one geographical locality and that the differentiation of man into different races occurred during the millenia of the same geological period during which man also spread to other regions of the globe. "There is no positive evidence for concluding that man simultaneously appeared in various places of the earth. The generally accepted assumption that humanity, just as every other species, has had a 'cradle,' a center of origin and extension, today meets no positive scientific argument in opposition to it."[38]

The monophyletic hypothesis of natural science does not imply monogenism. The question remains whether in that cradle of humanity there was only one pair of human ancestors for all humanity (monogenism), or whether there were more than one ancestral couple (polygenism). It is hardly possible for natural science to reach the idea of a single original couple. Nor can it on the other hand exclude the possibility of a single couple as the progenitors of all mankind. With the methods of investigation proper to it (at least with those at its disposal today), natural science is unable to decide either for polygenism or for monogenism. Thus there is room for knowledge coming from other sources; and this is of decisive significance for theology. We can thus reiterate our claim that science does not force us to abandon a doctrine of the Church.

---

[38] V. Marcozzi, *loc. cit.,* p. 402. — "L'hypothèse monophylétique est la seule acceptable." H.–V. Vallois in the collection, *La paléontologie et l'origine de l'homme* (Paris, 1950), p. 80.

B. *Theology and the Question of Man's Origin*

Until the advent of evolutionism, monogenism was generally taken for granted by theologians. The proposition that the biblical Adam was the first man and the unique ancestor of all humanity presented no special problem to theologians. As the conflict with the theory of evolution began and as individual representatives of the profane sciences came to hold polygenistic views, Catholic theology unanimously rejected polygenism as opposed to revelation; monogenism appeared to have been expressed in Holy Scripture and in the documents of the Magisterium as an undeniably revealed doctrine. However, as more and more theologians came to see that the teaching of the Church does not necessarily exclude moderate transformism, some began to ask whether a polygenistic view of the origin of man was compatible with revelation as interpreted by the Church or not. Was it not possible to suppose that the biblical reference to the one Adam reflects the concrete thinking of the ancients, particularly the Semites, who could portray the common nature and destiny of men only in terms of an ancestral unity of blood? If this were so, then this description of the revealed message could be abandoned as a temporally limited view and replaced by one which corresponds to the world picture of contemporary natural science. The right to ask this question was justified both on the grounds of advances made by scientific research into the origin of humanity and on the basis of studies by exegetes on the literary forms of Holy Scripture and the attitude of ancient peoples to the writing of history. There was grave concern lest the natural sciences should one day trace the origin of humanity to various prehuman progenitors or to many ancestral parents, and thus raise insuperable obstacles for exegetes. This concern led some theologians, before the encyclical *Humani Generis* (1950), to the point of proposing polygenism (polyphyletic or monophyletic) as a hypothesis compatible with the teaching of the Church.[39] By advocating this, these theologians sought to forestall a possible future conflict between science and faith. According to this polygenistic hypothesis, the "Adam" of the Bible and tradition does not necessarily designate a unique ancestor, but can be interpreted as the *collective* expression of a plurality of

---

[39] The exegetes and theologians who proposed polygenesis as a hypothesis are mentioned by K. Rahner, *op. cit.*, p. 238, note 1.

first men from whom all men descend.[40] Others proposed that the biblical Adam was indeed an individual human being, but they likewise held that after Adam men existed who did not descend from him. The unity of the human race should be understood, they held, not as a physical unity, but as a *moral* unity of origin.

The proponents of this hypothesis understood clearly that under no circumstances was doubt to be cast on the historical validity of the biblical account of the Fall. If the Church's doctrine of original sin was not to be given an entirely new and heterodox meaning, then the *historical character of the biblical and magisterial assertions regarding original sin* must be kept as the fundamental premise for original sin. The opinion of these Catholic theologians thus differs completely from the position of those Protestant theologians who choose to see in the biblical account of the Fall only a myth which tells us, in the form of a "story" of the remote origin of humanity, that from the very beginning every man has been found to be a sinner. The Catholic advocates of polygenism were forced to make their own interpretation of the Fall. They explained it as a sort of *collective sin,* either in the sense of the sin of the whole group of men or in the sense of God's attributing to all these "first" men the responsibility and guilt of the sin of an individual who represented them all.

This attempt to integrate polygenism into the teaching of the Church led theologians to a conscious investigation of the question, whether monogenism is really part of the binding, revealed content of faith or not. For the majority of theologians polygenism was definitely a contradiction to revelation. In many works and discussions every polygenistic proposal was rejected as an implicit or open denial of the unity of man's origin as understood by Holy Scripture and the Church. The majority of theologians thought that it led to an interpretation of hereditary sin contradictory to the teaching of the Church.[41]

The stand taken by the encyclical *Humani Generis* with respect

---

[40] The first humans would thus have been personified in the "Adam" whose history the biblical author is portraying.

[41] A great number of the almost countless treatments of the question of polygenesis in the years preceding and following *Humani Generis* are listed by K. Rahner, *op. cit.,* p. 234 f., note 1. — For the biblical notion of the "corporative personality," and its application to Adam, cf. J. de Fraine, *Adam et son lignage* (Bruges, 1959).

to polygenism is essentially different from its critique of the theory of descent.[42] Monogenism is not defined as dogma, nor is polygenism condemned as heresy, but the attempt to show that polygenism is compatible with the teaching of the Church is nevertheless rejected. Its carefully thought-out wording merely reflects the present state of theological knowledge: "it is not clear how this opinion . . . can be compatible" (without doubt this is less radical than if the wording were: "It is clear that this opinion is not compatible.")[43] Accordingly, the qualification of monogenism as "theologically safe" corresponds to theological thinking on the matter.[44] At times the Preadamite hypothesis, which first arose in the seventeenth century, appears. This predicates the existence, before the Adam of the Bible, of men who died out before Adam so that no part of the present humanity would have descended from them. These Preadamites (possibly of polygenistic origin) were not created for a supernatural end and were hence constituted in the state of pure nature as opposed to the supernatural and fallen nature proper to Adam and his seed.[45]

---

[42] "There are other conjectures, about polygenism (as it is called), which leave the faithful no such freedom of choice. Christians cannot lend their support to a theory which involves the existence, after Adam's time, of some earthly race of men, truly so called, who were not descended ultimately from him, or else supposes that Adam was the name given to some group of our primordial ancestors. It does not appear how such views can be reconciled with the doctrine of original sin, as this is guaranteed to us by Scripture and Tradition, and proposed to us by the Church. Original sin is the result of a sin committed, in actual historical fact, by an individual man named Adam, and it has a quality native to all of us, only because it has been handed down by descent from him," Denz. 3028. Cf. Rom. 5:12–19.

[43] E. C. Messenger synthesizes the sense of the encyclical's formula in this way: "Polygenesis is excluded as long as there is no evident way of bringing this doctrine into unison with the teaching of the Church concerning original sin. But this unison can never be found, "The Origin of Man according to Genesis" in *God, Man, and the Universe*, p. 240. The transformations undergone by exegesis and dogmatics since the seventeenth century prohibit, in any case, all apodictic judgments in the matter.

[44] No higher theological qualification is justifiable today. Were monogenesis clearly contained in an earlier dogmatic decision of the Magisterium of the Church, the Pope would certainly have evoked such authority. For a thorough justification and explanation of the qualification "theologically safe," cf. K. Rahner, *op. cit.*, p. 233, n. 2.

[45] "Leur rôle dans la vie future serait pour le théologien de marquer, plus nettement et plus diversement que les petits enfants des limbes, la place de la nature pure," Ch. Journet, *Petit catéchisme sur les origines du monde* (St. Maurice, 1950), p. 42. — Cf. E. Amann, "Préadamites," *Dictionnaire de Théologie Catholique*, XII, cols. 2793–2800.

Humani Generis apparently avoids intentionally the question of Pre-adamitism. According to the thinking of most theologians, however, this hypothesis has so many difficulties that it can in no way be considered as a solution to the problem.

Some of the principal concerns of any judicious review of the problem of monogenism can be briefly stated as follows:

1. Monogenism is an important instance in the *encounter between the Church's teaching and the scientific concept of the world.* Since scientific research can now speak with some authority on man's origin and unity, theology should naturally inquire whether the re-vealed doctrine on man's unity of origin is associated with any notions which should be pruned away in order to grasp rightly the meaning intended. The discoveries of present-day exegesis do not in principle exclude such a possibility. In view of the difficulty of defining exactly the provinces of natural science and theology, and in view of the present state of knowledge on both sides, it is also perfectly understandable that *as yet no final certainty has been reached on either side.*

2. As far as an evolution of animal forms up to man is concerned, Catholic teaching must insist that the actual creation of man was possible only through a new creative act of God. Consequently, it is implied that this divine intervention occurred as often as it suited the free will of the Creator. It is legitimate to ask whether this crea-tive will (the Author of the supernatural order) has really been revealed. This question cannot be resolved through simple exegesis of the accounts of Genesis concerning Adam and through an inter-pretation of references to these accounts in the New Testament. In his article, "Theological Aspects of Monogenism," which is perhaps the most significant work on this problem, Karl Rahner analyzes the problem exhaustively, taking issue with the usual scriptural proofs.[46] Only the *whole of revelation, completed by the New Testament,* and as authentically interpreted by the Church, can be considered here as a *valid criterion* (cf. above, pp. 41–42).

3. The application of this criterion leads us to the conclusion that polygenism — contrary to the theory of descent — requires an essen-tial change of the Church's teaching concerning original sin and

---

[46] *Op. cit.,* pp. 229–296. Concerning the possibilities and limitations of a direct proof from the Old and New Testaments, p. 275 ff. For a critique of the usual form of the indirect proof, pp. 293–299.

redemption. This is indicated in Pius XII's encyclical and is maintained by all proponents of monogenism. We cannot review here the difficulties and ungrounded assumptions of polygenesis which its critics have rightfully noted.[47] We shall rather attempt a general, but simplified, restatement of Karl Rahner's positive proof.[48] The proof will be presented indirectly, by showing that a Christological truth necessarily implies an "Adamological" premise.

I. Christ can be the Head and redeeming Mediator of all men with the Father only on condition that He, the eternal Son, became truly a member of a true community, the one human race. Certainly we become His brothers (with the hereditary claim to His glory before God) in the full sense of the word only by sharing in the redemption He accomplished, but this community unquestionably presupposes a true community of flesh and blood "from one" (*ex henos,* i.e., Adam — cf. Heb 2:11). This community is not based on a specific similarity of nature, but is a physical, substantial participation, by birth from a woman, in a comprehensive real history of the guilt of the whole race. It is no use to weaken this Christological assertion of the New Testament by insisting that its premise in the Old Testament represents a "Semitic" or "archaic" way of thinking (the impossibility of conceiving a common destiny and way of life other than in terms of a community of race), for the New Testament does not cite the Old here so as to derive meaning and importance from it, but seizes upon it with its own new meaning. The New Testament establishes the Redeemer's solidarity with all men precisely upon the intrinsic connection between the two Testaments.[49]

II. This Christological truth requires that the unity of race be understood in a strict sense, as a fact dependent on a first man who establishes the totality of the race in its historical origin. If we see the disastrous situation of all members (original sin) not as history but as something in the nature of man, then we shall end in Manichaeism. If, on the other hand, we see it as resting upon a purely free imitation of ancestors, rather than upon something preordained for every new member of humanity, we are guilty of

---

[47] Synthesized by K. Rahner, *op. cit.,* p. 286 f.

[48] *Ibid.,* pp. 286–296.

[49] And if the generations preceding Jesus go back, in the Gospel of St. Luke, to Adam, and if contemporary biblical criticism acknowledges no historical content, in the modern sense, in the discussions of Adam, one must ask all the more insistently what St. Luke intended to tell us with this listing.

Pelagianism. Such a "purely" historical situation, which must be conceived at the same time as an unconditionally universal tragedy (since all flesh stands in need of salvation), can have come about in no other way than through the free act of that man who — in an analogy to Christ which Paul rightly emphasized — is so veritably a link in the chain that he is simultaneously both its origin and its founding and permeating principle. And if Christ as a "later member" can (only as the Son of God) become the salvation of all, it is not possible to think that anyone other than the first man could bring about a disaster for all. Polygenism is necessarily excluded. If Adam is to be the principle demanded at all costs by this Christological dogma, he cannot be just any individual or typical exemplar of humanity. His history cannot be simply a piece of our history — as little as this may mean to our modern habits of thinking. It is to be expected, indeed it is to be postulated theologically, that Adam's world does "not fit into our world and its science."

4. Another fundamental contribution to this problem is found in Rahner's significant attempt to come to grips with this subject metaphysically. The principle of economy, already mentioned in connection with the problem of descent, can be used here to great advantage. In freely calling man into existence, God has established a "first thing," i.e., a being which — though in a different way than the Creator — can itself bring things into existence, a being which possesses, besides the power of action, the power of generation. Since the power of generation of a single human couple is sufficient in itself to constitute the origin of the whole of humanity, it would be against the principle of economy for God to call still other first parents into existence through subsequent free acts. For He would be doing what the creature itself was called into existence to do. As Rahner says: "Suppose it were possible for the animal kingdom to evolve in such a way that various animal forms were fit subjects for the reception of human life, for the creation of men. We must still assume that this miracle has taken place only once. It is the establishing of something metaphysically new (man) which was able and called upon to increase by multiplying itself. This event was never again to be repeated, otherwise true creation would have become a commonplace in human history."[50]

"Nor do these considerations," writes Father Rahner, "result in

---

[50] *Op. cit.*, p. 295.

any forced compromise between a moderate anthropological theory of descent and monogenism. Both repose in more or less the same way upon a metaphysical principle of economy. . . . What the world can do alone, it must do as completely alone as possible. This accounts for the preparation of the biological substratum for man's coming into being and for the propagation of the human race as well."[51]

Theological polygenism is an impossible and unnecessary accommodation of Church doctrine to hypotheses gradually formulated in the development of a scientific conception of the world and incapable of strictly scientific verification. These attempts are beneficial in that they lead to a more explicit grasp of the revealed truths (and of their significance) concerning the unity of the origin of humanity. But only two positions are open to us. On the one hand, there is the radical renunciation of the historical validity of the biblical and traditional assertions concerning Adam and the Fall. This necessarily involves a radical renunciation of the Church's doctrine of original sin and a denial of the doctrine of redemption. On the other hand, we can maintain the historical reality of a single ancestor, Adam, and of his Fall as the premise for the doctrines of original sin and redemption as they have always been understood by the Church. This upholding of Church doctrine places us, however, in no opposition whatsoever to scientific progress as certainly established.

III. THE QUESTION OF MAN'S ORIGINAL STATE

Essentially involved in the Church's account of the origin of humanity is the teaching that God called into existence, by creating a spiritual soul in matter (lifeless or living), a first man as the progenitor of all humanity. But even more is involved. For God

---

[51] *Ibid.,* p. 296. — Preadamitism seems at first to make possible a reconciliation between polygenesis and the Church's teaching concerning the historical fact of Adam and the Fall. These men, extinct before the appearance of Adam, could have had a polygenistic origin, while the humanity of which revelation speaks is traceable back to the sinful couple in Eden. Thus it seems that we could preserve the monogenesis of the Bible. With more careful examination, however, this view leads us to a dead end. The assumption of the existence of men on earth with no relationship of descendency with the present humanity contradicts the views of natural science, with the result that the conflict which was to have been avoided by means of this hypothesis is, as a matter of fact, not avoided at all. This theory is extremely arbitrary, and theology has received it negatively. Cf. K. Rahner, *op. cit.,* p. 257, note 1.

destined this new being, for whose welfare and life He had made the
the rest of creation, to a supernatural end which absolutely trans-
scended all the claims and natural potentialities of any creature. He
provided man in a seemingly wasteful way with graces and gifts
that corresponded to this supernatural destiny. He endowed him
with sanctifying grace, with the gift of immortality and of the interior
harmony of all powers (integrity or freedom from concupiscence).[52]
He protected man from suffering and pain, gave him a knowledge
which corresponded to his responsibility to his posterity, and conferred on him sovereign dominion over other creatures. God wanted
the recipient of His covenant to be more than a creature endowed
with spiritual faculties; He wanted him to be a highly graced son.
According to the Church, the placing of Adam in Eden did not only,
or even chiefly, mean that God surrounded the first man with a
terrestrial paradise; it meant, above all, that He gave him a nature,
at once spiritual and corporeal, which was at peace with itself and
which made him a full and perfect man, made to the supernatural
image of God. The "original man" of Church tradition possessed the
supernatural grace of holiness — which man can possess today
because of Redemption; but in addition he was gifted with "preternatural" qualities which lent him an inner harmony of nature,
qualities which man today does not possess in spite of the Redemption. Thus he was more perfect than any man will ever be until
the end of time.

Does not a contradiction appear precisely at this point? Is this
teaching not diametrically opposed to the empirically verified knowledge of natural science? For according to science man was quite
imperfect at the beginning; he was undeveloped, a being who was
to develop through immeasurable ages toward an ever higher perfection. Science can show us the millenia-old remains of the earliest
human forms unearthed by archaeologists. These fossil remains seem
to present no reason for doubting their primitive character and
similarity to animals. Can a man of today, whose glory, but also
whose problem is truly the scientific conception of the world, still
accept the traditional view in the Church of man's perfect original
state? Is it not obvious that in the religious view we find reflected
an old, mythical, metaphysically dated conception of the world,

[52] Cf. K. Rahner, "The Theological Concept of *Concupiscentia*," *Theological Investigations* (Baltimore, 1962), Vol. I, pp. 342–382.

according to which the perfect must stand at the beginning? Can we really conceive of the Adam of the Church's teaching, a man endowed with such perfections, as the first man pictured by science, a man quite similar to an animal? On the other hand, can the assertions of natural science regarding primitive man be harmonized with the supernatural gifts which the Church and theology attribute to the first man? At this point, it appears E. Brunner came to a standstill and called the attempt to think both positions at once: "a bastard conception," the fusion of the most heterogenous views. It appears, in fact, impossible to advocate simultaneously the new conception of the world and the old teaching of the Church — and if one attempts it all the same, then what results will necessarily be something other than the Adam of the Bible and tradition.

There is still not too much written about this matter in theological literature, although the question arises even if a genetic connection between man and the animal world is rejected.[53]

A. *Natural Science and the Question of Man's Original State*

The notion, long considered by many as self-evident, that the farther back one goes into the history of mankind, the more primitive and animal-like will man be found to be, is today being subjected to serious questioning. Recent findings have indicated that human forms, with the distinguishing marks that are characteristic of men today, lived at the same time as did those primitive types also unearthed by science. Hence we ask if there was at the origin of mankind, a type of man similar to present-day man or a primitive type

---

[53] The question is treated by M.–M. Labourdette, O.P., *Le Péché originel et les origines de l'homme* (Paris, 1953), Chap. V: "La perfection de l'état originel," pp. 169–181. — The question of the compatibility of the gifts of Adam's original state should be examined in more detail because as a result of widespread evolutionistic thinking there is the danger, particularly with specialists, that the doctrine of man's original paradisial state and of his supernatural privileges will no longer be taken seriously, that it will in fact be considered as at best mythological or even as a naïve fairytale. And the fact is hardly taken into consideration that with the relinquishing of this doctrine, one also excludes the Church's understanding of original sin, which faithful Christians naturally do not want to reject. On the other hand it may very well be that the faithful are holding to certain natural notions of the paradisial state of the first parents as if they were holding to truths of faith, and that they close their minds categorically before the knowledge of the natural sciences. — Cf. H. Rondet, "Croyons-nous encore au péché originel?" In *Problèmes pour la réflexion chrétienne* (Paris, 1945), pp. 9–39.

whose morphological and physiological properties were much more similar to the animal primates. Is the development of humanity to be understood as a purely progressive evolution (i.e., from a man*like* form up to *homo sapiens*), possibly with unequal rapidity of development in the various branches of humanity; or should it be regarded, at least partly, as a regressive evolution (i.e., from the *sapiens* form down to the various animal-like forms that have been found), or perhaps in some other way as yet not thought of? In recent years there has been a shift in the notions that natural scientists are able to formulate concerning the appearance of the earliest man and the course of his biological history. This shift was decisively influenced by the discovery that different groups of men existed, evidently from the very beginning, with either theromorphous (animal-like) or *sapiens*-tending characteristics. In this connection we shall quote P. Overhage, a noted expert in the matter as it stands today: "With the growing store of findings it seems ever more evident that the hypothetical succession and division of the great form-families (Anthropus, Neanderthal, and Sapiens) changed into an extremely complicated co-existing of groups with theromorphous and sapiens-tending features in the most diversified combinations throughout the entire ice-age."[54] "Instead of considering the fossil remains of humans as steps in a series of forms, as stages on the path from an original primitive form to a resultant higher form, one interprets them today, on the evidence of existing knowledge, principally as variants of a type or form-family. To be sure, this interpretation is not yet proved, but there is constantly more reason and justification for the idea that from the very beginning, and throughout the whole Ice Age, the development of man oscillated about a middle form type, about a 'forma typica' as Lebzelter called it, which, because of the less protruding nose and mouth, the less receding forehead, the higher hair growth over the eyes, etc., possessed much fewer theromorphous features, and which stood nearer to the sapiens form. Other forms, then, which developed more decidedly in the direction of the sapiens form, or in that of the theromorphous form, can be grouped about this middle type as variants."[55] "If it is as yet impossible to form any certain and

---

[54] P. Overhage, *Um das Erscheinungsbild der ersten Menschen* (Quaestiones disputatae 7) (Basel-Freiburg-Wien, 1959), p. 63.
[55] *Op. cit.*, p. 78 f.

final judgment concerning the appearance of the first man, then it would seem preferable to assume, on the evidence of the findings, particularly of such significant deposits of theromorphous and sapiens-tending fossils, which are found juxtaposed, that his appearance was not purely theromorphous, but tends rather toward the 'forma typica,' i.e., he had a number of sapiens features of weaker or stronger formation. This combination would then be the point of departure for the ins and outs and ups and downs of the feature mutations of man."[56]

B. Theology and the Original State of Our First Parents

We must limit ourselves here to the sketching of some essential viewpoints from which to judge the relationship between the scientific hypothesis concerning primitive man and the theological doctrine of man's original state. In order to avoid the criticism that theology makes things too easy for itself by assuming an advantageous scientific position even before it is proved, let us suppose — out of mere formality, without really asserting it — the theologically disadvantageous supposition that natural scientists should be universally of the opinion that the first man was definitely animal-like in nature.[57] Must such an opinion, we ask, be denied in the name of faith and theology? Does the Catholic doctrine of the supernatural and preternatural endowments of our first parents demand that we require the first man to have a physical appearance closer to ours than to wild beasts? It is impossible to give a definitive answer to this question today. But the opinion may surely be expressed that this question may be answered negatively.

1. First, it is certain that the teaching of the Church says nothing directly concerning the *biological constitution and appearance* of our first parents. Without doubt, the sacred writers as well as all Christendom until very recently, pictured Adam and Eve as persons at least as "perfect" in physical appearance as are men today. A cultural level — agriculture! — was assumed for them which the profane sciences are unable to claim for primitive man. But all these

---

[56] *Op. cit.,* p. 84.

[57] Anthropological research scientists naturally do not expect ever to find the truly first human couple. But they are convinced that the type of the absolutely first men corresponds somewhat to the oldest forms that have been found.

earlier notions are elements of the old conception of the world, and do not belong to the substance of the teaching of the Bible and the Church. Thus one who holds fast to the Church's teaching concerning the gifts of man's original state, without sharing the world view of the ancients, does not thereby surrender anything of the proper content of the traditional faith of the Church. His Adam is still the first parent of tradition, even if his concrete notions of Adam differ from the temporally conditioned views of the ancients.

Nor does the Church say anything concerning the geological epoch in which Adam lived. If we consider the plant and animal world of the early quaternary or of the late tertiary as the environment of the first man we indeed abandon the earlier conception of the world, but we do not thereby change any tenet of Church doctrine. The dogmatic notion "Adam" remains the same. Adam is and remains the first man and the one progenitor of humanity, provided by the Creator, because of his very special position, with advantages which natural science can neither discuss nor deny. The notion of time and space, which the believer today attaches to his belief in Adam, may differ from that of the ancients; what is proper and essential to faith, however, remains untouched. Only an identification of current notions (which in any case will always be found in our thinking) with essentials of faith can lead to the inference that the Adam of the Bible and tradition becomes, with a change of the notion of space and time, something fundamentally different.

2. Anyone who does not profess materialistic, monistic evolutionism (which is not only a conception of the world, but also a dogmatic, erroneous belief) knows that the spiritual soul animating the first man — and this was not present in brutes, even the most highly developed — provided the "point of departure" for the endowment of supernatural grace. Even if the first man were biologically "primitive," he was in any case a fully human person, capable of genuine personal behavior and action, and thereby a subject whom God could make a partner of His covenant and endow with those supernatural graces and preternatural qualities. And it is these qualities which are the proper concern of the Church and theology, and indeed not only because they are discussed in Genesis, but above all because they are an element of the New Testament revelation concerning original sin and Redemption. As man's progenitor

Adam was the sole bearer of that human nature which was to develop by procreation and which was to be extended out to a vast humanity. The gifts with which he was endowed were destined to all future bearers of the nature inherited from him (hereditary grace). The loss, through fault, of hereditary grace meant that Adam could pass on only a nature deprived of grace; he established, as K. Rahner has said, "a universal situation of disaster, binding for all men in advance of their own personal choice and freedom," into which every man, as offspring of Adam, is generated (original sin).

3. The doctrine of these privileges of man's original state is in no way conditioned by temporally limited conceptions, and cannot be abandoned without detriment to revealed doctrine (in the light of our changed world view). It is neither myth nor the invention of theologians.[58] The universal disastrous situation of humanity (original sin) has, according to the teaching of New Testament revelation (Rom 5), a human, historical origin, namely in Adam's sinful act. Without his supernatural elevation as a result of the hereditary graces of his original state, however, Adam would not have been able to bring about this disaster.

4. The biological history of humanity shows that the outward appearance of men was subject, in spite of the unchanging essential form of the spirit, to a great range of variation. Now it is our opinion that, neither on the grounds of any of the several supernatural and preternatural gifts of paradise, nor on the grounds of their totality, can it be proven that the first parents in paradise possessed, among all the morphological and physiological combinations possible, only one definite biological appearance, free of theromorphous characteristics, as the expression of their spiritual *raison d'être*.[59] An animal-

---

[58] In any case one cannot deny that Church Fathers and theologians were wont, influenced by their notion of the world and by their philosophy, to attribute at times excessive importance to certain single privileges of Adam, and that we need not agree with such exaggerations. Thus if St. Thomas, for example (*Summa Theologiae*, I, q. 94, a. 3), makes the statement that Adam surpassed in knowledge, because of God-given wisdom and science, all the generations of men who are ever to come after him, or if many Fathers thought it incompatible with the peace and harmony of paradise that animals should have consumed one another as food, we may simply refuse to agree. Cf. Labourdette, *loc. cit.,* p. 66 f.

[59] Cf. the exceptional study by K. Rahner published as an introduction to Overhage's *Um das Erscheinungsbild der ersten Menschen.*

like outward appearance of Adam would certainly fall short of
our ideal and sense for beauty. However, the latter can hardly
constitute a valid theological criterion.[60]

It follows from the above that the question of the morphology
and physiology, of the corporal nature, of the outward appearance
of the first man is not to be answered by theology, but by natural
science. This answer is not clear and definitive today; it will probably
never be finally decided.

5. The privileged original state of the first parents — which incidentally was of very short duration in comparison to the long history
of mankind's development — is genuine history, yet it lies *beyond
the area of history open to exploration by natural reason*. Rahner
says rightly that the "transcendence of the history of man's origin"
means "that the historical reality of man's early history is not
simply a piece of our homogeneously structured history (in spite
of all the variety and antithesis therein) but is a history with its
own peculiar structures. And it must be so taken (if it be taken
seriously), in spite of all the overlapping in both areas of history."[61]
Thus should research into nature and primitive history prove able to
provide us some knowledge concerning the first human beings, they
will nevertheless never be able to tell us everything, and especially
nothing about the essence and existence of the first parents in their

---

[60] It is known that St. Irenaeus depicted the first parents in paradise as
children, i.e., as human beings standing at the beginning of their individual
biological development. Thus it might be very well to think of them as human
beings standing at the beginning of a development of the whole human
descendency. The idea that Adam was the bearer of all the virtualities of
human nature which unfolded in his progeny in the vast millennia of human
descent and development constitutes no detraction from the high idea of the
great progenitor of humanity advocated by the Church. — Here also we
might make reference to the principle of economy. Through a creative act,
God gave man what the natural evolution of life could never attain: the
spiritual soul, plus preternatural and supernatural gifts. He did not, however,
give him directly what nature was able to accomplish through the unfolding
of interior powers: the full development of human nature.

[61] K. Rahner, *op. cit.*, p. 233, note 2. One of the elements which are
common to both areas of history is, of course, the biological structure of
man. One can hardly assume that the first parents were of a higher biological
structure than earliest men found by modern science, and that as a punishment
for their sin the first parents, or their immediate successors, fell to a lower
level. A rapid radical morphological change would require intervention from
above nature, i.e., a miracle. There is no reason for assuming such a "puni-
tive miracle" (which the sources of revelation indicate in no known instance).

original state that would be truly important for our life as men before God.

Thus if the profane sciences and theology stick to their particular provinces (which, to be sure, are not so easily distinguished one from the other) and each stays open to the genuine truth provided by the other, there is no reason to fear any real opposition between faith and modern science. Indeed the two should work hand in hand.

"For us, what pertains to original history (Gn 1–3) and to eschatology must possess, by their very nature, an enormous difference between the image, the picture on the one hand, and the thing meant on the other."[62] From the central point of history, i.e., the redeeming "hominization" of God, in which the "hominization" of man takes its true meaning and fulfillment, we can see a light shed upon both the beginning and the end of the history of every human being, of all human kind. From Christ, Who is at once the Proton and the ever-present Eschaton, we have not only the certainty that the story of Adam is true history, but also the certain faith that the history of man's disaster initiated by the first Adam, has been annulled and replaced by the history of redemption, instituted by none other than the second Adam, the Son of God.

---

[62] K. Rahner, "The Resurrection of the Body," *Theological Investigations* (Baltimore, 1963), Vol. II, p. 208. Cf. also A. Darlapp, art. "Anfang," in *Lexikon für Theologie und Kirche*, I (Freiburg i. Br., 1957²), cols. 525–529, and K. Rahner, art. "Aetiologie," *ibid.*, col. 1011 f.

ALOYS GRILLMEIER

THE FIGURE OF CHRIST IN CATHOLIC THEOLOGY TODAY

EVER since the first coming of the Holy Spirit, Christ has been the center of the apostolic message: "But we preach Christ, the crucified, for the Jews a stumbling block, and for the gentiles folly" (1 Cor 1:23; cf. Acts 1:22–36 *et al.*). Jesus, the crucified and risen, mediator between God and man, may lay claim to this central position in the faith and theology of every age. It is the duty of every generation of theologians to bring something lasting from their time to the incessant search of the Church for the true image of Christ. Let us survey what contemporary Catholic theology has brought, and is bringing, to the Christ-Image of the Church.

Catholic theology today need not shy from our inquiry. The course of theological pursuits in recent years gives us occasion to hope that the foundations of a *"Christological Age"* have finally been laid. Though Mariology and ecclesiology have entered into the foreground in recent decades, we have witnessed nonetheless an equally intense effort to examine and deepen the Christ-image. As a matter of fact, Christ, Mary, and the Church constitute in Catholic theology an indivisible unity. They are concentric circles, as it were, about the one order of the Incarnation.

The foregoing is one of the dominant themes in Christology today. It embraces salvation as the *raison d'être* of the Incarnation. The world and history are centered on Christ. Revelation, the saving act of redemption, preaching, and theology are stamped with Christ or are oriented toward Him. But where something is in a state of flux, Catholic theology, out of long experience and tradition, inquires further into the "substance and being" lying beneath appearances. Catholic theology prefers to linger and rise gradually from its foundations, a characteristic for which it has often been harshly

66

judged. Such inquiries into the roots have marked the Church for centuries, and now new questions centering around the "Person and consciousness of Christ" are being bridged in this spirit. In surveying these problems, we believe we shall be able to shed light upon some of the most important contemporary Christological endeavors both in scientific theology and in the proclamation of the "Good News" by the Church to the world. Much of it is handed-down matter still carrying the clear stamp of the past. This is not surprising in an age of such momentous theological breakthrough as we are witnessing.

I. SALVATION AS THE "RAISON D'ÊTRE" OF THE INCARNATION

The Christology that has been enshrined in theological manuals has received much criticism from within, in recent decades, and open reproof from without. Complaints are raised against an apparent separation of the doctrine of salvation by Christ from "Christology," considered as the theological study of the Person and nature of Jesus Christ. An overemphasis in Christology on the aged formulae of the old councils has perhaps hindered theologians from fully exhausting the richness of the Christ-image in Holy Scripture and even from seeing its basic contours at all. The Catholic doctrine of redemption, it is argued, is content with formal consideration of the redemptive work of Jesus Christ (seen as "atonement," "merit," "sacrifice," or "ransoming," etc.), and fails to attend to the actual working out of Redemption portrayed in the biblical "mysteries of the life of Jesus." It is urged that the image of Christ is unquestionably situated much more centrally in Catholic theology and that it performs the intrinsic function of fulfilling and bracing together all of theology's single parts.[1] Consequently, our first questions are subdivided into various individual themes, which appear to fall into two major groupings, of which the one is concerned with "Christocentric perspective" and the other with "redemption as event and history."

[1] Cf. Karl Rahner, "Chalkedon — Ende oder Anfang," in *Das Konzil von Chalcedon,* edited by A. Grillmeier and H. Bacht (Würzburg, 1951–1954, 3 ed., 1962), Vol. III, pp. 3–49; also in Rahner's *Theological Investigations* (Baltimore, 1962), I, pp. 149–200. J. R. Geiselman, *Jesus der Christus, Die Urform des apostolischen Kerygmas als Norm unserer Verkündigung und Théologie von Jesus Christus* (Stuttgart, 1951).

1. Christocentric Theology. We can speak of a subjective and an objective Christocentric theology. The first refers to a theological approach or to a subjective view of the reality of redemption. The second refers to this reality itself as effected by God.

Subjective Christocentric Theology. The call to shape the whole of theology according to the Christ-image has been raised more distinctly by Karl Barth than by anyone else. Nor has anyone answered his call more definitely than he himself. The coming of revelation and redemption in Christ constitutes for Barth the occasion of a vision up, into God, and of a vision down, into the world, man, the Church, and universal history. It is not the aim of these pages to test the peculiarities and richness of Barth's powerful synthesis. Hans Urs von Balthasar,[2] who gladly acknowledges the great caliber of Barth's work, has referred to it as an attempt to pack too much into Christology (*Christologische Engführung*). Basically it is a question of the true understanding of the relationship between God and the world, or between nature and grace. The danger of a radical "theology from above" is readily evident. A theology of this kind finds it difficult to give to the world and man, as distinct from God, their full, even if relative significance, as must be done if a supernatural monism is to be avoided.

Even Catholic Christocentric theology is aware of this problem and has difficulty in finding a solution. Such is the case when the call is heard for a more Christocentric *apologetics*. There is no doubt that Catholic apologetics — considered as an entrance and preamble to theology proper, which expounds revelation — is all too frequently compartmentalized and severed from the true science of faith. Hence the rationalistic character in many of its actual arguments. The other path was immediately tempting: "If apologetics is to be truly Christian and not something that could be constructed even by a non-Christian, then its presentation and defense cannot stand upon the level of natural reason and cannot be content with the same means. Natural reason as used here excludes faith. A genuinely Christian apologetics requires a reason upon which faith

---

[2] Hans Urs von Balthasar, *Karl Barth, Darstellung und Deutung seiner Theologie* (Köln, 1951), p. 253 f. Cf. H. Küng's article, "Christozentrik," in *Lexikon für Theologie und Kirche*, II (Freiburg, 1958²), cols. 1169–1174; F. Malmberg, *Über den Gottmenschen* (Quaestiones Disputatae 9) (Basel-Freiburg-Wien, 1960), pp. 9–26.

casts true light. An apologetics which is truly oriented toward essentials will have to take into serious consideration the original Christological constitution of human nature. It will need to consider seriously the fact that all men have been established as holding the place of the Son through the mystery of the Christ, and are in a hidden way bound up with Him, whether they now know Christ or not, whether Christ has been preached to them or not. . . ." A human being possesses, in virtue of the grace of faith within him, the "sense of Christ," which is not, however, to be confused with any form of "direct intuition." Here there is a "foundation" established by Christ Himself, "which we can presuppose" (cf. Tim 2:4).[3]

It seems clear that these assertions assume that grace is an "existential fact in the concrete man" and hence that it is in some way related to consciousness. It follows that there is in fact only the one order of salvation in Christ. Every human being stands in either a positive or a negative relationship to Him. But are we justified in unhesitatingly making this existential fact an item of reflective knowledge? Isn't the *fides ex auditu* at issue here (Rom 10:14)? The question must finally be referred to the theology of grace. Again we must return to the question of the two paths of theology, to the fundamental problem of our theory of theological method and knowledge. We are definitely still far from any final solution.

A subjective Christocentric theology requires a Christological hermeneutics.[4] A look at Protestantism may bring this home to us, for there a strong reaction against the extreme liberal spirit has taken hold and intrinsic to this trend is the search for a new hermeneutics.

---

[3] G. Schückler, "Die christologische Verfasstheit der Natura humana," in *Catholica,* XI, 1 (1956), pp. 51–64. The quotes above are from pages 51, 53, and 57. The reader is referred also to C. Nink, *Ontologie* (Freiburg, 1952), pp. 375–379; K. Rahner, "Der Christ und seine ungläubigen Verwandten," in *Geist und Leben,* 27 (1954), pp. 171–184; and *Schriften zur Theologie,* III (Einsiedeln, 1956), pp. 419–439. Schückler comes, in agreement with H. de Lubac, to the idea of a Christocentric hermeneutics. Cf. also K. H. Schekle, "Über alte und neue Auslegung," in *Biblische Zeitschrift,* Neue Folge, I (1957), pp. 161–177; A. Lang, *Fundamentaltheologie,* II (Munich, 1958[2]), pp. 269–274.

[4] See L. Malevez, S.J., "Cullmann's Functional Christology," *Theology Digest,* Spring, 1962 (X, no. 2), 115–121; O. Cullmann, "Functional Theology: a Reply," *Theology Digest,* Autumn, 1962 (X, no. 4), 215–219; D. Bowman, S.J., *The Word Made Flesh* (Englewood Cliffs, N. J.: Prentice-Hall, 1963).

The principal charge against liberalism was that it sought, by way of a positivistic process of historical negation and elimination, to discover the "Jesus of history." Its conception of God and Christ was limited to scientific abstractions and could not lead to the true (i.e., "supernatural" in the Catholic sense) encounter with redemption. Freed from a positivism which leveled everything down, and influenced by the existentialism of Martin Heidegger, Rudolf Bultmann proceeded to build everything upon the living act of "being addressed" by God and upon the divine action brought to completion therein.

The liberal approach must be rejected, because "revelation" is not an objective statement of truth at all, nor is the "redemption" objective history. Everything comes to depend, therefore, upon "being addressed," encountered in a living way, by the transcendental God: "The statement of truths rests not on isolated sayings but rather on the saying of them."[5] Everything is centered around the "significance, of a quest, for me," around "man's understanding of himself as confronted by God in Christ." The elaboration of this personal relationship gives Bultmann's theology its drive, its appeal, especially when it is contrasted with the sterile neutrality of liberalism. God's living action, encountered in Christ and designated as "revelation" must be brought into man's "existence." This is accomplished by the exegesis of New Testament texts and by a process of "demythologizing" revelation. Christology is not a matter "of communicating doctrines and facts, of questioning the possibility and reality of Christ's existence. . . . Rather, in asking questions about the meaning of a biblical text, I am really asking questions about myself. The question of Christ's existence is meaningful only if I am engaged with the greatest vitality and participation, with the most intensive existential involvement. Thus does the highest subjectivity guarantee — if it is understood correctly — the greatest objectivity."[6]

---

[5] R. Bultmann, "Die Bedeutung der 'dialektischen Theologie' für die neutestamentliche Wissenschaft," in *Glauben und Verstehen* (Tübingen, 1933) pp. 114–133), p. 116. For general reference cf. H. Fries, *Bultmann-Barth und die katholische Theologie* (Stuttgart, 1956); and J. Ternus, in *Chalkedon III*, pp. 577–611; H. Volk, *Die Christologie bei K. Barth und E. Brunner*, pp. 613–673.

[6] H. Fries, *op. cit.*

We mention these movements within Protestantism only to the extent that they help us put the right emphasis and perspective on some recent Christocentric tendencies within Catholic theology. There is also among Catholic theologians a call to shake off a methodology and hermeneutics which have been rightly accused of liberalism. We are asked to shake off pure philology, sterile scientific research, and neutral objectivity, in favor of a "theological," "interested," "engaged," dogmatic and finally Christocentric interpretation of Scripture. Hence the recourse to patristic exegesis and a pursuit of the "spiritual sense" of scripture.[7] The challenge regularly voices certain criticisms made in the nineteenth century by J. A. Möhler and M. J. Scheeben. Through modern historical thought, through a broadening of our theological methods with the categories of existential philosophy and the incorporation of biblical typology and patristic symbolism, contemporary theology should succeed in opening up this deepened understanding of Scripture and in rousing the whole of theology out of its torpor. According to Henri de Lubac the "spiritual sense" of Holy Scripture coincides with the methods of dogmatic theology. This, basically, was also Scheeben's contention. For there is an inner connection between Scripture, tradition, and the Church. Moreover, the inner dynamism of the spiritual sense leads us to the New Covenant, to the event in history when God's transcendence becomes concrete, palpable for us in Christ, the God-Man. Jesus Christ is the spiritual sense and content of Scripture. In Him is the unity of the Old Testament and the New brought to its fullness, and in Him is the sense of world history summed up. The methods of pure historical research are not sufficient for de-

---

[7] The literature here is vast, but cf. the Elenchus which appeared in Biblica, 35 (1954), pp. 7–13; 36 (1955), pp. 5–8; 37 (1956), pp. 8–13. Also A. Kerrigan, O.F.M., St. Cyril of Alexandria, Interpreter of the Old Testament (Rome, 1952), pp. 435–461; J. Coppens, Les harmonies des deux Testaments. Essai sur les divers sens des Ecritures et sur l'unité de la Révélation (Tournai, 1949); Coppens, "Nouvelle réflexions sur les divers sens des Saintes Ecritures," in Nouvelle Revue Theologique, 74 (1952), pp. 3–20; H. de Lubac, Catholicism (New York, 1955); and Histoire et Esprit. L'intelligence de l'Ecriture d'après Origène (Paris, 1950); and Der geistige Sinn der Schrift (Einsiedeln, 1952); R. E. Brown, The Sensus Plenior of Sacred Scripture (Roland Park, Md., 1955); F. Buri, "Neuere Literatur zum Problem der Hermeneutik," Schweizer Theologische Umschau, 24 (1954), pp. 66–72.

ciphering this final sense of Scripture. Such research leads merely
to a Christ-image devoid of content, attainable by purely natural
research. The inspired character of Scripture and the presence there
of divine revelation demand, in the sense of this hermeneutics,
that we approach Scripture with an epistemological apriori: We
must know beforehand that the full and sole content of revelation
is Jesus Christ, the Word of God spoken to us, the crucified and
resurrected. The interpretation of Scripture may not prescind in any
way from the sense of faith, but must rather possess faith as its
true strength, and must allow it to bear fruit. The full mystery of
Christ includes the *Corpus Mysticum,* the Church. This means that
the mystery of Holy Scripture is to be understood only in the spirit
of the Church, which is the Holy Spirit. The Holy Spirit was given
to the Church in order to lead her to the totality of revelation.

Objective Christocentrism. Today there is thus a demand for
an integration of "Christ-thinking" into our theological approach
and method. But even more is required, for there is raised the
summons to a more intensified, more substantial Christocentrism in
the separate branches of theology. A "methodological" centering of
the Christ-idea should, it is urged, bear fruit in the specific disciplines themselves. Here we are on more solid ground than we were
before, in the discussion of subjective Christocentrism. The question
concerning the "motif of the Incarnation," the so-called *prae-
destinatio Christi,* has not as yet been decided in favor of either the
one or the other party, whether Scotist or Thomist. Nonetheless,
the thought that history and creation in general are bound up in
Christ is winning more and more followers — and here Karl Barth's
theology is not the least influential factor.

The current controversy transcends the type of treatment usual
in traditional theology and preaching; and at the same time gains
in relevance to modern man. The knowledge that the classical passage for the *predestination of Christ* (Col 1:15 ff.) refers precisely
to the Word made flesh (and not the preexisting Logos as such)
acquires for this idea a strong biblical foundation.

We do not wish to attempt here even to sketch the structure
of a Christocentric theology. Serious efforts have already been
made elsewhere to complete various theological disciplines in the
light of Christology. This has been done with particular effective-

ness in the area of sacramental and moral theology.[8] And particular advantages are rendered ecclesiology (together with Mariology) and eschatology when they are given a Christocentric orientation.[9] The Christocentric idea will serve to deepen our recognition that redemption is incarnational in character. Christ, the Church, the sacramental life — and with these also our piety — together compose one indivisible whole. Christ's becoming man is not a mere phase in history, but is of "eternal significance." Upon it, upon His incarnation, is founded not only the eternal Church, but also the temporal Church. "The Lamb" belongs, like God, to the heavenly Jerusalem: "No temple did I see in her. The Lord God, the Almighty, *and the Lamb* is her temple. The city is in need of no light, whether light of the sun or of the moon. The glory of God enlightens her. Her lamp is the *Lamb"* (Apoc 21:22 f.). "The throne of God *and of the Lamb"* belong to heaven (Apoc 22:1, 3). The objective Christocentrism of the Bible has in fact not been harvested, or for the most part even considered by theologians. Theology can and must begin and end with Christ. Today's pursuit of a theology of history — as thorny and untrodden as the path may be — can find substance in these thoughts.

2. **Salvation as Event and History.** The same position taken by Rudolf Bultmann against liberalism, and historicism, and upon which he founded his new hermeneutics, was also the occasion of his special

---

[8] Cf. K. Rahner, "An Outline of Dogmatic Theology," in *Theological Investigations,* I (Baltimore, 1962), pp. 20–38; H. Schillebeekx, *Christ the Sacrament of Encounter* (New York, 1963). Cf. also J. Fuchs, "Die Liebe als Aufbauprinzip der Moraltheologie. Ein Bericht," *Scholastik,* 29 (1954), pp. 79–87.

[9] Cf. O. Semmelroth, *Kirche als Ursakrament* (Frankfurt, 1955²), and "Die Kirche als 'sichtbare Gestalt der unsichtbaren Gnade,'" *Scholastik,* 28 (1953), pp. 23–29; K. Rahner, "Die ewige Bedeutung der Menschheit Jesu für unser Gottverhältnis," in *Geist und Leben,* 26 (1953), pp. 279–288, and *Schriften zur Theologie,* III, pp. 47–60. Rahner rightly underscores the fact of grace as created, but accidental grace is always (as a communication "of God" to the created soul) simultaneously an "uncreated grace." As such it is most essentially and intrinsically the grace of God become man. Christ did not merely effect it "meritoriously" in a distant point of the past. He remains, in His glorious humanity, the permanent realization of this grace. At the same time every grace has also an ecclesial significance by means of which it orients one toward the Church. Cf. Rahner's "Die Gliedschaft an der Kirche nach der Lehre der Enzyklika Pius XII., 'Mystici Corporis,'" *Zeitschrift für katholische Theologie,* 69 (1947), pp. 129–188, especially 176–188; also in *Theological Investigations,* II, pp. 1–88.

understanding of revelation. This understanding goes under the term
of *Actualism.*

All proponents of dialectical theology are more or less familiar
with this idea. It is, in short, the viewing of revelation as the
deed and action of God disclosing Himself to His creation. Revelation is seen as an act, an occurrence, an event of this world which
comes from God. It is characteristic of revelation that it occurs
once and only once. It is essentially unrepeatable, "historical." It
is existential, actual. We have here an extremely neat reversing of
the scholastic *agere sequitur esse.* The question of an objective
being lying behind revelation is not even raised. We need not stress
here what consequences this pure actualism can have for our understanding of who or what Christ is. Karl Barth has tried to grasp
this character of revelation as act and to show the objective reality
involved and contained in it. He conceives of "actuality" as more
or less complementary to "nature." The action of God in Christ,
the Christ-event, is anchored and centered in the *person* of the
God-man. Thus the question of being has an important place in
the Christology of Karl Barth's church dogmatics — so much so
that for him the doctrine of salvation (viewed here as the work
of Christ) stands in a secondary position.[10] He thus takes up arms
against the universal *horror physeos,* the dread of nature.

We point to this state of affairs in order to show that the traditional direction of Catholic dogmatics, proceeding from Christ's
being to His work, can be thoroughly modern and has advantages
which cannot be easily foregone. Nevertheless it is proper and
necessary to integrate more closely Christ's nature with His work,
Christology with soteriology, being with doing. Not that this has
been entirely lacking in the past. But when, from the very inception
of our Christological efforts, we insist upon knowing the motif of
the incarnation, and ask: "Why did God become man?" then only
will we at last cast our inquiry in a soteriological framework. It
must not be peripheral; rather it should tend to permeate organically
every facet of Catholic doctrine concerning the person of Christ.
It is possible, without throwing over what has been handed down,
at least to draw the contours of a definitely soteriological image of

---

[10] K. Barth, *Kirchliche Dogmatik,* IV, 1 (Zollikon-Zürich, 1953), pp. 133–
170.

Christ — and one based upon the words of Holy Scripture. It can be extremely profitable for us to travel the road twice; once from His deed to His being, and again from His being to His work. Before we reiterate the classical doctrine of the person of Christ as expressed in the formulae of the ancient Councils, we should develop the features of the biblical figure of Christ, for they remain as standards for the theology of the Fathers. It will be especially fruitful to allow the salvation motif to cast light upon the being and nature of Christ, upon His natural humanity, and upon His supernatural accomplishment. In this connection it should be made clear that the hypostatic union itself should be taken as the fundamental figure and model of all union with God whatsoever. Doctrines concerning the "knowledge" and "power" of Christ should be carried beyond their formal abstractions to the concrete depiction of the figure of Christ, to the tangible image of Him bringing "revelation" and "redemption." The first chapter of John — indeed his entire Gospel — will uncover particular depths for us here. The question of His "one Sonship," His freedom, and His sinlessness reveal a Christ eminently stamped with the salvation motif. When this is seen, we can begin to investigate the offices of the Christ.

Christ as Event and Act.   If a doctrine of salvation in Christ is to be developed it should not be limited — unavoidable as this factor may be — to a formal inquiry into the satisfaction, merit, and sacrifice of Christ. For what salvation is, and how it is realized, is defined by God Himself in the Person of Jesus and in the happenings in and around Him. We are referring to the "mysteries of the life of Jesus," i.e., those events which focus the light issuing from Christ and which let it fall in a special way upon the world. For example, the virginal conception tells us that God, not man, begins things in the economy of grace; the happenings in and about the birth are so many inexhaustible occasions on the level of the theology of grace for an encounter with Christ; His baptism and temptation, His transfiguration and abandonment, His passion and death, His descent into hell and His resurrection, His ascension and sitting at the right hand of the Father. All this — as well as the fact of Christ's teaching and miracles — has still hardly been exploited for its soteriological content. And still there remains the very singular "event of salvation" which has its center in Christ's agony. In our everyday teaching on redemption only the effect of this death is considered, whereas the whole event as such is not analyzed. We have restricted our attention to its edifying aspects, and have not taken its theological characteristics seriously.

If our formal doctrine of salvation can thus be supplemented by a portrayal of salvation as an actual event it will thereby receive an enriching and deepening fulfillment. Redemptive salvation is an encounter between God and His creation, an event which God sets in motion. It is He who reconciles us with Himself in Christ (2 Cor 5:18). Here a theology of grace must develop the whole relationship of God to creation, to sin, and to damnation, so that the richness of our reconciliation will come into sight. A glance into theological manuals will show how little one is aware of the intrinsic interrelationship of such isolated catchwords of our formal doctrine of redemption one to the other. Does not even Holy Scripture speak of a redemption of the universe? Is it not a question then of an all-embracing event which established creation and the covenant anew, which stretches from the beginnings until the end of history, spanning both protology and eschatology, man's origin and destiny?

3. A Dynamic Christology. With all its new tasks, Catholic theology can still learn about its own past, and can reintegrate that past in a fresh way. Such a synthesis might confront East and West with each other, remolding and vivifying both.[11] Only too often in the past have academic polemics obscured our vision of the positive value found in various classical schools of Christology — the schools of Alexandria, Antioch, and Rome. What the West can learn from the East is above all an interpretation of the Incarnation which is dynamic and rich in tensions. What the West can give the East is the balance and precision of its Christ-image. Our two-sided idea of man can fulfill itself in both directions.

The preaching of the resurrection of Christ and of the reawakening of the flesh has created, above all in the East, the image of the glorious Christ, and has fixed the predominating Easter feeling

---

[11] Cf. the invaluable article by O. Rousseau, O.S.B., "Incarnation et anthropologie en Orient et en Occident," *Irénikon,* 26 (1953), pp. 363–375.

for life as the basic attitude of the Christian. The faithful Christian knows from the fact of the resurrection that God's power has become visible in the flesh of the Lord. Spirit and flesh have met in Christ; the Word (*logos*) has become flesh (*sarx*), has entered the flesh that was so sinful and mortal in us, but so glorious and immortal in Christ. The *Logos* has become flesh, has died in the flesh, but has also risen again living. In the Word this has also happened to our flesh. Thus speaks the Christology of the East, a Christology understood as "salvation event." The brilliance of the gloriously rejoicing Lord proves to be the dominant element in its image of Christ and man. Consequently the Greeks before and after Chalcedon — with its static-sounding formula for hypostasis — hold so firmly to the Alexandrians' central concept: the "one incarnate nature of the divine *Logos*." For considered in itself and not merely as the counterpart of the formula of Chalcedon, this concept expresses a happening or, as a matter of fact, the entire economy of salvation in Christ. It allows the glory of God seen in Christ to shine like a falling meteor. It expresses a Christology "from above," for the Alexandrian formula primarily focuses on the divine *Logos*, on its *one nature* (*physis*) in God. (It is true, too, that this Alexandrian formula is open to misinterpretation, and indeed can be viewed as objectionable as a result of the false meaning given it by Apollinaris and his followers.) Yet we should recall that the Alexandrians themselves took care to round out their formula by adding "incarnate." By this they made the *Logos* visible in its "leap of love" (*saltus amoris*), in its incarnation within the realities of the flesh and the earth. The Alexandrine formula is, in fact, only a paraphrasing of John 1:14: "the Word became flesh," i.e., the one indivisible *physis* or nature of the divine word became flesh, and remains this one *physis* even as an incarnate reality. It was only the polemic over the nature or *physis* of Christ — was it one or were there two? — that caused theologians to forget that this formula in Church use communicated a living, divine event. Chalcedon — dedicated to opposing any misunderstanding of the divine *physis* in Christ — expressed not the event but the being: a person (hypostasis) in two natures. We shall see how significant this was to become for the evolution of our interpretation of Christ. But if the formula of Chalcedon is not to lead to a one-sided view of

Christ, then it needs to be completed by the living dynamism of
the Alexandrian-Cyrillic vision. This does not at all mean that we
should return to the old "terminology." But an ideological synthesis is pressingly needed.[12] The Christ-image of Alexandria with
its emphasis on Christ's glorious reign as Lord and Word, should
extend its light both to East and West. A new emphasis upon
Easter elements in our liturgy can only serve to further these things.

II. The Nature and Being of Christ

Is it not true that our study of salvation, our study of the glorious
destiny (*doxa*) of human flesh is centered too much upon man?
Should we not be concerned first and foremost with God and His
Christ? For a theology which has devoted many centuries to sounding the depths of the being and nature of Christ can claim to have a
profound reverence for the mystery of the Incarnation. Asking about
Christ, the God-man, is a disinterested question. Yet it will lead
of necessity to direct knowledge about the questioner, man himself
Hence we may, in fact must, pose the question of Christ most
seriously. Consequently we may not pass over as insignificant the
new controversies which are arising over the nature and being
of Christ; and if we are to comprehend today's controversies, we
must turn briefly, at the very least, to the old disputes over this
subject. For theological insights within the Catholic Church are
reached only after a searching inquiry into the historical-theo-
logical consciousness of the totality of what has been handed
down. The more thoroughly the spiritual movements of the past
are comprehended, the more fruitful they will be for the present.
Here there has always been, and there is still today, much for
Christology to work on. We are, for example, all familiar from
our undergraduate studies with notions such as Monophysitism
and Nestorianism. For the most part we know little more than
their names and consider the doctrines for which they stand simply as monuments of the past. In reality they express tensions
which embrace in themselves the mystery of the Incarnation. The
human spirit cannot fathom the mystery of the Incarnation and

---

[12] Cf. A. Grillmeier, "Der Neu-Chalkedonismus. Um die Berechtigung
eines neuen Kapitels in der Dogmengeschichte," *Historisches Jahrbuch*, 77
(1958), pp. 151–166 (B. Altaner-Festschrift).

inescapably fails to express this mystery in its fullness. In the mystery of the Incarnation we are face to face with a new, special, incomparable relationship between God and creature, between God and the world. The Incarnation is the high point, and the prototype, of all relationships between God and the world.

1. Classical solutions. Here we must not neglect to evaluate the breadth and scope of the old heresies. They are fundamentally false, naturalistic definitions of the God-world relationship realized in Christ which fail to respect its character as *mystery*. On the one hand we encounter a solution (monophysite) which damages the transcendence of God, of the Word that becomes flesh. For it reduces the *Logos,* the Word, to a *partial principle* which is to be transformed, as it were, with another partial principle, human flesh (*sarx*), into a single new natural principle. Hence the real sin of monophysitism is that of reducing God to a part of the world. The notion of a "mixed nature," as it is described in many histories of theology, contains the very ideology of this heresy. This tendency in "monophysitism"[13] — to keep the old name for such a vast and complex idea — is not really evident in the works of the poor and simple Eutyches, who was not completely clear about the implications of his claims, even though certain of his formulae are extremely suspicious. Much more dynamic and virulent was the *synthesis in nature* between God and the world, as proposed in the fourth-century heresies of Arianism and Apollinarianism. Although these two heresies disagree over the question of Christ's divinity, their basic assumptions concerning the Incarnation are the same: the *Logos* is related to the human flesh of Christ as man's soul is related to his flesh. As body and soul together form one

---

[13] Dogmatic criticism of monophysitism has undergone profound changes in recent decades. Under the leadership of J. Lebon, the widespread Severian monophysitism was proven to be the consequence of Cyrillian-Alexandrian Christology (with pre-Chalcedonian terminology and a definite preservation of Christ's humanity). On the other hand this verbal monophysitism was never again replaced by the original ontological monophysitism after Chalcedon. Nevertheless, as a consequence of closing one's eyes to the Chalcedonian interpretation of the figure of Christ, certain dangerous and one-sided aspects of the Alexandrian understanding of Christ came out in Monotheletism and Monoenergetism. The mystery of the Incarnation is thus deprived of its full significance. Cf. J. Lebon, *Le Monophysisme Sévérien* (Louvain, 1909); and "La Christologie du Monophysisme Syrien" in *Chalkedon I*, pp. 425–580.

nature, so also do divinity and humanity unite to form one "nature."

According to Apollinaris of Laodicea "Christ" is constituted a "manlike unit" (*menschenaritge Synthese*) by the union effected through the addition of the *Logos* to flesh which lacks a human soul. God and flesh are, according to the words of the bishop, "partial principles." The actual denial of a human soul in Christ is not the basic error of this interpretation of the Incarnation; its falsehood stems rather from the unacceptable infringement on the transcendence of God implied in it. The Arians were quite logical here when they denied divinity to this flesh-united *Logos,* this *Logos*-soul. Apollinaris was, in fact, illogical in defending the Nicene doctrine of the divinity of the *Logos*.

This tendency toward a *synthesis in nature* makes God a part of the world and sees Christ's "humanity" only in the union of the *Logos* with flesh; and it is here that we see the virulent character of those doctrines which have been designated as "monophysitism." In the form given it by Apollinaris — and not in the so-called "doctrine of fusion" for which it is condemned in school texts — it was destined to become the great temptation of the Greek spirit.[14] The elements of such a "synthesis in nature" are found here and there throughout the history of Greek theology, until it became generally agreed that the union which is in Christ may not be adequately interpreted in terms of any created analogy.

The attempt to clarify matters was of prime concern to the Cappadocian Fathers and especially to the theologians of Antioch, who opposed the *Logos-Sarx Christology* of Arius and Apollinaris with a *Logos-Anthropos* doctrine. They merit our reverence for bringing to light, out of the old Church tradition, the absolutely full humanity of Christ. Their weakness, in fact their dangerous error, was to describe the bonds uniting Christ's humanity to the *Logos* in terms of a reciprocal moral relationship between "persons." This attempt should be condemned mildly in view of the fact that the theology of the time lacked the conceptual means to strike the center between the dreaded nature-synthesis of the Apollinarists and a merely moral, accidental union. However, the theology of the Church did eventually go this middle way which casts light upon the mystery of the Incar-

---

[14] For a more detailed treatment of this, cf. A. Grillmeier, in *Chalkedon* I, pp. 67–120, reprinted in *Christ in Christian Tradition* (London, 1964).

nation in its full dimensions. It assumed, on the one hand, that in Christ, God and man constitute a substantial, ontological unit, and acknowledged, on the other hand, that Christ was fully God and fully man. The Council of Chalcedon provided the solution by bearing witness both to the union and to the distinction of principles in Christ. The distinction — to the horror of Alexandrian theology — was made between *physis* (nature) and *hypostasis* (person), and upon this distinction rests the famous definition: In Christ there is one Hypostasis, one Person, one *Prosopon,* but two natures. The Council wisely added several popular descriptive explanations of its principles to this theologically new terminology. It underlined the fact that Christ, as God and man, is in the strictest sense "one and the same" Person and subject. With respect to nature He is, to use the terminology of Chalcedon, "inconfusedly" and "indivisibly" both human and divine: "inconfusedly," and consequently there is no "synthesis in nature"; "indivisibly," and consequently no duality of persons.

2. **Modern Christology and Christ's Unity.** Commencing with this fundamental definition, which by no means exhausted the whole of dogma concerning Christ, but which made clear its decisive principle, modern Christology strives to define more exactly this singular and most sublime case of a God-man relationship. Modern positions remain very close to the old, classical solutions, even though they employ an advanced terminology and metaphysics.[15] Here we can see what a stimulus Chalcedon actually meant for the history of theology. Alexandrian Christology could not have provided a basis sufficiently broad for theology. The principal question is still that of the definition of this ineffable unity of Christ. One interpretation begins with the idea of a "unified unity," as the Fathers were wont to call it, which sees the humanity of Christ as being one, indeed as being personally one with the *Logos,* bypassing any further inquiry into the metaphysical structure of the unity. This is the Scotist-Tiphanic school of Christology, whose principal concern is the loyal

---

[15] Cf. here K. Rahner, in *Chalkedon III,* pp. 3–49 (reprinted in *Theological Investigations, I* [Baltimore, 1962], pp. 149–201); cf. also J. Ternus, *Das Seelen-und Bewusstseinsleben Jesu.* For a systematic investigation of the whole problem, cf. *Chalkedon III,* pp. 81–237; and even more recently, R. Haubst, "Probleme der jüngsten Christologie," *Theologische Revue,* 52 (1956), pp. 145–162, especially pp. 155–158.

defense of Christ's humanity.[16] Proceeding from the opposite approach, others strive to investigate the "unifying unity." Naturally the difficulties involved here are enormous, though undeniable headway is being made. Let us take a look at the work of those theologians who have tackled more decisively than anyone else the question of unity in Christ. For these theologians, a fundamental principle is provided by St. Thomas, who maintained that in Christ there is *unum esse,* i.e., one, and only one act of being, of existence. Although there are truly two natures in Christ, He is in the strictest sense "one and the same," metaphysically "one subject" and "one being." But in order to explain this unity, it is necessary to deny any created existence whatever to the humanity of Christ. J. H. Nicolas, O.P., points out, in one of the most recent studies of this school, how close to despair theologians since Cajetan have been in their efforts to elucidate the classical Christology of Thomism.[17] Dom Diepen, O.S.B. has uncovered the fundamental limitations of the thesis according to which the uncreated existence of the *Logos* is identified with the existence of Christ's humanity. It requires an interchange or identification of efficient causality with formal causality. Thomism takes its point of departure in the fact that God is the efficient cause of Christ's humanity. As such, does not God virtually and eminently contain in Himself all that He effects outside Himself? Can the infinite act not become in this way the act of the very beings He created? P. Nicolas says rightly: "That the form of an effect is given beforehand in the cause does not mean that the effect is constituted through the form of the cause. . . . To cause means to confer being, and if the effect is distinct from the cause, then the being it receives must also be distinct from the being of the cause."[18] Suppose we were to conceive the unity of person in Christ in such a way that the *Logos* takes the assumed nature into His divine existence.[19] This would imply an equation of

[16] The most significant presentation of this Christology in German is that of K. Adam, *Der Christus des Glaubens* (Düsseldorf, 1954) (English tr. *The Christ of Faith* [New York, 1963]). The high value of K. Adam's Christology lies particularly in its biblical basis.

[17] On the occasion of a study by H. Bouëssé, O.P., *Le Sauveur du Monde,* Part 2, *Le Mystère de l'Incarnation* (Chambéry-Leysse and Paris, 1953). Cf. the review in *Revue Thomiste,* 55 (1955), pp. 179–183.

[18] *Ibid.,* p. 182.

[19] *Ibid.* Nicolas reproduces the thought of Bouëssé with the words, "Le Verbe attire à son exister divin la nature assumée."

the personal subsistence of the *Logos* with His divine existence. But "being" is an essential attribute of God and hence is absolutely common to all three Persons, whereas personal subsistence is *proper* to each one. How, then, can the divine *esse* or being be equated with the existence of the humanity of Christ without abrogating essential theological principles of the Trinity and the metaphysical laws of being? Would not this view require divine Being — the being common to all three Persons — to become the formal cause of the humanity of Christ in the strictest sense, because *esse* is not a mere point of reference, but an act?[20] It would be impossible in this way to bind the human nature of Christ to the *Logos* as Person. The whole Trinity would necessarily be incarnated and made the act of a created being. Dom Diepen has rightly invoked against such views the principles of St. Thomas, those principles which St. Thomas used to condemn the pantheism of an Amalric of Bène.[21] The path of Cajetan and Billot provides no through passage.

Does this render impossible every attempt to explain the unity of being in Christ in the "direction" of formal causality, or better, in that of a "quasi-formal" causality? M. de la Taille, S.J.,[22] makes another attempt by assuming that there is a created existence proper to the humanity of Christ. From the divine act of being, common to all three Persons, comes, as from its efficient cause, the *esse* or "act of being" of this humanity, and it comes forth precisely by way of the Hypostasis, the Person, of the *Logos*. The human nature of Christ is created and maintained as the creaturely existence of the hypostasis of the *Logos*. If there is any quasi-formal relationship, it is to be found only between the "subsistence" of the second Person of God and "His" humanity. The Incarnation must be considered the highest case of God-world relationship, but it is an analogous instance, as is the case of the inhabitation of the Holy Spirit and of the vision of the creature dwelling in God at the end of time. To be sure, there is in the Incarnation, as against these analogous types of this relationship, not merely a difference of de-

---

[20] *Ibid.*, p. 183.

[21] According to R. Haubst, *Theologische Revue*, 52 (1956), p. 156.

[22] M. de la Taille, "Actuation créée par l'Acte Incréé," *Recherche de Sciences Religieuses*, 18 (1928), pp. 253–268; and "Entretien amical d'Eudoxe et du Palamède sur la grâce d'union," *Revue Apologétique*, 48 (1929), pp. 5–26, 129–145; and in *Mysterium fidei* (Paris, 1931³), p. 514 ff.; cf. J. Ternus, in *Chalkedon III*, p. 229 ff.

gree, but one of essence. The humanity of Christ is "substantially" united to the *Logos* — and united in the unity of the one subsistence and consequently in that of "one subsisting reality" (*una res subsistens*). All other grace brings about only an accidental union with God. The unity of the personal act with the *Logos* is of critical significance for the humanity of Christ. If His humanity finds its autonomy in the *Logos,* the *Logos* in turn becomes, in this humanity, truly a man.[23] Here we have more than a mere orientation, more than an ordering of Christ's humanity to the *Logos.* If the *Logos* "is" in the world in and through the humanity of Christ, then this humanity is subject to an "actuating" by the *Logos,* an "actuating" which may not be considered as efficient causality. Every requirement for the subsistence of a spiritual being is thus fulfilled by the *Logos* in this humanity which is created by the act of the triune personal God. The *Logos* fulfills it by way of a quasi-formal self-communication which thus leads to a singular case of transcendental unity.

Consequently, the "Thomistic" approach of Cajetan must be abandoned, if we wish to explain the metaphysical unity of Christ as that of "one subsisting reality" through the singularity of the act of existence. Nevertheless, the solution — as far as the mystery of the Incarnation permits one at all — is to be sought in the area of "(quasi-)formal" causality, for otherwise we can come to no *unum* in the metaphysical sense. Indeed we may admit everything that Dom Diepen asserts in explaining the unity in Christ according to St. Thomas. He is working from the principles of integration, or the integral whole. He knows very well that Deity and humanity are no more "partial substances" in this whole than they are "constituents standing unto themselves." It is a question neither of a synthesis of natures nor of a disparate and heterogeneous conglomeration. "Christ is formally *one* more than anything else because of His one act of subsistence." Christ's human *esse* or act of being is distinct in its very nature from the divine act of being. Yet it forms, with the divine act of being *one being* proportionally as Christ *is* at once God and man, and as His human nature does not *sub*sist for itself. Thus "there is," as Diepen says against Duns Scotus and against Baslism, "in Christ only one unique existence — and this not as if every created existence in Him were elimi-

---

[23] *Ibid.,* pp. 213–215, 229 f.

nated, but because this created existence is integrated into the complete and personal Being of the Son of God."[24] Is the question of the "unifying unity" thereby fully exhausted? We believe the Theory of Actuation has still something further to add here, although metaphysically it may lack some thoroughness and detail. In any case it can make clear for us the fact that the unity of Christ as the actuation of Christ's humanity through the subsistence of the *Logos* contains dialectic elements worthy of our attention. The more interior the union and bond of this humanity with the subsistence of the *Logos,* the more it can be considered as a fully actuated, created, and individuated essence (and this does not mean that it is autonomous). This point may be fittingly directed against the old "synthesis in nature" which succeeded in conceiving of union only by sacrificing the natural and independent mode of operation proper to human nature. Expressed in a dialectical formula the view proposed here can be stated thus: the greater the union of human nature with the *Logos,* the more perfectly actuated is its distinct essence of "being a man." This formula alone does justice to the mystery of the Incarnation, without invoking it as such.[25] For it lays stress upon three things concurrently: "God" "becomes" "man." And therein lies also the kerygmatic significance of this theory — which surely has not as yet been thought through. For in Christ, the God-Man, "being a man" — which is not in the order of nature — is carried in its dignity, scope, and overall significance for the economy of salvation, to the level of Christ's personal reality. Forasmuch as grace is a supernatural "actuation" of nature for a supernatural purpose, so is it in fact the actuation of Christ's human "nature." The entire pattern of this nature is bent toward a supernatural end (whereby all rights of nature, as is emphasized today in all theology of grace, are to be preserved). But in Christ is found the highest of all graces, the *gratia unionis creaturae ad subiectum divinum.* Never can anything higher fall to a creature's lot. Hence the Incarnation means the highest actuation, realization, and fulfillment of this human nature in Christ.

3. **The Antitype.** This conception of the unity proper to Christ

---

[24] R. Haubst, *Theologische Revue,* 52 (1956), p. 157.

[25] Cf. K. Rahner, in *Chalkedon III,* p. 15; F. Malmberg, *Über den Gottmenschen* (cf. note 2), pp. 27–70; and B. Lonergan, S.J., *De constitutione Christi ontologica et psychologica* (Rome, 1956[1], 1958[2]).

and of His being as God-Man is a Christology of unification. A
school of theology has taken a stand in opposition to this view,
perceiving therein a threat to divine transcendence. It prefers to
consider itself the custodian of the ancient *Logos-Anthropos* tradition and the doctrine of the *Homo Assumptus.* The leader and
champion of this interpretation of Christ was the Franciscan Father
Déodat de Basly († 1937). For him the fundamental mistake of
the Cyrillic-Thomistic Christology of unification consisted in the
falsification of the true relationship between God and creation.
Basly saw the true problem, and saw it correctly. There is no doubt
that theologians of unification have advanced too precipitously,
as we have already pointed out and must continue to point out.
But here we encounter a direct and categorically expressed antithesis. It states that a nonabsolute, created thing, whether body or
spirit, cannot enter into an intrinsic union of being with the Absolute.[26] It cannot, and may not, come to the *una res subsistens*
of the Thomists. Instead, the only possibility of connecting the nonabsolute with the Absolute remains, according to Father Déodat,
a *subjonction déitante.* This should preserve both full divine transcendence and the corresponding autonomy of the assumed man
(the *Homo Assumptus*). The result is a very loose Christ-image
which is open to the accusation of Nestorianism and which needs
to be more carefully stated. Following, then, the official condemna-
tion of this interpretation of Christ the ecclesiastical world became
publicly aware of a true theological controversy, the background
of which is, even for the trained theologian, extremely difficult
to see.

In a unique novel, *La Christiade Française* (Paris, 1929), in
which even geological sketches are found together with appendices
on the patristic doctrine of the *Homo-Assumptus,* Father Déodat
attempted to represent the God-Man relationship in Christ as a
"love duel" (*duel d'amour*) of the *Homo Assumptus* with the
triune God. This love duel is peculiar, however, in that this "assumed man" is "placed below" (*subjoint*) the *Logos,* while the
Logos is "placed over" (*surjoint*) the assumed man. The "over"
and "under" relationship was certainly valid. The dubious part
was the suffix: *-joint.* Between both elements there was only an

---

[26] Cf. Déodat de Basly, O.F.M., "Inopérantes offensives contre l'Assumptus Homo," in *La France Franciscaine,* 17 (1934)(pp. 419–473), p. 456.

undefined bond, which appeared in further elaborations by the Franciscan to be altogether too loose. The "assumed man" is, as *agens,* completely autonomous. This autonomy means that the *Logos* exercised no influence whatever upon the human knowledge and willing of Jesus. This autonomy alone, Father Déodat claimed, could keep intact the teaching of Chalcedon on the two natures subsisting "inconfusedly" (ασυγύτως) in Christ. Up to this point the doctrine of Father Déodat seemed acceptable to many theologians who subsequently broke definitively with him. But Father Déodat went still further and shifted the weight of the autonomy so emphatically into the humanity of Christ that it is only there, as it were, that the "I" of the *Logos* comes into being. There is in God only "one" individuality, which is that of the one nature. Hence, on the level of the Absolute, which alone can explain the Incarnation as a phenomenon outside of God, the *Logos* is not an autonomous "I."[27] Although the *Logos* is thus certainly placed over (*surjoint*) the *Homo Assumptus,* it is still not placed in this superior position as an autonomous "I" (*Je, Moi*). For the Trinity is, as regards all that is outside of God, only *one* indivisible autonomy. Thus if Christ can be addressed as an "I," a *Je,* a *Moi,* then it must be in virtue of the autonomy of the "assumed man." Only in the latter is there an "I," a "*Je,*" and "*Moi.*" The Gospels always show, according to Father Déodat, the *human* "I" of Christ, who stands before the triune God, in His individuality and personality in no essential way different from every other man. Hence the Franciscan adjusts the notion of person to his application of this concept to Christ. "Who, then, in Christ is really the final subject by whom everything must be done or uttered? Who is the final bearer of the being and natures that are in Him?" If we ask these questions of Father Déodat we receive an answer totally different from that of the Christology of unification. With Aquinas, the theologians of unification say that Christ is the Word-become-flesh, the *Logos* in the flesh. Everything is centered in the one and only subject, which is the *Logos.* Thus is Christ not merely an *unus,* an only one, a "one and the same" personal subject, as Chalcedon exclaims with the whole of early tradition (see Denz. 148), but even an *unum* (neuter gender). Thus the unity of Christ in the transcendental

---

[27] I.e., He is not, according to Father Déodat de Basly, "un agisseur agissant des actions qui ne sont que ses actions propres" (*ibid.,* p. 463).

metaphysical sense is affirmed and the distinction between the two
natures is in no way denied. It is otherwise with Father Déodat
de Basly. The *Logos* and the "assumed man" are bound into a
type of complex "person" which de Basly defines as a "physical
and transcendent whole (*Tout physique et transcendant*)."[28] Christ
is a "connecting whole" between what is not absolute (man, soul,
body) and the Absolute (God). But the latter may not be regarded
here as triune. Above all, the *Logos* may not be taken as a complete, autonomous principle of operation (*parfait Agisseur autonome*[29]). This connecting whole, which is Christ, is thus inwardly
in part an absolute which is autonomous only as God (*qua Deus*)
but not as *Logos,* and partly a nonabsolute, the *Homa Assumptus,*
which enjoys perfect autonomy.[30] Strangely enough, Father Déodat
believes that he has, through his exposition, raised himself to a
level superior to that of Nestorius and Cyril of Alexandria. In spite
of all their differences, they are both, for Déodat, fundamentally
the same. They make of Christ, the God-Man, a synthesis which
exceeds the sum of His "components"; they make Him into a
"third being" (*Tiers-être*), as Déodat repeatedly asserts. For Nestorius, this *Tiers-être* is composed of *Logos,* regarded as an autonomous individual, and of Christ's human nature. And this *Tiers-
être* is concretely "man," i.e., autonomous in Déodat's view. Besides
his false notion of the Trinity, Nestorius is to be censured only for
this *Tiers-être*. Not a word is uttered concerning Nestorius' faulty
conception of the unity between the *Logos* and Christ's humanity.
Cyril of Alexandria, on the other hand, does not, we are told,
conceive of the second component in Christ as a concrete *homo,*
i.e., an autonomous man.[31]

---

[28] Déodat de Basly, "Le Moi de Jésus Christ," in *La France Franciscaine,*
12 (1929), pp. 125–160; 325–352), p. 148 f.; and "L'Assumptus Homo, *ibid.,*
11 (1928), (pp. 265–313), pp. 284–286. Father Déodat, referring here to the
words of Augustine, "Persona Christi, mixtura Dei et hominis," says, "C'est
le TOUT, mixtura, qui et la personne du Christ. C'est ni le Verbe, ni
l'Assumptus Homo, mais ce TOUT — là que les deux unis, font: persona
Christi" (cf. above).

[29] Déodat de Basly, "Inopérantes offensives," in *La France Franciscaine,*
18 (1935), p. 55.

[30] *Ibid.,* 17 (1934), p. 457. Only for this *Tout physique et transcendant* are
the *Logos* and the *Homo Assumptus* concurrently "interior." Otherwise, from
the standpoint of the latter, "L'Assumptus Homo perfectus est in obliquo le
Verbe qui lui est *extrinsèque,* mais qui lui est transcendentalement *surjoint.*"

[31] *Ibid.,* 18 (1935) (pp. 33–104), p. 45, "Le tiers-être théandrique de Nes-

Déodat's own position thus means that in the connecting whole which is Christ, the *Logos* itself, is not to be considered as an *individuum,* as a self-sufficient "I." The *Logos* can act in Christ only as God (*qua Deus*), not as *Logos* (*qua Verbum*). Thus Christ's individuality and autonomy are to be attributed to the *Homo Assumptus.* The latter also becomes the primary subject of words uttered by Christ or addressed to Him. When one says "Christ" in Déodat's sense, he is referring directly (*in recto*) only to the autonomous, individual *Homo Assumptus.* This is not the "whole" as such. The *Homo Assumptus* is only a part, it exists only "in the whole." Only of this "whole" can divine and human things be said. Only because this whole comprises both God and man, and precisely by a "placing over" of the one component and a "placing under" of the other, can divine and human things be attributed to it, and precisely by way of a *réciprocation prédicative.* Father Déodat never wishes to accept the traditional assertions (*communicatio idiomatum*) that this *Homo Assumptus* is the *Logos* or that the *Logos* is man. For he sees there the dreaded identity of the infinite with the finite, of the absolute with the relative.[32] Nor

---

torius comprend, comme ses deux composants, le Verbe et la nature humaine; concrètement homme! — Le Tiers-être théandrique de St. Cyrille comprend, comme ses deux composants, Le Verbe et la nature humaine, mais qui, concrètement, n'est pas un homme." — But Déodat misinterprets here both Nestorius and St. Cyril. In the end he draws very close to Apollinaris. (Cf. P. Galtier, "S. Cyrillus et Apollinnaire," *Gregorianum,* 37 [1956], pp. 584–609.) Both formed their Christ-image according to the principle that two complete dimensions could not grow together into a third. Hence the humanity of Christ must be made into something "incomplete" if it is to serve as a principle. Apollinaris is supposed to have taken from Christ's humanity the soul, whereas Cyril, leaving this intact, took the *autonomy* from His human nature. "Il faut que la réel inabsolut subjoint au Verbe ne soit qu'un réel imparfait, ou (according to Cyril) imparfaitement autonome (!), puisque déjà le Verbe est, lui le un réel parfait (with Apollinaris), ou parfait Agisseur autonome (with Cyril)." (See *La France Franciscaine,* 18 [1935], p. 55.) Nestorius thus unites, according to Father Déodat, two autonomous individuals to make a *Tiers-être,* and Cyril unites the *Logos* as an independent Individual with a nonautonomous humanity. Father Déodat himself wishes to unite an individual, autonomous "assumed man" with the *Logos* for which this *Homo Assumptus* is not individual, not an autonomous dimension. The two are not united to constitute a third which is above the original two and resulting from them, but are "Person" as a totality.

[32] Cf. Déodat de Basly, "L'Assumptus Homo," in *La France Franciscaine,* 11 (1928), p. 282; "Le langage in recto dirait l'identité de l'Infini et d'un fini: suprême erreur." Cf. R. Haubst, *Theologische Revue,* 52 (1956), p. 148.

may Mary be named "Mother of God" with logical immediacy and unequivocal meaning. In reference to Christ the term "Mother of God" refers first of all to the bearer of the *Homo Assumptus* as an autonomous *individuum*. With respect to the *Homo Assumptus,* Mary is directly and immediately mother; with respect to the *Logos* she is mother only indirectly, by way of inclusion, *in obliquo.* We must clearly distinguish that in Christ God and Man are related to one another as "one thing to another" (*un autre et autre quelqu'un*). Father Déodat attempted to support his doctrine with an appeal to the whole patristic tradition and to his master Duns Scotus.[33] Certain basic assumptions in the latter in fact lean in this direction, e.g., the Scotistic stress upon the wholeness and autonomy of the human spirit as efficient cause in Christ's humanity and on the absolute transcendence of the divine. But Dom Diepen has shown that Déodat goes beyond Scotus. For Scotus decidedly aligned himself to the so-called doctrine of subsistence and in the form expounded by St. Thomas in the renowned second *opinio* in *S.T., III,* q. 2, a. 6.[34]

The judgment of the Church — which we shall discuss further — against a follower of Déodat, Father Léon Seiller, O.F.M., showed that extreme *Homo Assumptus*-Christology is not compatible with Catholic theology. There is a genuine value in stressing the autonomy of Christ's humanity, as is to be seen in that type of Christology which is represented today by such theologians as Galtier and K. Adam. But Galtier clearly distinguishes himself from Déodat in building upon the foundation of the theory of subsistence and in assuming a substantial unity between Christ's humanity and the *Logos* — assumptions which Déodat most decidedly shuns. To be sure, the Christology of Galtier also fell under the reproach that it inquires in fact after the "unified unity" in Christ and not after the "unifying unity."[35]

4. The Christ-Image. What theologians provide as outlines to the Christ-image needs then to be filled out by the theologians themselves and by those who preach to the faithful. The resultant Christ-image will in any case differ in some respects from the

---

[33] In his work, "Scotus Docens," *Supplément à la France Franciscaine,* 17 (1934).

[34] Cf. L. Ott, in *Chalkedon II,* p. 906 ff., 913–915; I. Backes, *ibid.,* p. 928.

[35] Cf. K. Rahner, in *Chalkedon III,* pp. 11 ff., 32 ff.

original. Even the Gospels and Epistles show noticeable differences in their interpretation of Christ. There is a Christology "from above" and another "from below." The one stresses, above all, the prerogatives of the divinity in Christ, while the other lays emphasis upon the prerogatives of His humanity. Here the weight is laid upon "identity," there upon "distinction." This twofold approach has special significance in interpreting the deeds and life of Christ. Those theologians who hold for the one act of being in Christ also teach a more or less "strict, dynamic hegemony of the *Logos*." One of the most recent representatives of this point of view attributed an actuating and directing efficient causality to the *Logos* as its own, but not to Christ's humanity.[36] He thinks that an irrevocable principle of the theology of the Trinity seems inapplicable to Christ, the principle namely which asserts that every exterior act of the triune God is common to all three Persons. Now the humanity of Christ, regardless of its union with the *Logos*, remains a creature, an "exterior act," and hence cannot be excluded from the universal law of trinitarian operation. The doctrine of the hegemony of the *Logos*, therefore, has its limitations. The exaggerations which are to be noted in this new theology are a remnant of the old Apollinarist synthesis in nature. They have their origin in a false understanding of the mystery of the Incarnation. For the primary concern of God's intervention in Christ in human history is not to act according to His divine nature. It was not to this end that He brought about the Incarnation. His first intention is to be and act as man in the world. It is for this reason that, within the limits set by the Church's *magisterium*, we must consider as highly significant that other Christ-image which emphasizes the *difference* between the divine and the human, or at least strives to see this difference given equal stress with the unity. Paul Galtier therefore insists again and again that the human spiritual life of Jesus was in no way changed as a result of the hypostatic union. There is no

---

[36] Cf. R. Haubst, *Theologische Revue,* 52 (1956), pp. 158–162. Concerning the theological Christ-image cf. A. Grillmeier, *Der Logos am Kreuz. Zur christologischen Symbolik der älteren Kreuzigungsdarstellung* (Munich, 1956), Chap. 5. This book provides a survey of the formulation of Christological thought in earlier Christian depictions of the crucifixion. Its aim is to show, from the picture of the crucifixion, how there is also a *Theologia Monumentalis,* a theology of monuments. This also should help us to grasp the fullness of Christian tradition and to bring its content to life.

"hegemony of the *Logos*," in Parente's sense, since there can be no personally specific action of the *Logos* upon Christ's humanity. The hypostatic bond between Christ's humanity and the *Logos* proffers no occasion for the divine nature to act directly upon the human. Such a view nevertheless does not preclude the possibility of considering Christ's human nature — precisely in *its* truly human aspects — as an organ or instrument of the divinity.

Thus today, as ever in the past, the coloring varies in the figure attributed to Christ by theologians. All agree that the true synthesis is expressed by the two fundamental Chalcedonian principles. The "inconfused" must always accompany the "undivided." This synthesis is, however, without meaning as long as the above-mentioned dialectical principle which underlies every encounter and union with God is not taken seriously. This principle asserts that the highest union with God implies the highest fulfillment of created essence and being. For this reason it is from the Actuation theory that we can expect Christology to turn with a view to elaborating on Chalcedon. For it seems to hold the greatest promise of opening up the mystery of Christ's God-Manhood, and thus of integrating both these great themes in Christology.

III. Person and Consciousness

The true contribution of our time to traditional Christology is the inquiry into the human consciousness of Jesus Christ. Here the psychology of Christ is joined to and builds with and upon the ontology of Christ. Even in the new posing of the question required by this enterprise old tensions and solutions become particularly meaningful. We can summarize the first phase of the struggle — refraining from any attempt to give the reader an exhaustive description of it.[37]

---

[37] The first direction was led, in recent years, by the following: P. Parente, *L'Io di Cristo* (Brescia, 1951[1], 1955[2]); M. B. Xiberta, O.Carm., *El Yo de Jesucristo* (Barcelona, 1954); and *Tractatus de Verbo Incarnato I–II* (cf. note 10); H. Diepen, O.S.B., in numerous articles in *Revue Thomiste* (1949–1956). In the other direction: besides Déodat de Basly; J. Rivière; Léon Seiller, "Homo Assumptus bei den Kirchenvätern, Ausgewählte Texte," *Wissenschaft Weisheit*, 14 (1951), pp. 84 ff., 160 ff.; esp. "La psychologie humaine du Christ et l'unicité de personne," *Franziskanische Studien*, 31 (1949), pp. 49–76, 246–274; also separately (Paris-Rennes, 1950) (indexed: *AAS* 43 [1951], no. 12; cf. M. Browne, O.P., in *Osservatore Romano*, Vol. 19, 7, 1951). In a moderate way P. Galtier, esp. in *L'unité du Christ. Etre. Personne. Conscience*

1. The Question of Autonomy. Père Galtier raised the question of autonomy in the human soul and consciousness of Christ in his important work *L'unité du Christ* (Paris, 1939). In that book the author attributes to Christ a human psychological "I," distinct from His divine Person. The empirical, psychological "conscious I," lying at the surface of human life, has its roots farther back, in the individual human nature of Jesus. This "conscious I" does not represent the "personal I" to which this human nature, this vehicle of the whole human spiritual life of Christ is subordinated, but rather the "substantial I" of Christ's human nature.

Consciousness, according to Galtier, is the function of a spiritual *nature,* not of the *person.* Its immediate awareness is an awareness of that motion of the soul by which man first experiences himself as a spiritual being at all. Only indirectly, through reflection, does "being a person" come into the light of consciousness. Whether a nature becoming conscious of itself subsists or not is thus secondary. "Person" is of itself not an essential subject matter of the consciousness. If our consciousness is also aware of "being a person," it is only because, *in us,* "I" and "person" are identical. But there may also be an "I-consciousness" which in itself does not necessarily imply personality.

Now let us consider the fact that Christ is both God and Man. Both natures are "inconfusedly" united in Him. According to P. Galtier, we must commence with this "inconfusedly" if we are to understand something of the divine-human consciousness in Christ. The human "I" (understood as the psychological "I") has a special function in Christ since the divine consciousness is one of nature and is common to all three Persons. Christ's human consciousness thus becomes an organ by which the *Logos* truly assumes its most purely personal and proper domain. With regard to Christ's hu-

---

(Paris, 1939) and in numerous articles (cf. the bibliography in M. B. Xiberta's *Tractatus II,* pp. 671–739). Also K. Adam. For survey and general discussion cf. J. Ternus, "Das Seelen- und Bewusstseinsleben Jesu," in *Chalkedon III,* pp. 81–237. A. Perego, "Il 'lumen gloriae' e l'unità psicologica di Cristo," *Divus Thomas,* (Pi), 58 (1955), pp. 90–110, 296–310; R. Haubst, "Probleme der jüngsten Christologie" (cf. note 15); B. Lonergan, *De constitutione Christi* (cf. note 25); and "Christ as Subject: a Reply," *Gregorianum,* 40 (1959), pp. 242–270; J. Galot, S.J., "La psychologie du Christ," *Nouvelle Revue Theologique,* 80 (1958), pp. 337–358; F. Malmberg, *Über den Gottmenschen* (cf. note 2), pp. 89–114.

man nature, the "person" itself, the hypostasis of the *Logos,* is not
primarily an operating principle, but is above all a unifying principle. Hence the divine hypostasis is not directly relevant for the
analysis of the human consciousness of Christ. The "I" of the
divine Person does not flow over into Christ's human consciousness.
There is no transition. Hence in Christ's human nature there must
be a purely human "conscious I" which is not directly influenced by the divine consciousness. Indeed, because of this psychic
privacy, the humanity of Christ would have to be considered as a
nature standing purely of itself, as merely another human "person."[38]
In order to avoid this, Galtier holds that this human-psychological
"I" is "opened," "dilated," by means of the direct vision of God.
The humanity of Jesus sees that it is united to the *Logos.* The "I"
of experience, as seen in this vision, is bound to the Person of the
Logos. Thus is formed in Christ a psychological unity which is in
effect an expression of His ontological unity.

But this psychological opening of Christ's human nature to the
Logos, resulting from the Man-Christ's vision of the Godhead, is
not incompatible with a relative autonomy, on the level of consciousness, in His humanity. The interior life of Jesus is stamped
with freedom and privacy. But, according to P. Galtier, this changes
nothing, either of the hypostatic union, of the vision, or of any
of the other graces in the soul of Christ. Privacy is the principal
fact, and the openness of Christ's humanity to the *Logos* must remain a matter of secondary importance, although it is, to be sure,
present always. In 1949, when Father Léon Seiller, O.F.M., referred
to this Christo-psychology of Galtier, incorporating it into the ultra-
Scotism of Déodat de Basly — it is well to note this development
— there ensued an official declaration of the Church on the *Homo
Assumptus* doctrine of Déodat. The Christo-psychology of Galtier
also seemed to fall under the judgment. The inclusion became clear
in Pope Pius XII's encyclical on Chalcedon, *Sempiternus Rex
Christus,* as published in the *Osservatore Romano* on September 13,
1951, where the Pope condemns a doctrine which assumes two
subjects, at least psychologically distinct (*saltem psychologice*) in
Christ: "Although there is no reason why the humanity of Christ
should not be investigated further by way and reason of psychology,

---

[38] P. Galtier, *L'unité du Christ,* p. 350.

nevertheless there are not lacking those, who, in difficult studies of this kind, overlook old views more than is appropriate, so that they construct new teachings and fail to rely on the authority and definition of the Council of Chalcedon, so that the teachings elaborated by them may shine more splendidly. These (theologians) so promote the status and condition of Christ's human nature that it may seem to be regarded, *at least psychologically* (my emphasis) as a kind of subject *sui generis,* as if it were not subsistent in the person of the Word."[39] However, in the official and definitive edition of this encyclical, the words *"saltem psychologice"* were omitted and the question of the human consciousness in Christ was left unsettled. Only the old Nestorian doctrine of the two "ontological subjects" in Christ was condemned anew.[40]

2. Hegemony of the Logos and the Consciousness of Christ. We come now to the antitype of P. Galtier's Christo-psychology. It is advocated by P. Parente, B. Xiberta, O.Carm., Dom Diepen, A. Perego, S.J., and others, each with special modifications with respect to the Trinity and the ontology of Christ. Whereas Galtier's experiment is based upon a Christology "from below," Parente works out his antithesis from a Christology and Christo-psychology "from above." He first asserts that consciousness is an attribute not of nature, but of person. Even in the deity one can speak of a personal consciousness. Even the *Logos* has a personal consciousness, and precisely to the extent that He personally shares in divine

---

[39] *Osservatore Romano,* Vol. 13, 9, 1951 (No. 212), p. 2, cols. 1–2.

[40] Cf. *AAS,* 43 (1951) (pp. 625–653), p. 638: "Hi humanae Christi naturae statum et conditionem ita provehunt ut eadem reputari videatur subiectum quoddam sui iuris, quasi in ipsius Verbi persona non subsistat." Cf. P. Galtier, "La conscience humaine Du Christ," *Gregorianum,* 32 (1951), p. 562, n. 68. To be sure, the comment of the Master of the Sacred Palace, on the decree against the article of L. Seiller, leaves certain possibilities open. The distinction between psychological and ontological person (in both cases, the Italian expression: *personalità*) is allowed. But L. Seiller goes further. He speaks of the *eminente personnalité* of the *Homo Assumptus in Franziskanische Studien,* 31 (1949), pp. 50, 246 ff. and comes very close to making this into an ontological person. P. Galtier, customarily more prudent, of late tends to weaken the stressing of autonomy in this psychological "I," so much so that he designates the divine Person as a *Je* (i.e., ontological "I"), but allowing in the humanity of Christ only a *Moi.* Cf. *Gregorianum,* 32 (1951), pp. 525–568, esp. pp. 534–536. He furthermore underlines the fact that psychologically "autonomous" is not the same as *sui iuris.* Cf. here R. Haubst, *Theologische Revue,* 52 (1956), p. 152; J. Ternus, in *Chalkedon III,* pp. 141–142; J. Alfaro, *Gregorianum,* 39 (1958), pp. 222–270.

nature. This notion of the Trinity is proposed as a way whereby we can reason to certain activities proper to the *Logos* as against those of Christ's humanity. These activities must necessarily influence and condition the human consciousness of Christ so totally that the latter can in no way possess the psychological privacy or autonomy proposed by Galtier. Since the humanity of Christ subsists in the *Logos,* it can in no way be *sui iuris,* ontologically or psychologically. Furthermore the *Logos* is the only principle of all Christ's activity, including the activity of His human nature. Christ's humanity is the instrument of the *Logos,* and is ruled in full hegemony by the *Logos* (see above). In Christ there is only one *esse,* the *esse personale* of the *Logos.* Insofar as the divine Person shares this being with the humanity of Christ, it exercises an immediate, actuating influence upon all of Christ's human activity, and consequently upon His consciousness. Thus the latter is from the very beginning open to the *Logos* and centered in the divine "I." Between divinity and humanity in Christ there is no hiatus, no gap of consciousness. The divine "I" is immediately, totally centered in the humanity and is the sole focal point in the entire human-divine interior life of Christ. Thus the Person of the *Logos* alone is the psychological, as well as the ontological, center of unity. For this reason Parente does not need to have recourse to the direct vision of God in order to explain the one "I" of the consciousness in Christ. Later, of course, he attributes to the vision an integrating function of making more clear the direct perception of the Person of the *Logos* by Christ's humanity. Still he seems not to consider it really necessary for his interpretation of Christ's interior life.

This rejection of a psychological autonomy as an "I" on the level of the human consciousness of Christ has found definite acceptance with many theologians. The same cannot be said of Parente's concrete application of his thesis. His contention that there was an influence, personal and proper to the *Logos,* working upon the human nature in Christ was unequivocally rejected by all. Also his assumption that the created consciousness of Christ could apprehend the divine being by its "own power," by introspection (with neither the grace of the vision nor the *lumen gloriae*), was unacceptable. With this assumption, Parente stands practically alone. He seems to overlook the fact that human spirituality too is in need of a special interior provision of grace through the *lumen gloriae* in order even to come into contact, on the level of experience, with the Person of the Logos. Criticism also fell upon his over-emphasis of the unity of being in Christ in the sense of Cajetan's unity of the uncreated act of existence in Christ. Parente's "con-sciousness theory," set up against the "vision theory" of Galtier, is, as such, untenable. With Parente there is the danger that Chal-cedon's teaching on the "inconfused" presence of two natures in Christ may be lost; Galtier's theory seems, on the other hand, to threaten Chalcedon's principle of "undividedness" with respect to the two natures in Christ.

3. Actuation Theory and Consciousness. With a view to going beyond both these interpretations and to integrating them in their true substance, J. Ternus has recourse to the Actuation theory of M. de la Taille, so as to apply it — as an original Christological project — to Christo-psychology. The Actuation theory in fact al-lows us the opportunity of observing the problem from a more lofty vantage point. The dialectical principle it contains is of par-ticular significance here: the more perfect the union of a creature with God, the higher the consummation of the creature accord-ing to the plan meant for it by God. The highest conceivable union of Christ's humanity with the Person of the *Logos,* achieved through a quasi-formal causality and actuation, implies the most perfect "reali-zation" of Christ's humanity as such. This applies, in its own way, to psychology. From this viewpoint nothing stands in the way of assuming a psychological "I" in the humanity of Christ. This human "I" is so enlightened in the light of the vision, that it renders trans-parent in itself the "I" of the *Verbum Incarnatum.*[41] In so far as Christ's human "I" experience is shown to be the transparency of the "I" of the one divine Person, it is on the one hand preserved in its full human integrity and still, on the other hand, intrinsically oriented toward Christ's ontic center. The ontological actuation of the humanity of Jesus through the hypostasis of the *Logos* is paralleled by an actuation of Christ's noetic consciousness as spirit. The hypo-static "I" of the *Logos* is conscious of itself not only by its divine na-ture, but also in its human nature, *in* its human consciousness, and precisely *through* the resultant presence to itself of this humanity.

---

[41] J. Ternus, *ibid.,* p. 237; in general, pp. 208–237.

To be sure, the *Logos* neither formally brings about the act of the human consciousness, nor causes it virtually. In the dialectical unity of quasi-formal actuation, the human consciousness can be considered as a thoroughly closed-off area — even if it remains open by reason of the vision — but in the depth of being it exists as the actuation of the *Logos,* in fact as the consciousness of the *Logos.*

4. Lumen Gloriae.   In a comprehensive survey, A. Perego, S.J., took issue with the interpretations of Christ's consciousness which we have just sketched.[42] His major stress falls upon the distinction between knowledge of objects and consciousness, a distinction particularly neglected in the vision theory of Galtier. P. Galtier, Dom Diepen, J. Ternus, *et al.,* failed to attribute a true "consciousness" to Christ. The vision of God confers only an "object-knowledge," but no *conscientia,* no awareness of self. Particularly where a psychological or phenomenological "I" of Christ's humanity is concerned, the gap to the "I" of the ontological person can be bridged only by "knowledge." Even Dom Diepen falls under this proscription when he does not even assume this "I" of experience and thus seeks an immediate centering of Christ's human consciousness in the *Logos.* For neither the experience of the hegemony of the *Logos* in Christ's humanity nor the vision of God could justify inferring any "consciousness of being the Son of God." Perego himself seeks the solution in an appeal to the *lumen gloriae,* which is the necessary supernatural condition required for the created intellect to enjoy the beatific vision. In this light of glory the soul sees God, and furthermore is conscious both of the intuition and of the blessedness ensuing from it. Thus this *lumen gloriae,* this highest of all supernatural endowments of the created spirit, must be analyzed if we are to solve the problem of consciousness. For it is here that we encounter the first principle of Christ's consciousness. By virtue of the hypostatic union, Christ, the Head of Creation, enjoys this light in the fullest measure. Consequently, it can also constitute a perfect unity on the level of consciousness.

Various answers, therefore, have been offered to the problem of interpreting the human spiritual life of Jesus. They echo the tensions of the classical Christological questions. Theologians are

---

[42] A. Perego, cf. note 37.

again distinguishing between a Christology "from below," and one "from above," between the Chalcedonian antitheses of "the inconfused" and "the undivided," between a Christology of union and one of distinction. But what of a synthesis? Can it be said that any genuine reconciliation of divergent views is in sight?

To explain the consciousness of being the Son of God, as it existed in Jesus as man, we must doubtless start from His human spiritual life. And it is this human spirituality of Jesus which, as the principle of consciousness, concerns us here. But consciousness of self can also take the form of the mere knowledge of an object, being, as it were, the "self-awareness" of a spiritual nature. For spirituality is by definition connected with being conscious, with being present to one's self. "The higher the 'actuality' of a being, at least as far as the level and consistency of its being is concerned, the more it is intelligible to, and conscious of, itself."[43] In his natural spirituality man is not, by nature, fully "conscious of himself," since he experiences himself only in his acts. Man stands in need of a liberation and a profound regeneration from something above nature if he is to become completely self-aware, fully in possession of himself and fully transparent to himself. With mystics we often find the remarkable phenomenon of an increase in the experience of God together with an intensification of self-awareness. The latter will attain to its full measure only in the Beatific Vision of God, and this by virtue of the light of glory. This vision of God in the *lumen gloriae,* already substantially and fundamentally within us by virtue of faith and grace, means the highest actuation of human, spiritual being. Here again it is true to say that the highest union with God is the spiritual creature's fulfillment, its "most complete realization of itself." Everything is lit up, even to the last detail, by the *lumen gloriae.* God becomes clear for the soul, and in God the spirit becomes clear to itself. Experiencing God revealed to itself, the created spirit at the same time experiences itself as the vessel of this revelation — more intensely and more comprehensively than it could of itself.

Thus if it be true to say that the higher the actuation of a spiritual being, the more profound its self-awareness, then we can, indeed

---

[43] K. Rahner, in *Chalkedon III,* p. 21.

we must, claim the highest possible degree of spiritual self-aware-ness for Christ's humanity. He is doubtless the highest conceivable actuation of human spiritual being, for His humanity is united to the *Logos,* the divine principle of intelligibility. Indeed the union, since it is not "in nature according to nature" (*in natura secundum naturam*), can by no means be a monophysitic confusing of divine and human spirituality. But the union is nonetheless substantial — in fact hypostatic — and as such it leaves room in Christ for the clearest consciousness.

"The fact of the substantial union of the humanity of Christ with the *Logos,* insofar as it is a disposition ('act') of the human nature itself, cannot be simply 'subconscious.' Because this sub-stantial union is ontologically a higher reality, it cannot be simply subconscious, as long as its subject has attained that degree of actuality in being which implies an awareness of this very being."[44]

To no one do the following words of the Apostle apply more perfectly than to Christ: "For which man knows the essence of man, unless it be the spirit of man himself, which is in him?" (1 Cor 2:11.) This self-illumination of the human spirituality of Christ is brought about in His natural spirit through supernatural light. For the illumination of Christ's humanity makes possible the full inner liberation of the spirit which is otherwise, sharing as it does the common pilgrim lot of all men, bound to matter. The effect of this liberation is the presence to itself of this spirit as spirit, that is in its perfect naturality which is illumined by grace. Nor is that all. Everything in this spirit that is made objective in nature and grace must be brought into the light of consciousness. This includes of course, above all, and in a most profound way, the union with the Person of the *Logos.* All this is a theologically justified requirement ensuing from the doctrine of the perfect su-pernatural knowledge of Christ, which must also be applicable to the illumination of His consciousness. Thus we stand here upon safe and solid ground.

Now we come to the question whether, in the man Christ, the consciousness of the divine Sonship, or of divine Personality was a pure "consciousness," taking consciousness as "the immediate self-awareness of the human spiritual nature," or whether the jump

---

[44] *Ibid.*

over into the "object" is unavoidable. We must attempt here to approach, with all reverence and caution, the mystery of Christ. Everything that the spirit can present or reveal to itself stands as genuine "consciousness" (*conscientia*). We may count as part of Christ's consciousness everything which is revealed to Him, everything which is made objective in Him simply through the complete natural and supernatural illumination of His spirit. Thus it appears that we must extend the direct illumination of consciousness in Christ to embrace the ontological union with the Person of the *Logos*.[45] This presupposes the unifying unity as an ontological fact of His human nature. Truly "united unity" requires, in the transcendental order (not in the categorical order), a foundation in the created nature of Christ. This foundation consists, in fact, in this nature, as actuated transcendentally in its created being by the subsistence of the *Logos*. The human spirit of Christ experiences itself as the created existence of an uncreated Subject. Inasmuch as the human spirit of Christ is conscious of itself and of its total human reality, it grasps itself as ontologically not subsistent. In coming to itself, the human spirit of Christ points outside itself, to a bearer of its own self lying beyond the "province of its nature." We have intentionally referred to the direction of this orientation with the indefinite "outside." For we are inquiring after what can be revealed to Christ's humanity specifically from its self, i.e., in the strict sense of "consciously known" and not merely "known."

Here we approach a barrier. Up to this point we could advance unhindered, without considering knowledge of objects, and we were still in the province of the illumination of consciousness and the self-awareness of a spiritual nature. We needed attend only to the demands of that nature's own being and of any being objectified in it. But now we must change our course. For this illumination

---

[45] From this point of view as well, it becomes clear that the question of the united unity in Christ must be carried further back to the question of the unifying unity, i.e., that of the reason and ontology of unity. This stands as a prerequisite even if none of the existing solutions of these two problems are satisfactory. It is certain that unity is objectivized as a substantial oneness in Christ's humanity (in the realm of transcendental being). Thus the self-enlightenment of Christ's human being can comprise the substantial union as part of consciousness.

of the consciousness has not shed light upon the final Subject and Bearer of this nature, at least not as He is in Himself, in His immediateness. Even though we have considered the soul of Christ under the final, full illumination of the light of glory, we can nevertheless call "conscious" only that which the human spirituality of Christ possesses of itself. Even if it is aware of an orientation and ontological unity with a subject which lies by nature above itself, the experience of this subject as such remains something else. This may become clear by considering the words of Karl Rahner:

"To the extent that this hypostatic union means or implies that a human reality is united to the *Logos* as to an ontological determination of this human reality, *the human soul of Christ is immediately present, on both the ontological and conscious levels* to the *Logos* (my emphasis). The immediate vision of that unity . . . is the consequence, not the premise of the soul's conscious presence to the *Logos*. It is (finally) not a *donum* given as a moral prerogative to the human soul out of 'convenience' or 'fittingness' because of the hypostatic union, but *is* the hypostatic union itself, insofar as this union is necessarily that of an *intelligibile actu* in the *intelligens actu* which is the human soul of Christ. In other words, to the extent and in the way that the hypostatic union is a real and ontological determination of Christ's human nature, and is, in fact, ontologically its highest disposition (or implies such), and this human nature is, *of itself* 'aware of things' (my emphasis), then this union must also be a quality proper to this very human nature, and cannot be merely the content of an 'object knowledge given from outside.' "[46]

Difficulty arises at this point unless we determine more precisely how far the self-awareness of Christ's human nature can extend. We can without hesitation admit with Karl Rahner that every real ontological determination of Christ's human nature must, for this nature, be an aspect of its "being aware of itself by its own power." Part of this real ontological determination of Christ's humanity is the *fact* of being ontologically united, but not the term of the union the Person of the *Logos*. The latter does not enter into the objectified reality of Christ's spirituality and created nature in such

---

[46] K. Rahner, in *Chalkedon III*, p. 21 f.; cf. F. Malmberg, *loc. cit.*, esp. p. 112 ff., whose solution lies in the direction of K. Rahner without removing all difficulties there.

a way that it could of itself and through itself make the union visible as such. This could be possible only if the union of natures could really come about as it is conceived by monophysitism. Of itself, from the concrete constitution of its being as such, i.e., by way of strict consciousness, the self-conscious human nature of Christ can know only that it is not a being closed within itself, but the existence and being of a transcendent subject. To this inference it is forced directly, intuitively, and in the fullest clarity, indeed, by virtue of its "consciousness." But the vision of the Subject as such will not come from the creature's objective reality, even if the latter is viewed in its constitutional union in grace and being with the *Logos*. This "Subject" remains completely transcendental in its own reality, and it can never be objectified as it is in itself in a creature. Thus the jump to the "Object" must be made here, lest divine transcendence be destroyed. Christ's humanity can thus be fully "in the presence of the *Logos*" only when the *Logos* freely reveals itself in its own reality through the vision, and, in fact, reveals itself as Person-Subject of the Trinity. This object awareness, however, is intercepted by a spirituality which experiences itself, by virtue of self-awareness, as oriented ontologically to this *Logos*. Through this self-awareness of Christ's soul in the light of glory, through its openness, experienced also in the light of glory, of itself toward the *Logos,* and finally through the vision of this *Logos*-Subject itself is constituted Christ's consciousness of being the Son of God. The conscious and the known are bound together here in a union that simply cannot be expressed. With this the *Logos* shines forth in its inviolable transcendence and personal reality, free of the mediation of any representational likeness, in the center of Christ's spiritual being. But it is one thing to shine *in* Christ's soul, and something else to be aware of things *by virtue of* and *through that soul* itself. To be sure, the bond between that which comes from Christ's spirituality itself, and that which is there as a result of a direct illumination from the *Logos,* is so intimate that this direct object-vision of the *Logos*-Subject appears as the most harmonious fulfillment of the self-awareness of Christ's humanity. Pure conscious self-enlightenment on the part of Christ's humanity and revelation of the *Logos* as both Subject and Object in the substance of Christ's soul fit together into an inseparable unity.

Thus, since true "consciousness" of Jesus' humanity must neces-sarily remain limited *qua* creature, and the *Logos qua Logos* can reveal Himself only in inviolable transcendency, the psychological unity of the God-Man Jesus Christ is unattainable via a pure "consciousness" (as the complete self-awareness of a nature by itself and purely of itself). At this point an object-vision is un-avoidable. It is the gap, infinite in character, between the creature and God which is, in fact, essential to the "consciousness" of this humanity. This humanity knows itself as a creature and as such experiences itself united ontologically to a transcendent Subject.

No one experiences himself so much a creature, but also divine, as Jesus Christ. In spite of this infinite tension He claims an inimi-table psychological privacy. "Before Abraham was, I am" (Jn 8:58). Here lies the secret of the rarely seen eminence and self-assured-ness that shines forth from the Person of Jesus — and again the secret of the abysmal humility in which He bows before the Father: "The Father is greater than I" (Jn 14:28). Experiencing Himself as creature, He stands nevertheless as Son before the Father — infinitely elevated over our adoptive relationship to "His" Father. The interior range of experience in Christ's humanity is completely open to the *Logos*-Subject, and is so utterly fulfilled through the vision of the *Logos* that the psychological unity of Christ becomes the most intimate conceivable image of the ontological union, of the "inseparable" in the order of being — but at the same time also of the "inconfused." Hence, "Father, glorify me in your bosom with the glory I possessed in your bosom before the world came to be" (Jn 17:5). It is a man who utters these words. But since for the *being* of the God-Man, the Chalcedonian "inconfused" applies as well as the "undivided," then it must remain the governing standard also for the *consciousness* of Christ and our interpretation of it.[47]

---

[47] R. Haubst, "Welches Ich spricht in Christus?" *Trierer Theologische Zeit-schrift,* 66 (1957), p. 1 ff., shows, in a very clear presentation of the problem, how a "human psychological I" can be assumed in Christ here. We can accept the fruit of this interpretation from the standpoint of the position set forth above. "For in the perspective of this general view of the question, both types of Christo-psychology move back close together, the two types which we saw above very much removed from one another with the assump-tion of only one divine or even of a 'human I' in Christ. For on the one hand, the human consciousness of Jesus experiences, as we said, His psycho-logical I most intimately related back to the hypostatic I, and so much so that this latter is always present when Christ says 'I,' in that it is, as the

This inquiry into the consciousness of Christ brings to the fore the most recent and most important problem of contemporary Christology. A new aspect of the mystery of Christ is revealed — its interior, so to speak. Only Christology handed down from the Fathers provides us with a sufficiently sound foundation for the valid elaboration of a question raised only by the investigations of modern psychology. If it serves to reveal the mystery of Christ in a new depth and in its utter inexhaustibility, the question has not been asked in vain.

Since the Ascension the Church — and the theology which stands in her service — works in unbroken tradition to depict the figure of Christ in such a way that it should serve to propagate doctrine and honor God. She will still be wrestling with this task when the *Kyrios* Himself returns at the end of time to let His mystery shine forth in unveiled glory and clarity before the community of those bought with His blood. A basic law of the Church's understanding of Christ has been formulated in this struggle which often brings pain and heavy losses upon the Church: In Christ, God and Man are "inconfused" and nevertheless "undivided." This law must govern theology as well as the promulgation of the Gospel and the cult of Christ, if the image of the *Kyrios* is really to give forth its full strength upon the Church. Wherever this law is violated or ignored, the true figure of Christ is distorted.

In reforming the manner of promulgating the doctrine of the Church, particular attention in recent decades has been drawn to this fundamental law. A tendency toward idolatry and a one-sided anti-Arian polemic have from time to time allowed the rights of Christ's humanity to recede too much into the background. A true idea of Christ's mission and of its place in the totality of the Church's teaching had therefore to be worked out anew.[48] Of all

---

metaphysical basis for the subsistence of the psychological I, participant in consciousness. In another light the hypostatic I 'appears' or 'manifests itself' in the psychological I-phenomenon because of this metaphysical deepening" (p. 18 f.).

[48] Playing a directional role here was J. A. Jungmann, *Die Frohbotschaft und unsere Glaubensverkündigung* (Regensburg, 1936), pp. 67–80. This work also contains further suggestions toward the structuring of our Christocentric theology. Significant for the emphasis of Christ's humanity was K. Adam, *Christus unser Bruder* (Regensburg, 1930²). The most recent presentation of the problem is to be found in F. X. Arnold, "Das Gottmenschliche Prinzip der Seelsorge und die Gestaltung der Christlichen Frömmigkeit," in *Chalkedon*

the forms of the cult of Christ, the honoring of the Heart of Jesus is perhaps the most particularly apt to lead one into the mystery of Christ's God-Manhood, into the holiness of His consciousness. But this form of the cult of Christ is also markedly dangerous, in that it often brings one to an unreal confusion of principles. With some of the faithful, not to say with many, this cult thrives upon a secret, unclarified monophysitism. It is well to remember at this point that God became true man in His Son, so as to see the purest service and the fullest obedience rise up to Himself out of the heart of a man. The "attitudes" of Jesus' interior life, of His heart, are human attitudes which, constituting the obedience of the new Adam, have reestablished the dignity of man before God. Let us leave Christ in His humanity truly on the side of Man, since He wanted in fact to be like us in everything, excluding, of course, sin (cf. Hebr 4:15). He takes our place here, stands before God as the representative of sinners so as to be able to elevate us to that place which He Himself took as man before God. Thus we must continue to take the genuinely human life of Jesus Christ in all theological and religious seriousness. It will always be a holy task for us to penetrate the secret of His interior, which is the human interior of the Son of God, the interior of every child of God.[49]

Being our Brother and Mediator, Christ is, as the incarnate God, also the *Kyrios* of His community of faithful. He is therefore worthy of our *praying to Him*. As much as our prayer should go to the Father with and through Christ and in the Holy Spirit, it is nevertheless false to exclude Christ Himself, the God-Man, from this prayer. To pray only "through Him" to the Father, and not also "to Him," would not be in accord with true Church tradition.[50] Pope

---

III, pp. 287–340. Cf. K. Rahner, "Die ewige Bedeutung der Menschheit Jesu für unser Gottverhältnis" (cf. note 9); the special edition of *Lumen Vitae*, 7 (1952), No. 4, on the idea of Christ with the following individual essays: Chas. Moeller, "Jésus-Christ dans la mentalité moderne" (pp. 549–567); Dom Bernard Capelle, "L'union à Jésus-Christ par la messe et l'année liturgique," (pp. 567–672); J. A. Jungmann, "La place de Jésus-Christ dans la catéchèse et la prédication" (pp. 573–582). To be sure we must bear in mind that each of these authors here approach Christocentrics in theology and propagation of doctrine from a different standpoint.

[49] Cf. J. Stierli, *Cor Salvatoris* (Frieburg, 1954).

[50] In his well-known study, *Die Stellung Christi im liturgischen Gebet* (Münster, 1925), J. A. Jungmann rightly observes that the *liturgical* prayer of the Roman Church was, from earliest times, emphatically directed to the

Pius XII has spoken most clearly in this connection.[51] Jesus is the elevated *Kyrios* (cf. Phil 2:9–11) and sits at the right hand of the Father (cf. Act 7:56). Nothing greater has ever been said of any man. This "sitting at the right hand of the Father" is the divine confirmation of the cult given to Christ since Apostolic times. Prayer "through Christ" is a special recognition of His humanity; it is our peculiar consolation and establishes our new

Father, to whom it is offered *per Christum Dominum nostrum*. A second observation, added to this, is that, in the course of history, the so-called "mediator formula" was transformed so that Jesus Christ appears, not as the Mediator of prayer to the Father, but as the Object of precisely this prayer. This change, which can be observed both in the universal Church and in the separated communities of the East as well, is due above all to two important facts: (1) the anti-Arian bearing of Orthodoxy in the fourth century and (2) the monophysitic annihilation of Christ's human nature in the East. The inquiry was extremely fruitful, even if the results were subject to some later modifications. In a study of monophysitism in the oriental liturgies, H. Engberding (in *Chalkedon II,* pp. 697–733) comes to the conclusion that, "Not in the entire span of monophysitic liturgies is it possible to exhibit clearly as an essential element the diminution of Christ's humanity or the depreciation of his redemptive sacrifice on the cross, which our traditional notion of monophysitism would lead us to expect. Christ is ever there as a whole man, well familiar with everything human, even the most humiliating passion — sin alone excepted. Thus is best explained how the Church communities in union with Rome were able simply to take over, *in toto* and without reservations, the monophysitic Liturgies" (*loc. cit.,* p. 727). Differences in the delineation of the interior of Christ are, of course, admitted. Even within an orthodox framework, piety toward Christ can develop in extremely diverse forms (cf. O. Rousseau, *loc. cit.* [cf. note 11]; A. Grillmeier, "Der Logos am Kreuz" [Munich, 1956], ch. 5). At the instigation of J. A. Jungmann, extraliturgical prayer was also subjected to a special examination, with the result that there was found, already in pre-Arian times, a piety which turned directly to Christ in completely spontaneous prayers of praise, thanksgiving, and petition. The sources indicate clearly that the number of prayers to Christ outside of liturgical piety was much greater than those which have come down to us. There were for example the Christological hymns which flourished in the ancient Church. Alongside the prayer offered *per Christum* to the Father, which predominates especially in the liturgical area, there flows in the early Church the stream of a vigorous piety to Christ as well, which directed its prayers straight to the Redeemer and which was especially found in the private and popular piety of that time. The sources of this prayer lie, to be sure, in the New Testament (Mk 10:47; Lk 23:42; Acts 7:59, where reference is made to "Jesus standing on the right hand of the Father!"). Authoritative in this question are the studies of Jungmann's follower, B. Fischer, "Die Psalmenfrömmigkeit der Märtyrer," *Trierer Theologische Zeitschrift,* 62 (1953), pp. 19–32; *ibid.,* 60 (1951), pp. 178–188 (Jerome); 63 (1954), pp. 312–339 (Augustine); RömQschr, 49 (1954), pp. 21–55 (Origen-Ambrose).

[51] *AAS* 48 (1956) (pp. 711–725), pp. 723–725.

position in grace before God. The teaching of the "inconfused" union of natures in Christ, which must prevail in cult as well as in doctrine, is expressed here. Prayer "to Christ," makes us realize that God means in all earnestness the exchange that He has made with us. For man has thus been raised in Christ to the throne of God and enjoys there the rights of absolute Lord. Adoration of the God-Man is our gratitude for this incomprehensible act of God. The Church's principle of "undividedness" is our foundation for such prayer. Irrevocably earnest, then, is God's concern for our salvation.

Christ, the God-Man, is thus the most intense union of contrasts possible. He is the incarnate union between God and man.

ALOIS MÜLLER

CONTEMPORARY MARIOLOGY

MARIOLOGY was, until the beginning of Vatican II, unquestionably the most active area in dogmatic theology. To be sure, other questions were being attacked again with a fresh vigor — such questions, in fact, as one had until recently, perhaps, considered long settled. But while other questions matured slowly with a measured theological gravity, Mariologists were very active in their field. From the beginning there was a good deal of popular basis for the movement, a popularity often deliberately encouraged and characterized, unfortunately not without reason, as "publicity."

This development has definitely been promoted through the two great events of recent Marian faith and life: the papal definition of the corporal assumption (1950) and the Marian Year (1954). But both events were, at least partly, the outcome of an active process of several decades. It should be made clear that Marian doctrine is not a distinct theological discipline such as Patrology and Church history, for example, but simply a chapter of general dogmatic theology. In view of this, it is truly astounding that in many countries special theological societies have been expressly formed for the serious study of Mariology, e.g., in Germany, France, Belgium, Italy (where the "International Marian Academy" has its home), Spain, the United States of America, Canada, and others.

All these societies publish studies and the papers delivered at their congress, and the International Academy publishes concurrently seven different collections of Mariological studies. International Mariological congresses have followed one another at brief intervals: Rome, 1950; Rome, 1954; Lourdes, 1958. Identifiable groups attempt to promote a similarly rapid "frequency" for Marian dogmas. The writer recalls that, within weeks following the definition of 1950, religious houses and the like were urged by some quarters to collaborate in a follow-up petition for the definition of Mary's role as Mediatrix of all graces.

The impassioned atmosphere found in expressions of Marian life also carries over, occasionally, with impetus into Mariology. One sometimes receives the impression that something is always afoot in Mariological matters, that something must be "proven" or reached. And, varying with national temperament, "generosity" toward Mary is to all intents and purposes used as a theological criterion par excellence to determine orthodoxy in doctrine in general.

. This "Mariological phenomenon," which has anything but reached its high point, many theologians see fraught with dangers as well as promising in hopeful developments. They are not just imagining the danger. They wish to forestall these dangers through a simple "braking" action and restraint. One often detects, diametrically opposed to prevailing sentiment, an outspoken resentment. The success of these reactions is minimal, and they may not be the correct approach. Once such a broad movement has laid hold of the Church, there is no turning back. But the movement itself has a theological bearing and significance. Marian thought is a fact in the Church. It is the joint task of theologians and those who bear the teaching office of the Church to give this movement vision, to show it the right paths, the exact aims, and to provide it with a healthy growing pace, so that the results may contribute real illumination and clarification on the horizon of faith. This work is fully under way, and it behooves the pastoral-apostolic Christian, be he priest or layman, to be aware of the vistas which are opening up in a field whose significance for the Church can be misunderstood or belittled no longer.

Hence we shall attempt at the outset to survey prevailing thought in contemporary Mariology so as to determine things as they are today and to come to some idea of what the immediate future may hold for Marian questions. But we must first handle the question to what extent these matters are still open to discussion.

We are all acquainted with the inclination of some to advance Mariological tenets as quickly as possible to the status of doctrine binding on the Church. There is an eager counting of heads with the hope of coming to a "general consensus" (*sententia communis*) whereby a differing theological opinion may be checkmated without full discussion. One aspect of this is the attributing, in theological argumentation, to papal acts and statements a weight which they neither have nor were intended to have. For the most part papal utterances are less theological sources than applications of theology. And every pope speaks with those theological media which his age is able to place at his disposal. But it is fundamental to remember that what he does not "define" is not "closed," and remains absolutely open for further theological scrutiny. It can only bring harm to theology, and thereby to the Church, to remove questions from discussion before they are thoroughly investigated and cleared up. But they can be so clarified only if the various antitheses are allowed full expression and the time which the Church customarily gives to considering serious doctrinal matters is permitted to elapse

Above all it is unjust, in matters which are still in full state of flux, when one opinion claims for itself a sort of ecclesiastical tradition. One can often easily determine in a given question a numerical prevalence of one opinion. One may even express the well-grounded supposition that such an opinion will finally enter, in some form, into the doctrinal treasure of the Church. But it would contradict the *disputatio* stage to make theological argumentation of such possibilities. At this stage the Church does not *want* to commit herself to an irrevocable definition and she must never be enlisted for the purposes of unilateral argumentation. In this connection it is worth mentioning, for example, that Pope Pius XII, contrary to the practice of Pius XI, exercised uncommon restraint in the use of the title *Co-redemptrix* (we shall discuss this further). He evidently wished to *avoid* his statements from being rewrought in theological workshops.

Thus we must maintain unwaveringly that a theological question should stand open to theological discussion until the ordinary or extraordinary teaching office of the Church takes in it a position *binding in faith*. A mere adoption of notions does not constitute any such binding position, nor, what is more important, does the occurrence of a term imply a confirmation of its various theological explanations. The general assent to a truth does not infer the canonization as well of all conclusions drawn therefrom.

I. The Principal Questions in Mariology Today

All the Mariological efforts of our day could be placed under the heading: *Mary and the Redemption*. No longer are the inquiries into the inner "privileges" of Mary's person so very important theologically, but our attention is directed rather upon her active relationship to the redemption of humanity. This claim appears to be contradicted by the dogmatic definition of 1950, which fell upon an inner privilege of Mary, and by the celebration of the Marian year and its congress, which had a similar object — the Immaculate Conception. But it is particularly indicative that both these privileges in grace are seen and explained today mainly in the larger framework of Mary's special position in the work of redemption. It is perhaps essential to the development of Marian doctrine that we depart from a concentration on Mary as an individual with her privileges and proceed to see her role in the entire work of salvation. It was long overdue that the relationship of Mary to the Redemption should be recognized in Catholic Mariology. Its main feature is, in fact, that Mary's connection to Christ is personal, which by consequence bespeaks a personal relationship to the redemption.

In this fundamental concern — and it is this concern which most frequently comes up in relevant papal announcements — may well lie the genuine dogmatic development in which the Catholic Christian sees the working of the Spirit of God. *Theological treatments* of these matters, however, are themselves only contributions to a common effort.

A. *Mary, Co-redemptrix With Christ*

The question of the co-redemption of Mary is no longer entirely new. Certainly it has not yet come to rest. It calls forth from time to time new explanations and trial solutions, and, as will be shown, could be considered as the ensign of a fundamental direction of Mariology today.

The expression "co-redemptrix" comes down to us from as recently as the fifteenth century. Indeed Mary was given, as early as the tenth century, the truly astonishing title of "redemptrix." To be sure this meant nothing more than "mother of the Redeemer." Today's problem of the collaboration of Mary in the sacrifice of the cross goes back to Bernard of Clairvaux, who approached it by his notion of *com-passio* with Christ. As soon as the relative independence of Mary became accepted in theological reasoning the term *redemptrix* was felt to be unsuitable, and it was gradually replaced by the more qualifying term *co-redemptrix*. Since the nineteenth century only the latter expression has been in use. In the acts of St. Pius X this term appears once in passing, whereas Pius XI uses it more often, though never in official documents. We recall that Pope Pius XII refrained from using the expression at all.

Hence we must say that as a *word* it has not yet attained to any real gravity in ecclesiastical tradition. Many theologians have a positive reserve with respect to the expression. It is, however, quite another matter with respect to the reality signified by the term *co-redemptrix*. The idea of a collaboration of Mary in the working of redemption is very commonly assumed in theology, and more frequently in papal pronouncements.

1. Let us first of all consider the so-called "maximalistic" thesis. This thesis teaches a direct merit of Mary in the redemption as such, in the "ransoming of man." It is admitted that the doctrine is not theologically traceable to revealed sources. Its existence and justification is based upon a (growing) ecclesiastical tradition. For biblical corroboration reference is made especially to the *protoevangelium* (Gn 3:15), to the intimate union of the woman with her Son in enmity toward the evil one, and then to Mary's standing under the cross and there suffering with her Son. Theologically, the principle, "Mary is the new Eve," is taken in the sense that Mary is in all things the new Adam's helpmate, above all in the work of redemption. The theory is stated (the different authors being reduced here to one common denominator) thus: through her consent and her compassion at the sacrifice of the cross, Mary, the new Eve and companion of the Redeemer, has comerited the entire redemptive grace that Christ merited.

Naturally it is stressed that Mary is not in any way a redemptive principle of equal rank with Christ, but that she was herself capable of collaborating in His work only through His power. It is furthermore made clear that the redemptive work of Christ would have of itself no need of this collaboration of Mary. The enlisting of Mary rests upon the free pleasure of God, and serves, as it were, for the ornamentation and elegance of the work of redemption. Thus one of the extreme proponents of this thesis, G. Roschini, comes then to the following qualifications: "The Virgin collaborated really and directly toward the objective redemption of humanity, but in a secondary, accidental, subordinate, relatively universal, only conditionally necessary way; not toward the essence of the redemption, but toward its perfection."[1]

One difficulty in this theory required a radical solution: how could Mary comerit the redemption as such, whereas she is in fact herself redeemed, and was capable of meriting grace only when in the redeemed state, only after the redemption was in effect? ("Before" and "after" are here intended not in a temporal, but in a logical — *prioritas naturae* — sense.) At this point the proponents of the "objective co-redemption" have introduced a new and extremely significant *theologoumenon*. The redemption has two "effects" or "schemes": in the first, Mary is redeemed through Christ alone, and in the second all other humanity is redeemed through Christ *and* the already blessed Mary.

As testimony for this form of the co-redemption theory we can refer to Roschini. Another significant advocate of the maximalistic thesis, more circumspect and discreet than Roschini, is Clément Dillenschneider C.Ss.R.[2] In a pamphlet published in 1951, he very soundly incorporates into his thesis the idea that Mary's co-redemption lies in her *communio* with the Church, wherein she acts in the name of all the redeemed, partaking thereby in the entire work of Christ. M. J. Nicolas O.P.[3] also sees Mary's co-redemption as the ideal stage of the general capacity of the Church for collaboration, and would prefer that the expression *corredemptio* not be suppressed, but extended to apply to the entire Church.

2. The maximalistic thesis called forth a "minimalistic" reaction, whose classical proponents were, among others, W. Goosens[4] and

---

[1] G. Roschini, *Mariologia,* II/I (Rome, 1947[2]), p. 263.

[2] Dillenschneider's principal work on co-redemption is: *Marie au service de notre rédemption* (Hagenau, 1947). In response to criticism he followed this up with: *Pour une Corédemption mariale bien comprise* (Rome, 1949) and finally: *Le mystére de la corédemption mariale. Théories nouvelles. Exposé, appreciation critique, synthèse constructive* (Paris, 1951). Here we find a most rapid orientation and consideration of Köster's ideas (cf. note 6).

[3] M. J. Nicolas, *La doctrine de la corédemption dans la cadre de la théologie générale de la rédemption,* found in: *Marie corédemptrice,* 5th National Marian Congress (Lyon, 1948), pp. 105–129. The same author takes a critical position with regard to the problem of co-redemption: "Chronique de la théologie mariale," *Revue Thomiste,* 53 (1953), pp. 164–179.

[4] W. Goosens, *De cooperatione immediata matris redemptoris ad redemptionem obiectivam quaestionis controversa perpensatio* (Paris, 1939).

H. Lennerz, S.J.[5] Their arguments turn about the notions that, according to the traditional doctrine of the redemption (which knows no two "effects"), Mary, who is herself one of the redeemed, cannot comerit the redemption; that a comeriting by Mary next to Christ would be superfluous, since the merit of Christ is more than sufficient; that such a juxtaposition of Mary next to Christ would detract from the singularity of Christ as Mediator and Redeemer; that if we are to speak of a comeriting by Mary in the redemption, then we can refer only to the "subjective" redemption, to the granting of grace; that Mary has only an indirect collaboration in the objective redemption through being the Mother of the Redeemer.

3. Except for slight variations both these views were advanced vigorously for years. Then from Germany came a completely new proposal by H. Köster, S.A.C.,[6] which attempts to preserve on the one hand the title Co-redemptrix, and on the other the traditional teaching of the Church concerning the redemption. According to this thesis, Christ is in fact alone the meritor of the redemption. Mary did *not* collaborate in the reward of redemption. But it is not enough to see the redemption in such a neutral, anonymous way, as the mere meeting of a demand. The reality of the redemption is something much more personal; it is the covenant and engagement of God with humanity, biblically so clear in both the Old and the New Testaments. Now Christ came to us as God's Son who offered us peace and a new covenant with God in His blood. To bring redemption — to be sure, *objective* redemption — about a personal counterpart in humanity is also needed, a partner in the covenant who will *take on* the redemption as a whole. This *personal summit* of humanity countering to Christ, the Son of God and Redeemer, is Mary. In the name of all humanity she has taken on the redemption in its totality, has entered with humanity into the new covenant of God, and it was only in this way that the redemption happened, i.e., the possibility for every human being to make the redemptive grace subjectively his own. For this reason a true, direct, and necessary role in the objective redemption is to be attributed

[5] H. Lennerz, "De cooperatione Beatae Virginis in ipso opere redemptionis," *Gregorianum*, 29 (1948), pp. 118–141.

[6] H. M. Köster, *Die Magd des Herrn. Theologische Versuche und Überlieferung* (Limburg, 1947). The reaction, in part critical, to this book occasioned a second: *Unus mediator* (Limburg-Gossau, 1950). The first was reissued in a thoroughly rewritten second edition (Limburg, 1954).

to Mary, but her part is that of receiving. She is the receptive co-redemptrix.

This solution was reproached for not respecting the principle that Christ, as Man and Head of humanity, is Himself God's "Partner in the Covenant," and conceives in Himself, in the name of His brothers, a reconciliation with God. Critics held that a latent monophysitism was implied by overlooking this point and attributing to Mary an essential task which is the affair of Christ. The originator of this new theory maintained, however, that his proposal is justified even with full deference to Christ's humanity, and that his thesis may stand. For *fundamentally* the "marriage of the king's son" is the union of the Son of God with the nature of man, but formally it is His marriage with the Church, if these distinctions are appropriate here, which we shall return forthwith to discuss.

It has not yet been decided whether this third solution can effectively bridge the gap between the other positions, or simply becomes a third front of opposition. The basic idea is certainly new in the dispute as it stands today, and will not disappear from the scene.

B. *The Co-redemptive Merit of Mary*

There are today quarters where the question whether one can speak of Mary as a true, immediate co-redemptrix is not so much as raised. For Spanish theologians today it is a self-evident principle and the point of departure for new inquiries. Mary has co-merited the redemption "under Christ and in Christ." Hence one can inquire further into the specific nature of this merit. Theology distinguishes between the merit of one equal in rank (*meritum de condigno*), to whom a reward is due by right because the meriting deed is worthy by virtue of the doer, and the merit of one "equal" by fitness or adequacy (*meritum de congruo*), for whom a reward is due not out of equality in rank, but only out of gracious, amiable evaluation of a lesser, even if, *comparatively speaking,* still significant deed.

According to this distinction it is perfectly clear that Christ has merited the redemption *de condigno* for us. For His act is at once the act of God and of the head of the human race. Thus it has in itself infinite value for all men. On the other hand, most proponents of the objective co-redemption thesis maintained that Mary's co-redemptive merit is only *de congruo,* due to a gracious consideration of her immediate connection with the head of humanity. For sanctifying grace confers on the bearer, through God's disposition, the power of the merit of one of equal rank only for the bearer himself. Only the head of humanity can merit for others through equality in rank. All others merit according to their fitness. Such is the theological teaching of St. Thomas.

For several years now Spanish theologians have been teaching unanimously that Mary's co-redemptive merit is also a merit *de condigno.* This position was the object of a lively discussion in the International Mariological Congress of the Holy Year in Rome. It is also, as a result, a leading position in the Mariological controversy today.

In that congress, P. Llamera, O.P., presented the following arguments:[7] "Because of the hypostatic union the Mother of Christ is the Mother of God; because Christ is the Head of Christians, Mary is their spiritual Mother. Mary's spiritual Motherhood or maternal fullness of grace is consequently related to her salutary mission just as Christ's grace, whereby He is Head, is related to His salutary mission. Thus as Christ has merited grace *de condigno* by virtue of His being Head of the whole human race (*gratia capitalis*) (and in fact absolutely because of the dignity of His Person), so also has Mary, by virtue of her grace of Motherhood, merited grace *de condigno* for all men, for all her children, even if not absolutely (since, although she is the Mother of God, hers is a finite person), nevertheless out of equality in rank ('*ex condignitate*')."

This theory has, as of the date of the present writing, won little sympathy outside the Spanish school. Its future development remains to be seen. But it is only the extreme consequence, drawn with Spanish inexorability, from the autonomy into which Mary is placed by the maximalistic thesis of co-redemption. One should note how Mary's maternity is taken as an absolute category in the argument. We shall come back to this point.

---

[7] *Alma Socia Christi: Acta congressus mariologici-mariani Romae anno sancto MCML celebrati* (Rome, 1951), Vol. I, pp. 163–164. Cf. also Vol. I, pp. 243–255: *de solemmi disputatione mane diei 30ae octobris habita,* and Vol. 4, pp. 81–140: *El mérito maternal corredentivo de Maria.*

C. Mary and the Church

Meanwhile, starting almost from nothing and appearing simultaneously everywhere, the problem of the relationship between Mary and the Church has risen like a comet in recent years. The rapidity, indeed the suddenness, of this development is shown by the fact that fifteen years ago truly nothing of importance concerning it could be found in the Marian literature of the day. Then the *Societé Française d'Etudes Mariales* dedicated three annual congresses to this theme (1951 to 1953), and in 1958, "Mary and the Church" was the object of the third International Mariological Congress at Lourdes.[8] Besides the extremely significant documents of the *Societé Française*,[9] O. Semmelroth, S.J.,[10] H. Rahner, S.J.,[11] and, mainly in a patristic investigation, the present writer,[12] have already submitted their comments on the subject. From these publications many others, even in Spain, take their departure.

For dogmatic history the problem is patrological and biblical in nature, but it is also of the greatest speculative importance, as Scheeben (whose Mariology has just been republished)[13] first recognized after it had been forgotten for many centuries. It will be surveyed here as briefly as possible.

The elements from which the parallel between Mary and the Church proceeds, even from an historical point of view, are the analogous attributions to each of divine maternity, virginity, and the

---

[8] The acts of the Congress of Lourdes appeared under the title *Maria et Ecclesia: Acta congressus mariologici-mariani in civitate Lourdes anno 1958 celebrati,* Academia mariana internationalis (Romae, 1959 ff.).

[9] *Marie et l'Eglise,* I–III. *Bulletin de la Societé Française d'études Mariales* (Paris, 1951–1953). The first volume is dedicated to the history of Marian thought, and Volumes 2 and 3 to the theological problems involved.

[10] O. Semmelroth, *Urbild der Kirche. Organische Aufbäu des Mariengeheimnisses* (Wurzburg, 1950).

[11] H. Rahner, *Maria und die Kirche,* ten chapters concerning the spiritual life (Innsbruck, 1951).

[12] A. Müller, *Ecclesia — Maria,* the oneness of Mary and the Church (Paradosis V) (Freiburg, 1955[2]). — H. Coathalem, S.J., was the first to investigate the history of the parallel of Mary and the Church. But his thesis, defended in 1939, was first published years later: *Le parallelisme entre la Viérge et l'Église dans la tradition latine jusqu'à la fin du XIIe siècle* (Univ. Gregoriana, Romae, 1954).

[13] M. J. Scheeben, *Handbuch der katholischen Dogmatik,* Vol. 2: "Erlösungslehre" (Freiburg i. Br., 1954[2]), pp. 306–499. This reissue is particularly commendable for its extensive, up-to-date bibliography.

title of New Eve. Mary bore the Child of God, conceived by the Holy Spirit, in a miraculous, virginal birth. But children of God continue to be born, conceived likewise by the Holy Spirit; the womb which now miraculously bears them is the baptismal font, the maternal womb of the Church which conceived in the Easter night the strength of the Holy Spirit. Thus the Church continues to be the Mother of God. And in clear allusion to Mary there was an emphasis, early in the history of the Church, that the Church is a virgin mother belonging exclusively to her Bridegroom Christ in the undivided dedication of her pure, unadulterated faith. Similarly Mary has long been recognized as a new Eve who brings back to all humanity that which had been lost by the old Eve.[14] But the thought is similarly present that the Church is the new Eve, created for the new Adam out of His pierced side of the sleep of death. However, because, as is evident, Mary and the Church were called the new Eve for different reasons, their consequent paralleling in this connection was not drawn as early as were the parellels of their maternity and virginity. The thought that Mary is the bride and helpmate of Christ first arose at the turn of the fourth century, and then only in isolated cases (which should be better borne in mind by many who are too eager to demonstrate positions through the Fathers).

Biblically, the designation of the Church as bride and virgin is generally verifiable, and for her role as Mother of God perhaps these words of Christ should be noted: "Whoever does the will of my Father is my brother, sister, *and* mother" (Mt 12:50).

These parallels used by the Fathers are more than mere superficial analogies or metaphors. Between Mary and the Church there is a relationship which corresponds to the relationship and union of Christ's human nature with His Mystical Body, as Augustine explained in the greatest detail. And upon this relationship is based also the great sign of the Apocalypse, the Woman clothed with the Sun, the sign which expresses with utmost clarity the identity of the Mother of Christ with the Mother of Christians. Hence it is the task of speculative theology to elaborate on this subject. And speculation knows that if the Church is humanity *redeemed* in Christ, the humanity which shares in the human nature of Christ, and which

---

[14] Cf. *La Nouvelle Eve*, I–IV. *Bulletin de la Societé Française d'Études Mariales 1954–1957* (Paris, 1955–1958).

is likewise also the humanity which continues to *redeem* in Christ, then both these factors, redeemed and redeeming, have been fulfilled in the most perfect way in Mary. She has the most intimate possible share in the human nature of Christ, namely, the mother's share. As immaculately conceived and corporally assumed into heaven, she is the most perfectly redeemed, and, as Mother of the Redeemer, she has the highest, most universal share in the redeeming action of the Church. And all this came to her out of personal, faithful dedication to God, in which she is again similar to the Church.

It is of the greatest significance that from this aspect the God-Motherhood itself is not in any way absorbed in the order of grace, as is often feared, but takes rather the same direction as every encounter of humanity with God in Christ. Thus we see that Mary and the Church form only one single mystery in a twofold plan or shaping of things: the mystery of human salvation in Christ. issuing from God, taken on and taken up by man, and handed on throughout the history of the human race.

Theologically undreamed-of insights are afforded us if Marian and ecclesiological doctrines can mutually coordinate and fertilize one another, as Scheeben claimed. Hence we find ourselves here before one of the most significant developments of our day.

D. *The Fundamental Mariological Principle*

As a final problem let us point to the ever persisting search for a "first principle" in the theology of Mary. By this is meant a basic truth back to which all Mariological theses can be traced, through which they are made comprehensible, and of which they prove to be an unfolding and fulfillment. Such a principle is no mere theological *jeu d'esprit*. It is much more a bid for theological clarity and purity, a signpost and a warning. Basically it is a search for knowledge of the perfectly simple wisdom of God.

It is traditional to construct the entire theology of Mary upon the divine maternity, not upon maternity from an exclusively physical perspective, but upon maternity in its *adequate* sense. This requires us to pay heed to the complete spiritual-personal privileges and attitudes of Mary with respect to the divine maternity. But with this as a first principle too much is already made explicit; nevertheless Mary's active collaboration in the redemption will never find sure footing here. This collaboration is more properly linked to another principle whereby Mary is seen as the helpmate of the new Adam. But this principle, in turn, would not include her maternity.

A synthesis of both points of view was proposed by Scheeben when he (and his interpreter, Feckes) explained Mary's "personal character" as a "divine maternity of a betrothed," making of this personal character a fundamental principle. This notion has a true unity in that Mary's motherhood has a "betrothed" character through the *fiat,* and in that her first deed as betrothed was to conceive the Christ. This is a profound, truly theological insight. Nevertheless it could be substantiated more precisely, and more thoroughly.

Another synthesis of the mother and helpmate roles has been proposed by G. Roschini[15] with the principle that Mary is the Mother of God and Mother of humanity, and consequently the Mother absolutely. Characteristic of this imposing principle is that it makes Mary into a category all her own, attributing to her a fully autonomous role. It is thus a workable first principle only if one refrains from searching for any connection with the rest of theology.

Opposed to this attempt to view Mary as autonomous and Mariology as independent of other tracts are the proposals which grew out of the efforts to see Mary's privileges in her relation to the Church.

O. Semmelroth defines Mary as the model-image of the Church, as the conceiving and transmitting vessel of salvation, from which follow on the one hand all the mysteries of divine maternity and personal holiness, and on the other her active role in the transmission or mediation of grace. The present writer set the same thoughts in a formula whereby Mary is absolutely the person full of grace, the person participating in the highest way in the humanity of Christ,[16] from which again the entire theology of Mary can flow. And in the same vein we find K. Rahner's[17] principle: "Mary is the fully redeemed person, she who most fully realizes and exemplifies what the grace of God works in human nature and in the Church."

---

[15] *Mariologia,* 4 vols. (Rome, 1947–1948[2]), Vol. I, p. 337.

[16] A. Müller, "Um die Grundlagen der Mariologie," *Divus Thomas* (Fr.), 29 (1951), pp. 385–401.

[17] K. Rahner, "Le principe fondamental de la Théologie mariale," *Rech. Sc. Rel.,* 42 (1954), pp. 481–522. The quote is from page 503. Cf. also C. Dillenschneider, *Le principe premier d'une théologie mariale organique. Orientations* (Paris, 1955). I. Alfaro, *Significatio Mariae in mysterio salutis,* Greg. 40 (1959), pp. 9–37.

Finally there is H. Köster, who finds his fundamental principle[18] in the fact that Mary is the delegated member and personal summit of the expectant and redeemed human family (the Church). She is this by reason of her bond as betrothed to God before the one Mediator, the incarnate Son of God. Common to each of these versions is the notion that all the individual truths concerning Mary can be comprehended best, and in their correct place, and in the right measure, when one sees Mary as the person in whom God's whole order of grace for men has been fully executed, as the high point of human salvation.

II. Assessment and Prospects for the Future

Irrespective of relative weight, the problems discussed above are decisive in Mariology today. From them will proceed the further development of this branch of theology. It is therefore urgently necessary, after cataloguing them, to look more closely and afford ourselves a glance into the future.

Although, as mentioned in the beginning, there is always a question of Mary's precise role in the redemption, a fundamental distinction can nevertheless be made with regard to the approach taken to this question. According to one approach, Mary is a subject unto herself, a separate dimension and category in the theological order. For the other, she belongs to a larger framework, and one is concerned with her for the sake of the whole, because it is the whole which always concerns us most. This is chiefly a question of method, of inner attitude, of an unexpressed "basic principle" within, which is felt more or less explicitly in every Mariological thesis. But proportionate to this potential "more" or "less," the "spheres of interest" of the two approaches are distinguished and divided. It is immediately evident that the question of co-redemption can be profitably discussed as a factor contributing to the notion of Mary's autonomy, just as the Mary-Church theme can be enriching for the synoptic approach. If, therefore, in the following, we place ourselves at odds with both these points of view, it will be mainly because of their thematic expressions. Nevertheless it is not our intention to set our sights directly upon the themes themselves. For there are good reasons to believe that even the theme of co-redemption — which

---

[18] *Magd des Herrn* (2nd ed. Limburg, 1954), p. 296.

will occupy us more than any other — can be set in a universal framework.

The inclination to isolate and make Mary autonomous thus proves to be advantageous for the "maximalistic" thesis of co-redemption; of course it is even more so for the doctrine of co-redemptive merit *ex condigno*. Since fundamental attitudes and theses support one another mutually, we must first of all test the validity of this thesis to make a judgment regarding the soundness of the attitude basic to it.

When it is said that the active direct collaboration of Mary in the work of redemption cannot be deduced from Scripture or from theology, but solely from the tradition of the Church as it is being formed at the present moment, it can be maintained in opposition that this "tradition" largely consist in the utterances of the very theologians who invoke it. This applies at least for any *theological specification* of the collaboration of Mary, as the term is used. It is in fact no more than a *petitio principii,* a premise of what is to be demonstrated, when these theologians invoke this tradition. It is certain that no genuine tradition can as yet be considered as the *locus theologicus* of a precise doctrine of co-redemption. Nor can tradition therefore justify the necessity of developing such a doctrine in a certain direction. This is significant for what follows.

The pivotal point of a maximalistic doctrine of co-redemption consists in assuming that the redemption has two effects or objectives: (1) the redemption of Mary through Christ alone, and (2) the redemption of all men through both Christ and Mary. This assumption appears, however, to assert something concerning the plan of the Redemption, in support of which nothing precise is to be found in the real tradition of the Church. The interior as well as the exterior grounds for this explanation of Mary's collaboration in the Redemption are thus hardly sound, nor do they therefore recommend convincingly to us the image of Mary which rests upon them.

With this notion of a doctrine of co-redemption, Mary has become a fully self-sufficient dimension in the plan of salvation. In the theology of salvation, consequently, it is not enough to speak of Christ and His redemptive act on the one hand and of the receiving human race, i.e., of the Church and grace, on the other. It is also considered necessary to say that a unique human person, who is isolated from the remaining humanity, and who is the Mother of the Redeemer in an absolute sense, is required alongside those to be redeemed. The Redemption is seen to be Christo-Mariological in nature. This unexpressed yet basic idea is unmistakable in many a Mariological statement. It may have its source in the Scotist contention that the incarnation of Christ and hence the divine maternity of Mary were absolutely predestined, so that Mary possesses, regardless of humanity, an absoluteness which is contingent only upon the absoluteness of Christ. But in reality Scotus' doctrine of the incarnation would not have suggested such a conclusion concerning Mary. For even though the thought be thoroughly legitimate (Aquinas does not reject it) that the incarnation was absolutely predestined, even without the Fall, Christ could in fact not have been the Redeemer in today's sense, but He would have been simply the head of the human race. He would have become man anyway for the sake of man, and Mary's relationship to the whole human race and the identity of her act with that of all humanity would not have been changed in any way.

A theory of co-redemption which isolates Mary finds itself in a perpetual dilemma. Stressing and making autonomous the Marian part in the redemption logically implies considering her as something necessary. On the other hand the orthodox faith in the sufficiency of the redemptive act of Christ alone requires that Mary's task rest upon the "fully free divine decree of grace," that we therefore acknowledge the nonnecessity of the position of Mary in the divine plan. Naturally, this has always been acknowledged. But tension develops here and some theologians tend to move in the direction of a necessary co-redemptive role for Mary.

This is evidently the case with the Spanish thesis concerning merit *ex condigno* on the part of Mary. To be sure the proponents of this doctrine take all the necessary measures of precaution; but it is in this very precaution that we detect the pinch in the boot. For the overall tendency of their assertions tends peculiarly toward a full absoluteness in the role of Mary. It is indeed very significant that P. Llamera reproaches the opponents of this theory with considering Mary "only" as a member, even if the first, in the body of Christ, and not as the mother of the Head and the members. Here, indeed, the idea is expressed that Mary's maternity over head and members gives her *no mere member's function,* but something autonomous, a new category of relationship to Christ. This opinion reached its highest development when Roschini made it the fundamental principle of Mariology in general.

We must once more draw attention to the relative silence of the earliest Church tradition regarding Mary. Although it is unwise to deduce from this silence an argument against developing any theology of Mary whatsoever, it is equally unrealistic simply to overlook this fact. There is surely a good reason behind its being thus.

Negatively, Mary's role in the achievement of the world's redemption cannot have been both essential and independent. If this were the case, if the picture of the redemption were incomplete without Mary as an individual immediately co-meriting alongside the Redeemer, then the *Credo* of early Christianity lacked an article of faith. For *this specific* fact had been nowhere germinally included, nor is it today deduced from any of the old dogmas, but from some other "tradition."

Positively considered, however, the key to the silence of the first centuries lies in the fact that *whoever has the Church, has Mary.* During the early centuries the theology about the Church was extraordinarily rich. Even in popular devotion, in the more lyrical expressions of early religion, the Church took to a great extent the place which Mary takes today. It is a fact that in a millennial loosening-up process the figure of Mary gradually took the place of the Church in Christian thought, prayer, art, etc. Mary was not forgotten or lost in the first centuries, but held as it were in safekeeping and trust in the theology about the Church, in a place, therefore, where her honor and greatness would not be diminished. Doctrine concerning her remains therefore *in medio ecclesiae,* and does not necessarily lead to a deadend. We must here once again mention the Eve-Mary parallel, probably the oldest postbiblical element of theological doctrine concerning Mary. It is only too readily employed as the basis for a Mariology of absolutist tendencies. This use of the parallel overlooks the fact, however, that Mary plays precisely in this parallel, the role of the human race as did Eve herself, "the Woman" of the creation story who is in every instance an individual not closed, but open to the entire human race.

If we keep our sights on this horizon, we shall remain in the Church tradition of Marian teaching. Dillenschneider, who seeks to do justice to the new ecclesiological standpoint in approaching the doctrine of co-redemption, insists that in Mariology we must give more consideration to Mary's relationship to Christ than to her relationship to the Church. But the best solution would probably be that of seeing Mary's relationship to Christ as the completion of, and against the background of, the Church's relationship to Him, beginning with the fundamental principle of the relationship between Mary and the Church. The relationship of Mary to Christ does not run parallel to that of Mary to the Church, but the two form an organic, coherent unit, and between them we encounter no real competition at all.

The tendency to make Mary into an absolute can hardly have a rich future. One such tendency has already come up against impassable limits. And certain symptoms of a breakdown are also beginning to appear, much like the decadence of an art style. Or what else can one say at the present with regard to a "privately tolerated" opinion of Spanish theologians, that the privilege of immaculate conception is attributed even to St. Joseph? . . . And more recently, what of careful cultivation of the theme of Mary and the Sacrament of the Altar? Certainly there are well-founded and beautiful things to say about this. But we must admit that in the first place such themes hardly contribute to a genuine development of Mariology, and that, second, there is no reason to believe that anything of significance would accrue therefrom in Eucharistic piety. For the mystery of the altar is so full of the encounter with Christ that a retrospective glance to His Mother really seems out of place there. The fact is that Mary has brought us Jesus, not vice versa. The telling characteristic in these signs of decadence is that, especially in pious Marian tracts, the stress makes it seem more important that Mary co-redeemed us than that Jesus redeemed us.

Here we might observe that this absolutist movement does not so much lead to strictly dogmatic considerations as to attitudes of tone, atmosphere, and proportion. Such factors may not be overlooked or disregarded. Theology is in fact not simply a collection of theses varying in credibility and certainty, but a living organism in which our faith must be able to live. Nor is it exclusively a mathematically exact registering of supernatural facts, but much more a human work of art (which fact does *not* detract from its "scientific character"). And it depends upon not only the fact *that* something is asserted, but also upon where it is asserted, when and how, how often and why it is asserted. Here also, perhaps, lies a deeper reason for the insolubility of the discussion between the "maximalistic" and the "minimalistic" theses of co-redemption. It is the difference between scholastic method, which arrives, through analogous application of philosophical, precisely defined notions, at precisely defined (and therefore also "limited") propositions and conclusions in theology, and the mode of expression found in Scripture and in the Fathers, where the analogy proceeds by images and from one level of being to another, coming to propositions which perhaps lack scholastic precision but not clearness and a content of truth. Nonetheless, the borderlines between the two methods blend and interlace in countless instances, and neither may be omitted in a universal theology.

It now appears that the doctrine of Mary's co-redemptive suffering under the cross belongs more to early symbolic thought than to scholastic rational thinking. This has perhaps been overlooked by both parties, in that the "minimalists" attempted to measure with the scholastic yardstick what the latter cannot measure, whereas the "maximalists" on the other hand essayed to invest something with scholastic thematic quality, which would not be forced in this way. We cannot stress sufficiently the fact that one may not consider a proposition to be less "strictly theological" simply because it has no place in the scholastic system.

Thus we view as unqualified all scholastically formulated deductions which, for all their precise validity, lean toward making Mary an absolute. They are unqualified, that is, to point the way of the future for the Marian movement *of the Church*. (It is not only *in* the Church). Essentially it is not a question of defining Mary as an autonomous dimension in the history of salvation, which she most certainly is not, but to see her glory and splendor in the great harmony of all the other glories of God's works. It is this which animates the other general movement in Mariological thought today, which sees Mary as the Church (and which may not be reduced to mere scholastic formulae). Here also much discussion is already underway concerning the details or composition of this idea, but the essential view is that of Mary as the first and highest recipient of all graces destined for the human race.

If one sees Mary as the personally perfect realization of the Church, then the entire significance of traditional doctrine concerning Mary comes into light. It is then no more a mere question of ornament and chivalry, but one of serious inquiry into the reason, essence, and purpose of every grace. Hence it is an affair which *applies* to us.

If one sees Mary as the person full of grace, then one recognizes in her, conversely, the measure of every grace. In this light we can see what it means to define everyone who does the will of the Father as not only the brother and sister, but also the mother of Christ, which means that the whole theology of grace and the Church has its yardstick in Mary.

Here, moreover, lies the safe way of recognizing Mary's glory without falling into error. Complete participation in the human nature of Christ constitutes the highest privilege of Mary, and it nonetheless stands firmly rooted in the solid ground of the theology of the Body of Christ. An answer will be given to the thorny question of Mary's collaboration in the work of Redemption, but only as a complement to the role that has been given to the Church as a whole by grace, i.e., *a maternal cofiguring of the divine,* which means of the redemption. Nicolas and Dillenschneider tend clearly in this direction.

An essential motif is restored to ecclesiology with the knowledge that the Church is always represented in persons, in personal experiences of grace, and, conversely, that every personal experience of grace is endowed with the dimension of the Church, because this dimension has its measure in the Person full of grace.

Rich possibilities of development and balance are offered to both movements by mutual collaboration. Marian doctrine will always stand solid in the Church's universe. Doctrine concerning the Church and grace, on the other hand, can always be daring, and remain sure, in the light of the image of Mary.

With such prospects, no one has anything to fear from the further spread of the Marian movement. By integrating their movement with the rest of theology, a sure guide for further progress is provided. And so it may be hoped that current Mariology, viewed in the ecclesiological and universal perspectives of all humanity, will be the theology of Mary for the future.

OTTO SEMMELROTH

THE INTEGRAL IDEA OF THE CHURCH

To EXAMINE in detail every question treated in recent dogmatic studies of the Church would exceed the scope and capacity of this essay. Our recovered vision of the essence of the Church as the Mystical Body of our Lord has indeed given new life to many questions: the necessity of the Church and membership in the Church for salvation; the relationship between the clergy and the laity, which in turn called for a more precise definition of the role of the layman in the Church; the nature of the hierarchy and the relationship of its various functions one to the other; and a vast number of other questions which suggest themselves in a discussion of the essence of the Church.

But perhaps we can do all these questions an indirect service if we treat here a most significant and central question in matters *de Ecclesia,* a question which touches on some important notions concerning the essence of the Church. Thus, although all the separate questions are not taken expressly into account, the attempt to derive, from the sacramental nature of the Church, a theme which unifies several aspects grounded in revelation, may yield interesting implications for these and other questions.

I. THE PROBLEM

1. The Inquiry Into the Mystery of the Church. The Church was, until the late Middle Ages, a reality which one lived without making it the object of speculative theological treatises. There are, of course, in the writings of the Church Fathers and Doctors any number of passages which cast light upon the mystery of the Church, hymns which praise her mystery, and admonitions drawn from a knowledge of her essence. But a strictly dogmatic treatise on the

Church is found neither in the Fathers of early Christianity nor in the theologians of the Middle Ages.

In the life of the Church today it is not fundamentally different. The Church lives in her faithful. The faithful live in the Church. And this life is little, if at all, determined by a reflective knowledge of the mystery of the Church. One may regret the Christians' meager knowledge of the mystery of the Church. That the Church lives in spite of this ignorance should also be regarded in its positive aspects. Were the life of the Church dependent upon a reflective knowledge of her essence, then this life would be condemned outright. And this not only because only few concern themselves with such reflective knowledge, but also because a clear and definite knowledge of this essence is not easy. Even professional theologians must wrestle to comprehend it.

Attempts to investigate the mystery-laden essence characteristic of our Church are not uncommon in our day. Those who live as mature persons in a society subject to attack from so many sides, yet which does not crumble thereunder, must feel compelled to a thorough and penetrating sounding of this mystery. St. Peter's injunction has pertinence here: "Be ever ready to justify yourselves against anyone who demands justification from you concerning the hope that lives in you" (1 Pet 3:15). At times the Christian's own heart seeks, perhaps even pressingly needs, this justification, this understanding of the belief by which he lives.

But one encounters grave difficulties here. Contemporary man is constantly tempted to consider the Church as completely explained by her social aspects. This would suit nicely the pragmatic tastes of our time. Beside this, Church theology in recent centuries could very well indeed give the impression that this social explanation exhausts the Catholic's belief in the Church. On the other hand for the living, believing members of the Church it has always been self-evident that her visible social character is only an exterior which belongs, to be sure, to her essence, but which does not alone constitute that essence. They have long since learned to take the Church as a divine mystery — not merely in her origin, but even in her essence.

But a mystery, if it is to be believed, must be at least partly comprehensible. It must be able to make itself understood, at least to a certain depth. And here again, we encounter further difficulties.

The believing Christian can accept the fact that the sources of revelation express the true mystery of the Church only in images and analogies. He knows that God's supernatural order cannot be completely contained in human categories. But the difficulty lies in the fact that the similes in which revelation speaks of the Church seem not to complement, but rather to contradict one another. Whoever compares the various images and similes used to describe the Church might receive the impression that the same Church is not meant at all in every case. Or can it be that the same Church which presents itself to our eyes as an apparently static social structure is nevertheless the same Bride of Christ referred to in Holy Scripture? Should it not therefore be depicted as a person, and not as a society? Animated by love, not by a juridically stamped structure? Or can the Church be the Bride of the Lord and also be His Body? Does not a bride, all union of love notwithstanding, always remain, over against her bridegroom a proper and full person, whereas a body possesses no autonomy at all when separated from its head?

Even when one grants that the same reality is signified by all the various symbols, from various viewpoints to be sure, the difficulties seem to grow more intense. For to see one and the same reality designated in terms that seem to contradict one another brings the observer into serious confusion. When he views the visible social structure of the Church, how shall he think that he is standing before a mystical reality hidden within this society? How shall he think simultaneously of the bridal character of the Church and of the organic unity of a body with its head, and acknowledge this unity as a characteristic of the Bride herself?

2. Contradictory Response? Let us describe briefly the various designations with which the Church is commonly presented to us, and whose unity is often sadly missed. Holy Scripture and tradition refer to the Church principally under three different images or figurative descriptions.

A. *The Church as the People of God*

We begin with the notion which has dominated for centuries, in a not wholly satisfying way, the thinking of the faithful regarding the Church. It is the idea of the Church as a social dimension, as a body of men, which was constituted a society through the positive institution of Christ and through the further development of the ecclesiastical authority itself, and which thus enters into competition with numerous other societies including, above all, the state. There is no doubt that we have been made conscious, in recent centuries, of the fact that this visible, social Church stands in the service of a divine, transcendent reality, a service which raises her up above all other societies of earthly life, in spite of any similarities she may have to them. But this service has been regarded, for the most part, as something extrinsic, much as a means or instrument is related to the end. As a result, the divine, transcendent reality served by the Church is made to appear not as the interior principle governing the life of the socially characterized Church, but as a completely distinct reality lying beyond the social Church and infallibly attainable through her assistance. Then one attempts to define the essence of the Church without even mentioning this divine reality. Such, for example, is the renowned definition of the Church given by Cardinal Bellarmine in the sixteenth century: "The Church is a body of men who, bound together by the confession of a Christian faith and the partaking of the same sacraments, stand under the direction of their lawful pastors, particularly under that of the only Vicar of Christ on earth, the Roman Pope" (*Controversiae*, II, lib. 3, cap. 2). The Church described here is only an outwardly perceptible, social reality. Later we shall see that the Church is sacramental, and that as a result any description of the outward sign, i.e., of the Church insofar as she is a visible society, necessarily embraces the divine substantial reality of the Church, which is signified, and made present, by that outward sign. And it would be a misinterpretation of the Bellarminian definition to conclude from it that its author had overlooked or forgotten this God-given inner substance of the Church. But even though the symbolism of the sacraments reveals their content clearly only to the person who is enlightened by faith, one can nevertheless expect to find in a definition, even a merely descriptive definition, some indication of the invisible substance lying beneath the visible form. Otherwise we should not wonder that the Church is regarded as an extremely external reality, that she is seen only as accidentally, not essentially associated with divine grace. This is an error into which many Catholic Christians have frequently fallen. It is not surprising that such an externalized view of the Church is often opposed by an equally one-sided ecclesiological spiritualism (frequently this spiritualism has good effects). Here again is an indication of the dire straits of the Christian who, while struggling for his Church, is unable to reconcile the various terms and images through which the Church is presented to him.

This social view of the Church has its biblical foundation in the naming of the Church as People of God[1] or *ecclesia*.[2] The Greek translation of the Old Testament had already rendered the Hebrew word *qahal* by the Greek *ekklesia*. And the early Christians adopted it to designate their own entity. They wished to express thereby above all the fact that the Church of the New Testament founded by Christ is the continuation and completion of the People of God of the Old Testament. The same idea was expressed in the early Church by referring to the Apostles as "the twelve," thinking of the twelve tribes of the Chosen People in the Old Testament. The Church, the People of God of the New Testament, is of course not divided into twelve tribes with regional boundaries, as were the Chosen People of the Old Testament. It has no regional limits at all. The perfection of the People of God in the new covenant consists precisely in the fact that it penetrates all peoples as the life principle of the entire human race and makes them holy from within, because by it they belong constitutionally to God. But the number "twelve" in reference to the Apostles has for the Church the functional significance of reminding Christians that the mission of being God's People has now passed over to Christ's Church, and will be carried out by her alone.

In his book *Ekklesiologie im Werden* (Paderborn, 1940), published before the encyclical *Mystici Corporis*, M. D. Koster, O.P., proposed "The People of God" as the most adequate definition of Church, at least as far as its essence is concerned. He considered it preferable to the designation "Mystical Body of Christ." The encyclical of Pius XII, however, speaks of the Mystical Body of Christ as "the most exalted and divine" definition of the Church, and as such does not appear to be very favorable to Koster's point of view. On the other hand, the biblical origin of the designation of the Church as God's People and its roots in early Christian tradition may not be taken too lightly. To be sure, it views the Church —

---

[1] Cf. Acts 15:14; Rom 9:25; 1 Cor 6:16; Ti 2:14; Heb 4:9; 8:10; 1 Pt 2:9 f.; Apoc 18:4; 21:3.

[2] Cf. Mt 16:18; 18:17; Acts 5:11; 12:5; 20:28; 1 Cor 4:17; 10:32; 14:4; Eph 1:22; 5:23 ff.; Col 1:18, 24; 1 Tim 3:5, 15; Jas 5:14.

and rightly so — above all from her external, juridical, and social aspects. The people have definite characteristics by reason of their place within the social organization of the Church, and accordingly are capable of being designated as members of the Church. Hence the Church's understanding of herself as the People of God leads us directly to an understanding of her social character, to her likeness to a political state. That this people is designated as belonging to God is surely a reminder of divine reality in the background to which the visible Church is connected. But it reveals nothing of the nature of this relationship of the Church to God. In the possessive "of God" any variety of relationships can be intended; as a matter of fact, a religious body founded by men might very well call itself the people of God, in the sense that its aim is to lead its members to God by directing them religiously. And the designation would be even more justified if it referred to the divine origin of the society, as is actually the case with the Church. But the expression "people of God" is, as such, ambiguous. It leaves undecided the question whether this relationship to God is a strict ontological bond effected through His grace or not. It obviously tends to stress that the reality of the visible Church *can* be discerned by men.

B. *The Church as the Mystical Body of Christ*

The mysterious interior reality of the Church is illuminated by the notion of the Church as Christ's Mystical Body. It was this concept which Pius XII, in his encyclical of 1943, made the keynote of his description of the Church. In his *Mystici Corporis* and in the subsequent encyclical, *Humani Generis,* of 1950, the Pope expressly rejected the attempt to distinguish the Mystical Body of Christ, as an invisible reality, from the reality of the visible Catholic Church. (This attempt had been made by some Catholics prior to 1943, and today it is frequently made by non-Catholics.) Even the pattern of problems which especially concern us in these pages — how the various names and definitions of the Church can be brought into a unity where they complement and not contradict one another — could also be a temptation to make such a distinction. Whoever thinks of "the Church," thinks first of all of the juridically organized, visible society which the Church actually is. But the faithful Christian is convinced that this external society is a shrine, as it were, which hides the unseen divine substance. Is it not plausible to conclude that this inner reality is what we want to signify by the notion "Mystical Body of Christ," particularly since the word "mystical" seems to point to an inner reality removed from, and in a way beyond, the sense and understanding of men? Should we not indeed say then that this invisible "Mystical Body of Christ" and the visible Church were intended by Christ to coincide, or in any case to belong together as inner content and outward expression, but that as a matter of fact this unity breaks down from time to time only to be mended again, and that the "Mystical Body of Christ" is broader in scope, embraces more men than the visible, social Church? This is apparently an approach to solving the problem of the necessity of belonging to the Body of Christ in order to be saved, and it is apparently a thought commonly entertained by sincere men who stand outside the visible Church through no fault of their own.

Some believe that the concepts of the Church as the socially organized people of God and as the Mystical Body of Christ can be united without any great difficulty, much as we conceive the living person as a union of body and soul. It is supposed that whoever refers to the Church as a visible society is speaking of her physical exterior, and that whoever refers to her as the Mystical Body of Christ is referring to her invisible interior. However, since the premise of this solution rests upon an error, we cannot be satisfied with it. The encyclical *Mystici Corporis* leaves absolutely no room for doubt that the "Mystical Body of the Lord," as understood by the Church, refers not only to the interior invisible reality in the depth of the Church but is just as essentially applicable to the social corporality of this Church. Again in the encyclical *Humani Generis* Pius XII condemns those "who hold that they are not bound to the doctrine of the identity of the Mystical Body of Christ and the Roman Catholic Church, even though the doctrine stands upon revealed truth and has been restated in our encyclical of several years ago."[3]

Thus it is crucial to determine how the notion of the Church as the Mystical Body of Christ is related to that of the Church as God's People, as a religious society. The two notions are, at least on the surface, too different for one to admit immediately that they

---

[3] Cf. A. Hartmann, *Bindung und Freiheit des katholischen Denkens* (Frankfurt, 1951), p. 242, no. 27.

must really mean the same thing. But since the Church tells us that
the same reality is intended by both notions, we can ask whether
they might not differ in emphasis rather than in meaning, pointing to
different components of the total reality of the Church.

C. *The Church as Bride of the Lord*

A third and final designation of the Church seems to contradict
the two previous descriptions. How shall one imagine that the very
same Church can be Christ's own body — the Mystical Body of
Christ — and at the same time His Bride?[4] Regardless of how profoundly she may be united in love to her bridegroom, a bride is
nevertheless inviolable and sacrosanct in her private personal being.
An organic living whole, as the notion of the body implies, and personal (or quasi-personal) inviolability, as is proper to the bride, appear to be mutually exclusive principles. How shall we see the one
Church identified in both? That we must identify them, however, can
be deduced from the fact that St. Paul, precisely when he refers
to the Church as the Bride of the Lord, also says that this Church
is one Body with the Lord. Thus we have scriptural assurance that
our notions of the Church as Body of Christ and as Bride of the
Lord do not exclude one another. But it is not easy on first sight
to comprehend the unity of such ostensibly incompatible views. Such
a comprehension would be of incalculable significance. For it is
we ourselves who are called upon to live the life of the Church,
who are summoned to bring about the social existence of the People
of God and the mystical and living union with Christ, and furthermore to encounter the Lord as our Spouse. To be sure, we need
only to live as disciples of Christ and as the Church directs in
order to make actual all the elements in the concept of the Church.
But on the other hand, God's revealed word has set the Church
before us in the various images mentioned above, so that we recognize the essence of this Church solely in them. We must therefore
take these words in their full spiritual vigor and regard the Church
in their light to see her from all her different sides at once and
perhaps come to a more complete picture of her. We should live
and build the Church not only unconsciously, not only in virtue of
a grace granted us without our knowledge, but also by conscious

---

[4] Cf. Jn 3:29; 2 Cor 11:2; Apoc 18:23; 19:7; 21:2, 9; 22:17.

and personal decision. And this means that God's revelation itself has laid upon us the pressing obligation of uniting, of integrating, our notions of the Church.

II. THE UNIFYING PRINCIPLE

1. The Church as Sacrament. Ecclesiology has recently come to an understanding of the Church which seems extremely new, but which is, in fact, most ancient. It is the notion of the Church as a sacramental reality.[5] The Church is, of course, sacramental in the sense that she was instituted by Christ for the administration of the seven sacraments. But this is not all. Even more, the Church is herself the living root and principle of the seven individual sacraments. She is the power, founded by Christ, from which come the efficacy and actuality of the seven sacraments.

This designation of the Church as the "primordial Sacrament" (*Ursakrament*) is not simply another "notion of the Church," but is the meaning and ontological sense of the mystery expressed in the statements found in revelation regarding the Church. To see the Church as a sacrament is to grasp the connection between the various partial aspects of the Church, particularly those of her mysterious, divine interior and her social, human exterior. For as the Church has taught through the centuries, the essence of a sacrament is to bind together a complex of realities, interior and exterior, human and divine, in the relation of sign to signified, of cause to effect.

This "ontology" of the Church, which is expressed by the notion of sacrament, gives us the principle we need for uniting the various notions of the Church which presented our problem. This principle functions like the soul, which gives living unity to the multiplicity of the human body by permeating and unifying all the sundry parts of the body.

2. The Significance of the Sacramentality of the Church. If a person understands sacramentality correctly and does not lose sight of this understanding when he considers the Church as a sacrament, he will never fall into the danger of making light of the visible Church as a social and juridical reality. This is true, first of all, because the visible Church owes her existence to the institution of

---

[5] Cf. O. Semmelroth, *Die Kirche als Ursakrament* (Frankfurt, 1955²).

Christ — and naturally, new emphasis is given in the sacramental view of the Church to the fact that only Christ Himself can establish a genuine, sacramental reality. Moreover, the sacramental essence of the Church gives a much more spiritual foundation to her visible and social structure. A sacrament is essentially a symbol incarnating divine, invisible reality in a tangible visible way. But only he who takes the visible Church seriously can take sacramentality seriously and esteem it justly. To grasp the Church as sacrament, one must not conceive the Church as simply a useful means, a step toward attaining divine graces which of themselves have nothing to do with this Church. If the Church is a sacrament, she makes visible and incarnate our community of grace with God and we consequently obtain grace from God, not in any unmediated way, but rather we — men of flesh and blood ourselves — grasp it in the material form it has received from God, in the form which *is* the Church, in the life which is essential to her. Nor should we think that the Church is simply for children who need the order and direction of the Church lest they should forget to open themselves personally and decisively to God, whereas there is no need of the Church for adults, since the latter are supposed to be living near to God. If the Church is a sacrament, then she is the "outward sign of inner grace," as the Council of Trent says of all sacraments (Denz 876).[6] To see the Church as a "symbol" does not mean the undoing of the visible Church, as many fear, misunderstanding the nature of a symbol. On the contrary, it is to shed the light of day upon this Church, in which the reality of God's grace, like the soul in the body, is conditioned by space and time and is made present to men in a tangible way.

But at the same time the concept of the Church as sacramental reality counteracts an exaggerated emphasis on the visibility of the Church. When we regard the Church as a sacrament, we truly take her visibility seriously, regarding it not simply as an apologetic for manifesting in an empirical way the corporate existence of the Church but as a genuine incarnation of her union with God through grace. If someone wishes to honor a person, he tips his hat, shakes his hand, or gives him something as a token of his esteem. These physical actions bear directly on the physical body of a person,

---

[6] Cf. O. Semmelroth, "Die Kirche als 'sichtbare Gestalt der unsichtbaren Gnade,'" *Scholastik,* 28 (1953), pp. 23–39.

but they do not terminate there. Rather, they are symbols of the invisible life of the person, evidence of his intelligence and will. Similarly, when we view the Church as a sacrament, we indeed refer to her materiality, her visibility. But we see that this materiality is a value precisely because it is matter seized by God, that in this matter God encounters man in a mode suitable to his nature as a being at once physical and spiritual. If we see the Church as sacramental reality we shall not be tempted to separate her physical, visible elements from her divine, invisible features; we shall be prevented both from an extreme spiritualism which would deny the role of matter in mediating our encounter with God and from a materialism wherein the external organization becomes an absolute unto itself. When we grasp the significance of the Church as sacrament, we shall recognize in a fresh and eye-opening way the unity and living interrelatedness of all else that can be said of the Church: visible society and incarnation of efficacious grace, structured organization and life, a human and divine reality.

3. Primordial Sacrament and Individual Sacraments. First we should say a word or two concerning a possible misunderstanding. Let us state unequivocally that there is no question here of erecting an eighth sacrament next to the traditional seven. This is strictly forbidden, the Council of Trent limiting the sacraments instituted by Christ to seven, no more and no less (Denz. 844). Nor will anyone who considers the nature of the Church and that of the seven sacraments ever think of placing them next to one another on the same level. The Church is not a sacrament in the same way as baptism, confirmation, etc. But the difference is only in one aspect and does not belong to the essence of sacramentality: the seven sacraments are actions which, carried out in a moment, are soon done with and gone, persisting only in their effects, whereas the Church is not a passing action, but an enduring institution.

Nor may these two realities, the dynamic reality of the individual sacraments and the static reality of the permanent Church, be separated too much from one another. They belong together because of an inner, supernatural vitality given to His work by Christ: the enduring Church dispenses the individual sacramental actions from its bosom by virtue of this supernatural vitality. She is the lasting power whose supernatural life principle lends supernatural authority and vital efficacy to all actions that are essential to her — which means above all the individual actions of the seven sacraments. Nor are these specific sacramental acts *purely* temporary, isolated actions of the moment. On the contrary, since they are performed by the power of the Church, they unite the cooperating receiver in a new and vital way to the permanent Church, out of whose bosom they in fact came forth.

If those sacramental actions essential to the Church are vital functions of her divine life, then that institution which carries them out by God-given authority must necessarily have a sacramental nature. For power is recognized in its execution, and vital actions are determined by the life principle from which they take their origin.

Thus we do not consider the Church as an eighth sacrament next to the other seven. The Church is much more the "primordial Sacrament" or, according to K. Rahner, "root Sacrament" (*sacramentum radicale*) out of which, as out of their living principle, the specific acts of the seven sacraments are always invested with sacramental power.[7]

III. THE RESULTANT UNITY OF OUR NOTION OF THE CHURCH

Three things are required for the execution of a sacrament. To begin with, only a genuine symbol or sign which is part of our world of experience can be a sacrament. Second, a sacrament is distinguished from other symbolic signs in that an essentially human, earthly, token reality is made by God a guarantee and cause of the divine grace symbolically represented in the sign itself. And finally the human person must bring to the symbolic sign that disposition whereby the notion "reception of the sacrament" will be given its full meaning. These three elements must also determine how we are to regard the Church as sacrament. And with closer examination we see that each of the different partial notions of the Church discussed in the first part of this essay correspond to one of these three elements in a significant way.

---

[7] Cf. K. Rahner, "Kirche und Sakramente," *Geist und Leben,* 28 (1955), pp. 434–453. A. Winklhofer, "Kirche und Sakramente," *Trierer Theologische Zeitschrift,* 68 (1959), pp. 65–84.

1. The Outward Sign. The consideration that the Church is an experienceable society subject to sociological laws makes us realize that there is a real sense in which the Church can be perceived and experienced with the physical senses. Of pertinence here are those biblical passages which liken the Church to realities of the political order, such as the "Kingdom" or "People of God." The "of God" element in these expressions is not the chief object of our inquiry here — after all, it simply asserts the fact that a community belongs to God without determining the nature of this relationship. We are rather concerned with the emphasis these assertions place on the *People* or *Kingdom,* for this directs our attention to the physical reality of a visible human society whose members are socially organized more or less after the manner of a state.

In view of the sacramental dimension of the Church, this visible, institutional Church is recognizable as the sensibly perceptible sign essential to a sacrament. Thus the importance of seeing the Church as a real society, as the organized People of God, takes on added meaning; for we see that the Church so conceived is nothing less than the outward sign of a tremendous sacrament, is, in fact, that meeting point at which God with His grace and the human person with his devotion should encounter one another.[8] Here, and here alone, is man given, by God-instituted order, guarantee that his devotion has found acceptance, that he is in communion with the God from whom he has received everything. Nor is the chief significance of this visible Church to be found on the level of pure sense experience. The Church is important not because of her clear social order and juridical organization, but because, through her, God communicates His devotion and grace to men, and because, conversely, He has made the Church the context in which man is to express his dedication and devotion to God and thus encounter Him. If the Church is a sacrament, and as such a sign, she must necessarily point beyond herself, or better, point through her visible exterior into a hidden divine interior of which she is the incarnation and expression.

As the term "sign" is used in referring to miracles in the New Testament and to the sacraments instituted by Christ, it does not merely mean *that* there is some reference to an invisible divine

---

[8] On "the Church as place of encounter" between God and man, cf. O. Semmelroth, *Gott und Mensch in Begegnung* (Frankfurt, 1956), p. 191 ff.

reality. Signs should also indicate *what* is inferred or represented, *what* it is that they are meant to indicate. In other words, they must make present the *reality* they signify. The sacramental signs are symbols, sensory representations of that which they communicate to men. "The sacraments impart those graces which they signify" (Denz. 489).

Thus, if the Church is a sacramental sign, the salvation which she makes incarnate must also be somehow imprinted in her visible structure. In fact, that great salutary act by which the Son acquired for us the grace of God the Father is physically represented in that unfailing structure which Christ gave to His Church. This work of salvation was accomplished by the Son, who, sent by the Father, set out to bridge the gulf separating men from their Creator. He is the Word that the Father addresses to men, inviting them thus to a new dialogue, to a new sharing of His life. From the time that the human race — principally and fundamentally through Mary, who, in behalf of all humanity, spoke the *fiat* — believed this Word of the Father, and received it with piety, the Word of God came into the midst of men. This act consummated the first phase of the redemptive dialogue between God and men — the encounter of the approaching Word of God with the believing, receptive Virgin Mary. But there must be a response: Christ Himself, who is God's Word to men in the first phase of salvation, now as the God-Man-become-member-of-humanity, utters with His sacrifice the response of humanity to the Father. But men are not exempted, through Christ's sacrifice, from sacrifices of their own. The voice of assent, with which they (the Virgin Mary at their head) received the coming Word of God, must continue to speak in this second phase of the redeeming dialogue. Men must make Christ's sacrifice their own; they must make Christ their offering, bring Christ's sacrificial action to the Father as their own. Thus in the second phase also, since men must join the sacrificing Christ, the keynote is again found in encounter, communion. For our salvation stems from the work, from the encounter made by the Mediator Christ, who crossed the gulf from the Father to men and returns from men to the Father, taking with Him those men who, like the Virgin Mary, receive the coming Mediator with faith, and who accompany the departing Mediator in His sacrifice.

Because the visible Church is to be the sacramental outward

sign of this work of salvation, and because the life of the Church is to be an enduring figure of the salutary encounter between Christ and the Virgin Mary, Christ established His Church in that polarity which is required for encounter, that duality which is always found in a people organized in a society similar to a state. This duality in the Church is a symbolic representation of the poles which join in the work of redemption. And the essential life of the Church consists in the two poles, the one representing Christ, the other representing humanity, meeting one another on their own account. Thus when the Church pronounces, by virtue of her teaching pastoral office, God's revealing and reminding Word to the Church community (to the "people"), she represents the revealing advent of the Word of God to men; she is bringing the Word of God again into the proximity of those men who come to meet Him with open and humble spirit. And when the Church, by virtue of her sacerdotal office, places before the community the sacramental cult of Christ's sacrifice in the celebration of the Eucharist, she is representing in a sensible, tangible manner before the community the sacrificial departure of Christ to the Father; and the community is being called upon to imitate and fulfill the co-offering of the Virgin Mary by assembling around the altar of the Church. Thus the Church, in her essential polarity of religious office and community, in having the single destiny of perpetuating the encounter of grace with nature, men with God, is a sacramental outward sign of salvation. This is the more profound significance of the organized social nature of the Church.

2. The Salutary Power of This Sign. A sacramental sign has the quality of not only representing the grace of Christ symbolically, but also of imparting it to men in the very act of representing it. That encounter which is represented in the polar life of the Church reconciles and unites the two dimensions represented there. It begins with that mere fact of adjacency, of duality-unity entailed in any encounter. But in the Church this natural unity is endowed with deeper vigor than are purely human encounters. When, within the Church, the community (or a separate member thereof) encounters the bearer of religious authority as representing Christ by hearing his Word and celebrating with him the cult which he performs, then this encounter is animated by a twofold source of life: the *wish* on the part of the community to hear what the promulgator of God's

Word says, and the *will* to bind itself to the cult of Christ which the consecrated priest represents in the sacramental framework. This is the first fruit of the encounter. It belongs to the natural order more or less as that "unity of intention" produced by faith and loving desire, that unity which leads to complete union in every true encounter between two opposite poles.

But when the life of the Church reaches full realization, it entails a supernatural union which is not the work of man, but which is infused as the grace of God into the human will to effect a meeting. In the life of the Church, the sacramentally represented encounter of the community with an officeholding representative of Christ effects a true union with Christ, the Head. Nor is it a mere moral union; it is a real, a mystical union. Pius XII spoke in detail of this union in the encyclical *Mystici Corporis.*

This objective salutary power in the sacramental sign of the visible Church is thrown into relief when we refer to the Church as the "Mystical Body of Christ." This notion refers to the very same reality designated when the Church is considered as a religious society, as the People of God. As the encyclical *Mystici Corporis* makes clear, this notion corresponds exactly to the visible, organized, social Church. The Church is a "body" and as such is tangible, organized. The one notion, however, complements and fulfills the other. For thinking of the Church as a society or people tends to stress her outward aspects, those elements which constitute the sacramental sign. On the other hand, the "Mystical Body of Christ" directs our attention more to the intangible reality of grace figured in the tangible; it urges us to consider that intangible substance with which God gives a new spirit to the human community of the Church, constituting it thereby a "mystical body." The visible reality of the social Church is designated by the word "Body." But the fullness of grace proper to this "Body" is also asserted, for the visible society is the sacramental vessel and guarantee of divine grace. We are reminded that the visible Church renders something more than the simple service of preparing and disposing men in their spiritual life. Her function is not simply that of inducing them, through instruction and reminders, to open themselves up for God's grace. We are reminded that the Church, above all, leads men to grace by incorporating them into herself as members of a Body which lives by the breath of the Holy Spirit. For she is, as a society founded by Christ, herself the embodiment of grace, the mystical Body of Christ Himself, and in a certain way the God-Manhood of Christ, the archetype and model of all sacramentality, extended in space and time to all men.

3. The Human Disposition. For a sacrament to have its full effect, a knowledge of its essence is not enough. A sacrament becomes a vessel of salvation only in its concrete realization. But for this, more than the outward sign itself is necessary. Two dimensions must meet: the one, a sacramental representation of Christ's encounter with Mary; the other, the actual making of salvation present here and now through that representation. What is required for the sacramental realization of salvation is the correct administration by the minister of the sacrament as the representative of the offering Christ and, in addition, the proper response on the part of the one who receives the sacrament. For the latter is the one for whom the sacrament is ministered and he thereby imitates Mary as she makes the sacrifice of her son her own personal sacrifice. This collaboration is what theology refers to as the proper "disposition." It must be twofold in nature. On the one hand, some sort of objective disposition is necessary for a sacrament to exist at all (e.g., it is necessary, for the reception of the other sacraments, that one be baptized; for the reception of the Anointing of the Sick, that one be seriously ill; for the reception of Holy Orders, that one be of the male sex). But if a sacrament is to attain its full effect, it is also essential that, beside this objective prerequisite and beyond the minimum personal intention, there be present a consciously open attitude before God, corresponding to the sacrament in question. Hence the visible sacramental sign is the exterior form of an inner reality which is a harmony of two poles. On the one hand, the sacrament is a divine guarantee that God does in fact unmistakably express His sincere devotion to men (which we call grace) in the sacramental sign; on the other hand, the human person expresses his devotion and self-giving, thus constituting the other interior pole of the sacramental sign. The sacramental sign is truly and essentially an expression of the encounter between God and man. What both give of substance to one another in this encounter must be contained and expressed in the outward sign of the sacrament.

This is the case with the individual actions of the seven sacraments. For since their *raison d'être* is the *sacramental* Church, they

too must be marked by these two interior principles. What God
gives to the Church makes this society of men into the Mystical
Body of Christ. And what the human persons give, if they are in
the Church in the full sense implied by membership, makes the
Church a bride which encounters the Lord in love. And with this
we come to the last "notion of the Church" which we must reconcile
with the others, the notion of the Church as bride.[9]

The mystical unity that makes the Church the "Mystical Body
of Christ" does not nullify the polar character of Christ's encounter
with man. The Head, Christ, represented by the religious office of
the Church — "we administer our office in Christ's stead" (2 Cor
5:20) — and the community of the faithful become "one Body"
through the efficacious grace given by God to the visible Church,
but they nevertheless remain "two in one flesh" (Eph 5:31). In
considering the mysterious unity of the Church, we must not forget
that the Church is differentiated into Head and members, with the
latter embracing hierarchical office and faithful community. The encyclical Mystici Corporis takes pains to depict the unity of the
Church (which is far more than a moral unity) in such a way that
she should not appear as exclusively or even predominantly visible,
as inhibiting the personal autonomy of individuals. On the contrary,
the Holy Father depicted the permanent autonomy of the Church's
members in such a way that her substantial unity does not break
down as a result into an at best morally united multiplicity.

The attitude toward God symbolized by the use of the "bride-
bridegroom" figure is essential. It should be expressed both in the
individual sacraments and in the Church as primordial sacrament,
and its expression depends upon the personal wills of the individual
members of the Church. But this bearing or attitude of the individual has its divine value from the fact that it is the attitude taken
by the individual to the God present in the community of the Church.
But that is the very reason why both the prototypal "Church" of the
old Covenant and, with even fuller significance, the Church of the
New Testament is called "the Bride of the Lord" (Eph 5:22–33;
Apoc 19:7; 21:9).

Thus we see in this notion of the Church as Bride of the Lord,
that the reality signified is identically that same visible, social

---

[9] On the Church as the Bride of God and of Christ, cf. O. Semmelroth,
op. cit., p. 214 ff.

Church which, as the "People of God," cuts across and even enters into competition with the peoples of the world. The notion of the Mystical Body of Christ, in particular, refers to this visible Church as a sacramental sign possessing a mystical, redemptive power available to men if only they enter as members into this Church. In a parallel way the notion of the Church as the "Bride of Christ" underlines the fact that the visible Church also contains a human principle which encounters, in belonging to this same visible Church, the divine reality of grace.

Let it be reemphasized that the notions of the Church discussed above are not mutually exclusive. Although the one always contains elements of the other, each tends to give to the Church a new emphasis, a differently nuanced meaning. The person who prefers to call the visible Church the Mystical Body of Christ should bear in mind that this Body involves two elements — Christ the Head and we the members; he should think immediately of the bridal character ascribed to the members of this Body. And the person who, on the other hand, prefers to call the visible Church the Bride of the Lord also knows that in the New Testament the Bride appears as showered with gifts and jewels (Eph 5:26 f.; Apoc 21:2) and as such has become one flesh with her Bridegroom, the God-Man Jesus Christ.

Summing up, the notion of the Church as the socially organized People of God underlines the Church as an outward sacramental sign. The notion of the Mystical Body of the Lord stresses the inner grace sacramentally welling up in this sign. And the notion of the Church as the Bride of Christ emphasizes the personal disposition in which the Church, in the devotion of her members, meets her Bridegroom. But all three stand for, and declare to the world, the one sacramental Church.

THE CHURCH AND THE CHURCHES

THIS book seeks to offer an insight into the living issues of contemporary theology. And the dynamic and fermenting character of theology today is evident particularly in the dialogue that is being carried on with separated Christians. This activity appears in an ecumenical theology whose object is to arrive, both in theological expositions and in the practical promulgation of doctrine, at an ecumenical or "catholic" truth, at a truth which embraces in an absolute way all data of revelation and tradition, at a truth which disposes of all one-sidedness and discrepancies by integrating the partial truths of the communities of Christians separated from Rome into the full vision which satisfies the requirements of all. The significance of such an ecumenical theology consists not only in its importance for the Christian communities separated from Mother Church but also for Catholics, since it tends to correct one-sided attitudes inspired by the counterreformation and misplaced emphases in preaching and in the affirmations of so many schools of theology. It is certainly possible that, after rejecting a heresy, one can lose sight of the legitimate message lying therein for revelation; it is possible for one to respond to an heretical formula overemphasizing one element of revelation by putting too much stress on another; in short, it is possible to reply to an heretical part-truth with another. It will always remain the sacred task of Catholic theology to teach the truly Catholic truth, i.e., the total truth. It may surely be considered as a value of our time that divided Christians have entered into a dialogue with one another, a dialogue which has left behind the centuries-long polemic of Christendom.

This dialogue becomes more impassioned when we turn to a consideration of the article in the Creed wherein we profess belief in the *one, holy, catholic,* and *apostolic Church.* In this essay we shall attempt to present a picture of this dialogue as it is carried on both with our separated brothers and within Catholic theology itself, with a view to determining the connection and possible value this dialogue may have for our understanding of Church unity and membership. Obviously our analysis cannot be executed in one comprehensive sweep, for the most diverse religious communities with the most varied notions of the Church are in disagreement with the Catholic Church. The Orthodox, the Anglicans,[1] the Swedish Church, the Lutherans, the Reformed Church, and the Baptists each have their own understanding of what the Church of Jesus Christ is. One cannot speak of an all-inclusive "Protestantism," even though a common prevailing characteristic can be pointed to in statements concerning the Church and unity made by all of these communities — leaving the Orthodox out of consideration for the present. I think it preferable to limit our study to a confrontation of the notion of the Church proposed by the Evangelical Lutherans with that proposed by Catholics.

I. The Evangelical Lutheran Understanding
of the Church[2]

If we want to put our finger on the Lutheran idea of the Church, then we must first of all ask whether there is such an idea at all. Ernst Kinder shows in his treatise[3] that, in Luther and in the confessional literature which followed upon the Lutheran Reformation, there is no reference to a "notion of the Church" in the sense of

---

[1] On the Orthodox and the Anglican Churches, see Yves M.-J. Congar, O.P., "Position des orthodoxes et des anglicans au regard d'une position 'protestante' en ecclésiologie," *Irénikon,* 23 (1950), pp. 302–308.

[2] On the Lutheran understanding of the Church, cf. Ernest Wolf, *Peregrinatio. Studien zur reformatorischen Theologie und zum Kirchenproblem* (Munich, 1954), in particular pp. 146–182, "Die Einheit der Kirche im Zeugnis der Reformation"; Regin Prenter, *Spiritus Creator. Studien zu Luthers Theologie* (Munich, 1954); Edmund Schlink, "Christus und die Kirche. Zwölf Thesen für ein ökumenisches Gespräch zwischen Theologen der evangelischen und der römischen Kirche," *Kerygma und Dogma,* 1 (1955), pp. 208–225; Peter Brunner, "Die Kirche und die Kirchen heute. Thesen zu einer konkreten Ekklesiologie und einem ökumenischen Ethos," *Evangelische-Lutherische Kirchenzeitung,* 8 (1954), pp. 241–244; Ernst Kinder, "Zur Frage des lutherischen Kirchenbegriffs," *Evangelische-Lutheranische Kirchenzeitung,* 10 (1956), pp. 67–69; Leslie Newbigin, *The Household of God. Lectures on the Nature of the Church* (London, 1953).

[3] Kinder, *loc. cit.*

a positive, universally valid definition of the Church in its essence. The sources contain too little in this area, and Evangelical theologians have always felt the lack of a clearly documented position here. We can speak of "notion of the Church" only in the sense that there are critical and normative affirmations of certain decisive points relating to the reality of the Church, whereas the latter, in her living fullness, is greater than the sum of these affirmations. "The Lutheran notion of the Church chooses not to attempt any satisfactory definition of the essence of the Church; it chooses rather to apply regulatory standards critically to situations affecting the Church in history."[4] Consequently no true definition of the Church is given in the seventh Augsburg Confession but the reality of the one holy Church is recognized as something given. The assertion is made here not ontologically, but critically and noetically. It is a question of the identifying marks of the existing and enduring reality of the Church, of the concrete mode making evident her legitimate status. In other words, it appears to be a question of identifying the *ecclesia vera* as opposed to the *ecclesia falsa*. But these regulative specifications are unable of themselves to provide an enduring basis for a concrete superstructure for the Church.

"Developments led to the consolidation of a specifically Lutheran church structure. This, however, was due in part to the misdirected shift from a regulatory to a constructive notion of the Church, and also to an unavoidable historical choice which can be justified only when understood eschatologically."[5] Thus in the very existence of a Lutheran Church there is a paradox, a contradiction. "It was necessary for the Lutheran Church, in order to be at all, to be something which, according to its principles, it cannot really be."[6] This indeed is a paradox.

Kinder's proposition seems to me to be of a grave significance. But Kinder's views are isolated, unique within the realm of Lutheran theology. Were they general attitudes, they would surely constitute an exceptional basis for a dialogue between the Evangelical and the Catholic Churches.

The Evangelical Lutheran understanding of the Church has been described by Edmund Schlink in his twelve theses for an ecumenical dialogue.[7]

---

[4] *Ibid.*, p. 67.   [5] *Ibid.*, p. 68.   [6] *Ibid.*, p. 69.   [7] Schlink, *loc. cit.*

I. The Church is the people summoned from the world through Christ to God.

II. The Church is the Prophetic-Priestly-Royal People sent by Christ into the world.

III. The Church is the worshipful congregation in which Christ acts in the present.

IV. The Church is the Bride who awaits Christ and partakes even now in the worshipful congregation of the coming wedding banquet.

V. The Church is the Body of Christ which is being built up as a worshipful congregation into a universe renewed, re-created by Christ.

VI. The Church is the community of the gifts of grace, through whose multiplicity the one grace of Christ works, making itself present.

VII. The Church is the congregation led by Christ Himself through the pastoral office.

VIII. The Church is "one, holy, catholic, and apostolic" (Nicene Creed).

IX. The Church is indestructible.

X. The Church is visible in this world.

XI. The threat of judgment is meant for the Church.

XII. The promise of glory with the second coming of Christ is meant for the Church.

On hearing these theses, a Catholic is inclined to exclaim, "Why, these are Catholic assertions!" The Church is the people of God, the worshipful congregation, the attendant bride of Christ, the body of Christ, the community of graces, the congregation led by the Good Shepherd. She possesses the four attributes of unity, holiness, catholicity, and apostolicity. She is indestructible, visible, threatened with judgment, and has the promise of glory at Christ's return.

Nevertheless these affirmations are understood by Evangelical theologians in a sense that is completely different from that assigned to them by the Magisterium of the Catholic Church. To see precisely where this difference in understanding lies, we shall examine Schlink's theses closely and critically.

Let us first fix attention on one point which is of particular significance to the ecumenical dialogue; this is the question of the *notae ecclesiae*.

It is traditional Catholic doctrine that the Church is visible and recognizable in the marks or *notae* which set her apart from other religious communities.[8] These marks are the unity, holiness, catholicity, and apostolicity of the Church.[9] The essential things, as far as Catholic faith is concerned, is that these marks constitute the Church as a visible society.

The attitude of the Reformed Churches is quite different. "The reformation's antithesis to this doctrine of constitutive marks of the Church is summed up in Luther's sentence: 'The sole, perpetual and infallible mark of the Church has always been the Word.' "[10] This sole mark is, according to Wolf, "the sharpest expression of understanding of the Church by the Reformers" and is "directed squarely against the teaching essential to the Roman notion of the Church of the four marks."[11]

How does Schlink look upon these four attributes or properties of the Church? First of all, he distinguishes between properties of the Church and the marks or *notae* of the Church. *Notae,* or distinguishing marks, "by which the reality of the Church can be unmistakably recognized in the world, are the Gospel, Baptism and Communion, i.e., Word and Sacrament,"[12] whereas the properties or attributes are merely effects of the *notae.* Schlink refers the attributes of the Church (unity, holiness, catholicity, and apostolicity) to the domain of faith, and apostolicity assumes a prominent position because he understands it as apostolic witness to the Church, or as apostolic Gospel. While the attributes *una, sancta, catholica, et apostolica* belong, according to Lutheran thinking, only to the Church in its proper sense — and this is the *ecclesia invisibilis,*[13] the visible Church is recognizable in its "distinguishing marks," which are the fitting promulgation of the Word and the

---

[8] How very different meanings can lie behind the similar sounding expressions — something which should call for careful scrutiny on our part — is illustrated by the recent controversy over F. J. Leenhardt's "Ceci est mon Corps. Explication de ces paroles de Jesus-Christ," *Cahiers theologiques,* 37 (1955). See the critique leveled against this article in *Istina,* 2 (1956), pp. 210–240. We will come back to this later.

[9] Cf. Denz. 86, 223, 247, 347, 430 f., 464, 468, 1686, 1793 f., 1821 ff., 1955.

[10] E. Wolf, *Peregrinatio,* p. 150.

[11] *Ibid.,* p. 157.

[12] E. Schlink, *loc. cit.,* p. 221.

[13] Cf. Christian Ernst Luthardt, *Kompendium der Dogmatik* (Leipzig, 1937), 2 ed. with revisions by Robert Jelke.

orderly administration of the sacraments. Hence we may ask Schlink whether he assigns the attributes of the Church to the Church as an invisible society. The Catholic Church identifies the attributes and the distinctive marks, holding that they are simultaneously both visible and invisible. The decisive question concerns the formal visibility of the Church, her form and appearance. Schlink himself knows very well where criticism will fall upon him. In his *Theologie der lutherischen Bekenntnisschriften*[14] he mentions an attempt by J. Stahl to complete the Seventh Article of the Augsburg Confession by considering the office and government of the Church. Stahl criticizes the neglect of this Article to heed the organic aspects of the Church: "Our notion of the Church includes only the spiritual powers and their free efficacy and not the institutional structure which should support and bear them. We stress only the divine factor, the working of the Holy Spirit in souls and God's Word and Sacrament, and not the human factor, the exterior ordering and disposing of persons, through which the Word should be kept pure and promulgated in a fitting manner."[15] To this Schlink responds that the Seventh Article of the Augsburg Confession may not be taken out of context, that it should be seen in its relationship to Articles V and XIV. "But then it becomes clear that the proper distinction between law and Gospel necessarily leads to an emphasis on the 'divine factor,' and to a bypassing of the 'human factor,' at least of constitutionally fixed and stabilizing Church activity, as Stahl has in mind. For this activity and its juridical effects cannot be put alongside Word and Sacrament in our notion of the Church, but, being mere human action can always be sacrificed and suspended for the sake of the Word. We cannot claim that the visible structure of the Church, however proved as historically legitimate and rooted in a divine foundation, is 'founded and fitted out by God' and in this sense represent it to the congregation as an alleged 'higher thing.' "[16]

Still sharper criticism has been leveled against this reformed notion of the Church by the Bishop of the South Indian Union, Leslie Newbigin.[17] He begins by asking how contemporary man,

---

[14] Munich, 1948.

[15] J. Stahl, *Die Kirchenverfassung nach Lehre und Recht der Protestanten* (Erlangen, 1862), p. 43 f.

[16] *Theologie der lutherischen Bekenntnisschriften*, p. 275, n. 9.

[17] Leslie Newbigin, *loc. cit.*, in footnote 2.

who lives 1900 years after the death of Christ, can become a member of Christ; in other words, he asks how Christ can become present today. The Lutheran response is that Christ becomes present through the "event" of Word and Sacrament. But the Bishop replies that this is insufficient, for Word and Sacrament do not come to us naked, as it were, but through those who represent Christ and who act in His place. Newbigin urges us to take seriously the social dimensions of the Christian faith and the visible, continuous, and factual structure of the Church. The Church does not consist in a series of disconnected human responses to the supernatural acts of divine grace in Word and Sacrament. The basis of the Lutheran conception is, for Newbigin, the false and unbiblical dialectic of exterior and interior, visible and invisible. A deeply rooted tendency to "spiritualize" the Church on the part of Luther and of Article VII of the Augsburg Confession is the root of this notion.

Is it possible that Schlink conceives the relationship between Christ and the Church too mechanistically, too rigidly? In final analysis, does he not fail to give to ecclesiastical office any fundamental significance of its own? The visibility of the Church is more than visible action, and here the question is essentially concerned with offices within the Church. Schlink's understanding of office is too vague. An office of function within the Church is by its essence an organized reality, an aggregate of privileges and obligations. But these privileges and obligations are conferred by direct mission and authorization. A person is entrusted with ecclesiastical power in a definite historical act wherein the power is conferred.

Thus we ask, "Is the Church an objective datum with juridical status?" or, to put it differently, "Is the official who has been commissioned with divine authority part of the visibility of the Church?" Basically we are asking whether the human, the visible, the legally determinable has any genuine meaning for salvation.

Before we take up this profound question, we would like to examine briefly what Lutheran theology understands by *Body of Christ*. "The mystical Body of Christ is the 'invisible,' i.e., empirically indeterminable communion of saints, understood as the Church of Faith in Article III of the Augsburg Confession. One does not become a member of this body through a sacrament conferred by a priest, but through the faith worked by the Holy Spirit by means of the exterior Word — and the sacraments are included in this external Word. Word and Spirit establish our contact with the Body of Christ, and we remain attached thereto by faith."[18] The Evangelical understanding of the *Corpus Christi mysticum* is fundamentally distinct from the Catholic. According to Wolf, the difference lies in the following elements of the Evangelical notion: "1. the denial that the unity of the Mystical Body of Christ — the unity making it a genuine *body* — is to be understood in the sense of an organism hierarchically structured; 2. the Word of God, which is identical with Christ and the Holy Spirit, takes the place of Peter's successor as the center and ground of unity."[19]

Protestant theologians seem to misunderstand, or indeed not even to consider, the mystery of Christ's Person and His gifts, the redeeming function of Christ as Legislator. In the opinion of these theologians, there is no juridical element at all in grace,[20] or conversely, nothing divine is genuinely operative in the realm of the visibility of the Church.

Why does Schlink believe that he must, because the attributes of the Church are a matter of faith, refer them to its purely spiritual or invisible aspect? I think that he does so because he relates these attributes to the Lutheran notion of the *Law* and the *Gospel*. In his article, "The Visibility and the Hiddenness of the Church according to Luther,"[21] the Swedish theologian Herbert Olsson analyzes Althaus' statement, "There is not even the possibility that we can know God apart from faith."[22] Olsson comes to the conclusion that such a position is not Lutheran: "For Luther there is a knowledge of God through the Law; or in other words, a knowledge of God which the man who has no faith also possesses." Here we become aware of the gap between contemporary Protestant theology and the attitude of the Reformers. Contemporary Protestant theologians understand "The external as a sphere which is essentially unrelated to the divine. The divine is understood as if it lay behind the external, or beyond it, and as if it becomes real only by being

---

[18] Wolf, *Peregrinatio*, p. 175.

[19] *Ibid.*, p. 172 f.

[20] Karl Barth is of another opinion. Cf. his *Kirchliche Dogmatik*, Vol. II, Part I, p. 591.

[21] In *Ein Buch von der Kirche. Unter Mitarbeit schwedischer Theologen*, edited by G. Aulen, A. Fridrichsen, A. Nygren, H. Linderoth, R. Bring, translated into German by G. Klose (Göttingen, 1951), pp. 338–360.

[22] Paul Althaus, "Theologie des Glaubens," *Zeitschrift zur systematische Theologie*, no. 2, p. 305.

actualized by faith." Olsson rightly observes that "This is a spiritualistic and subjectivistic point of view which necessarily undermines thought concerning the Church." In any case I am of the opinion that Luther himself provided the source for Olsson's criticism and that the ideas of modern Evangelical theologians effectively close off the genuine Lutheran conception of the Church.

This basic ecclesiological position is, in my opinion, profoundly related to a corresponding understanding of Christ. We are concerned here with the question of the Person and work of Jesus Christ. It would appear that Protestants and Catholics do not share the same faith in Jesus Christ.

If I see it correctly, the Christian confessions are divided primarily on their definitions of faith concerning Jesus Christ, true God and true Man. In 1951, the year commemorating the 1500th anniversary of the Council of Chalcedon, there were dynamic discussions regarding our understanding of Jesus Christ.[23] Since then Catholics have continually asked Evangelical Christians to elucidate their understanding of Christ's human nature. In his studies of reformed theology and the problem of the Church, Ernst Wolf writes: "One cannot say that Luther remained entirely content with the formula of Chalcedon."[24] The basic formula for Luther's Christology is Col 2:9: "For in him is embodied and dwells the fullness of the Godhead" and Jn 14:9: "He who sees me sees the Father." "Christ's human nature is God's sign of revelation, under whose protective cover the whole majesty of God as God is present for us . . . it is a mask for God's majesty."[25] Catholic theologians in no way accuse the reformers of denying Christ's human nature. It is more a question of the part played by Christ's human nature in the work of salvation. The humanity of Christ is the revealed sign of the Godhead. With this we can agree. But it is more than that. It is the instrument, the organ of salvation, the efficacious or real sign of the grace of the Godhead. The Protestant will reject the expression

---

[23] Cf. Yves M.-J. Congar, O.P., "Regards et refléxions sur la christologie de Luther," in *Das Konzil von Chalkedon III,* edited by Grillmeier and Bacht (Würzburg, 1954), pp. 457–486; Thomas Sartory, O.S.B., *The Ecumenical Movement and the Unity of the Church* (Westminster, Md., 1963).

[24] Wolf, *Peregrinatio,* p. 52.

[25] Prenter, *Spiritus Creator,* p. 263. I regard these books of Wolf and Prenter as specially significant. A genuinely ecumenical dialogue should be made in coming to grips with them.

"efficacious sign of grace" because in his opinion this notion is rooted in an anthropocentric way of theologizing.[26] Catholic theology understands Christ's human nature in the work of salvation as an *instrumentum unitum*.[27]

At an East-West Congress of the *Una Sancta* organized in Berlin in the summer of 1956, the Lutheran Pastor Max Lackmann addressed the following questions to his fellow Evangelicals:

"Does Luther's understanding of the two natures of Christ leave room for the human person and personality of Jesus? Does it really leave room for the *proprietas* of His human nature? Does the stress not lay, in a way, on the efficacy of God alone in the person of Christ, which person now must absorb the horizontal? To quote Luther: 'The Kingdom of Heaven is not entrusted to Christ the man because of His humanity but because of His divinity. In fact, His divinity alone created everything; His humanity did nothing. It was not Christ's humanity that conquered sin and death, but the fishhook hidden under the bait of Jesus' humanity, which the Devil swallowed — this fish-hook was the divinity hidden under His humanity. Hence his humanity consummated the work only because of His divinity.' Luther's meaning here is clear: God alone redeems, but to be sure only in the theater of Christ's humanity, in His 'mask,' as Luther was wont to say. God Himself in Christ makes the needed reparation; the man Jesus does not redeem.

"Is there perhaps a tendency in Luther and the Lutheran Church to overstress the theocentric element in their concept of Jesus.

"Does Luther sufficiently value the commitment of a member of humanity, Jesus, next to the commitment of the Son of God, who for our sake parted even with his own glory? The *'pro nobis'* — this is an absolutely decisive question — can in no way mean that God's mercy suspends, in the case of Christ, the responsibility of the human nature for itself. There is no suspension of His need to accept His destiny in the sense that the life and suffering of the Lamb of God becomes a divine substitute and reduces human nature to nothing on the scale of real justice.

"The substance of our traditional Evangelical hymns to the Passion

---

[26] Cf. Prenter, *op. cit.,* p. 259.

[27] Thomas Aquinas, *Summa Theologiae,* III, q. 13, a. 5; *Summa Contra Gentiles,* III, 41. On this whole question cf. the outstanding work of Theophil Tschnipke, O.P., *Die Menschheit Christi als Heilsorgan der Gottheit* (Freiburg, 1940).

lies doubtless in such statements as: 'true *God* hath given Himself
verily for me, lost man, unto death, oh great tribulation, God's Son
lies dead,' etc. This is a legitimate biblical reference to the *'pro nobis';*
but does not 1 Tim 2:6 necessarily retire here, subdued, into the
background: 'Christ Jesus the Man, who gave Himself away as
ransom for all'? And what of those passages which speak of the
suffering, self-sacrificing, self-giving *Man* Jesus? And do we forget the
importance of one of us, indeed the new Adam, a creature born of
the very dust and who vouches for us without reserve? How are
we to interpret the key passage in Isaiah 53 where no mention of
divinity is to be found? No, we are here in the imposing
presence of a servant of God suffering in his full humanity and in
his unconditioned dedication to us and all humankind."[28]

Again, in considering Christological questions, we are concerned
with our understanding of Christ and of His *offices.* The Christology
of the reformers is in the main a soteriology. This means that Christ
is looked on principally as our Redeemer, our Saviour. But is not
Christ also our Lawgiver?[29] Does He not act with authority in
virtue of His anointing and His offices? The Lutheran antithesis
between the Law and the Gospel, between the two kingdoms, the
orders of creation and redemption, comes into play here. We must
investigate the Christ-image found in Paul's Epistles to the Ephesians
and Colossians. Catholics have tended, in recent years, to direct
their attention to this important point.[30] The Protestant cry, "Either
the Law or the Gospel," is not genuine. Is it not possible that an
unjustifiable extension of St. Paul's polemic against the Mosaic Law
(Law as a substitute for the salvation of Christ) underlies the
Protestant position? But then let us compare it to Augustine's classical
solution of this problem: "The Law was given so that grace might
be sought; grace was given so that the Law might be fulfilled." It
is a question of the second and third uses or functions of the Law,
and with the latter it is a question of the use of the Law for the
reborn. Werner Elert writes that the Church "understood Christ as
Lawgiver, His legacy as law, and herself as His instrument for

---

[28] Cf. also Max Lackmann, *Ein Hilferuf aus der Kirche für die Kirche*
(Stuttgart, 1956).

[29] Werner Elert strenuously denied this in *Der christliche Glaube. Grundli-
nien der lutherischen Dogmatik* (Hamburg, 1956), p. 141.

[30] Cf. J. P. Michael, "Jesus Christus, Erlöser und Gesetzgeber," *Wort und
Wahrheit,* 10 (1955), no. 8.

disseminating the Law of Christ among the peoples.[31] This understanding of herself and her mission may explain the fundamental importance that the Roman Church has given to the principle of natural law. For if the Church is to represent the power of God among men, then she must also claim eternal and immutable validity for her norms and laws. Luther destroyed this theological premise and from this stems his significance. "Luther laid bare the falsification of the Christ-image. Christ is not a second Moses. He is not a lawgiver. His legacy is not the law, but the Gospel. Nor can the Church be a lawgiver. Her statelike structure is anti-Christianity. If Christ is the Redeemer, then He brings that freedom to which men are called by their Creator. The believing person acts in fact from practical motives, and not from the pressure of laws. He is released into freedom."[32] It is evident what implications this doctrine has for ecclesiology, particularly for the juridical character of the Church, and for one's understanding of Christian ethics.

Furthermore, all this is connected with the *notion and meaning of grace*. We have already seen that the Reformation's chief concern about the part played by Christ's human nature in the work of salvation is the exclusive efficacy of God and the exclusion of anything human that might derogate from God. St. Thomas Aquinas understood Christ's humanity as an "instrument united" to Christ.[33] This has, to be sure, its implications for our doctrine concerning Word and Sacrament and the role of the Church in the economy of salvation. Regin Prenter understands Word and Sacrament solely as signs of Revelation.[34] In any case — and here, as I see it, is fertile material for a dialogue — he later writes: "This sign is also an instrumental sign, the means through which God has made our being like Christ's"[35] But he also points out that the young Luther, especially in his teaching concerning baptism, gives unusual emphasis to the instrumental function of the outward sign; the mature Luther, however, stressed much more the revelatory function of the sign.[36]

Let us consider this preoccupation of the reformers. It is a question of the primacy of grace versus a supposedly synergistic doctrine of salvation in scholasticism which attributes to free will a significance which would constitute in fact a limitation of God's domain of

---

[31] Elert, *op. cit.*, p. 20.
[32] *Ibid.*, p. 21.
[33] Cf. note 27.

[34] Prenter, *Spiritus Creator*, p. 258.
[35] *Ibid.*, p. 259.
[36] *Ibid.*, p. 259.

activity.[37] On the Protestant side there is fear either of attributing to man an activity which in effect rivals that of God, or of positing a metaphysical and causal relationship between God and His means of conferring grace. The notion of secondary causes is pointed at as *the* great heresy of Catholicism.[38] "A secondary cause is not purely and simply an instrumental cause through which the First Cause, God Himself, acts with exclusive responsibility, but on the contrary it competes in the effect, independently and responsible to its own self, with the First Cause."[39] One sees how difficult it is for a Protestant to understand scholastic language. For the Catholic it is perfectly obvious that the elevation, by grace, of creation to a genuine partnership in the action of God does not necessarily mean a "competing," synergistic secondary cause. It seems, in fact, that in stressing the absoluteness of God, Lutheran theology falls into a theorizing which is not less "scholastic" than the scholasticism which it condemned.[40]

Another test case for the difficulty of understanding scholastic terms is the notion of *gratia creata*. Every theology of grace must respect, in fact defend, the primacy of God, who alone justifies and sanctifies man, and must also maintain the reality of rebirth. The reproach by Protestants — it always comes up in ecumenical discussions — is that Catholics drop the primacy of God in their doctrine of "created grace," as well as in that of the "state of grace." It may be that Catholics give some occasion to this reproach. For example, Bernhard Bartmann says, in a footnote to his *Abriss der Dogmatik:* "The cause of grace is God alone," and then adds in italics *"de fide."*[41] It would be important for the ecumenical dialogue, and beyond that for all work dealing with this notion of "created grace," to know how and when the notion came into being historically. Space is lacking here to go into the matter in detail, but we wish to refer the reader to an instructive essay by Charles Moeller entitled *Théologie de la Grâce et Oecuménisme.*[42] It is not at all pointless to familiarize oneself with the various ap-

---

[37] *Ibid.*, p. 180.
[38] Wolf, *Peregrinatio*, pp. 322, 327.
[39] *Ibid.*, p. 382.
[40] On this entire problem, cf. Lackmann, *op. cit.*
[41] Cited by Charles Moeller, "Théologie de la Grâce et Oecuménisme," *Irénikon*, 28 (1955), 19–56.
[42] *Ibid.*

proaches to the question of grace taken by such thinkers as Albert the Great or Bonaventure. Luther denied the *habitus* (state) of created grace because he wanted personal, subjective contact with Christ and God, not an impersonal objective contact. It was Luther's misfortune that as a consequence of the nominalism which dominated the thinking of the sixteenth century, both with Catholics as well as with the Reformers, he never really grasped the meaning of created grace. In the thinking of such men as Biel or Ockam this *habitus* was conceived as separated from God and, as it were, closed up in the walled world of human affairs. The *habitus* appeared as a middle being, closed unto itself, belonging to man, outside of true grace. Moeller rightly notes that "Luther rejected the *gratia creata* in an attempt to repudiate Pelagianism, whereas the medieval theologians had projected this *gratia creata* with a view to resisting Pelagianism more effectively. Luther would not have rejected created grace, had it been well presented, such as in the formulae of Bonaventura."[43] An eminently significant point for the ecumenical dialogue today!

II. THE CATHOLIC UNDERSTANDING OF THE CHURCH

The preoccupation of Protestant theology with the true nature of the Church cannot be overlooked or scorned in these pages, despite any errors associated with the Protestant. In contemporary Catholic ecclesiology, which takes seriously the dialogue with separated brethren, statements about the Church are thought through anew and reworded to make them more "catholic" and to transcend the position taken during the Counter-Reformation.[44] Hence we shall direct our attention here to the problems facing ecumenical ecclesiology.

1. A Protestant recoils from the notion of a direct, unbroken, and absolute *visibility of the spiritual reality of the Church.* Perhaps, therefore, one should make more clear to the Protestant that the Church, while truly visible, discernible,[45] is an object of *faith* both

---

[43] *Ibid.,* p. 35.

[44] Certainly the victory over the Counter-Reformation in matters of ecclesiology is shown in the encyclical *Mystici Corporis,* since this encyclical binds together in one grand vision the diverse aspects of the Church. This becomes evident if one thinks that prior to this encyclical ecclesiology (along the lines of Cardinal Bellarmine?) had been too one-sided and overconcerned with the juridical and visible elements in the Church.

[45] "The Church must be something tangible and visible, as our predecessor of happy memory Leo XIII, in his encyclical *Satis cognitum* pointed out: 'for just as it is a body, so is the Church perceptible by the eyes.' Consequently

in herself and in her marks or notes. We would like to extract from Schlink's extreme and consequently erratic definitions the message which may be considered as legitimately founded upon revealed sources.

The *Roman Catechism* states: "Finally we must show just how and why it is an article of faith to believe in a Church. For though everyone knows by the testimony of his reason and senses that there is a Church on earth, i.e., a community of men who are consecrated to and made holy by Christ the Lord, and although it seems unnecessary to have faith in order to grasp this since neither Jews nor Turks doubt it, still only an understanding enlightened by faith, without being forced in any way by reason, acknowledges those mysteries which are comprised in the Holy Church of God. Thus since this article no less than the former transcends the capacity and powers of our knowledge, we confess with the fullest right that we acknowledge the origin, offices, and dignities of the Church not by human reason, but see them solely with the eyes of faith."[46]

The *notae ecclesiae* are both visible and invisible at once. Catholic "visibility" is not exactly "absolute," because it is a *sacramental visibility*. The treasures of salvation are not to be reduced to mere visibility, nor coupled mechanically to the domain of man's natural faculties.

2. The Protestant also complains of the lack of an *eschatological* character in our notion of the Church. Take the statement of the Bavarian Regional Bishop, Hermann Dietzfelbringer, as an example: "The notion of the Kingdom of God is stronger with them [with Roman Catholics] than with us, but stronger in such a way that it is taken out of its eschatological perspective and often thereby dreadfully changed. Has this Church lost its eschatological vision of itself and of earthly things?"[47] In our ecclesiology it should be made very

---

he wanders far from divine truth who so describes the Church as if it could neither be grasped nor seen, as if it were, as some maintain, only something 'pneumatic,' " Pius XII, *Mystici Corporis,* as cited in Cattin-Conus-Rohrbasser, *Heilslehre der Kirche* (Fribourg, 1953), no. 764, p. 475.

[46] Part I, Chap. 10, ques. 17. Karl Barth noted with pleasure that even the Catholic Church can speak *fide solum intelligimus ecclesiam.* Cf. his *Kirchliche Dogmatik,* IV, I, p. 736.

[47] "Toleranz und Intoleranz zwischen den Konfessionem," *Una Sancta,* 11 (1956), p. 115.

clear that the Church and the Kingdom of God are not identical, that the Church is made up of sinful members, and that the day of completion is not yet come. We should work much more on the notion of "the Church as God's People." The Church is God's People far from home. To be sure, the Church has the truth (*veritas*) and the life (*vita*), but they are conditional, in the Church, by the way (*via*). The Church stands between spirit (*pneuma*) and flesh (*sarx*), and her position is consequently located between synagogue and Kingdom: between the synagogue, which was all expectancy and promise, and the Kingdom, which will be the completed reality. The eschatological character of the Church consists in the fact that the Church is rooted in the reality of the Principle and in the first appearance of God's efficacious Substance.[48] The essence of the Church is unfolding; it is the transformation of the substance of the first Adam into the entire substance of the second Adam.

3. The Protestant concern is for the *sovereignty and free efficacy of God*. Prenter expresses this in extreme form when he utterly repudiates a metaphysical (and for him this means rationally comprehensible) union of the spirit with the outward sign as an anthropocentric idea. "The sovereignty of the spirit over the 'means of grace' must be maintained unconditionally and unfettered."[49]

Catholics must also be careful not to identify the work of the Holy Spirit with the actions of the ecclesial body. "One could say that the heritage of Protestantism is that element of Christian Revelation which was undervalued by an ecclesiology which equated, without the necessary reservations, the working of the Holy Spirit with the activity of the Church apparatus. To an extent this heritage justified the reaction of the Protestant Reformers."[50] But, continues Congar, one may not make this element of the free act of God into a law, making use of it, after the manner of an acid, "to break down the very structure of the Work of God, to dissolve what He most certainly created to bring salvation and the life acquired in Jesus Christ to us: His Church which continues His corporeal presence and His corporeal work until He returns."[51] This means that the proper structure of the Church must be preserved unconditionally and must

---

[48] Cf. Yves M.-J. Congar, O.P., *Vraie et fausse reforme dans l'Eglise* (Paris, 1950), p. 470.

[49] Prenter, *Spiritus Creator*, p. 57.

[50] Congar, *Vraie et fausse reforme* . . . , p. 482.

[51] *Ibid.*

be strongly emphasized against Protestantism; nevertheless, this structure must not be made such an absolute that in the end a complete hierarchization of the Church should again emerge![52] The encyclical *Mystici Corporis* lists in fact as one of the juridical bonds of the Church "still another principle of unity. It is those three virtues through which we are most intimately bound to God and to one another, Christian faith, hope and love."[53]

4. A further concern of Protestant theology is the *superiority of Christ over His congregation*. The Catholic stresses Christ's *being in* the Church; thus the Catholic gladly describes the Church as Christ living on, as the continuation of the incarnation, i.e., he describes it in incarnational terms. If we should fail to keep Christ's humanity sufficiently in view,[54] we run the danger of an ecclesiological monophysitism, i.e., a deification of the Church. We cannot speak of the Church as possessing divine nature or divine personality. Therefore, no direct equation between Christ and the Church is possible, and it is furthermore impossible, without careful precision, to speak of the Church as the continued incarnation of Christ. Pope Pius XII speaks in his encyclical *Mystici Corporis* of the danger of this identification. He designates as a "misleading doctrine in full opposition to Catholic faith" a view which ascribes divine attributes to men ("they make the divine Redeemer and the members of the Church into a single physical Person"). The Pope counters this view with the teaching of Paul (Eph 5:22 f.): "who, though he combines Christ and His mystical Body in a marvelous union, yet contrasts the one with the other, as Bridegroom with Bride."[55] This Bride has, on the one hand, the divine dowry in the sense defined by the Vatican I[56] of the preservative teaching office through which she

---

[52] Cf. Congar's remarks that ecclesiology up to the present has been simply a hierarchology (*ibid.*, p. 60). Martin Ramsauer has shown how closely the Church has been identified with the hierarchy in catechisms and, as a result, in the popular mind, in his article "Die Kirche in den Katechismen," *Zeitschrift für katholische Theologie*, 73 (1951), pp. 129–169, 313–346. Cf. also Franz X. Arnold, *Grundsätzliches und Geschichtliches zur Theologie der Seelsorge* (Freiburg, 1949), pp. 80 ff., 106 ff.; cf. the same author's "Die Stellung des Laien in der Kirche" in *Una Sancta*, 9 (1954), no. 4, pp. 8–26.

[53] Cattin-Conus-Rohrbasser, *op. cit.*, no. 813, p. 504.

[54] Karl Rahner showed this danger for Catholics in his *Schriften zur Theologie*, III, p. 57 f.

[55] Cattin-Conus-Rohrbasser, *op. cit.*, no. 825, p. 511.

[56] Denz. 1800.

remains, because of the assistance of the Holy Spirit, unconditionally free of error and infidelity. This aspect of the Bride shows the Church as essentially loving. But, on the other hand, in her personal actions, this Bride can become untrue and apostate, as prophets have described her again and again, and as we have in fact again and again experienced as a result of the sinfulness of the members of this Bride, this congregation. It would be a genuine task for Catholic theology to investigate references in the Old Testament to the Church as a bridelike congregation (the New Testament supposes these Old Testament notions as premises), because we might then speak more biblically and more realistically with regard to man's sin and God's grace which is even greater than that sin.

The relationship between Christ and the Church is not univocal but *analogical*. And with analogies the unlikeness is always greater than the similarity.[57] This entire matter must develop with our understanding of grace.[58]

5. Protestant ecclesiology strives to connect the Church with an act of God and with the heavenly Christ, while Catholic ecclesiology prefers to see the Church under the light of the economy of salvation, with the salutary work consummated by the incarnate Word. The Protestant loves the *Category of Immediacy*: God and Christ raised up to the right hand of God, both work and act *immediately, directly* upon the Church. That the Catholic also knows this *immediacy* is shown in the encyclical *Mystici Corporis*: "But because Christ is so exalted, He *alone*[59] by every right rules and governs the Church . . . our divine Savior governs and guides His community also *directly and personally*.[59] For it is He who reigns within the minds and hearts of men and bends and subjects to His purpose their wills even when rebellious. By this interior guidance the 'Shepherd and Bishop of our souls' not only watches over individuals, but exercises His providence over the universal Church as well."[60]

What Protestantism exaggerates, Pius XII compensates for by pointing out that "One must not think that He rules *only*[59] in a hidden or extraordinary way. On the contrary, our divine Redeemer *also*[59] governs His mystical Body in a visible and ordinary way

---

[57] Cf. on this entire problem, Sartory, *The Ecumenical Movement and the Unity of the Church*, pp. 152–158.

[58] Cf. Charles Moeller, *op. cit.*

[59] Our emphasis.

[60] Cattin-Conus-Rohrbasser, *op. cit.*, nn. 782, 784, p. 485.

through His Vicar on earth. . . . Nor may one argue against this that the primacy of jurisdiction established in the Church gives such a Mystical Body two heads. Peter, in virtue of his primacy, is only Christ's Vicar; so that there is only one chief Head of this body, namely, Christ. He never ceases personally to guide the Church by an unseen hand, though at the same time He rules it externally, visibly through him who is His representative on earth . . . they, therefore, walk the path of dangerous error, who have taken away the visible head, broken the visible bonds of unity, and they leave the Mystical Body of the Redeemer in such obscurity and so maimed, that those who are seeking the haven of eternal salvation cannot see it and cannot find it."[61]

How void of content, therefore, in the light of the above, is the Protestant reproach that the Church is in competition with God as a *causa secunda* in an autonomous way, responsible only to itself.[62] But a personal responsibility and a relative independence of the human instrument in the economy of salvation cannot be denied in the light of the New Testament: "Christ makes no mechanical use of the members when He brings His will into effect in the community through them."[63]

III. THE UNITY OF THE CHURCH

Our notion of the unity of the Church depends upon our notion of the Church itself. Is it, indeed, legitimate even to speak of the "Church and the Churches"? We said that unity is a note of the Church. And corresponding to the different interpretations given to these notes, the notion of the unity of the Church will differ among the various confessions.

1. The Protestant Standpoint. With certain differences among themselves, the Evangelical Christians believe it possible to speak legitimately of "Churches." An instance of this is an essay by Peter Brunner, "Die Kirche und die Kirchen Heute" (*Thesen zu einer konkreten Ekklesiologie und einem ökumenischen Ethos*).[64] "It can never be the task of Christians on earth to *bring about* the unity of

---

[61] *Ibid.,* n. 785, p. 486 f.
[62] Wolf, *Peregrinatio,* p. 328.
[63] J. Horst, article "μέλος," in Kittel's *Theologisches Wörterbuch zum Neuen Testament,* IV, p. 569.
[64] In *Evangelische-Lutherische Kirchenzeitung,* 8 (1954), pp. 241–244.

the Church, because this unity of the Church is immediately *given* with the being of the Church. That the Church is one, is an affirmation that is self-evident (*praedicatio perseitatis*)."[65] A Catholic can agree with this statement, for he also knows that the Church's unity is a gift of God's grace. But here again it becomes clear how the apparent identity of the two theses can be destroyed when one comes to explain them separately. What specifically is this *given unity* for Peter Brunner? He also refers the unity, holiness, and catholicity of the Church to the domain of the intangible, the indescribable: This unity is a "spiritual unity of the intangible Church."[66] "One cannot proceed from the spiritual unity of the Church to a demand for constitution of the Church which joins juridically all congregations and churches on earth into a lawfully constituted Church Body with a common direction at the head."[67] Peter Brunner believes that "there is an absolutely legitimate plurality of Churches." And Ernst Kinder agrees with him: "Because of history and for reasons of expediency, different Churches can and may stand next to one another without the true unity of the Church being hindered. If the Churches are in basic agreement solely in their common confession of the Gospel and in a religious instruction according to the precepts of the Gospel, then with all their differences the true unity of the Church is nevertheless expressed in essential and decisive matters."[68]

Behind this view advocated on the Evangelical-Lutheran side lies the idea of the *ecclesia universalis invisibilis*.[69] The Lutheran view sees the unity of the Church not as the unity of her members but as the unity of Christ acting in these members.[70]

Thus Lutherans will say that there is only one Church as far as faith is concerned, but that there are many in an empirical sense, i.e., insofar as this faith is experienced differently by members of different "Churches." Reference is made to the New Testament according to which there have always been divisions and contentions among Christians, and to the history of the Church, which attests to the same fact. Thus, says Bishop Dietzfelbringer in his address on tolerance: "Divisions in the Church, as the New Testament and,

---

[65] *Ibid.*, p. 241.   [66] *Ibid.*, p. 241.   [67] *Ibid.*, p. 241.

[68] E. Kinder, "Die Einheit der Kirche und das Dogma," *Evangelische-Lutherische Kirchenzeitung*, 8 (1954), p. 245.

[69] Cf. G. Ebeling, "Zur Geschichte des konfessionellen Problems," *Ökumenische Rundschau*, 1 (1952), p. 107.

[70] Cf. E. Schlink, *loc. cit.*, p. 215.

if you will, the Old Testament show, are as old as the Church herself. They did not commence only with the Reformation. The great split between the Roman Church and the Eastern Orthodox Church took place a full half-millennium before the Reformation, and we find even as early as in the Codex Theodosianus (428) the juxtaposition of the great number of Christian confessions."[71]

It cannot be maintained that Christianity has ever known any absolute, complete unity. May one conclude, however, that the Body of Christ is necessarily divided in itself and that the plurality of the "Churches" is justifiable in Revelation? Karl Barth has energetically rejected the idea of a variety of Churches. After an examination of Eph 4:1–7, 1 Cor 12:4–31 and Rom 12:3–8, he concludes that a real plurality of unities in the New Testament does not come into question. There is only one, single unity.[72] "There is *no* theological, spiritual, or biblical justification for the existence of a multiplicity of such really separated, interiorly and therefore also exteriorly mutually exclusive Churches. *Many* Churches in this sense means many *Lords,* many *Spirits,* many *Gods.*"[73] If history contradicts the *una ecclesia,* then it is speaking only of the fact, not of the truth.[74] And Barth also says that in asserting "I believe in the one Church" one may not take refuge in the unity of an invisible Church.[75]

It is unbiblical when one attempts, on the grounds of opposed unities, to read contradictions into such passages as 1 Cor 12, where the one is contrasted with the many, the body with its members, the unity of spirit with the diversity of gifts. It is illicit to transfer the schisms and heresies denounced by the Apostle into the notion that the Christian reality can be plural. The distinction between the signification and the thing signified is often forgotten. In the signification there is a legitimate plurality. But what of the content? It is a matter of the problem of truth, which must in my opinion be posed more explicitly and energetically, as is done with questions concerning the correct promulgation of the Gospel and the administration of the sacraments. According to Eph 3, unity presupposes the one faith. And this means faith in the sense of the formulated Credo.[76] If one

---

[71] *Loc. cit.,* p. 113.   [73] *Ibid.,* p. 754.
[72] *Kirchliche Dogmatik,* IV, I, p. 746.   [74] *Ibid.,* p. 756.
[75] *Ibid.,* p. 756. Hans Asmussen also warns of this danger in his *Warum noch lutherische Kirche* (Stuttgart, 1949).
[76] On this cf. Heinrich Schlier, "Uber das Hauptanliegen des 1 Briefes an die Korinther," *Die Zeit der Kirche* (Freiburg, 1956), pp. 147–159.

argues on the premise of a spiritual or invisible unity of the Church, then one has the difficulty of recognizing the heresies which the New Testament in fact categorically denounced. The reference to the "juxtaposition of a large number of Christian confessions" in the Codex Theodosianus overlooks the fact that these confessions (except for one) were considered as heresies, and were placed by imperial law under liability to punishment.

2. Catholic Teaching. The Catholic Church therefore asserts nothing other than a biblical fact when she teaches that the Church is essentially and numerically one and when she denies that the Body of Christ can be divided. The only divisions are separations from this one Body of Christ. Hence history is consistent in pointing out that in early Christianity the name "Churches" was never applied to those corporate entities which had separated from the visible Catholic Church. The "Church" existed only where the four notes of unity, holiness, catholicity, and apostolicity were found. This practice prevails even today. In official Roman documents only the Eastern Christians are designated as *ecclesiae*.[77] Gregory VII and Urban II held that the aim of the first Crusade was the *liberatio orientalium ecclesiarum*. Gregory IX spoke of the *ecclesia Graecorum,* as did the fourth Lateran Council in 1215. The Council for Union in Florence named the Greek Church the *Ecclesia orientalis*. Leo XIII spoke of the *ecclesiae orientales,*[78] whereas he referred to the Protestant communions as *congregationes*. Pius XI spoke in his consistory address on December 18, 1924, *de orientis ecclesiarum doctrinis institutisque;* and with Pius XII the expression *ecclesia orientalis* was used with particular frequency.[79] Thus we can point to different manners of expression in referring to Orthodox and Protestant Christians.[80]

How are we to explain this distinction? First, it must be pointed out that a number of elements must be verified before we can speak of a "Church" (no matter whether the Church be completely or

[77] On this cf. Yves M.-J. Congar, O.P., *Chrétiens désunis. Principes d'un 'Oecuménisme' catholique.* Collectio Unam Sanctam (Paris, 1937), appendix.
[78] Encyclical *Praeclarae gratulationis* of June 20, 1894.
[79] Cf. the encyclical *Orientalis Ecclesiae decus* of April 9, 1944, and *Orientales omnes Ecclesias* of December 23, 1945.
[80] A distinction of this kind is valid also in non-Catholic circles. Cf. J. Burn-Murdoch, *Church, Continuity, and Unity* (Cambridge, 1945). The latter maintains that the term "Church" cannot be properly applied to Baptists, Quakers, and similar sects.

partly realized). The decisive question is: *how has Jesus Christ instituted His Church?* The elements of this Church correspond to the threefold office of Christ as Prophet, Priest, and King; and they are:

1. The revelation and transmission of *Faith*.[81]

2. The institution of the *Sacraments,* in the first instance Baptism and the Eucharist, but also those which we find performed by the Apostles, particularly the laying on of hands for the imparting of the powers of office.

3. The institution of the Apostolic office to which the *depositum fidei* and the celebration of the sacraments is entrusted.

If these elements are present, we can speak of a Church; one can even say that they form the very structure of the Church.

One may wonder why the primacy of Peter and his successors is not mentioned here. To me it would seem wise to mention the See of Rome only when one speaks of the universal Church. What we have primarily in mind here are the Churches of the local bishops. Thus in the New Testament there are references to the "Church" of "Corinth" or "of Jerusalem," and today we can speak of the "Churches" of Paderborn, Passau, or Aachen, of New York, Chicago or St. Louis. Each is of course truly a Church, since each has the essential structure of the Church, a structure which is bound to apostolic succession in the episcopacy, through which the *depositum fidei,* the sacraments, and the apostolic authority are transmitted. This local church is in fact the Church of God, to the extent that the latter is to be found in the place.

True, the Lord did not build His Church on the level of local communities, but rather on the level of the universal Church. Nor is the latter a mere sum total of all the local churches joined, as it were, in a confederation.[82] Just as the whole college of the Apostles is

---

[81] Congar believes that this is essentially a matter of trinitarian faith. Cf. "Note sur les mots, 'Confession,' 'Eglise,' et 'Communion,'" *Irénikon,* 23 1950), pp. 3–36.

[82] K. L. Schmidt writes, in his article "Ekklesia" in Kittel's *Theologisches Wörterbuch,* III, pp. 506, 508: "It is not true that the *Ekklesia* can be disintegrated into *Ekklesiai.* Nor is it true that the *Ekklesia* would first arise only through an addition of *ekklesiai.* Rather it is true that in the places where we find *The Ekklesia,* we find something which neither can nor should be regarded as an assemblage of *ekklesiai.* . . . For it is not an addition of individual communities which results in the universal community, the Church, but it is rather the latter which exists even when it is a small community."

comprised in Peter (in the Gospels, Peter comes forth again and again as spokesman for the Apostles: when Peter speaks, the whole college of Apostles has spoken in him, whereas when the Apostles speak without Peter, then only the various single Apostles, not the entire college, have spoken), so does the worldwide episcopacy in postapostolic times require a visible principle of unity. If "being the Church" belongs to the local churches by reason of their participation in the "being the Church" proper to the universal Church, then the episcopal office in the local Churches must be a participation in the episcopal office of him who stands visibly at the head of the universal Church. This does not mean that the local bishops are delegates or general vicars of the bishop of the entire Church, any more than the Apostles were delegates of Peter. It was rightly noted at Vatican I that the episcopal dignity is not limited by the power of the Pope, but rather receives from the papacy its absolute warrant and guarantee.[83] Vatican I set this truth forth as follows: "But, that the episcopacy itself might be one and undivided, and that the entire multitude of the faithful might be preserved in the unity of faith and communion through priests closely associated with one another, [our Lord] placed the Blessed Peter over the other apostles, establishing in him the perpetual principle and visible foundation of both unities, upon whose strength the eternal temple might be built and the sublimity of the Church to be raised to heaven might rise on the firmness of his faith."[84]

Now if we consider the Orthodox Churches and ask just how they can be called Churches, we find it impossible to say that they are Churches in the full sense of the word. For they have in fact severed their ties with the true successor of Peter. Congar believes that the situation of the Orthodox Churches must be interpreted on the basis of local Churches: "The structure of a local Church is somehow incomplete, particularly on the level of the teaching office as well as on that of the criteria and means of the universal community, when this local Church is not united with the Petrine Apostolic

---

[83] Denz. 1828.

[84] Denz. 1821. On this question see the extraordinarily instructive article of Karl Hofstetter, "Der römische Primatsanspruch im Lichte der Heilsgeschichte," *Una Sancta*, 11 (1956), no. 4. On the question of Peter and his successors, cf. Otto Karrer, "Apostolische Nachfolge und Primat. Ihre biblische Grundlage im Lichte der neuren Theologie," *Zeitschrift für katholische Theologie*, 77 (1955), pp. 129–168.

principle, with the center and criterion of the unity realized in the Roman Episcopate. . . . Thus there can be Christian communities which are really local Churches, but Churches in an incomplete way, since they lack communion with those principles which the Lord instituted with a view to forming the total Church. To me, this seems to be the situation as regards the Orthodox Churches."[85] Congar goes on to remind us how difficult it is to say just how much the integrity of the apostolic *depositum* (especially with respect to belief and sacraments) can be distorted before the character of a local Church is effaced. The Orthodox communities would be called Churches in any case because of their trinitarian belief, which is surely the basis of everything. But in the strict sense, what of Nestorians and Monophysites or of a community which does not recognize all sacraments? We can say with certainty only that a community lacking apostolic succession can be called neither Church nor local Church in the strict theological sense of the word.

Let us summarize Catholic teaching on this point with the words of Pope Pius XII in *Mystici Corporis*: "Now since this social Body of Christ was intended by its Founder to be visible, the cooperation of all its members must be manifest externally through their profession of the same faith and their sharing of the same sacred rites, through participation in the same sacrifice and practical observance of the same laws. Above all, everyone must be able to see the Supreme Head, who gives effective direction to what all are doing toward attaining the desired end, that is, the Vicar of Jesus Christ on earth."[86]

Thus it is clearly impossible for Catholics to speak of the unity of the Church as spiritual, invisible, or eschatological, or in the sense of the branch theory (whereby religious communities are branches on a tree of the Church, etc.), or as the "sum of the different religious experiences" of separate communities. A Catholic can speak of "Churches" only with respect either to local Churches in the sense described or to Orthodoxy. But in the latter case the Church can be affirmed only with definite reservations and distinctions.

Thus it must be understood that Catholic teaching identifies the

---

[85] Congar, "Notes sur les mots 'Confession,' 'Eglise,' et 'Communion,' " *loc. cit.*, p. 28.

[86] Cattin-Conus-Rohrbasser, *op. cit.*, n. 812, pp. 503–504.

Mystical Body of Christ with the Roman Catholic Church.[87]
But this brings us to the question of membership in the Mystical Body. What does Revelation allow us to say of non-Catholic Christians and non-Catholic religious communities? In other words, can we speak of a membership in the Mystical Body of Christ outside of a visible Catholic Church?

IV. MEMBERSHIP[88]

In his book *De Ecclesia Christi,* the Roman theologian T. Zapelena opens the section dealing with this question with a sentence to which everyone who concerns himself with these problems can assent: "The question on the members of the Mystical Body is obscure and very complex."[89]

The Protestant world has not given the question of membership any special attention. It has come to the fore more as a result of the ecumenical movement. When it is said, for example, in the Toronto Statement, that the member Churches of the World Council of Churches should recognize other "Churches" not "as Churches in the true and full sense of the word," this necessarily implies that

---

[87] Cf. T. Zapelena, S.J., "De coextensione corporis mystici et Ecclesiae R. catholicae," *De Ecclesia Christi* (Rome, 1954), Vol. II, p. 359 ff.

[88] On this question cf. the following: J. Beumer, S.J., "Ein neuer, mehrschichtiger Kirchenbegriff," *Trier Theologische Zeitschrift,* 65 (1956), pp. 93–102; N. Hilling, "Die kirchliche Gliedschaft nach der Enzyklika 'Mystici Corporis' und nach dem CIC," *Archiv für katholisches Kirchenrecht,* 125 (1951), p. 127 ff.; Charles Journet, *L'Eglise du Verbe Incarne* (Paris, 1951), Vol. II; Clement Lialine, O.S.B., "Une etape en ecclésiologie. Refléxions sur l'encyclique 'Mystici Corporis,'" *Irénikon,* 19 (1946), pp. 129–152, 283–317; 20 (1947), pp. 34–54; A. Liégé, "L'appartenance à l'Eglise et l'encycliquè 'Mystici corporis Christi,'" *Revue de Sciences Philosophiques et Théologiques,* 32 (1948), pp. 351–358; V. Morel, "Le corps mystique et l'Eglise romaine," *Nouvelle Revue Theologique,* 70 (1948), pp. 703–726; Klaus Mörsdorf, "Die Kirchengliedschaft im Lichte der kirchlichen Rechtsordnung," *Theologie und Seelsorge* 1 (1944), p. 116 ff.; M. Nothomb, "l'Eglise et le Corps du Christ. Dernières encycliques et doctrine de Saint Thomas," *Irénikon,* 25 (1952), pp. 226–248; Karl Rahner, S.J., "Die Zugehörigkeit zur Kirche nach der Lehre der Enzyklika Pius XII, 'Mystici Corporis Christi,'" *Zeitschrift für katholische Theologie,* 69 (1947), pp. 129–188 (reprinted in *Theological Investigations,* II, pp. 1–87); L. Richard, "Une these fondamentale de l'oecumenisme: le baptême, incorporation visible à l'Eglise," *Nouvelle Revue Theologique,* 74 (1952), pp. 485–492; Thomas Sartory, O.S.B., *The Ecumenical Movement and the Unity of the Church,* chapter on "Membership"; Theodore Strotmann, O.S.B., "Les membres de l'Eglise," *Irénikon,* 25 (1952), pp. 249–262; T. Zapelena, S.J., *De Ecclesia Christi* (Rome, 1954), Vol. II.

[89] Chapter entitled "De membris Corporis mystici," p. 341 ff.

Christians of other religious communities are not to be considered in every case as true and full members of the Church. The problem also must be posed by Protestants when Lutheran Christians ask themselves just what the members of the Roman Catholic Church really are.[90]

With Catholics, on the other hand, there is general agreement on the interpretation of the doctrine of "No salvation outside the Church"; this is particularly true since the release of the letter of the Holy Office on August 8, 1949, to Archbishop Richard Cushing of Boston,[91] concerning the rigorous interpretation of this doctrine by Father Feeney.[92] This letter first of all reaffirms the unshakable conviction of the Roman Catholic Church that outside of herself there is no salvation; but the letter points out that this dogma must be understood in the sense given it by the Church itself. No person can be saved who knows that the Church is an institution founded in a divine way by Christ and yet refuses to be subject to her and to practice obedience to the Roman Pope. God wished in His immeasurable mercy that in certain cases the salutary effects of the Church be attainable, however, even when the means of salvation are no more than the object of a desire or wish. The letter refers here to the Council of Trent with its doctrine of the *votum* with respect to the sacraments of baptism and penance.[93] The same must be said also of the Church as the "universal means of salvation." That a person should attain to his eternal salvation, it is not always required that he be factually (*reapse*) incorporated into the Church as a conscious member, but it may in certain cases suffice for him to be bound to her by desire or wish, although nothing less than this desire or wish may suffice. This *votum* need not always be expressed. When a person lives in invincible ignorance, God's requirements may be met by an implicit desire. We may call this desire implicit because it is implied in the disposition of the soul to the

---

[90] What, for instance, is the significance, from the theological point of view, of Luther's statement in his great commentary on the Epistle to the Galatians regarding the Roman Church: "So also we call the Roman Church and all its bishops holy today, even though this Church is perplexed and its officials godless. For 'God is master even in the midst of His enemies' (1 Thes 2:4)."

[91] The text of this letter is found in *The American Ecclesiastical Review*, 127 (1952), pp. 2, 307–311.

[92] His excommunication followed on February 13, 1953 (*AAS* 45, 1953, p. 100).

[93] Denz. 797, 807.

good. We are speaking of a disposition in which a person wishes to assimilate his own will to that of God. But in no case may we suggest that just any form of desire to enter into the Church can be sufficient for salvation. Besides being a desire oriented toward the Church, it must be stamped by a perfect love and by supernatural faith.[94]

This brings us then to a controversy among Catholic theologians with respect to the notion of membership in the Church. It is an ecumenical problem which takes the following form: Are schismatics and heretics members of the Mystical Body of Christ?

The answer appears to be extremely complicated. The controversy at present turns on the interpretation of the encyclical *Mystici Corporis*. The encyclical teaches that membership is constituted by baptism.[95] And then further conditions are defined: "Only those are truly to be considered members of the Church who have been baptized and profess the true faith and who have not unhappily withdrawn from the unity of the one body, or for grave faults been excluded by legitimate authority . . . Those who are divided in faith or government cannot be living in one body such as this, and cannot be living the life of its one divine Spirit."[96] Thus, besides baptism, we have the positive conditions of the true faith and unity under juridical Church authority, and the negative condition of freedom from excommunication. Excommunication, according to the encyclical, cancels membership in the Mystical Body. The sinner remains a member, while schism, heresy, and apostasy "by their very nature sever a person from the body of the Church."[97] "The Spirit of Christ refuses to dwell with sanctifying grace in members that are wholly severed from the body."[98] Of those who do not belong to the visible community of the Catholic Church, the Pope asserts that they could, through an unconscious longing and wish, stand in a valid relationship to the Mystical Body of the Redeemer. The Holy Father exhorts them to incorporate themselves into the Catholic unity so

[94] Cf. also Bishop Julius Döpfner, "Die alleinseligmachende Kirche. Predigt zur Weltgebetsoktav 1955," *Una Sancta*, 10 (1955), no. 2, pp. 3–7. Thomas Sartory, O.S.B., "Die katholische Kirche und die getrennten Christen. Papst- und Bischofsworte zur Wiedereinigung im Glauben," *Religiöse Quellenschriften* (Düsseldorf, 1956).

[95] Cattin-Conus-Rohrbasser, *op. cit.*, n. 768, p. 4–77.

[96] *Ibid.*, n. 769; p. 478.

[97] *Ibid.*, n. 770; p. 479.

[98] *Ibid.*, n. 799; p. 496.

as not to miss so many telling divine graces and aids which one can enjoy exclusively in the Catholic Church. He expresses his wish that they may "return not to a stranger's, but to their own, their Father's house."[99]

Thus on the one hand one becomes a member of the Church through baptism and is directed toward the Mystical Body of Christ through the *votum ecclesiae;* and on the other one is excluded from the Church by heresy, schism, and apostasy. How is the obvious contradiction to be resolved, since heretics, schismatics, and apostates are baptized?

There are indeed theologians who deny membership in the Mystical Body to heretics and schismatics, whether they are formal or material, private or public. Yet other theologians see the need for a distinction in our definition of the notion of membership. Thus, for example, Father Zapelena, S.J., construing with particular effectiveness the words of Eph 4:4 ff., sees thorough agreement between the doctrine of St. Paul and that of Pope Pius XII. He shows how St. Paul lists *faith* as the first condition of membership in the Body of Christ, therefore excluding from the Mystical Body all who lack faith. St. Paul's second condition, continues Zapelena, is that it be that *one faith,* the confession of which is the prerequisite of baptism, therefore excluding all believers who deviate from the truth (*in doctrina dissidentes*). And third, St. Paul sees in his listing of Apostles, prophets, evangelists, shepherds, and teachers within the Mystical Body an external principle of the unity of faith, which is *the hierarchical and charismatic ministry.* Thus, reasons Zapelena, all those are excluded from the Mystical Body who, though possessing faith, "do not adhere to the ecclesiastical hierarchy or the authentic magisterium of the Church." Finally, St. Paul lists the condition of the one baptism, excluding from membership in the Mystical Body all heathens or pagans, the faithful of the Old Testament, and the catechumens.[100] Except in virtue of the *votum ecclesiae,* heretics cannot, according to Zapelena, be called true members of the Mystical Body,[101] any more than the *excommunicati vitandi*[102] and schismatics.[103]

The question as to whether we can legitimately read as much as

---

99 *Ibid.,* n. 838; p. 520.
100 T. Zapelena, S.J., *op. cit.,* II, p. 348.
101 *Ibid.,* p. 389 f.

102 *Ibid.,* p. 392.
103 *Ibid.,* p. 391 f.

Zapelena from Eph 4:4 ff. is a matter for biblical exegetes to decide.

Other theologians reason differently in this question (probably because they orient themselves, as a result of direct experience, toward the "phenomenon" of separated Christians). In general, they are working with the notion of "levels," which are distinguished one from the other something like this:

1. To the first and lowest level of the Church belong *all members of the human family* because, in His Incarnation, the Son of God assumed human nature, and an essential bond was thereby cemented between Christ and all humanity. Hence one could refer in a certain way to the whole of humanity as the "Church."

2. The second level is built upon the first, adding to it the *bond to Christ in grace and love,* i.e., the grace of justification. This level rests upon doctrine developed above concerning the possibility of receiving grace and attaining eternal salvation even outside the visible Catholic Church.

3. On the third level we come to the visibility of the Christian community. On this level belong *all who profess the true faith, partake of the sacraments, and are united in obedience to the papal authority.* At this level the *sinner* also belongs to the Church.

4. The fourth level further adds the *true life of grace within* the Church community.

And corresponding to these levels there are various gradations of membership. An analogy is taken from Thomas Aquinas who maintains that Christ is the Head of all men, but by degrees. Above all, He is the Head of those who are united with Him in eternal glory; second, He is Head of those united to Him *in actu* by love; third, of those united to Him by faith; and, fourth, of those potentially (*in potentia*) joined to Himself.[104] The analogy then takes the following form:

1. Whoever is baptized, professes the true faith and is not excommunicated is visibly and actually (*in actu*) a member of the Mystical Body.

2. Whoever is wanting in one of these three visible elements is visibly and potentially a member of this Body.

3. Whoever is wanting in all three visible elements, but who is

---

[104] *Summa Theologiae,* III, q. 8, a. 3.

invisibly ordered to this Body through an unconscious longing and desire, is invisibly and potentially a member of this Body.[105]

Johannes Beumer, S.J., has subjected this "multilayered notion of the Church" to a critical analysis.[106] He found himself forced to admit that this notion of the Church has the following advantage: "The particular facts in question (unity of men through the Incarnation of the Son of God, accessibility of salvation even to those outside the visible Church, preeminence of sanctity in the community as a whole) *cannot be challenged on theological grounds.*"[107] And it provides, he points out, the further advantage that a new aspect of the Church comes into view from the juxtaposition and connection of the various factors involved, all of which could eventually lead to an answer to pressing ecclesiological questions of our day. "It seems, to mention only one example, that a reversion to the multiplicity of levels is unavoidable if we are to come to a definition of Church membership."[108]

Beumer's principal concern is with a "certain lack of conformity to tradition" pervading this multilayered notion of the Church. "We can and must admit that no objection may be made to the particular facts which make up the notion of a layered Church, but the overall approach results in a picture of the Church which is, as such, new and unfamiliar to say the least."[109] On the other hand, there is the possible danger of an abstract construction which may be exciting and felicitous in itself, but perhaps inadequate to theological expectations and needs. Above all, Father Beumer sees in this notion of the Church the danger of making us forget the visible Catholic Church.

I am not so sure that this multilayered notion of the Church, for all the surprising novelty of its terminology, is so weak in tradition as Father Beumer assumes. There is, for example, St. Augustine, who says, "He knows His own. For His incalculable providence there are many within who appear to be without, and many without who appear to be within. Those who are, as it were, *within in a hidden way,*[110] form the closed garden, the sealed well of which the Scriptures speak. They also partake of His inexhaustible Love in this world, and of eternal life in the next."[111] And of course proponents

105 Cf. C. Lialine, *op. cit.*, p. 44.   109 *Ibid.*, p. 96.
106 Cf. J. Beumer, *loc. cit.*   110 Our emphasis.
107 Our emphasis.   111 *De baptismo contra Donatistas*, V, 27.
108 Beumer, *loc. cit.*, p. 96.

of the idea of a multilayered Church take ready recourse to the teaching of St. Thomas mentioned above.

It may well be that, with this "new" notion of the Church, much must be thought through and formulated more carefully. I personally consider the version of the Canonist Mörsdorf[112] of Munich as the best up to the present time (it demonstrates clearly that a distinction of various layers, or of concentric circles, does not contradict the encyclical *Mystici Corporis*).[113]

Mörsdorf bases his notion upon the definition of membership in Canon 87 of the Code of Canon Law, which reads as follows: *"Baptismate homo constituitur in Ecclesia Christi persona cum omnibus Christianorum juribus et officiis, nisi, ad jura quod attinet, obstet obex, ecclesiasticae communionis vinculum impediens, vel lata ab Ecclesia censura."* With the jurisprudential term *persona* (meaning *membrum*), the Codex describes two orders: the order of *being* in which the person stands either actively or passively in its juridical power, and the order of *function,* which is built upon the order of being and in which the person occupies itself according to its active or passive power. On the premise of these two orders Mörsdorf proceeds to various levels of membership, which are either constitutional (of being) in nature or pertain to function. The determining factor for constitutional membership is baptism. A person does not come into the Church through his own deed, but through a "birth from above." Because of the indelible character of baptism this constitutional membership is irremovable and hence cannot be lost. Mörsdorf sees this constitutional indelible membership delineated in the encyclical where the Pope refers to the sacramental rebirth of the children of the Church through baptism, and where he speaks of the separated members not as strangers, but as sons who should return to their own parental home.[114] Thus heretics and schismatics belong to the Church in virtue of this constitutional membership.

Then Mörsdorf speaks of a functional membership in the inner sphere and in the outer sphere. In the functional order the Church community strives, in taking up the salutary provisions afforded it by God, to bring about the Kingdom of God on earth. When the

---

[112] Klaus Mörsdorf, *loc. cit.,* p. 116 f.
[113] Sartory, *The Ecumenical Movement . . . ,* p. 137 ff.
[114] Mörsdorf, *op. cit.,* p. 130.

functional membership is realized in the inner sphere, it remains secret, invisible. But when it is realized in the outer sphere, it is officially known and effects the well-being of the community as such. Mörsdorf now points out that there is a sphere which is *most interior*, "the sphere of the invisible working of the Spirit of God which is consequently the most interior principle of the unity of the Church. It is before this forum of the Spirit of God that is finally decided whether a constitutional member of the Church is to be considered functionally active or passive."[115] It is thoroughly conceivable that a member function at once passively in the outer sphere and actively in the inner, and vice versa. According to Mörsdorf, active members are those who are in unimpaired possession of their essential rights of membership. With passive members there has been a fundamental curtailment of general membership rights, but even passive members do not cease to be constitutional members of the Church.

As to the encyclical *Mystici Corporis,* Mörsdorf finds that "the notion and definition of membership as used in this papal document refer to functionally active membership, and first and foremost to that of the outer sphere." The *reapse* of the encyclical looks to the area of functional membership. It embraces the fullness of membership, leaving room for a membership which may stand only in its initial stages, limited, partly or even fully invisible, abnormal, but nevertheless genuine.[116]

Thus, in summing up, we can say that the heretic, the schismatic, the apostate, and the excommunicated belong, or do not belong, to the Church depending upon the sphere from which one examines the specific case. It is necessary, when defining membership, to bear in mind that there is, besides the visibility of the Church, an invisible aspect of the Church to take into consideration, and that beside the external juridical structure of the Church there is the reality of grace which pervades the whole. We have seen that *Mystici Corporis* also recognizes, besides legal bonds, other principles of unity consisting in the theological virtues. It is fundamental to refrain from separating these two aspects except for purposes of analysis, and above all to shun all tendencies to make either aspect into an absolute.

---

[115] *Ibid.,* p. 128.
[116] Cf. M. Nothomb, *loc. cit.,* p. 242.

In applying these considerations to our separated brethren, we must pay extremely close attention to the following matters:

1. They profess trinitarian belief (Lutheran confessional literature, for example, contains the ancient Christian symbols; one may say, with respect to the Orthodox Christians, that they have no universal formal doctrine differing from the belief of the Roman Catholic Church).[117]

2. They participate in sacramental life (the Orthodox Churches in all seven sacraments; the Lutherans in the sacraments of baptism and matrimony).

3. Some religious communities have preserved apostolic succession (the Orthodox Churches certainly, and with the Swedish Lutherans the matter is as yet undetermined; thus the Orthodox Christians celebrate the Eucharist validly, and their priests appear, "from the tacit consent of the popes,"[118] to possess true jurisdiction with respect to absolution of sinners in the sacrament of penance, and not merely in cases of imminent danger of death).

4. Not a few non-Catholics are indisputably really faithful and pious persons. What of this faithfulness and piety in the question of membership? The answer given here by Bishop Marius Besson is daring to be sure, but nonetheless true: "By the grace which works within them they are nearer to God — and to us — than are Catholics in the state of mortal sin. And in this sense a faithful and pious Protestant or Orthodox Christian belongs more profoundly to the Church than a freethinking Catholic living on the edge of his religion. Augustine goes so far as to say that 'those who live in error not through any fault of their own, but because of their parents and rearing and who are ready to identify themselves with the truth if they can discover it, cannot be counted among the heretics' (Epist. XLIII, I)."[119]

Catholic teaching attempts to cope with these matters by speaking of an orientation to the Church through a *votum* or desire. In any case the question arises, posed with the utmost reticence indeed,

---

[117] Cf. M. Garriloff, "Gibt es echte dogmatische Unterschiede zwischen der katholischen Kirche und der Orthodoxie?" *Una Sancta*, 9 (1954), no. 2, pp. 26–32.

[118] Zapelena, *op. cit.*, p. 390.

[119] Marius Besson, "Le Mystère de l'unité," *Discours et lettres pastorales*, Fribourg, pp. 122–130.

as to whether this *votum* doctrine does not perhaps place baptized and unbaptized non-Catholics all too definitively on the same level.[120] Must we not take extreme care, when applying the doctrine of the desire to our separated brethren, to avoid taking their baptismal status all too lightly?

In any case it is of fundamental importance that we refrain from relativizing absolute realities and neglecting necessary distinctions. A genuine "Catholic" ecclesiology will encounter great challenges in this area.

V. VESTIGIA ECCLESIAE

Thus far we have spoken of individual non-Catholic Christians. And the question of evaluating their communities has forced itself upon us in the process. For Christians separated from one another live in fact in confessional groups or communities, and their personal belief is determined by the profession of faith and sacramental reality of these confessions. The Church's teaching concerning the desire or *votum* applies mainly to the subjective stand of the individual. But we must inquire more deeply into the *objective* values which characterize the faith of the individual and of the community to which he belongs. The New Testament does not permit us to speak of "Churches." But we must ask whether some *traces* of the one true Church, *vestigia Ecclesiae* as they are called, are not to be found in these separated Christian communities.[121]

What are *vestigia Ecclesiae*? Thils defines them as "certain authentic Christian values which are proper to the Church and which are encountered in non-Roman Churches or confessions because of the structure of these communities."[122] These *vestigia Ecclesiae* are not just some optional treasures of the Christian religion, but

---

[120] See how Zapelena in one breath speaks of "pagani et christiani," *op. cit.*, p. 362.

[121] On this question cf. the following: Congar, *Chrétiens désunis*, Chap. 7, Appendix VI; the same author's "A propos des 'vestigia Ecclesiae,'" *Vers l'unité chrétienne*, Nr. 39 (January, 1952); J.-C. Dumont, O.P., "Vestigia Ecclesiae," *Vers l'unité chrétienne*, Nr. 32 (April, 1951); Jerome Hamer, O.P., "Le Bapteme et l'Eglise. A propos des 'Vestigia Ecclesiae,'" *Irénikon*, 25 (1952), nr. 2.; Thomas Sartory, O.S.B., *The Ecumenical Movement and the Unity of the Church, ch.* "Vestigia Ecclesiae"; Gustave Thils, *Histoire doctrinale du mouvement oecuménique* (Louvain, 1955), ch. "Les Vestigia Ecclesiae," pp. 183–197.

[122] Thils, *op. cit.*, p. 187.

more specifically legacies of *ecclesiastical* nature. We can speak of invisible elements of the Church — such as the presence of the Holy Spirit — and of visible elements — such as uninterrupted apostolic succession. We could distinguish further between essential and accidental elements. Essential elements can never be lacking to the true Church, and she must possess them all, and possess them absolutely. The accidental elements are the manners and ways in which the individual essential elements are actually realized. In this latter area, the stamp of history may come forth in infinite possibilities of shading and variation. And this means the possibility of development and progress, of decadence and regression.[123]

Even though entire Christian communities stand separated from the Church, they nevertheless preserve in various proportions and degrees something of those realities which properly belong to the Church.[124]

Let us take, for example, the means of grace which, by their objective presence, cause the Church to be an institution. These means of grace are many, and are to be found whole and entire, all together, only in the Church of Christ and the Apostles. But one or another part can be severed from this totality. And it can be present as a holdover in a separated community, fulfilling the same function as in the true Church: effecting and communicating grace. Thus, for example, with the Orthodox Churches, the Utrecht Jansenists and the Old Catholics — all outside of the true center of Christianity — there is a priesthood, by reason of apostolic succession, which guarantees the validity of the Eucharist. And so we may conclude that although all non-Catholic Christian confessions not acknowledging the supremacy of the Pope are by definition outside the Catholic Church, they can share "in various degrees in those elements, some being visible and some purely spiritual in nature, which constitute this community and make of it — and it alone — the Church of Christ."[125]

Thus there are *vestigia,* authentic Christian values, basic elements of the Church in non-Catholic Christian communities. What, we ask with Thils, of the case of a return?[126]

---

[123] Cf. J.-C. Dumont, O.P., *Les voies de l'unité chrétienne. Doctrine et spiritualité.* Collectio Unam Sanctam 26 (Paris, 1954), p. 70.

[124] J.-C. Dumont, "Vestigia Ecclesiae," *op. cit.*

[125] Dumont, *Les voies . . . ,* p. 127.

[126] Thils, *op. cit.,* p. 193.

Catholic theologians are in agreement on two points. Separated communities are in possession of Christian values and sometimes even of fundamental elements of the Church. But this possession would never constitute in any case a substantial or essential addition to the Church should it "come home,"[127] for otherwise we should have to suppose that the Church might have ceased to exist *quoad substantiam,* which would contradict Christ's promises (e.g., Mt 16:18 ff.). Many theologians say that such a return would constitute an "actualizing of the universality of the Church, which in this case had always been potentially present in her."[128] A profound theological examination of these matters would prove very fruitful. Our view of the ecclesiological realities that exist in non-Roman Christian communities is in need of review. The Catholic Church undoubtedly realizes the true Church of Christ in her essential elements, but not fully and universally in the same way. All the other Christian communities show essential shortcomings, but have often proved themselves effective in realizing to the full those elements which they find in their possession.

We might conclude from this view of things that the question of reunion can be considered not only from the standpoint of individual conversions, but also as a question of reinstating these elements of the Church as members again of the one Church, as sharing parts of the fullness of the true Church.

An investigation of the *vestigia Ecclesiae* possessed particularly by separated Lutheran communities would probably throw the following into relief:

1. The Presence of Christ. This is an essential *vestigium Ecclesiae,* for where Christ is, there also is the Church. Though we must deny them the real presence in the Eucharist, there remains nevertheless Christ's presence by faith and grace (Eph 3:17).

With respect to the *real presence,* Hans Asmussen directed this serious query to Catholic Christians:

"What do you say of our sacrament of the altar? You could say that a Lutheran clergyman is in no way authorized to consummate the sacrament of the Eucharist. We Protestants must try to

---

[127] Cf. the instruction of the Holy Office, *De motione oecumenica,* of December 20, 1949.

[128] Cf. Tyszkiewicz in *Unitas* (1948), p. 102; P. Llamera in XII *Semana española de teologia,* p. 320; C. Colombo, "E Possible la riunione dei cristiani?" *La scuola cattolica* (1949), p. 302.

understand you in that. And who would hesitate to discuss this matter seriously with a Catholic? I can imagine no Lutheran pastor who would not be seriously troubled by Catholic interrogation on this point. In any case, it troubles me. But that does not exhaust the matter. I want to state the question even more pointedly. Just what do you Catholics and the Catholic Church want with respect to our divine services? Do you wish that as few as possible participate in it, or as many as possible? For if it is no sacrament at all, for what purpose should the people receive it? I formulate it in this way so as to show that in every possible answer the emotional factor contradicts the rational. I wish to cite here one of the greatest living Catholic theologians, who gave me in all seriousness the following answer: 'The Lutheran sacrament of the altar is *not nothing.*' I think, in the face of the past 400 years, that this modest statement, which was given honestly, is a happy response. And what we need is for you to make your judgment so clear that it takes hold of us. If we simply repeat the formulae of earlier epochs, formulae which miss their mark and pass us by, what have we accomplished? It is my suggestion that the Catholic Church is in a new ascendancy only because the number of those is growing for whom this question has come to be one of real significance."[129]

This is in truth an extremely serious and important question, and I must confess that our traditional theology lacks the categories required to answer it validly. We may continue to say that there is no *sacramentum* here, but we must nevertheless admit that there is an orientation by desire (*in voto*) to the *res* of the sacrament (and with the Eucharist it is union with the Mystical Body of Christ) and that this can surely be received before reception of the sacrament itself, namely through the desire to receive the sacrament itself. Aquinas maintains that the reception of the Eucharist is essential to the perfection of the spiritual life. "Nevertheless it is not necessary that one receive it physically; it suffices to have it by desire, much as one possesses one's end by longing and intention."[130]

Can we conclude from this that the dissenting Christians partake of the *res* of this sacrament when they celebrate the Lord's supper,

---

[129] Hans Asmussen, "Fünf Fragen an die Katholische Kirche," *Una Sancta*, 11 (1956), pp. 127–130.
[130] *Summa Theologiae*, III, q. 73, a. 3.

because they stand as constitutional sharers of an essential orientation to the Eucharist? However that may be, Catholic theology must face the task of coming to a more detailed understanding of the expression, "The Lutheran sacramental communion is *not nothing.*"

2. The Working of the Holy Spirit. The Holy Spirit is present in the Church in the infallible teaching office, in the sacraments, in juridical reality,[131] and in the various charisms. Let us single out the last for consideration. According to *Mystici Corporis* these charismatic gifts are essential properties of the Church.[132] Though we must refuse to acknowledge the total presence of the Holy Spirit in separated Christian communities, we can nevertheless not deny that they have charismatic graces in the way indicated by Pius XII.[133] Is this not an example of a true *vestigium Ecclesiae?*

As regards the true teaching office in the Church, we cannot say that it is to be found at all in separated communities. Just how far will we go in our understanding of the universal priesthood? And what is the significance of prophecy in the Church? It seems likely that there may be a noninstitutional office of prophecy in the Church, much as Paul received the Gospel "not through the mediation of men, but through the direct revelation of Jesus Christ" (Gal 1:12). Catholic ecclesiology has the task of working out, beside the institutional and juridical aspects of the Office, its singularly prophetic aspects more thoroughly, as is generally attempted anyway. Must not a genuine ecclesiology incorporate the sovereign discretion of the Holy Spirit into its view of the Church? Otherwise it could one day happen that "with the faithful around Peter," we could be scandalized "that the Holy Spirit should also pour His gifts upon heathen" (and before they were baptized at all) (cf. Acts 10:45 f.).

3. Baptism. In this essay we have referred often to baptism as an "ecumenical sacrament." There is no baptism outside the Church. Where a person is baptized, the Church is there sharing in the baptismal act itself. This is particularly evident with the

---

[131] Cf. H. Volk, "Das Wirken des Hl. Geistes in den Glaübigen," *Catholica,* 9 (1952), pp. 13–34.

[132] Cf. Cattin-Conus-Rohrbasser, *op. cit.,* n. 767, p. 476.

[133] Cf. Albrecht Volkmann, "Evangelisch-katholische Gedanken zur Frage der Successio Apostolica. Über das Problem der Kontinuität und Legitimität der exousia des Amtes," *Una Sancta,* 10 (1955), n. 1, pp. 42–54.

baptism of an infant, where the Church, acting in the place of the minor child, professes belief on behalf of the child.[134] Even though in necessity any person can legitimately perform the rites of baptism, the community in question is represented by its officeholder. Hence the significant words of Bishop Döpfner: "Let us not forget that in God's plan, by the holy legacy which they took with them, these communities carry out the task of the Church for many persons."[135]

4. The Word of God. Where the Word of God is rightly communicated, it becomes, by virtue of its intrinsic dynamism, a structural part of the Church. God has entrusted His Word to His Church. "The effective proclamation of the Word possesses power to form and preserve the community; such proclamation is an essential element in the structure of the visible Church."[136] But what Protestantism has done with the Word of God! How right is the Evangelical theologian O. Dilschneider when he says that as a result of an idealistic enervating of the Word which takes of it only a spiritual extract, "the spiritual forces which the biblical Word contains have dwindled away."[137] "The substance of Christ in Evangelical Christianity lacks, as far as preaching is concerned, indispensable elements, so that the development of sound faith and community life in the sense found in the New Testament is severely inhibited."[138]

The Christ-substance is impoverished.[139] And for this reason, as far as our separated brethren are concerned, we can speak only of *vestigia Ecclesiae,* only of a partial reality of the Church of Christ.

VI. The Question of the Being of the Church

When making a diagnosis, a doctor not only considers the symptoms of the disease in question, but looks also for a way of healing it. A diagnosis of our divided Christianity must reach deeper than

---

[134] J. Hamer, "Le baptême et la foi," *Irénikon*, 23 (1950), pp. 387–405.

[135] Bishop Julius Döpfner, "Apostolat im Geiste Christi," *Una Sancta,* 11 (1956), p. 51.

[136] E. Eichmann-K. Mörsdorf, *Kirchenrecht* (Paderborn, 1953), Vol. I, p. 23.

[137] Otto A. Dilschneider, *Gegenwart Christi* (Gütersloh, 1947), Vol. II, p. 257.

[138] Max Lachmann, *Zur reformatorischen Rechtfertigungslehre* (Stuttgart, 1953), p. 79.

[139] Cf. T. Sartory, *The Ecumenical Movement . . .* , pp. 147–194.

the fact of a different interpretation of New Testament Revelation. A different interpretation and the correction of theological axioms would not cure the essential illness. In a discussion concerning ecclesiastical office between Catholic and Evangelical theologians, the Protestants asked, after hearing a presentation of the Catholic doctrine, "What can we do to bring our office into order?" A Catholic answered, "One can bring the administration of an office into order, but not the office itself. For one either has the office entire, or one has it not." Evangelical Christians do not find this answer easy to comprehend, because it presupposes the question of ontological categories.

What stands between the Catholic Church and those Christian communities separated from her remains, in the last analysis, an ontological question, a question of being.

Leslie Newbigin, bishop of the Church of South India, whom we have already quoted in other connections, once made the remarkable statement that communities suffer a *loss of being* when they separate from the Church. Referring to Luther and the reformers, he says that because of obstacles resulting from sin a break in continuity was unavoidable if the truth of the Gospel was to be preserved. But once the break has occurred and a new structure is raised based upon the particular doctrine of the Reformers or the particular spiritual experience of a group, then something *essential is lost from the true being of the Church.* The body which ensues is necessarily subject to the spiritual caliber of the founders.[140]

The Evangelical Christians should hear more from us about this being and its loss.

In any case we come here to the enormous problem of how we can make this notion of being clear to Protestants. This seems to be all the more difficult in our day when certain Protestant theological currents tend toward a theological personalism which has a predilection for such terms as subjectivity, relation, actuality, etc. What is proposed as transcending subjective, relational, or active values is categorically rejected as unbiblical by any number of Evangelical theologians. And anyone who is even relatively familiar with Luther will know that these theologians cannot turn to him. For his concrete personalism "presupposed the ontology of the

---

140 L. Newbigin, *op. cit.,* p. 74.

ancient Church, particularly its Trinitarian and Christological dogmas."[141] Gloege has subjected the theological personalism of modern Protestant theology to sharp criticism. "There can and must be no 'pure,' 'efficacious,' 'abstract' personalism."[142] Regarding the Church, Gloege says — and this sentence may be revolutionary in the Protestant conception of the Church — "We live as a Church which is not only an 'event,' but which also has an 'institution' — we live as a visible and as a concurrently invisible reality."[143] This is the criticism directed to Schlink when he speaks of an "is" in the statement quoted above.[144] Gloege shows as well how biblical this talk of "being" is with references to both the Old and the New Testament and asks — to give an example — "What is the ontological significance of John's speaking not only in the categories of 'becoming,' but also in those of 'being'? that the Word 'became' Flesh? (1:14.) that Grace and Truth 'became' (or came forth, appeared)? (1:17.) What of the 'exegete' who interprets as personal and actual what is designated in Scripture as 'being' in the bosom of the Father? What is he to say when Christ describes Himself by means of the self-predication I am (*ego eimi*)? What is the meaning of: 'Before Abraham came to be, I am' (8:58), with its paradoxical juxtaposition of 'becoming' and 'being'?"[145]

And looking to the relationship of Christ to the Church, we ask what it means ontologically when Christ says of Himself, "I am the true vine, and it is my Father who tends it. The branch that yields no fruit in me, he cuts away . . . you have only to live on in me, and I will live on in you. The branch that does not live on in the vine can yield no fruit of itself; no more can you, if you do not live on in me" (Jn 15:1 f.).

Even the few references cited here show that one can come up against ontological terms and notions in Holy Scripture, and need not look to Roman theological tradition for such categories.

This brings us to a new, weighty problem which is causing untold theological controversy today. It is the question of the pre-

[141] Gerhard Gloege, "Der theologische Personalismus als dogmatisches Problem. Kerygma und Dogma," *Zeitschrift für theologische Forschung und kirchliche Lehre,* 1 (1955), p. 39.

[142] *Ibid.,* p. 41.

[143] *Ibid.*

[144] Schlink, *loc. cit.,* pp. 208–225.

[145] Gloege, *op. cit.,* p. 36.

suppositions to reading Holy Scripture, and it places us face to face with the very question of theology and its method. I think two works are extremely significant here, namely, *Teologiens metod-fråga*[146] by Professor Gustaf Wingren of Lund, and *Ceçi est mon Corps. Explication de ces mots de Jésus Christ*[147] by F.-J. Leenhardt. Wingren attempts to criticize contemporary theologians (Nygren, Bultmann, and Barth) on the grounds of their method and presuppositions. Confronting their theology with the New Testament, he finds that they fall short of extracting the full content from the revealed Word. Their methodical presuppositions hinder them from understanding the biblical text as it understands itself. In the name of faith — for theology is for Wingren a science so bound up with faith that it must take the assertions of faith as seriously as the most serious believer — he withdraws from Nygren, Barth, and Bultmann. He accuses Bultmann of having read the New Testament with an eclecticism conditioned by prebiblical criteria, and that he furthermore misinterprets the New Testament completely as a result of a faulty notion of the "Law." The attack against Karl Barth is similar; the latter's theological method leads him astray. And against Nygren, Wingren claims that he proceeds without reservations from the theories of knowledge of Kant and Schleiermacher, and works the truth right out of religion.[148]

With what does Wingren counter these interpretations of Bultmann, Barth, and Nygren? Nothing more, in fact, than his own notion of the New Testament. His confrontation of the Barthian conception with the Bible is in reality a confrontation with that of his critic. For Wingren cannot escape, any more than those he criticizes, "conceiving" in some specific sense the New Testament with which all are working. This brings the whole Protestant dilemma before our eyes. For in the end it proves to be a comparison not of conception with text, but of conception with conception. A Catholic critic of Wingren's book made these valuable observations: "Upon what does Wingren's system rest? With what does he demonstrate his claim to the only justifiable interpretation? Where is the criterion which determines Barth's position to the unbiblical, and his own to be right? Is there any approach to the New Testament

---

[146] Lund, 1954.
[147] Neuchatel-Paris, 1955.
[148] Wingren, *op. cit.*, p. 32.

at all which can prove itself, in the face of the naked word of Scripture, to be the only adequate interpretation? Is not every reading of a text in fact an uncovering, a definition of its content? But then the words interpreted and explained by a living man contain something more than the 'naked' words, and the words taken in themselves can neither justify nor limit this 'more.' "

Out of this controversy which is carried on within the framework of one school of theology (both Nygren and Wingren are professors in the University of Lund) emerges the problems of epistemological presuppositions, a problem which can be posed, and is posed, in all serious theology.

Now does not "epistemological presuppositions" mean the question of the *philosophy* with which any and every theology must, willy-nilly, approach the assertions of Revelation? Philosophy in theology is a horror for most Protestant theologians. But it is my opinion that some philosophy which *serves* theology in an ancillary capacity is a *sine qua non*. Moreover, we must admit that Protestantism has always been influenced by certain philosophies. Nominalism, Kant, Schleiermacher, Hegel, Kierkegaard, and Heidegger come immediately to mind.[149]

Let us consider here the example of the book of Professor Leenhardt[150] mentioned above. At first this work seems to contain some very "Catholic" statements. Its author uses, for example, such terms as "transubstantiation,"[151] "the Lord's Supper as sacrifice,"[152] "efficacy of ritual,"[153] "opus operatum,"[154] "objective character of the Church,"[155] etc. Nevertheless I believe that the criticism to which this book was subjected by French Dominicans[156] was apt and to the point. For it is a question of the sense or meaning Leenhardt gives to these expressions. Again, it is a question of the "being," or of the meaning of reality and facts. For Leenhardt, the reality of things does not lie in the things themselves; it does not lie in that which is presented to our senses. He is of the opinion that the essence of any reality consists in the divine intention, and that

---

[149] One of the most important "ecumenical" works that must be written would be an all-embracing and critical description of the influence of philosophical systems on Protestant theology.

[150] See note 145.
[151] Leenhardt, *op. cit.*, p. 34.
[152] *Op. cit.*, pp. 47–48.
[153] *Ibid.*, p. 53.
[154] *Ibid.*, p. 55.
[155] *Ibid.*, p. 59.
[156] "Un debat sur l'Eucharistie," *Istina* (1956), n. 2, pp. 210–240.

faith alone is capable of grasping what things are in the will of God. ("The essence of things is . . . in the will of God, which holds them in being."[157]) The *raison d'être* of things would appear, therefore, to lie in the divine intention which realizes itself in them. The *raison d'être* of the bread in the Eucharist, for example, would appear to lie not so much in the sustenance of the body as in Jesus' wish to extend His presence in this bread.

The criticism takes its departure at this point. For if reality lies exclusively in the *raison d'être* stemming from the divine intention, and is changed by the will of God, as Leenhardt claims for the Eucharistic bread, then nothing is changed in the thing itself, in this case in the bread. "Nothing changes in the bread. This means that only the role attributed to the bread, its *raison d'être,* its function in the divine plan is changed." This is the axiom which forms the keynote of Leenhardt's proposition.[158] It is true, of course, that such an "extrinsicist" interpretation of transubstantiation is imbued with nominalism of the purest sort.

Thus we are confronted here with a philosophy which places the reality of things outside the things themselves, locating it in the will of God. That alone counts which is "willed" by God. This voluntarism makes clear how utterly Leenhardt divests "Catholic" terms (transubstantiation, etc.) of their capacity for communicating reality (it follows with perfect logic that for him the sacramental "sign" plays no important part in things).

The *fundamental issue* around which the entire ecumenical dialogue seems to be turning is, in my estimation, nowhere better described than in these words of a French Dominican critic:

"Protestants generally take pleasure in denouncing the water of philosophy with which Catholics are accused of diluting the wine of Holy Scripture, the implication being that they had preserved their wine pure and undefiled. But they deceive themselves. For all of us, both they and we, we and they, have a philosophy. And philosophy, even though it be the most sublime and most complete, can become most dangerous and most corrupt, when one knows not what it is, and when one does not even know that one has it. Only too frequently, I fear, Protestantism betrays nominalistic or idealistic presuppositions. Is not Karl Barth, who supposes him-

---

[157] Leenhardt, *op. cit.,* p. 33.
[158] "Un debat sur l'Eucharistie," p. 219.

self as so removed from the devices of philosophy, himself a clearly marked son of nineteenth-century idealism? The time has come for us to analyze more in detail the implicit philosophic structuring in the theologies of our reformed or Lutheran brothers. Surely such a study, seriously executed, would be to the good of all, both of them and of us. And could one not well wish that, for the sake of fresh and more fruitful collaboration, the ecumenical dialogue would look less to distinguishing the various systems of exegesis of the one side from those of the other, and more to defining the philosophies that lie at the root of all our religious notions and all our intellectual postures and orientations?"[159]

When one considers all the many problems and questions raised in this essay, one begins to realize the difficulty of an approach, not to speak of a reunion, between Christians divided in belief. In many points, we seem to stand only at the very beginning. But I would hasten to say that it is a beginning full of promises. For we are broaching the issues which first occasioned, and which today perpetuates the rift between us. We are looking straight into the real problem. Perhaps Aristotle's observation, formulated positively, is to the point here: "He alone grasps the solution who knows the problem."

And the interfaith dialogue means in any case an enrichment for Catholic theology, for it can thereby become all the more certainly what it ought truly to be, namely, a theology which is eminently and genuinely *Catholic*.

---

[159] *Ibid.*, p. 220.

EDWARD H. SCHILLEBEECKX, O.P.*

THE SACRAMENTS: AN ENCOUNTER WITH GOD

THE SACRAMENTAL PRINCIPLE OF REVELATION

IT MAY be true that Rudolf Bultmann's attempt to demythologize the Christian kerygma, that is, to abandon its objective character and interpret it existentially, is unacceptable. It is true, nonetheless, that traditional theology has not always brought out clearly enough the distinction between the mere physical presence (*Vorhandensein*) of the things of nature and the unique character of conscious human reality (*Dasein*) and human existence (*Existenz*). The personal call which the living God addresses to man in his human situation often seems endangered by a reduction of religious life to the impersonal level. And it was precisely in the theology of the sacraments that this kind of approach resulted in treating sacramental life too exclusively as an impersonal cause-effect relationship. This led to the idea that our reception of grace in the sacraments is mainly a passive affair.

Our aim in this present work is to throw some light on the essential sacramental character of the Church from the standpoint of *intersubjectivity* or *existential personal encounter*.[1] Religion, after all, is a dialogue between God and man. By his created powers man can reach God only through the medium of his creation as its First Cause. At the utmost, all man can do is arouse only a powerless longing for the person of the living God (in reality, the three Persons) and for the immediacy of an I-Thou relationship with

---

* Reprinted with the kind permission of Sheed & Ward, Inc., from *Christianity Divided*.

[1] This article gives the main themes of our book *Christus, sacrament van de Godsontmoeting*, translated as *Christ the Sacrament of the Encounter With God* (New York: Sheed and Ward, 1963).

him. But by reason of the gratuitous, saving initiative of the living God, the religious man finds himself in direct converse with his God. In this divine encounter or personal fellowship with God — called saving grace — consists *salvation*. This encounter is, from God's side, *revelation;* from man's side, his *religious response.*

Revelation and religion — or, in other words, the mutual encounter of man, created and situated in history, with the uncreated God — of their very nature create history and hence, in the widest sense of the word, are truly sacramental. We call sacramental every supernatural saving reality which presents itself in our lives historically. God directs what he plans for man through history, and he does it in such a way that his interventions can be recognized by men as divine. God's giving grace to man makes history by revealing itself, and it reveals itself by becoming history.

Precisely because the supernatural saving reality, veiled in historical events, and surrounded by the darkness of mystery, is present to us only in earthly form (*sacramentum*), it demands the revealing word (*verbum*) as the interior aspect of its earthly appearance. Only in and through the prophetic word is the divine dimension of saving history brought to light. "Word" and "sacrament" are therefore the fundamental constituents for revelation in the Old Testament as well as in the New and, after this revelation has been brought to an end, for the life of the Church which grows out of it.

Christianity as Personal Communion of Man With the Living God in Christ

Intersubjectivity or the dialogue structure of revelation (as "Word and sacrament") appears already in the Old Testament. Yahweh is the God of the Covenant. He personally intervenes in favor of the one determined people he himself has freely chosen out of the community of nations — Israel. He intervenes *personally,* not just as the Creator who by his power guides the historical course of all nations in creative transcendence, but as one who takes part in the vicissitudes of history and who stands on the side of Israel. The core of Israel's history, as it was interpreted through the prophetic word, is set forth over and over again in the Old Testament as: "I will be *your* God, you *my* people" (Lv 26:11–12; Jer 7:23; 11:4; 24:7; 31:33; Ez 11:20; 14:11; 37:27; Os 1:9; etc.).

The burden of all God's revelation in the Old Testament is exactly the course of history which results from the alternation between God's constant fidelity and the ever-recurring infidelity of his people. This revelation, then, is accomplished in a dialectical situation. Out of the dialogue struggle between God and his people, in fidelity and infidelity, the concrete content of revelation takes shape. In one way, of course, this arises from a decision of the living God which is completely and sovereignly free. But looked at from the viewpoint of history, this revelation remains the result of a dialogue of acts: between the invitation and proposal of love by God and the personal, loving response or refusal of love by God's people.

Through all the vicissitudes of this history God desires to lead his people in spite of everything to a final and definitive fidelity. This intention of God appears to be a failure — at least for the majority: The Jews reject their Messiah. The revelation which leads up to Christ, then, evolves in history as a dialogue in which God wrestles with human freedom in his desire to save mankind. It is an existential, two-way struggle between God who calls and man who resists — until this God who invites to a faithful love, himself personally responds as true man to this courtship, with a return of love whose fidelity knows no bounds — which does not shrink even from the death of the Cross.

In the man Jesus is realized the fidelity of the covenant in a twofold way. At last the dialogue which was ever breaking down finds a full and perfect human resonance. In a single person both elements are fulfilled: the invitation, and the reply of perfect fidelity, and in such a way that both the invitation and the response constitute the completed revelation of God.

The man Jesus is not only the one sent by the Holy Trinity, he is also the one called to be the representative of all humanity. He is not only the visible embodiment of God's wooing of man, but also the representation and highest fulfillment of the human response of love to God's courtship. Jesus, the free man, who in his humanity reveals to us the divine invitation of love, is at the same time, as man, the person who in the name of all of us and as our representative accepts this invitation. As head of redeemed humanity, he is in a sense the whole of mankind. That is why it is possible for his sacrifice to be at the same time our redemption. Only by uniting ourselves to the man Jesus does our own personal fidelity to the covenant become possible. Our personal communion with God can only take place, explicitly or implicitly, by an inter-personal relationship with the man Jesus.

Sacramental Encounter With God Through Encounter With the Man Jesus

The encounter of man with the invisible God through the medium of the visible embodiment of the love of that same God in a man we call a *sacramental encounter with God*. To be personally addressed by the man Jesus is for the believer personal encounter with God; for God himself, the eternal Logos, is *personally* this man. Whoever touches with faith the hem of Christ's garment is immediately healed. That is why the human interchange, the interpersonal relationship between Jesus and the men he encounters, is the sacrament of their encounter with God. It means grace and redemption for all who in living faith actually come face to face with the man Jesus.

Social intercourse between men, however, occurs through and in bodily forms. Spiritual influence on a fellow man requires bodily means of communication; it remains a human activity which must find its bodily expression. Jesus was a real man. He was the Son of God appearing in a truly human form, an incarnated human spirit. His contacts with other men required, as do every man's, bodily means of communication. Nevertheless, the encounter of Christ with his fellow men and his properly human activity remain a personal deed of the Son of God, although in human form. It is consequently a divine encounter with men in a truly human form. And as the activity of the Son of God, this encounter of Christ as man with men possesses divine saving power; it is the friendship of God himself for man, translated and transformed into the form of human encounter. Although this is true of every truly human activity of Christ, it is especially true of those human actions of Christ which are exclusively actions of God, although accomplished in a human manner, that is, his miracles and, more especially, redemption itself which finds its consummation in the sacrifice of the Cross.

But since the translation of God's encounter with man into an encounter between men includes bodily elements making it visible, this human encounter of Christ with his fellow men possesses not only *divine* saving power in a very general way (since it is a personal action of the Son of God) but divine saving power which is specifically *sacramental;* for the human actions of Jesus in their visibility and corporality are the human outward manifestations of the divine bestowal of grace. They are "signs and causes" of grace, and this in such fashion that the same reality which is externally visible (the sign) is the inner saving power itself in visible form: the concrete embodiment of the offering of grace.

That the human actions of Jesus have sacramental saving efficacy in themselves means, finally, that our "body-spirit" encounter with the man Jesus is the sacrament of our encounter with God. And because redemption through the man Jesus is achieved "once and for all," and in such a way that every communication of grace remains essentially bound up with this man, therefore, every bestowal of grace or encounter with God will come about in an encounter with this man Jesus. The intersubjective relationship of the believer with Christ, the primordial sacrament (*Ursakrament*), remains the basic event of the Christian religion as personal communion with the three divine persons.

Sacramental Encounter With Christ as the Full Development of Religious Encounter With God

In the appearance of the man Christ, the anonymity of the living God is removed. The man Jesus shows us the true face of the living God in such a way that the universal religious themes come to the fore only in Christ. For in fact God reveals himself not only interiorly through his mysterious appeal to our souls (the impulse of the Holy Spirit drawing us to belief); he has, as we have said, concretized his inner invitation to personal communion with him in saving history and (fully at last) in the human appearance of Christ in this world. God desired not only to be God for us, he wanted to be God for us in a *human* way. For the first time we can fully grasp what sanctifying grace means; how it reveals, on the one hand, God's boundless desire for a personal communion with us, for the man Jesus who longs to befriend us is precisely revelation of God. On the other hand, it also reveals how profoundly meant our human response to that divine love ought to be, for the man Jesus whose devoted, childlike intimacy with his Father remaining faithful even unto death is also a vicarious realization of our devotion, the highest realization of religious intimacy with the living God which man has ever undertaken.

The bodily manifestation of divine life through Christ's human soul, the Incarnation, also plays a decisive role in solving the mystery of God's anonymity in the world. That its sacramental character makes Christianity the perfect form of religious life can be elucidated from insights into the true nature of man.

The human body is not only the appearance and countenance of the human person who reveals himself, it is also that in which and by which the soul develops into a full-fledged person. To join both ideas together: in and through the body the soul externalizes its process of becoming a person. By going out into the world, the human person gains self-consciousness. It is only in incarnation, becoming-flesh, that personal activity is completed. Thus, embodiment serves as the sign, although a sign that also veils, of the most intimate personal activity.

The point here is that dynamic personality constitutes itself in and through an activity which externalizes itself also in bodily form. In the body the soul presents itself to another. "What we in encounter call body is that through which we situate ourselves, express ourselves, and make ourselves known; in short, the form of man's being-in-the-world. The person we encounter *has* this form, but he also *is* this form."[2] It is through the body and in the body that human encounter takes place. In virtue of this, human relationships of a spiritual nature, no matter how independent they are in themselves of bodily encounter, nevertheless do attain their high points in such an encounter because in it the spiritual interrelationship is made fully present.

Of course, we should by no means overlook the unique characteristic of the man Christ. He is truly God-man, divine in a human way and human in a divine way. Nonetheless, he is truly man. What we have said about the human dimension pertains also to Christ in his personal relations with his fellow men. For the apostles,

---

[2] F. J. J. Buytendijk, "Zur Phänomenologie der Begegnung" in *Eranos-Jahrbuch*, Vol. 19 (1950), p. 468. See also G. Gusdorf, *La découverte de soi* (Paris: Presses universitaires de France, 1948); L. Binswanger, *Grundformen und Erkenntnis menschlichen Daseins* (Zürich: M. Niehans, 1952); K. Rahner, "Personal and Sacramental Piety," *Theological Investigations* II (Baltimore, 1963), pp. 109–134.

the moments of their companionship with Christ in both soul *and* body were the decisive high points of their experience of Christ. The Last Supper is a typical example, or Jesus' glance to Peter after his denial, which was enough to move him to tears.

In such bodily-spiritual encounters Christ himself makes the gift of his presence an intensely vivid reality, while in those bodily encounters the disciples also experience their spiritual bond with Christ more deeply than ever. On both sides the bodily personal encounter is the point at which spiritual encounter culminates. And since the spiritual intervention of the man Jesus, the redeeming God, is an intervention in grace, this means that the sacramentalizing or the embodying of this gracious intervention is the culmination of Christ's will to bestow grace and bring salvation. Conversely, whoever in faith encounters the man Jesus and is offered his mercy in a visible and tangible form can achieve through this a fully developed religious attitude.

In the encounter with Christ the anonymity of man's experience of God is removed. In religions outside of Christianity man cannot normally reach to an experience of God except in a vague and often nameless way. It is only in the sacramental encounter with Christ that this experience of God can develop into a mature and fully personal religious worship. The full unfolding of religious life has, therefore, a sacramental basis: the primordial sacrament (*Ursakrament*), Christ Jesus.

Against this one could object: Christ himself has said that "the Spirit gives life and the flesh profits nothing" (Jn 6:63); or, better: "It is good for you that I go. . . . If I do not go, the Consoler will not come to you" (Jn 16:7). The corporal absence of Christ seems to be the very thing which ushers in the perfection of religious life.

It is true, of course, that Christ had to go where we cannot yet follow him. He rose and vanished out of our visible world of empirical experience. But it is not his invisibility as such that "is good for us," but his *glorification* out of death. For us, this necessarily involves his withdrawal because we have not yet been glorified ourselves. But this means precisely that the definitive, eternal, and unsurpassible fulfillment both of the Incarnation and of our religious life takes place there where we ourselves enjoy the privilege of being together with Christ in transfigured *bodily* form, after his return. From this very fact it is clear that our earthly Christian life and (since this life, as we will see, demands sacraments) our sacramental life must fundamentally be an eschatological advance toward the Parousia. What at first seemed an objection, in reality confirms our position; precisely since the fullness of religious worship can only be realized in the sacramental, bodily-spiritual encounter with Christ, therefore Christianity, as the life which elapses between Pasch and Parousia, is fundamentally eschatological. In the last analysis the saying of Tertullian proves true: *"Caro salutis est cardo."* (It is on the flesh that salvation hinges).[3]

The Sacraments of the Church as Human Encounter With the Glorified Kyrios (Lord)

Another objection may perhaps be raised: Must we who have never encountered Christ in the flesh and who have not yet been taken up in glory — must we manage to get along meanwhile without bodily encounter with Christ? Must our Christ encounter occur in a purely mystical fashion, in the purely spiritual contact of faith, as our Protestant brothers in the faith suppose? The first answer that suggests itself is: in a certain sense, yes; just as those of the Old Covenant and also the other non-Jewish and non-Christian religions had to and still have to get along without any bodily encounter with Christ, although all of these were and are already indebted to Christ for everything. This makes Catholic life fundamentally a life of *waiting:* "waiting for the blessed hope" (Ti 2:13). Our eschatological eagerness is a vigil, an advance toward a meeting, an encounter not yet complete. Christianity is the religion of *Maranatha:* "Come, Lord Jesus!" (Ap 22:20); "Thy Kingdom come!" (Mt 6:10; Lk 11:2.)

But this is only one aspect. This active expectation of the perfect encounter is not sustained merely through an encounter with Christ which is only spiritual, or achieved through a mystical act of faith; but it is sustained just as much through an encounter with the living *Kyrios* (Lord) which, though unique, is nevertheless real and quasi-bodily — this encounter takes place in the sacraments of the Church and through them. And this quasi-bodily or strictly sacramental encounter with Christ is for that very reason a pledge and anticipation of the eschatological and perfect encounter with Christ.

---

[3] Tertullian, *De carnis resurrectione,* 8; Migne, *Patrologia Latina (MPL)* 2, 806.

From behind the cloud of his glorification, behind which he with-draws from our still earthly eyes, the Lord in his visible Church reaches for earthly, unglorified elements which for that very reason are visible to us, elements as unpretentious as the child in the crib: a little bread and wine, oil and water, a warm, fatherly hand upon the forehead, in order to make his heavenly, saving act effectively present to us here and now. The Church's sacraments are, therefore, our quasi-bodily encounters with the transfigured man Jesus, a veiled contact with the Lord but, nonetheless, one which is con-cretely human in the full sense because both body and soul are in-volved. Therefore, based on the historical redemptive event of Christ who is himself the *Eschaton,* the sacramental encounter is a celebra-tion in mystery of the Parousia.

From this we see the "why" of the Church's sacraments. The man Jesus, the visible, fully human image of the redeeming God is, as we have said, the "once-for-all" sacramental sign in which the mystery of the divine redeeming love is visibly represented to us and through which the redeeming God introduces us into existential, personal communion with himself. Since the Ascension has with-drawn the man Jesus from the visible horizon of our lives, our encounter with the living Lord Christ, our perennial mediator, would take place purely mystically by faith if there were no sacra-ments. Irremediably one of the human dimensions of the Incarnation would in fact be lost for all of us who have never encountered Christ in his earthly life. But God has remained true to his pedagogy. With sympathetic consideration for the characteristic situation of the human person who, because of his bodily nature, lives in a world of men and things, and reaches spiritual maturity in them and through them, God ever offers us the kingdom of Heaven in earthly garb. Thus it was in the days of the covenant; thus it was at the *ephapax* (once and for all) (Heb 9:12) of the human appearance of the redeeming God; and this is what the divine padagogy requires now in the sacramental Church which is the earthly, visible instru-ment of salvation employed by the living, invisible *Kyrios.*

The divine plan of salvation is essentially a sacramental economy of salvation. It is true that the spiritual Christ can meet us and in-fluence our lives outside the sacramental visibility of the Church. Nonetheless, *by reason of his glorified body,* he can only make him-self *fully present for us and to us* (and thus exploit his grace-giving approach to the full) by using earthly, untransfigured elements as visible symbols, prolonging and manifesting his invisible, heavenly, saving act. The concrete presence of this heavenly saving activity of Christ demands that the *Kyrios* embody his invisible, saving efficacy in this earthly world by employing unglorified corporality which becomes an interior element of his heavenly, symbolic action. The sacramentalism of the Church bridges the disproportion between our untransfigured world and the Christ: the world, that is, which at one point, at its center, is already glorified.

In the context of the historical milieu in which we live, the sacraments are a visible expression of the celestial, present, saving action of Christ, the *Eschaton*. In the sacraments we encounter Christ, though he be bodily absent, in a tangible, bodily way. The Eucharist is for us the crowning point of this actual encounter with Christ.

Thus we see immediately that the so-called *sacramenta separata* (separated sacraments) are not things, but rather personal encounters with the glorified man Jesus and in him with the living God. We now wish to investigate, first, the objective structure of these sacraments, and then reflect on the religious spirit in which we personally should celebrate them.

THE SACRAMENTS OF THE CHURCH

Their Objective Form as Mysteries

The man Jesus himself is the primordial sacrament (*Ursakrament*). The redemption wrought through him is "once for all" and conclusive. The sacraments of the Church have no new and additional meaning; they merely bring us in their own way into living contact with the "perennial Christ," who through the power of the Holy Spirit remains the permanent mediator between the Father and men. The sacraments of the Church, consequently, rest on an essentially Christogical foundation: "For there is no other Sacrament of God but Christ."[4]

If the sacraments of the Church are only the points of contact on earth with Christ the primordial sacrament (*Ursakrament*), that means that they *sacramentalize* the redeeming work of Christ for us and in us here and now: "What was visible in Christ passed over

---

[4] "Non est enim aliud Dei Sacramentum nisi Christus." Augustine, *Ep.* 187, 34; *MPL* 38, 845.

into the sacraments of the Church."[5] The significance of the Christological dimension of the sacraments can be made clear only after we have explained their ecclesiological basis.

a. The Ecclesiological Dimension of the Sacraments

We have already said that in God's economy of salvation the man Jesus represents the whole human race. In the sense of being its origin, he himself, as head of the human race he has redeemed, is personally the Church. In the fullest sense of the word this means that in the sacrifice of the Cross of Jesus, the whole human race became "Church." "Christ died so that by His death might arise the Church."[6] Christ's sacrifice on the Cross has meaning as a real fact only if it is at the same time the sign of the sacrifice of all mankind; and it has this value as a representative sign effectively only to the extent that it is at the same time a real fact. In this respect the Church exists only in germ, that is, in the representative humanity of Jesus, sacrificed, yet glorified.

The earthly Church is the sign, present within the world, of this victorious and definitive redemption which introduces the *Eschaton.* When we spoke of the sacraments as that which makes present in the world in earthly garb the saving action of Christ in glory, we meant, first of all, the sacramental *Church* herself. She is the visible, historical representation in the world of the definitive redemption. Christianity is essentially a belief in earthly realities as the appearance in mystery of the supernatural realities of the redemption.

Accordingly, the Church as the institution of salvation is essentially sacrament and Word. Both form the specific area of endeavor for the hierarchical ministry. The norm for ministry, sacrament, and Word is, on the one hand, the *ephapax* (once-and-for-all character) of the historical appearance of Christ and of the apostolic, primitive tradition, and on the other hand the earthly form of the saving action of the glorified *Kyrios* through his Spirit. The whole visible Church is ruled by the glorified *Kyrios* who, through the mediation both of his Holy Spirit and of the apostolic ministry of his earthly Church, brings to completion in this world the building up of the

---

[5] "Quod conspicuum erat in Christo, transivit in Ecclesiae sacramenta." Leo the Great, *Sermo* 74, 2; *MPL* 54, 398.

[6] "Moritur Christus ut fiat Ecclesia . . . mortuo Christo." Augustine, *In Evangelium Joannis,* tr. 9, n. 10; *MPL* 35, 1463.

people of God. Christ *sends* the Holy Spirit (Jn 14:16, 26; 15:26) and he also *sends* his apostles (Jn 13:16, 20; 17:18).[7] Both of these sendings are organically connected with one another. Pentecost, the day on which the Church with her sacramental and kerygmatic activity stepped forth into the full light of day, is the mystery event of the manifestation of both these missions precisely in their conjointly acting unity, a unity which is vitalized from a single source of life, the *Kyrios* himself. What the visible Church does in the order of historical, external visibility, the Spirit sent by Christ does interiorly both in her authorized ministers and in the souls of the faithful. That is why the Church as the representation of the mystery of Christ can herself be called a primordial sacrament (*Ursakrament*) insofar as she is (1) *sacramentum humanitatis Christi* (sacrament of the humanity of Christ) or the sacramental Christ, and (2) the subject in which the seven sacraments, the specific ministerial actions of the sacramental Church, are found.

This means that the seven sacraments, even before they are this or that particular sacrament, are first of all and primarily the visible official action of the Church or, better, the action of Christ in heaven sacramentalized in the visible action of the Church. They are the activity of the *Church* from a sevenfold perspective. This is the reason why the power of orders and the power of jurisdiction are interwoven in every sacrament and why the validity of an action of the power of orders can be limited, altered, or nullified by the power of jurisdiction. The validity or authentic sacramentality of the seven sacraments, therefore, fundamentally depends on whether or not the sacrament in question is truly an action of the Church of Christ. The so-called "matter" and "form" point out two complementary ways of giving concrete form of the ecclesial character of this celebration in mystery, which being "sacrament" includes "sacramental Word" as an inner constituent because the supernatural dimension of the earthly event is only made fully present to us in the Word.

The primary aspect, which reveals itself in a variety of shadings, in the reception of each of the seven sacraments, is the setting up of living contact with the visible Church in the actions as Christ's

---

[7] On this point see Y. Congar, *Esquisses du Mystère de l'Église* (Paris, 1953[2]), pp. 129–179. (English trans.: *The Mystery of the Church* [Baltimore: Helicon Press, 1960].)

representative which are characteristic of her as the Church. It is precisely this visible contact with the Church through the reception of her sacraments in faith that *is* the encounter with Christ.

This already implies that the *main* lines of this economy of the seven sacraments were established by Christ when he founded the Church. The fullness of the gift of redemption is bound up, through Christ's founding of the Church, with the great external sign: the Church as the historical reality which renders the achieved redemption present. Thus, Christ's founding of his Church as primordial sacrament (*Ursakrament*) is basically also the institution of the seven sacraments. What the sacraments do is nothing more than make concretely present here and now what the Church herself is in her essence. True enough, Christ himself also said, implicitly or explicitly, that the sevenfold treasure of the grace of redemption should be shared in and through the visible activity of the Church. But apart from the fact that for a few sacraments he himself also determined the outer form of the visible action (e.g., washing with *water,* the sacrifice of *bread* and *wine*), he gave full scope to the Church to determine for herself the external symbolic form of her visible action which would be the outward sign of the sevenfold sacramental grace. But the fundamental and decisive factor, the joining of the sevenfold grace to a visible action of the Church — *that* comes directly from Christ. The *substantia sacramenti* (essential element of a sacrament) — that element in the external sign which cannot be changed by the Church[8] and hence was determined by Christ himself — signifies, simply, the sacramental meaning as expressed in external form, that is, the sacramentalizing of a sevenfold grace. (With regard to certain sacraments this can also involve the concrete determination of the external symbolic form.)

The fact that the sacramental meaning is expressed in an *action* of the Church implies, as we have said, that it has as an intimate constituent element the sacramental Word. It is this alone that makes fully present to us in a visible action the supernatural saving presence. Both together — the liturgical action joined to the sacramental Word of the Church, made one in the liturgy — are the elements which go to make up the external symbolic action of the Church and turn it into a sacrament where we meet Christ. The sacraments are,

8 Pius XII, "Constitutio Apostolica 'Sacramentum Ordinis,'" *Acta Apostolicae Sedis,* Vol. 40 (1948).

therefore, the specifically churchly actions which make visible on earth the fulfilled messianic activity of her high priest in heaven.

That there are *seven* sacraments derives, in the last analysis, exclusively from the saving will of Christ. But this number seven should be explained not so much anthropologically, through an analogy, with human life on a biological level, as ecclesiologically i.e., from the essence of the Church as the kingdom of God existing on earth in historical form. For the sevenfold sacramental grace is the grace of redemption which comes to us in visible form, in the seven dimensions presented us by the Church. The fundamental reality which takes on a special shading in each of the seven sacraments is the personal contact with the inner dynamism of the holy Church, which contact itself is the effective sign of our personal encounter with the glorified man Jesus and in him with the living God. The special symbolism of each sacrament's liturgical action, taken as a whole in which the Word elucidates the symbol, highlights that special aspect under which the one redeeming action of Christ reaches us in the Church through the various sacraments.

On this account it is the progressive realization of the kingdom of God in each individual person and in the human race as a whole which demands a sevenfold, sacramental saving activity of the Church.[9]

b. The Christological Content of the Sacraments of the Church

The necessity of the sacraments is based upon the fact that grace continues to be mediated through the man Jesus. Since Christ's Ascension, this further continuation demands, as we have seen, the introduction of the sacramental Church with her sacramental activity (*sacramenta separata*) in which this mediation of grace visibly enters into our earthly world. Therefore, even after the Ascension, the conferring of grace continues to be on the basis of intersubjectivity between us men and the man Jesus, which is the sacrament of our personal fellowship with God. Since the Ascension, the perfect form of this intersubjectivity with the man Jesus takes place only within the sacred domain of the Church of Christ. This proposes for us the problem of "presence in mystery" (*Mysteriengegenwart*).

---

[9] We cannot analyze further here the ecclesiological foundation of each sacrament in particular. On this point see K. Rahner, "Kirche und Sakramente," *Geist und Leben*, Vol. 28 (1955), pp. 434–453.

Without allowing ourselves to become involved in the numerous and various opinions concerning this theory which have grown out of the discussion of the work of Dom Odo Casel, nor in the problem of what exactly Casel meant to affirm, we present a solution which immediately suggests itself from the standpoint of a sound Christology.

To put it in terms of time: When God became man, the eternal Redeemer entered into time. Now time is irreversible. What has happened historically can, in no way, be made actual again, not even by God. As an historical incident it is irrevocably past. Since, therefore, Christ was *really* man, the sacrifice of the Cross as an historical event is also a reality that is past; and it cannot actually be made to be present again even "in mystery." Of course, it is true that an historical action of a human person, being a personal action, in a certain respect surpasses time because it is a *spiritual* act and it had a part in fashioning the person into what he now is. But this does not alter the fact that the historical element of that act as a human act belongs irrevocably to the past and as such it can no longer be made actually present, not even in a mysterious way. The past of the human acts of Jesus inescapably shares in this irreversibility of the time event, otherwise we fall into a kind of Docetism.

On the other hand, the historical human acts of Christ, who is personally God, are the *personal* acts of the second divine Person, even though performed through his humanity. Therefore, Jesus' sacrifice on the Cross, as a personal action of God, is an eternally present actuality which is imperishable. The sacrifice of the Cross, not in its historical form as human act, but as *this* kind of human act which proceeds from the *Son of God* who *personalizes* the *human* act of Jesus — this sacrifice of the Cross, in its inner nature a truly divine act of sacrifice (although performed in the humanity and therefore in time) is — as is everything which is divine — eternal, and not past. Redemption, therefore, if considered *exclusively* as an action of God (only God can redeem us), is, although achieved in this humanity, an eternally present divine act. The death on the Cross, then, itself possesses a "mystery" content which transcends time.

Since Jesus did not cease to be man after the Resurrection but remains man, we must also speak of the *permanence* or perennial character of the *Kyrios:* "Christ yesterday, today, and forever!" (Heb 13:8.) To be sure, the eternally present redemptive act has in itself a "changing" human mode of expression — a "movement" which we, of course, cannot measure by earthly time because it is the human act of a man who has risen and shares in the vision of God. There is a difference between the mode of expression in the historical sacrifice on the Cross and in the Christ in glory. The historical human mode of appearance of the inner act of sacrifice of the Son of God is forever past; but it remains in its mystery content as an action of God. It possesses an eternal contemporaneity in the now living Christ, in whom it becomes humanly incarnate in a new "heavenly" manner. Rooted in an act of God, the death on the Cross has, therefore, an eternally permanent content, a content which had us in view in the sacrificial death and which still presents itself to us now.

The man Jesus is in a glorified state and is for that reason (to us) invisible. We, on the other hand, find ourselves in an untransfigured earthly condition. Consequently, the eternally-present redemptive act of the sacrifice of the Cross indeed can have a direct influence on us, but it can no longer be made present to us "in Christ's own body." The eternally-present divine redemption consummated in human nature can be rendered present now, as has been shown, only through sacramental, earthly symbols, especially those of the Eucharist. From this it automatically follows that there is inescapably a "presence in mystery" in the seven sacraments — and in a very special way for the Eucharist.

The whole redeeming mystery of Christ, not in some way or other in its historical content, but as the act of God, becomes actively present in the sacrament, so that in these sacraments we are immediately encompassed by the redemptive efficacy of the "redeeming Incarnation." It thus becomes clear that the core of the sacramental efficacy is the eternally-present act of redemption of the Son of God; and that this is *identical* with both the mystery content of the saving action of the historical sacrifice of the Cross and with the mystery content of the saving activity of the living, glorified *Kyrios* and, finally, with the mystery of the saving power of the sacramental Church; although in all of this the *human* form given to the divine redeeming act of the man Jesus is different in each case. From this viewpoint the *ephapax* and the sufficiency of the historical event of redemption is shown to be in no way threatened or cancelled out by the sacraments of the Church; and it becomes

clear that to support this we do not have to call on the questionable
theory which says that a past, temporal event can be made somehow
actual again in our own time *in mysterio* or in some "mystical" way.

Yet for all this the sacraments are truly also a celebration in
mystery of the past *acta et passa Christi* (actions and sufferings of
Christ) and always contain a reference to the historical coming of
Christ. For on the Cross — and *only* there — at that historical moment, God offered for us his human life. Therefore, the eternally-
present redemptive act of God retains a reference to the past sacrifice
on the Cross. The eternally-present redemptive act of the Son of God
made man is actively made present in the sacraments precisely as
referring to the historical sacrifice of the Cross. That is why St.
Thomas says with all Tradition that the sacraments draw their saving
power from the death of Christ. We must maintain at the same time,
however, that it is the glorified Christ now living who gives to the
sacraments their saving efficacy. "It is Christ himself, who, through
his Church baptizes, teaches, rules, absolves, makes sacrifice."[10]

The sacraments as a medium between Christ and us should be
situated, then, not so much between the historically past sacrifice
of the Cross and our present situation in the twentieth century, as
between the now living, glorified Christ, the *Eschaton,* and our own
human world which is not yet transfigured and which strains toward
the *Eschaton.* In other words, we should conceive of the sacraments
as a "medium" in a real encounter *between living men*: between
the man Jesus and us men and, therefore, *as this very encounter itself.* For although personal encounter through the medium of the
body in a certain respect is indirect, it is, nevertheless, also *immediate*
since in the body subjectivity immediately and directly expresses
itself.

It is only this encounter with Christ in and through the actual
presence in the sacraments of the eternally-present redemptive act
of the living Christ (and of the redeeming Christ himself in the
Eucharist) which explains the historical perspective in the sacraments insofar as they are: (1) an *Anamnesis* (commemoration) or
celebration in mystery of the past sacrifice of the Cross (*signum re-
memorativum*), because precisely at the sacrifice of the Cross the
eternally-present redemptive act of the Son of God amounted to

---

[10] Pius XII, Encyclical *Mystici Corporis, Acta Apostolicae Sedis,* Vol. 35
(1943), p. 218.

really giving up his life; (2) *actual bestowal of grace* (*signum demonstrativum*), because the receiving subject is here and now really drawn into the eternally-present redemptive act; (3) an *anticipation,* in germ, of the eschatological Parousia (*signum prognosticum*),[11] because they are the sacramental act of rendering the *Eschaton* itself present (in the Eucharist) or at least of making present the eternally-actual redemptive act of the Son of God in his efficacy as the glorified *Kyrios* (in the other six sacraments); they allow our own time to be grasped in a visible way by the *Eschaton* itself. The sacramental encounter of man with Christ in the Church is, therefore, on the basis of the historically-past redeeming event, the beginning or the *arrha* (pledge) here and now of eschatological salvation; and the supporting substratum of all this is the permanence of the redeeming man Jesus, who is God and who, through his sacraments, receives us into his redeeming mercy.

Sacramental Mystery of Worship and Sacramental Sanctification

In the concrete, the man Jesus is not only the person who offers us in his humanity the grace of God; he is also the person who in his humanity as our representative and in our name in obedient religious love accepts the offer of grace. Tradition expresses this by saying: "The man Jesus *gives* us the grace that as man he *merited* for us on the Cross." In the saving acts of Christ we find, therefore, a double aspect: worship for God and sanctification for man. These are two aspects of the same *mysteria carnis Christi* (mysteries of Christ's flesh). This idea must now be further developed.

Even to the very core of what is most human in him, Jesus is the Son of God the Father. In grace, therefore, he enjoys the perfection of the intimacy with the three-in-one God. He is the consummate actualization of the communion of love of man with God. He is "grace become man": As God-man, he is essentially dialogue between the holy man Jesus and the Father in the unity of the Holy Spirit. As God, Christ is the second Person, the Son of God, in all things like to the Father. "Living through the Father" (Jn 6:57), receiving all things from him, the Son is nevertheless true God and, in this sense, not "dependent" on the Father. There is question here

---

[11] Cf. *Summa Theologica,* III, q. 60, a. 3.

of an intimacy by which (without prejudice to full equality) the Father is the source without origin. We find ourselves, then, before the incomprehensible mystery of a divine and, therefore, "independent" person who, nevertheless, "derives" from the Father and possesses all things from him (derivation of origin without proper dependence) *a Patre* and *ad Patrem* (from the Father and to the Father).

Now the *human* existence of Jesus is the revelation of this divine inner-trinitarian life relationship: its translation into human forms of appearance. What is translated onto a human level in the man Jesus is primarily this divine intimacy of love of the Son for His Father. In the humanity of the Son the divine intimacy of love between Son and Father is brought to the *created* level, and thus in the man Jesus a real dependence toward the Father now comes into existence *in* this loving intimacy of the Son become man. "The Father is greater than I" (Jn 14:28). In and through this condition the Son reveals to us his divine loving intimacy with the Father — to the "principle without origin." The "being-from-the-Father" of the Son is made known to us by the man Jesus in His *obedient* or *dependent* love for the Father. The man Jesus is essentially *obedient* love and adoration of the Father as the human translation of his divine relationship of origin. Thus considered, the whole earthly life of Jesus is spent before the Father in "living out" this childhood which he acquired by becoming man. In obedient love for his Father, he has accepted his whole human existence (*Dasein*) which, through the intrigues of his fellow men, ended in his being murdered, as the religious expression of his ever-unshaken devotion to his Father. Through this supreme religious worship of Christ we have been redeemed.

But Christ reveals to us through and in his humanity not only his divine relationship to his Father but also his relationship to the Holy Spirit. The Son of God is also a *coprinciple of the Holy Spirit*: "who proceeds from the Father through the Son." The mission of the Holy Spirit *to us* is also the externalizing of this inner trinitarian structure. The "from the Father through the Son" as expressed in the Incarnation signifies that the Holy Spirit is given to us from the Father in and through the perfection of the Son's religiously obedient love (the human level of divine filiation as *a Patre* and *ad*

Patrem). That is why John twice mentions that Christ could send us the Holy Spirit only after his Resurrection from the dead (Jn 16:7; 7:37–39; cf. also Acts 2:33). Theology says the same when it tells us that Jesus through his human life has *merited* for us the Holy Spirit. Only with the final closing, the crowning of his earthly obedient life, is the "incarnation" concluded; only then is the *a Patre* and *ad Patrem* character of the Son fully translated on the human level. "Into thy hands I commend my spirit" is the consummate incarnational translation of the *"ad Patrem"* which is the Son. The Father's responding acceptance of His Son — on the level of the Incarnation — is the Resurrection and Ascension which concludes the cycle of loving intimacy between the Father and the Son become man. Only now can the Son — who on the trinitarian level in his *"ad Patrem"* is the coprinciple of the Holy Spirit — only now can he on the level of the Incarnation send the Holy Spirit to us, too. Thus, through the worshipful mystery of his life which culminated in death, the man Jesus "merited" for us *"the spirit* of sonship" (Rom 8:15); and thus he effectively bestows on us, as *Kyrios,* his own Spirit.

In this primordial sacrament (*Ursakrament*) which is Christ himself, who is personally God, we see that the redemptive act is a *mystery of worship* which is *liturgical* because it was done in our name (*leiton* or *laiton ergon* [work of the people]), and at the same time is the gift of redemption or *sanctification.* Both are achieved by God in human nature.

We find these two aspects again in the sacraments of the Church as celebrations in mystery of the Redemption; in them the Church celebrates the "mysteries of Christ's flesh," a liturgical mystery of worship in which Christ in and through the Church remains the actual high priest. In and through his Church, Christ sacramentalizes his intercession for us in heaven. It is the way he as Lord manifests his eternally-present divine redeeming act, so that every sacrament that is performed for one of the faithful is a *sacramental prayer for grace* for this believer: the prayer of Christ himself to which the Church joins her prayer here and now (*sacramenta fidei Ecclesiae* — sacraments of the faith of the Church). On the other hand, the sacraments are also the sacramentalizing of Christ's *effective sanctification* from heaven in and through his Holy Spirit. In virtue of the eternally-present redeeming act of the *Kyrios,* both efficacious and an act of worship, the sacraments *bestow* the grace which they *ask* of God by this act of worship.

Thus the sacraments of the Church give grace because the Church herself is visibly and perceptibly full of grace. She is, after all, the historical, tangible presence of the redeeming grace of the Cross here and now in the world. In her sacramental activity the Church is not only the effective instrument of salvation employed by the living *Kyrios* by which he establishes on earth among men a community in faith and love (i.e., the Church as a community in grace) and interiorly intensifies and deepens the life of her members, but this visible sacramental expression also makes visible the inner community of faith and grace of *the ever-holy Church* itself. The Church is community of worship and community of sanctification in such a way that in the very act of giving expression to her holiness in sacramental worship she is seen to be *carrying on the work itself of sanctification.* The grace which operates in the sacraments is Christ's fullness of grace shared in his living Church. The sacraments, therefore, are not only the saving sign of the sanctifying worship of Christ, but no less the worship of the Church herself, the expression of the Church's life of grace as community with Christ. The *pleroma Christi* (fullness of Christ) operates in each sacrament. In and through the performance of a sacrament, Christ and his whole Church surround with prayer the man who receives the sacrament. "The *faith* of the Church contributes to the efficacy of baptism,"[12] a faith which is always vivified by charity.[13] In every sacrament the believer enters more deeply into the living bond which the community of the Church has with the "mysteries of Christ's flesh." The mystery of worship, precisely because of its sacramentality, is not only the worship of Christ himself in and through his Church, but by the very fact a *liturgical* mystery of worship of the Church: the liturgical expression of the inner worship of God by the Church's community of the faithful in union with Christ. All this belongs to the constitution of a *sacrament* considered *valid* by the Church and which, consequently, if the receiving subject sets up no obstacle —

---

[12] "Operatur ad efficaciam baptismi *fides* Ecclesiae," *Summa Theologica,* III, q. 39, a. 5. Emphasis added.

[13] "Fides Ecclesiae est (. . .) fides formata [caritate]," *Summa Theologica,* II–II, q. 1, a. 9, ad 3m.

i.e., if the recipient also joins himself in a religious spirit with faith to this mystery of worship — through the very fact of the liturgical celebration (*ex opere operato*), efficaciously bestows the grace prayed for in this act of liturgical worship.

From this we can see the meaning of the traditional formula *Sacramenta causant quod figurant* (the sacraments cause the grace to which they give visible expression). As distinguished from the holy humanity of Jesus, which is hypostatically united to the Son of God, the sacraments are *sacramenta separata, i.e.,* earthly manifestations in symbolic signs of the invisible, saving act of the man Jesus in heaven. They are truly, therefore, the personal acts of the God-man in and through the minister of the Church. They are, in visible sacramental form (*signum*), the redeeming will of Christ himself with respect to the man who receives them. The eternally-present redemptive act as designed for us personally is sacramentalized by the glorified Christ in and through his Church. Essentially, therefore, this visible proof of Christ's redemptive love is meant for the believer to whom it is directed: the receiver of the sacrament. That it be directed to this definite man belongs to the essence of a sacramental proof of Christ's love.

Because they are the visible appearance on earth of this celestial saving act, the sacraments have, as a natural consequence, the same divine saving efficacy. The earthly symbolism of the Church visibly represents the heavenly salvific activity. If we consider the sacraments "from below," we can say that they are symbolic acts of worship of the Church in which Christ accomplishes a deeper mystery. Seen thus, the symbolic acts of the Church are *charged* with divine saving efficacy. But if we look at the sacraments "from above," from the standpoint of the saving act in heaven which is sacramentalized in the Church, as the personal human act of Christ through the official mediation of the Church, then the sacraments are the visibility in the Church, or the historical "incarnation," of the sanctifying will of Christ; they are this saving will itself in visible and tangible form. And thus because of their sacramental visibility, they are the effective bestowal itself of grace made manifest in a visible and therefore meaningful way. Just as the body is the soul itself made visible (but in such a way that the proper activity of the body can in no way be made equivalent to the spiritual activity of the soul), so also at Baptism, for example, the corporal washing of

the Church is the divine grace of reconciliation made visible on earth. As the action of Christ manifest in symbol, the washing is more than what it is on the merely physical level; insofar as it is symbolic activity, it is a bearer of salvation because it is a *sign*. It is only when we consider the physical aspect just in itself and then afterward proceed to give it a higher significance that we unnecessarily complicate the relation between "sign" and "saving causality." Because we are dealing with *sacramenta separata,* we can rightly call this symbolic causality an instrumental saving causality.

We should not forget, however, that this saving efficacy can be viewed in a twofold respect: as mystery of worship and as sanctification. In every sacrament, but especially in the Eucharist, both aspects operate *ex opere operato;* that means that in its sacramental manifestation the power of the redemptive grace of Christ operates *of itself,* both as prayerful *worship* and as efficacious *sanctification.* As sacramental mystery of worship, every sacrament, since it is supported by Christ and the whole community of the faithful in the Church, wins *ex opere operato* the sacramental grace for the one who is to receive it. This grace is then bestowed *ex opere operto* through the same sacrament as long as the man puts no obstacle in the way (i.e., if the adult recipient joins himself actively and religiously to the request included in this act of worship — a point which we will deal with in a moment). Precisely because of the efficacy of this act of worship or the sacramental value of the sacrament as prayer, as the sacramentalizing of the prayer of Christ in and through his Church, a valid sacrament that was received unfruitfully can *subsequently* "revivify." Even when a sacrament is perhaps unfruitful at the moment of reception, still, in a certain respect, no sacrament is *completely* unfruitful because of its value as a sacramental prayer of Christ and his entire Church.

The Sacrament as Religious Experience

The inner religious condition of the receiving subject is not merely a disposition which precedes or parallels the sacrament; it enters into the very essence of the fruitful sacrament. Of course, the religious experience contributes in no respect to the *validity* of the sacrament. Christ's demonstration of love has absolute priority over every human response and does not depend on it; rather, this response is supported by Christ's love. However, it remains true that only when some inchoate religious ardor is present in the believer who is to receive the sacrament will his sharing in the mystery of worship of the Church be a worthy sacramental expression of his inner spirit. Then this worthily received sacrament will become not only the worshipping petition of Christ and his Church but also that of the receiver: the sacramental expression of his religious desire for grace and his will to encounter Christ. If such a religious desire for encounter does not exist, the valid sacrament (i.e., Christ's will for encounter in and through his Church) cannot develop into a real mutual encounter. As a personal encounter with the glorified *Kyrios,* the sacrament which is completely genuine, therefore, necessarily implies the religious ardor of the receiving subject.

The personal religious dispositions of the receiver (which differ depending on whether we are dealing with a sacrament of the living or of the dead) will, therefore, be sacramentalized *in* the worshipping activity of the Church, which, then — solely by virtue of the redemption of Christ — bestows sacramental grace *ex opere operato,* that is, brings about the actual encounter with Christ. From this we see that the sacraments do not work automatically, but rather that, as a result of faith and a deep religious longing, they lay hold of the sanctifying power of Christ which is at work in the sacramental Church. But this grasping of salvation in faith is actually the person's *being* grasped by the redeeming Christ. ("The passion of Christ obtains its effect in those to whom it is applied through *faith and charity* and through the *sacraments of faith.*")[14]

The sacraments are, therefore, no easier path to holiness, as though they could dispense us from a part of that religious striving which is demanded in order to attain the grace of reconciliation or interior intimacy with God outside the sacraments. As we have seen, the significance of sacraments as incarnations of the religious disposition is rather that they bring about *moments of supreme ardor* in the everyday Christian life. In contrast to the extrasacramental communion with God, the sacramental life of grace and love is the full and mature stature of the Christian life. As modern anthropology points out, there are in human life, besides the *decisive* or *mo-*

---

[14] "Passio Christi sortitur effectum suum in illis quibus applicatur *per fidem et caritatem* et per *fidei sacramenta," Summa Theologica,* III, q. 49, a. 3, ad 1m. Emphasis added.

mentous actions in which the person achieves more intensive self-expression, also *everyday* actions in which personal freedom expresses itself in a lesser or more moderate degree. So also there are decisive Christian acts and also everyday acts of grace. Because of their sacramental incarnation, the sacramental acts of worship are intended to be decisive and momentous actions of the Christian life. They demand, therefore, more intensive deliberation and reflection; otherwise they become flat and are reduced to a soulless formalism. On the part of Christ too, the sacraments, as earthly embodiment of his heavenly saving act, are the tangible and complete intervention of his gracious will. Therefore, what is normally experienced as something *ordinary* outside of the sacraments should grow in and through the sacraments toward a special crowning experience, toward full and complete maturity.

Thus, the seven sacraments indicate the high points of our Christian existence (*Dasein*). They give sharp and clear dimensions to everyday Christian life, which at regular intervals raise up the level of everyday spiritual life to new heights. In them the ordinary day-to-day pattern must once again be left behind and surpassed if it is not to fade into that colorless anonymity which, once sacramental practice is abandoned, leads in time to the surrender of Christianity itself and, finally, of all religious spirit.

The sacraments are God's own saving act as it manifests itself in the sacred realm of the Church, as it concretely addresses man and takes hold of him as perceptibly and visibly as a mother embraces her child. Although the child already realizes that his mother loves him, still this felt embrace gives the experience of love in its fulness "Now we truly know." On our way to Emmaus which leads to the *Eschaton,* the sacrament is the veiled encounter in which our heart, listening with eager and ardent faith, burns within us. "Were not our hearts burning within us while he spoke to us on the road?" (Lk 24:32). Precisely because of their sacramental character, i.e., because the sacraments are an authentic, visible proof of Christ's desire to give grace to the one who receives them, they give us a tranquil, moral certitude of the reality of this gift of grace — a certitude which is lacking in grace bestowed outside the sacraments. This very fact makes us experience the divine graciousness of redemption even more intensely than the bestowal of grace outside the sacraments.

ANALYTICAL DEFINITION OF THE SACRAMENTS OF THE CHURCH

On account of the different levels and the numerous factors which we discovered in the sacramental order of the Church, it is impossible to put together into a single sentence all the elements which go to make up a sacrament. The definition which has become classical, *signum efficax gratiae* (an efficacious sign of grace), is only a schematic cross-section of the abundant riches contained in the notion of sacrament. In concluding, we can now attempt to give a descriptive definition which progressively indicates the different essential elements of a sacrament.

A sacrament of the Church is (1) a personal saving act of the glorified Christ, an act of worship as well as sanctification — (2) in and through his Church which, in virtue of the authority and the sacramental character given to her by Christ, *sacramentalizes* this invisible act of the glorified Christ in a sanctifying mystery of worship of the Church. In this way, the once-for-all, eternally-actual redeeming act of the God-man is given a public, historically situated visibility on earth which renders it present among us and for us, and which is at the same time the manifestation of the Church's holy participation in it. The Church does this through the medium of her authorized minister who, therefore, must have the intention of "doing what the Church does." This intention is necessary to authentically sacramentalize the celestial saving act of Christ. What is essential to this earthy sacramentalizing is the ritual action of the Church in liturgical unity with the sacramental word of the Church. The symbolic signs and actions are borrowed from ordinary human life and, for the most part, they are things which already had a sacred meaning for religious man (ritual washing, anointing, imposition of hands, sacred meal, etc.). But through the word, this basic symbolism is caught up in the higher vision of the Church and thus elevated to the specific sacramental symbolism of the Church. In this ordinary *matter* supplied by man, which of itself is lifeless and impotent, Christ accomplishes in his Church, by the power of his salvific *word,* a deeper, divine mystery of salvation.

(3) This sanctifying act of worship of the glorified high priest in heaven, sacramentalized in and through the Church, is *directed essentially* to that particular man in whom the sacrament is per-

formed (consideration being made for the unique character of the
Eucharist as sacrifice of the Church and for the entire Church). This
is so completely true that this personal involvement is part of the
very essence of the sacrament; for this reason, the intention of the
person to receive a sacrament also contributes toward determining
the validity or authentic sacramentalizing (i.e., the making visible in
an earthly way in the ministry of the Church) of Christ's will to
sanctify this person. These first three elements are what constitute a
valid sacrament.

(4) However, this sanctifying sacramental mystery of worship
of Christ in and through his Church can only develop *ex opere
operato* all the rich fecundity for which it was established when the
subject for whom the sacrament is intended also actively enters
with a religious spirit into this mystery of worship with faith and an
earnest longing for grace. Thus it will also become the sacramental
expression of his personal desire to encounter Christ in faith.

This vital religious participation by the (adult) recipient in the
sacramental mystery of worship — a participation which is itself
already the fruit of grace — now grows, through the saving efficacy
of the sacramental celebration, toward a more interior, personal
communion with Christ, toward a deeper bond with the Church's
community of grace, and, therefore, to an increased intimacy of
grace with the living God: with the Father, the Son, and the Holy
Spirit.

From all of this it becomes quite clear that the sacraments are
neither "things" nor "automatons" but rather, by virtue of genuine
incarnation, a mutual personal involvement on the part of Christ
and his Church (through the medium of her authorized minister)
and also on the part of the believer who receives him, and who in
his longing for grace lays hold of the living power of Christ which
alone sanctifies and which is actively present in the Church. He does
this through his reception in faith or, more correctly, through the
active part he also plays *in the celebration* of the sacrament. The
one same objective reality appearing in veiled sacral symbolic actions,
namely, the sanctifying sacramental mystery of worship, thus becomes the expression of both the condescending *agape* (charity)
of God and of the longing of the man of faith who strives to reach
above and beyond himself. In the liturgical, sacramental mystery
of worship the theophany of the redeeming God is accomplished

and man succeeds in returning home to the Father in Christ through the Spirit of sanctification. "You have showed yourself to me face to face, O Christ; it is you that I find in your sacraments."[15]

Translated by Rev. John L. Boyle, S.J.

---

[15] "Facie ad faciem te mihi, Christe, demonstrasti, in tuis te invenio sacramentis." Ambrose, *Apologia prophetae David*, XII, 58; *MPL* 14, 875.

ESCHATOLOGY

I. THE SITUATION

ESCHATOLOGY is the "weather nook" of theology today. It is here that those thunderstorms begin which threaten the whole country-side of contemporary theology with either the havoc of hail or the refreshing shower of gentle rain. If Tröltsch, speaking in behalf of nineteenth-century liberalism, could say that "the eschatological office is usually closed," we can now say that it is working overtime. Starting from eschatology, de Wette, Weiss, Albert Schweitzer, and Martin Werner succeeded in radically recasting liberal theology by centering it on "the parousia that has yet to come."[1] The reaction of Karl Barth and his school was in fact a recasting of theology in an eschatological mold. And if Barth has rejected[2] all one-sided eschatology since writing his *Kirchliche Dogmatik,* it remains true that his reconstruction of all Protestant theology has taken its departure from eschatology. The third "ground wave" in theological thought, which gave birth to Bultmann's demythologizing and existentializing of theology, also began with eschatology: negatively, since the breakdown of "the mythical" essentially affected the status of the last things — *the eschata* — and positively, since all faith is reduced to a realization of the death and resurrection of Christ in the believer.

It is understandable that this eschatological plowing up of theology has not been conducive to any calm, systematic presentation of the question. The "Last Things" are much more apt to be that locus which sooner or later makes the real problem, the aporia, of theology apparent. There is no "system" of the Last Things. When the

---

[1] F. Buri, *Die Bedeutung der neutestamentlichen Eschatologie für die neuere protestantische Theologie* (Zurich und Leipzig, 1934).

[2] *Kirchliche Dogmatik,* III, p. 2.

Last Things become the focal point of theological thought, the closed lines of previous schools open up and even become entangled. Emil Brunner was able to state in 1953: "If we ask what this theology, my own included . . . has contributed to the formulation of eschatology, we must confess with shame and amazement that only a great void has been uncovered. And hardly anything of greater significance has been done."[3] Now appearances are perhaps deceiving. It is not without significance that a whole generation of theologians learns, in the face of an *opening* horizon in eschatology, to engage in genuine theological work, only then becoming aware of the whole form-giving character of the Last Things for theological thought.

Catholic theological thought has not plunged headlong into the extreme positions reached by Protestant theology, but it has not been able to preserve itself from a relatively mild concern (and actually less mild as time goes on) with the same questions. Here too — often behind emptied show windows "temporarily closed for rearrangement" — a lively activity is going on. It is so manysided and so profound in significance, that it would be presumptuous to attempt in these few pages anything like a "progress report" on the situation, let alone any predictions of future developments, which at the moment are still definitely far from view. All that is possible, in the few pages we can dedicate to this essay, is to point to some *directions* of that theological thought and research which may be fundamental for the Catholic world of our day, and which may become even more so. From the immeasurable flood of publications (in eschatology the most differing streams come together to form a powerful delta[4]) only a few works can be named. We must limit our attention to those which will allow us to see the lines which are likely to prove to be decisive.

Writings on the subject of eschatology can be divided into four main categories, and of course some topics tend to overlap:

1. Works which carry on as if nothing fundamental has happened in the past fifty years, or as if everything fits easily, with a few added remarks, into the old frames of medieval or Counter-Reformation

---

[3] *Das Ewige als Zukunft und Gegenwart* (Zurich, 1953), p. 231.

[4] The abundant literature of the past decades can be found in the works of M. Schmaus, *Von den Letzten Dingen* (Münster, 1948) and *Kirchliche Dogmatik IV, Von den Letzten Dingen* (Munich, 1959).

treatises. These are for the most part practical manuals of theological teaching, either newly published or newly revised.

2. An extensive literature of "haute vulgarisation," in which most authors endeavor to present, in essay form, a short crosscut or survey of the whole problem area, or an important part thereof, in order to contribute to what they see as a needed change or improvement in the whole structure.[5]

3. Important fruits of individual research, which point up new questions in all fields of eschatology, teach us to see old questions anew, excavate questions which were once crucial and are now forgotten,[6] or teach us to see the utterings of Scripture and tradition in a more vivid light. As long as this individual research remains alive, seriously testing what is standing, or setting foundations for what is coming, we need not lament, in fact we should perhaps greet with open arms the fact that the new building blocks have not yet been brought together into any finished structure.

4. Attempts at a comprehensive and representative eschatology of our time are practically nonexistent. On the Protestant side, the repeatedly republished and newly revised work of Althaus, *Die Letzten Dinge,* might be considered as such, but it has been sharply criticized and it reveals inner weakness in many points. On the Catholic side, however, there is nothing of the sort, for even that work which more than any other might lay claim to this title: *Von den Letzten Dingen* (1948) by M. Schmaus, is, with its more than seven hundred pages, more a valuable and weighty gathering of extended viewpoints than a speculative examination and elaboration of these positions. Catholic theology also lacks at present representative partial treatises, whereas in the Protestant world

---

[5] We should mention the following: Friedrich Muckermann, *Von der Wiederkehr des Welterlösers. Religiöse Überlegungen über die Letzten Dinge des Menschen* (Regensburg, 1937); J. Staudinger, S.J., *Das Jenseits. Schicksalsfrage der Menschenseele* (Einsiedeln, 1939); A. Winklhofer, *The Coming of His Kingdom* (Eng. tr.) (New York, 1963), and the same author's *Ziel und Vollendung. Die Letzten Dinge* (Ettal, 1951); Ph. Dessauer, *Der Anfang und das Ende* (Leipzig, 1939); R. Guardini, *Die Letzten Dinge* (Würzburg, 1949); J. Pieper, *The End of Time* (Chicago, 1958) (Eng. tr.); E. Walter, *Das Kommen des Herrn,* I (Freiburg, 1942); II (1947).

[6] "How much the living questions have been left behind by us becomes evident when we are faced with the eschatology of the Fathers" (Winklhofer, *Ziel und Vollendung,* p. 9).

there are works which point out the direction of the results of the intense eschatological discussion. Among such books are Cullmann's *Christus und die Zeit* (1948; Eng. tr., 1950) and the work of the Swedish school.

We shall restrict ourselves chiefly to the third category of individual works, in order to extract from them — more would be impossible — some indication of the directions taken by the research of our epoch.

It should be superfluous to assure the reader at the end of this introduction that nothing dogmatically defined by the Church — such as the universality of death as consequence of sin, the cessation with death of opportunities for merit, the particular judgment, the immediate presentation of the soul either to the eternal Beatific Vision of God after expiation in purgatory of all temporal punishments due to sin and of all remaining sins, or to the state of its eternal damnation in hell, the parousia of the Lord at the end of time, the corporal resurrection of all men at the last and universal judgment — none of these are even questioned, let alone doubted, in current attempts to examine them objectively by modern theologians. For those parts of eschatology belonging to the unshakable deposit of our faith the reader can be referred to any good dogmatic work; their presentation is not the concern of the present essay. It is, however, easily understandable that that province of theology where one reaches and passes the limits of the world of space and time, where man and the world are decomposed, where heaven and earth pass away, where history ceases and its yield is reaped into the eternal barns, where creation is judged and delivered in its final state to God; it is reasonable, we think, that such a field of thought should be subjected to constant review and qualification. Perhaps some sense-image or scientific or other hypotheses may have slipped in unnoticed. Even though elements of this kind may help in shedding light upon a part of the truth, they may in time prove to be only of passing or limited value. One may justly point out that research in our day at least attempts to uncover the message of Revelation in its entirety and true magnitude, precisely through those simplifications which, as we shall show, may prove to be the principal characteristic of present-day eschatological thought. It may be the mission of a following generation to bring forth, out of the resultant seed, a still more enriching and more exhaustive speculative product.

II. Eschatology and Modern Man

The modern view of the universe, both in the structure of nature and in its "history," is something different from the anthropomorphism common to the entire ancient world, including Israel. The extraction of the revealed truth of Christianity from this ancient set of concepts and its transfer over into the modern is an audacious affair, necessarily subject to frequent challenge. Theology did not have to wait for Bultmann before coming to grips with this task. In a certain way it is necessary for us to experience what an Origen experienced during the Patristic age when he saw himself and the short centuries of the biblical account of divine redemption standing before the gulf of time, before the eons of gnostic speculation and resolved this confrontation to the profit of his faith through a Christocentric (perhaps better a Logocentric) idea of the world. For men of the nineteenth century the world disclosed by science seemed utterly irreconcilable to the world of the Bible — how could the biblical account of creation and the end of time be understood in face of what was then discovered about the span of human history from "Adam" to Abraham, about the eons between creation of the universe and the appearance of the first man, about the vastness of the cosmos? It was hopeless to think of locating the eschatological "places" (heaven, hell, purgatory, limbo) within the limit of the one world — to do so would make a physical universe out of a theological cosmos whose upper and lower limits reached from the divine to the demonic. Even more was it no longer possible (although this was less clearly seen) to regard the "end of time" (e.g., of the planet earth) as a theologically important event. It became necessary to view the Last Things of man, of his history and of the universe in general, in a new dimension, one which could be, in its essence, exclusively the creation of revelation and faith. One result of this was the new way in which the Last Things (*Eschata*) became "unseeable" for the mind (the whole world system, the whole earthly, birth-conditioned, living and dying man are ordered to this dimension that is open to the world only through the revealing acts of God). Furthermore, and precisely for this reason, theology itself fell entirely into the grip of the Last Things, becoming "eschatologized": they were now essentially *the* world, *the* human family, *the* history etc., to the extent that this decisive, transforming act of God takes place within them.

In other words, the so-called Last Things became actual, real, active, and they did so precisely because they had become, humanly speaking, "unclear." They now were seen as the Last *Events,* having a bearing upon the being and history of man.[7] No more were the Last Things included within the universe as it had been conceived in ancient theology. Rather was the universe raised, transformed to the level of God's activity. This reversal in thought doubtless carries as a logical consequence the danger of a certain "Acosmism,"[8] i.e., a virtual annihilation, theologically speaking, of the physical universe and an immediate relating of the creature to God alone, who becomes, in place of "things" and "states," the creature's Last Thing. But did not this mean that one had to face up to the decisive thesis of all revelation? Long before Bultmann, the great exegete P. Lagrange had commented on that most wonderful statement of Old Testament hope at the end of Psalm 72 ("Yet with you I shall always be. Whom else have I in heaven? But for me, to be near God is my good." Ps 72:23, 25, 28). "No description of hell or paradise at all," Lagrange wrote. "God alone remains before the eye of the Psalmist, and he desires God only. To be with God in heaven or on earth, that is sufficient. Nothing cosmological! We are standing here at the center of Israel's faith."[9] We should not forget that with the great the-

---

[7] "Eschatology will again become in theological thought what it is in Scripture and the Fathers: the essential sense of history; that which the whole mystery of the Church enlightens, a leaven in the entire order of the present world which will become fully understandable only in the tradition of the Church. . . . This meaning of eschatology is what Ecclesiology has most lacked since the inception of this science in the 16th century. Without a feeling for eschatology one saw in the 'last things' less the goal and the completion of the entire order of theology than an accumulation of 'things' which in some way follow death and which one can study in the same way as he can 'earthly' things. . . . One asks: 'What is the fire of purgatory? Is the vision of God through an intelligible species?' and the questions are posed in the same way as those about the essence of fire in physics or the meaning of conceptual knowledge in epistemology. In short, we have tried to answer eschatological questions with the methods of natural knowledge. The eschatological tracts in most of our manuals are of this kind." So writes Y. Congar in *Revue de Sciences Philosophiques et Théologiques* (1949), p. 463.

[8] As one can experience this as the "consequent eschatologism" in the young Barth of the *Römerbrief* (1922).

[9] *Revue Biblique* (1905), p. 195 f.

ologians, as with Scripture itself, everything cosmological has ever been of necessity a mere adjunct to the main theme. As St. Augustine put it: *Ipse Deus post hanc vitam sit locus noster.*[10] God is the Last Thing of the creature. He *is* its paradise gained, its lost hell, its trying court of justice, its cleansing purgatory. He it is in whom the finite dies and through whom it rises to Him, and in Him. And He is all this in His Son Jesus Christ, through whom He has turned to the world. Christ is both the revealability of God and the essence of the Last Thing.[11] Eschatology permeates, almost more than any other *locus theologicus,* the entire doctrine of the redemption. This principle, as shall be shown, is central and basic.

Here we can see why contemporary eschatology has been anti-Platonic (often to the extent of resentment). The "philosophical solution" to the eschatological problem, how man and the world can be eternal in spite of death and time, reached its highest expression in the Socratic-Platonic dichotomization of man into a "mortal" (body) and an "immortal" (soul) part. This teaching presupposes, by the term "immortality," that "man" does not really die, only his body. Thus the "mortal" falls away from the "immortal," but how this occurs in the phenomenon of death, which is of course the decisive point, was left obscure. The Psalmists and Prophets take upon themselves the enormous burden of showing why redemption requires that salvation belongs to the *whole* man, that it is man's total union with God. The claim of being whole with God cannot be seen clearly. It must remain philosophically unjustifiable. Yet this claim unfolds logically into the expectation of the resurrection of man and world in the New Testament.[12]

[10] Article "Ciel" in *Dictionnaire de Théologie Catholique,* II, 2, 2486.

[11] Jean Daniélou has seen this and described it in general in his "Christologie et Eschatologie" in *Chalkedon,* Vol. III, pp. 269–286. He shows that the apparently unhistorical formula of Chalcedon in reality conceals a biblical-patristic theology of history and presupposes as self-evident that Christ, in the hypostatic unity of the two natures, is *the* Eschaton, the End of all things, who rules both the time of promise and the time of fulfillment and is — as the coming Lord — He who brings all things to completion.

[12] Platonism, up to the threshold of modern times, has dominated both Western thought in general and Christian thought in particular (its emphasis is placed, and placed mistakenly, on the "immortality of the soul" and for it the resurrection of the body comes as an unexpected accidental happiness added to the substantial beatitude of the soul; cf. Denz. 530). The crisis of Platonism depends on the choice of a world view: in spite of the objections of philosophers the ancient world was constantly viewed as a "house," a

Precisely because the "surmounting" of the universe into the "Last" is itself not an act that is cosmological or historical in significance, the final redemptive action of God is directed to His creation, to giving it an utterly new determination *in itself*. The "other" of the new age is the "otherness" and "new" of the old; it is not a matter of casting away the present world and setting up a second unknown world in its place. Since one of Bultmann's basic concerns is that all revealed truth be verified existentially in man and his world, he will be in complete agreement with this contention. But Bultmann tends to view the transition from the old to the new eon on an equal plane with the death and resurrection of the Son of God: His "return" to the Father is the *creation of the dimension* into which man and universe begin, through God's free grace, to transform themselves: "becoming heaven's own."[13] The death of the believer (and through it the death of men in general) is the "incarnation" of the deceased soul into this heavenly body, this heavenly "house" of the risen humanity of Jesus Christ. On the one hand, we can see (and here we can count on a long theological tradition for support) the event of "resurrection of the dead" as the midpoint of history, begun with Christ's resurrection (with the resurrection of the "saints" mentioned in Mt 27:52 and Mary's assumption as incidental accompaniments, made possible by the social character of Christ's redemptive corporeality).[14] Or we may, with Feuillet, take the "heavenly house not built by the hand of man" (2 Cor 5:2) to be the glorified humanity of Christ and therefore the "Middle-state" of which Paul would speak. Whether we interpret these things in the one way or the other is not a "purely intellectual" question.[15] Jesus' resurrection and consequently the

---

body for the soul. The ancient Greek and medieval man could never really divorce their thought from their conception of the universe. Only when this world view broke down did two things become necessary: the explicit elevation of the reference of the whole universe to the dead soul (cf. Rahner, *Toward a Theology of Death* [New York, 1962]); and the equally explicit incorporation into the transfigured humanity of Jesus (cf. Rahner, "Die ewige Bedeutung der Menscheit Jesu für unser Gottesverhältnis," *Geist und Leben,* 26 (1953), pp. 279–288.

[13] K. Rahner, "The Resurrection of the Body," *Theological Investigations* II (Baltimore, 1963), p. 207.

[14] H. Zeller, "Corpora Sanctorum. Eine Studie zu Mt 27, 52–53," *Zeitschrift für Katholische Theologie,* 71 (1949), pp. 385–465.

[15] Feuillet, "Destinée des Chrètiens et Fondéments de l'Eschatologie paulinienne" (Institut catholique de Paris, hectograph): "La demeure céleste est

whole burden of eschatology, are becoming more than ever the center of Catholic dogma. F. X. Durrwell,[16] without side glances at Barth[17] or Bultmann, has refashioned the whole dogma around this center, and the Church, the sacraments, the Eucharist, and even justification allow the Christian life to proceed from it as from a universal center.

Before we pursue further how Jesus Christ as the *Eschaton,* i.e., as God's absolute action toward man, brings man and world to their finality, the transformations which take place in Christ must be understood in such a way that the Last Things appear as aspects of the "Christ and Church" event.

A refurbishing of a principle fundamental to the theology of the first centuries was required in order to show that the descent of the Redeemer into hell after His crucifixion and before the resurrection was an indispensable moment in the act of redemption (viewing this event, however, not as an isolated incident of history in the making on Good Friday but as the culminating and closing moment of Old Testament history, as the ending of Sheol on Holy Saturday[18]). And this refurbishing was needed in spite of all the interpretations of historians,[19] of all demythologizing,[20] of all attempts to show that this event was unbiblical.[21]

It is important to remember here that there was, contrary to all

---

le corps glorieux du Christ, mais a titre de premices de la nouvelle creation, c'est à dire en tant qu'incluant virtuellement le corps glorieux de tous les chrètiens" (p. 34). "Incorporation into Christ constitutes the foundation of pauline eschatology" (p. 49). Cf. "La démeure celeste et la destinée des chrètiens," *Recherches de Sciences Religieuses* (1956), pp. 161–192.

[16] *The Resurrection* (English translation by Rosemary Sheed [New York, 1961]).

[17] I have shown in my *Karl Barth, Darstellung und Deutung seiner Theologie* (Hegner, 1951), that the "consequent Christology" developed by Barth can and must also be taken in a genuinely Catholic sense (cf. p. 335 f.).

[18] A. Grillmeier, "Der Gottessohn im Totenreich. Die Descensuslehre in der älteren christlichen Überlieferung," *Zeitschrift für katholische Theologie,* 71 (1949), pp. 1–53, 184–204.

[19] Cf. the masterful but little recognized work of J. Kroll, *Gott und Hölle. Der Mythus vom Descensuskampfe. Studien der Bibl. Warburg XX.,* edited by Saxl (Leipzig-Berlin, 1932).

[20] Somewhat in the manner of the novel historical apercus of Riviere on the doctrine over satisfaction.

[21] W. Bieder, "Vorstellung von der Höllenfahrt Jesu Christi," *Abhandlung zur Theologie des Alten und Neues Testaments,* 19 (Zurich, 1949).

eschatological projections of late Judaic[22] moralizing, no entrance to heaven (Heb 11:39–40) "beyond the grave" "before" (in the logical sense, not temporal!) the death of Jesus on the cross and His descent into Sheol. Indeed the graces of salvation (such as faith, love, hope) — if we should suppose them at all possible — could be imagined in Sheol at best only as a sort of "anticipation" of the enlightening descent of Redemption into that "temporary *poena damni*" (Pohle-Gierens, *Dog. III*, 660). It is necessary to say that the believer most properly understands what damnation, in the strict theological sense, is when he views it from the standpoint of the *terminus a quo* of the redemption, when he sees it as the goal that would have been his had there been no redemption. The darkness into which sinful man must fall becomes manifest at the precise moment that this darkness is opened to the illumination of redemption. And this moment was Christ's descent into the *state*, not the *place*, of loss.[23] The mystery of Holy Saturday is at once both the final end, the death of suffering, and the commencement of glory even before the resurrection. The Fathers were of this mind, and thus is redemption pictured in the Eastern Church to this day. Only the movement initiated by Christ in Sheol could make possible the notion of "Way," "Entrance and Passage," "Beyond." This means that the "purgatorium," i.e., that aspect of divine judgment which permits the sinner a purifying passage through this fire, did not this event exist in the Old Covenant (taken logically, not temporally), but could be brought into being only through the annihilation of Sheol? In this connection the doctrine of St. Thomas, where the fire of hell and the fire of purgatory are identified, proves to contain valuable truth. On the other hand, it is this piece of medieval theology, which lays such emphasis on the "place" of purgatory and hell, that has proved to be particularly in need of revision.[24]

---

[22] Naturally later Judaism had a subtly different doctrine on the Last Things, on the "Beyond" (cf. P. Volz, *Die Eschatologie der Jüdischen Gemeinden im neutestamentlichen Zeitalter nach den Quellen der rabbinischen, apokalyptis-chen und apokryphen Literatur dargestellt* [Tübingen, 1934]). But Plato also possessed a teaching of this kind.

[23] Naturally this in no way agrees with the doctrine of Calvin.

[24] M. Jugie expresses the situation correctly — unfortunately! — when he (perhaps not without an unconscious humor) says: "St. Thomas . . . maintained that this visit of the Savior to those on the other side of the grave did not change in any way the normal course of divine justice in regard to purgatory" (*Le Purgatoire et les moyens de l'éviter*, Paris).

Actually very little would be accomplished by reducing purgatory from a "place" to a "state," unless the "purifying power" of this state became the encounter of the as yet unpurified sinner with the Lord who is appearing to judge him. On the one hand, we must agree with Joachim Gnilka who interprets the "trying fire" of the "day of the Lord" in 1 Cor 3:10–15 as presaging the coming Lord of the last judgment, even if this fire is considered as a mere "image for the majesty of the self-revealing God . . . the unapproachableness of the All-holy."[25] On the other hand, we may not deny that, for the Bible, there are not two judgments and two judgment days, but only one, and that we must therefore view the particular judgment after death as dynamically connected with the last judgment. If we succeed in making the so-called purgatorial fire comprehensible as a *dimension of the judgment and of the encounter* of the sinner with Christ, whose glance is like a "flame of fire" (Apoc 1:14 = Dan 10:6), we may suppose that much has been won for the ecumenical dialogue. In his important study of purgatory,[26] Yves Congar has presented the situation so ingeniously that he not only demonstrates how little the Church says about the state, but he also shows that purgatory must be interpreted as soteriologically connected with the descent (of the Mystical Body in this case).[27] If this theme of encounter is sustained, judgment will be seen as the face-to-face confrontation of sinners with the Redeemer-Judge of the Bible.[28] The unshakable unity between judgment and redemption, between justice and mercy on the cross, is the guarantee of the New Testament demand that Christians await the judgment as the realization (parousia) of the truth of the cross and the resurrection. And Christians are to await this culmination of salvation history in a spirit of unextinguishable and indivisible unity of fear and hope (trust, fearlessness); they are to persevere in this attitude, in this effortful, highly responsible, wakeful and prayerful expectation

---

[25] Gnilka, *op. cit.*, p. 126. According to Nicholas of Cusa "Christ is as the purest fire, who is inseparable from the light . . . and he is that spiritual fire of life and intellect which consumes all things, receives all things within itself, tests and judges all things as it were with a judgment of material fire. . . . So Christ the judge (acts) according to his unique, most simple and indivisible judgment in one moment . . ." (*Docta ignorantia*, III, 9).

[26] In *Le Mystère de la Mort et sa Célébration* (Paris, 1951).

[27] *Ibid.*

[28] Cf. D. Mollat, article "Jugement," *Dictionnaire de la Bible, Supplement.*

of the *Lord*. This, for the Bible, is the last, absolutely unsurpassible Christian attitude.

The existential attitude of the New Testament toward the Last Things has nothing at all to do with the expectancy of what is near at hand and cannot be reduced to this by any comparison with supposedly parallel texts. As man's final attitude, it is the last thing a person does, the last thing known by faith. And this attitude is not strengthened, but weakened, not deepened, but becomes more shallow if the believer presumes that beyond this hoping-fearing, active-receptive trusting in the Redeemer-Judge, he has a foreknowledge of the outcome of the judgment.

Whenever theologians, in good faith and response to the questions posed by faith, think it necessary to speak with a "certainty of faith"[29] about the outcome of the judgment, it is suddenly apparent that many things previously settled were closed off prematurely. Yet these presuppositions necessarily influence all theological questions, even those seemingly farthest removed. These theological consequences, which cannot be avoided, are then seen to be distinct from the biblical account of salvation; their questionable theological character is brought to light. The power of knowing the outcome of judgment (in the sense of a sure knowledge that the Judge *will damn*) leads to at least three consequences (all logically force themselves into theology at the historical moment when eschatology assumes this fundamental form, namely with Augustine): (1) One must burden oneself, despite the positively stated (open-ended) notion of predestination in Scripture, with a doctrine of a twofold predestination, either prior to or subsequent to foreseen merits. One is burdened with that terrible obscuring of Christian faith under which the medieval and Reformation man and the Counter-Reformation man as well — totally opposed to the man of early Christianity and of the age of the Fathers — has so unutterably suffered.[30] Only today are we beginning, in

---

[29] Fulgentius is somewhat of this mind. See his *De Fide,* rule 35: "Hold fast with an unshakable and firm faith that not only all the pagans but also all Jews, all heretics and all schismatics who end their life outside the Catholic Church are cast into the eternal fire prepared for the devil and his angels" (Migne, *Patrologia Latina,* 65, 704). But it is not the extreme position taken here that is to be noted, but rather the fact that Fulgentius makes the *knowledge* of the results of the Last Judgment an article of faith!

[30] As one example of this, one can read the *Disputations* of Simon of Tournai (ed. Warichez, Spicil, Lovaniensis, 12 1932).

obedience to Scripture, to look for a more suitable fashioning of
the subject, and this requires the greatest patience and care. (2)
If Christ, the Redeemer-Judge, is not seen as the *Eschaton, the final
end,* and if one presumes to handle the outcome of judgment as
a knowable "object," the character of faith is distorted. Faith is
meant as a loving, trusting, subjection of the whole person to
the personal truth of God the Father in His Son; yet if this attitude
prevails, faith necessarily takes on the aspect of an intellectual,
neutral act comprising truths both of salvation and of damnation
without any specific commitment to either. Faith can include love
and hope and trust only when it is directed toward a personal
truth of salvation.[31] Closely allied to this is a smug notion of hope,
which would seem to make it an affront to faith to hope for the
salvation of all men. This attitude is further connected to the fact
that Christ cannot have prayed for the reprobate, since His prayer
is infallible.[32] (3) Finally, with respect to significant series of scriptural texts, which place the salvation of all in the realm of what
may be hoped (but never known!), decisions made on the basis of
this prejudgment are interpreted in a way which robs the words of
the texts of their force.

Human thought inclines by nature toward a "system." Scripture,
however, does not attempt to reconcile the unpredictable outcome
of judgment with the possibility of a universal reconciliation of all
men with God, and there is no suggestion of either line of thought
being subjected to the other. Origen attempted this in one sense
— equating hell to a sort of purgatory and thus weakening the
notion of judgment advanced in Scripture — and Augustine (and
the theology which followed him) in the other sense, by removing

---

[31] "On the contrary, one can yet believe in something for which he no
longer hopes. Which of the faithful, for example, does not believe in the
punishment of the godless? Yet he hopes not for this punishment. . . . On
the good and on the evil faith can be fixed, since one can believe both the
good and the bad — and to be sure, he believes in both with good and not
bad faith." Augustine, *Enchiridion,* c. 8.

[32] St. Thomas, *Summa Theologiae,* III, q. 22, a. 4, ad 2: "The Lord did
not pray for all who had crucified him nor even for all who were to believe
in him, but for those only who were predestined, so that through him they
might attain eternal life." If this judgment were correct, then the prayer of
the Church according to 1 Tim 2:1 ff. would have greater extent than the
prayer of Christ, which nevertheless in Jn 17 appears to be absolutely universal (cf. v. 2, and this in spite of v. 12).

any ground for hope in a universal reconciliation. Indeed this tends to enervate the eschatological attitude of faith. This was seen by Charles Péguy better than any other Catholic. Because of the "insufferability" of the doctrine of hell, Péguy left the Church, only then to return to her upon finding a sort of "solution." He expressed this solution in his *Mystère de Jeanne d'Arc* where Joan, with her interior rebellions against the possibility of damnation for her sinful brothers, suddenly knows in her prayer that she is, in her revolt against the loss of any man whatsoever, in agreement with God Himself. Biblically speaking, Christ's utterances concerning judgment (particularly Mt 25:31 ff.) are not meant to communicate a calm "knowledge" of "unfortunately inalterable facts" which, like the damnation of a part of humanity, "must be accepted" with resignation. Against Madame Gervaise's[33] "incredible effort, terrifying in its immense will to humility," Joan states in words of liberating, revealing power: "Deep down, she is taking her position. She suffers much for it, but deep down, deep down at the bottom, she is taking her position. . . . They resign themselves. They grow used to it all. But you, my God, you never accustom yourself to it all. Nor do your saints accustom themselves. Jesus, your Holy One, did not accustom himself. You never resign yourself . . . my God, I have secret prayers. You know it. I trust you."[34]

Naturally this text supposes serious theological reservations. No man, even a "saint," can think of identifying his own basically worldly desires and hope with the hope of God and of Christ Himself, without interjecting that absolute Christian indifference, that reservation in the face of judgment which cannot be equated, however, with a mere passive "accepting." It may well be said, however, that Péguy's breakthrough into an eschatology leaves the outcome of judgment open, centers around the person of the Redeemer-Judge, avoids a closed system at all costs, and leaves room for an all-pervading Christian hope. And it is the same breakthrough that has always marked the eschatology of those spiritual writers and mystics for whom the "night" and "hell experiences" have always had a soteriological character (one thinks immediately of the two Mechthildes, Gertrude, Brigitte, Theresa, John of the Cross, but also of Eckhart, Nicholas of Cusa, and of the many who were

[33] Peguy, *Oeuvres poétiques* (ed. Pleiade), p. 151.
[34] *Ibid.*, p. 1347.

known to have experienced the darkness of God). Péguy, Bernanos,[35] and Claudel[36] stand squarely in the light of Lisieux and the open hope which broke through there.[37] The whole Christian existential "theology of hope," as it has been in the process of development for a decade in France and now also in Germany,[38] is sailing in this eddy. However, this movement remains obedient to the faith by avoiding the abyss of an esoteric Origenism[39] (and Origen's thesis is to be avoided), which has dared on occasion to cast proud invectives against the supposedly absolute eschatology of the Church and her preaching (*Kerygma*).[40] When one seriously considers this "reduction" one cannot think of opposing it directly with a (secretly gnostic) parallel system.

The reduction or rehabilitation of eschatology must also take hold of the *limbus puerorum,* a theological inference which has not as yet been validated. The question has been raised anew in conjunction with others through the work of Peter Gumpel, S.J.[41] Nowhere are the limits proscribed to eschatological thought during our pilgrimage made more clear than here. Finally Karl Rahner has repeatedly and vigorously pointed out that the connection between the Beatific Vision, between "heaven" in general, and the risen hu-

---

[35] Cf. my *Bernanos* (1954), esp. pp. 224, 291, 385, 414 f.

[36] For example, the Canticle of Palmyrus in "Conversations dans le Loir et Cher."

[37] Cf. my *Thérèse von Lisieux* (1950), p. 231 f.

[38] G. Marcel, *Homo Viator.* Cf. also the discussion given at the *Semaine des Intellectuels Catholiques,* 1954.

[39] Cf. G. Koepgen, *Gnosis des Christentums,* 2 ed. (Salzburg, 1940); W. Michaelis, *Versöhnung des Alls* (Bern, 1950).

[40] "No one can guarantee with absolute authority that there is no hell, but it will nevertheless no longer be taken into account" (*Wort und Wahrheit,* XI, Mai, 1956, 330b). Consequently it is right that contemporary "theology of hell" should be discussed very carefully (the best, although it is only a provisional study, work is the symposium by Bardy, Carrouges, Dorival, Spicq, Heris, and Guitton: *L'Enfer* [Paris, 1950]; although one should note the opposing views set forth in the symposium on *Satan* taken from the *Etudes Carmelitaines* in 1948). That the majority of theologians avoid the matter only shows that they are clearly conscious of its difficulties. Whoever tackles it must not only be up on the whole of manual theology but much more in systematic and historical theology. Cf. Rahner, "Outlines of a Dogmatic Theology," in *Theological Investigations* (Baltimore, 1962), ch. 1.

[41] "Unbaptized Infants, May They Be Saved?" *Downside Review* (1954), pp. 342–458 (excellent bibliography). "Unbaptized Infants, A Further Report," *ibid.* (1955), pp. 317–346. Cf. also Dyer, *Limbo: Unsettled Question* (New York, 1964).

manity of Christ has been almost entirely neglected by theologians.[42]

We can, by way of closing, say that only when one has come to understand the Last Things in a fundamentally Christological way — and this means, if one goes to the bottom of the matter, a trinitarian way — and to understand judgment, purgatory, hell, sheol, in the same framework, only then will eschatology be sufficiently decosmologized (not to mention demythologized), i.e., freed of human and time-found notions of the universe. Only then will it no longer contain an unelaborated residue of a sub-Christian philosophy of religion, and only then will eschatology have become an integral part of the personal obedience demanded by faith in Jesus Christ.

III. EXPANSION

The inferences which follow from the Christological structuring of eschatology, for the several parts of theology, and even beyond this for a philosophical interpretation of man and the universe in the light of revelation, are so vast and interlaced that we must forego attempting to present even the most sketchy description of them all. Only a rapid and approximate listing of the most imposing and most engaging questions of our time is possible here. The questions fall into three categories. First, those of eschatology itself; second, questions of the effect of eschatology upon the rest of theology; and, last, questions rising as a result of the encounter of theology with philosophy for the purpose of bringing about a convergence of a natural and supernatural end of man and the universe, or, in other words, an integration of the acceptable elements of natural eschatology with those of the Christian faith. Needless to say, these three areas frequently overlap. Whoever will recognize the progress of research must keep all three simultaneously in view at all times.

1. A projection of today's eschatology can be effected only in terms of the whole structure of theology in general and in terms of our contemporary understanding of man and of the universe. As in every decisive hour of history, the Church today is turning to the Scriptures of the Old and New Covenants with a fresh look. She is acquiring more comprehension for the place-value of certain state-

---

[42] K. Rahner, "Die ewige Bedeutung der Menschheit Jesu für unser Gottesverhältnis," *Geist und Leben*, 26 (1953), pp. 279–288; cf. "Problems in Christology Today," *Theological Investigations*, I, Chap. 5.

ments in history, history of religion and even history of revelation, and therefore is in a position to extract from these values and new insights a certain critique of traditional interpretations, but she can also — through slight transpositions — win new and valid views of the wealth of thought received from yesterday.

Instead of "demythologizing" Scripture (which results, as experience has shown, in separating the soul from the body of revelation, and in holding to an existentialism devoid of the sweep and power of conviction), it is a question above all of interpreting the Word of God as it was stated and embodied in its external form. Let us take for example the Old Testament presentation of Sheol. We know its "place-value." We can cite parallels in the Near East, and we can even show that Platonism presents, from the standpoint of the history of religion, a higher level of thought. We know that the eschatology of the Judaism of the time of Christ was far more subtle than the eschatology of the great prophets and psalmists. Nevertheless, *this doctrine* of Sheol, "imperfect" as it may appear, is the theologically decisive and unavoidable occasion for the revelation of Christ's saving act, which was in many ways obscured by the more subtle eschatology of the Greeks. Even the concrete images of Sheol in their anthropomorphic character are not to be dispensed with, but will and must be theologically interpreted. This is essential if a full and concrete eschatology is to take shape. The same may be said for the whole messianic expectation,[43] and the same for the various biblical notions of time in the Old Testament and between the Old and New Testaments. And thus the scheme of notions already known to the Fathers as the time of the promise and time of fulfillment can be reinstated, in the three ages of: mere promise (Old Testament), fulfilled promise through promised fulfillment (the Church of the New Testament), and fulfilled fulfillment (eschatology). Dodd's "realized eschatology" and its opposite, Cullmann's "advancing time" lead, in their dialectical confrontation directly into the time-notion of the Bible.[44] Then the biblical notion of

---

[43] Cf. Cerfaux, Coppens, de Langhe, *et al., L'Attente du Messie,* 1954; W. G. Kümmel, "Verheissung und Erfühlung. Untersuchung zur eschatologischen Verkündigung Jesu," *Abhandlung zur Theologie des Altens und Neues Testament,* 6 (Zurich, 1945).

[44] Cf. E. C. Rust, "Time and Eternity in Biblical Thought," *Theology Today,* 19 (1953), pp. 327–356.

time intersects the time-notions of nations and philosophers which Revelation judges as well as it opens and adjusts them to itself.[45] The situation proves here to be more complicated, from the standpoint of religious history, than was expected. The "revelation-religion" of Iran is in apparent agreement with the Judeo-Christian religion by favoring a finalizing, end-approaching historical time over against a cyclical, nature time. Here — as in the case of the notion of the "resurrection"[46] and in the "individual eschatology" (known as "particular judgment," "immortality")[47] — we are faced with the phenomenon of a *praeparatio evangelica,* the theological content of which has not yet (or no longer) been sufficiently investigated.

Still more broad in scope are the endeavors to deal with those specifically eschatological statements found in Scripture, i.e., the prophetic form and its historical completion, the apocalyptic form. Jesus and the Apostles resume indeed the apocalyptic manner of expression of their contemporaries, but this only to bring the prophetic vision to a fulfillment in a far more essential way.[48] It is not a question of exhuming an obsolete form, but of pouring the central revelation of the fullness of time into the form prepared by prophetism. This is the form referred to by Martin Buber as that of the "proposal of the alternative,"[49] and which intrinsically resists conversion into a "system" because it is fundamentally "dialogical" in nature. Interpretation of the apocalyptic form becomes especially difficult when we set out from this solid argumentation. The discussion is in full swing and the prospect of a valid resolution is dim for the present. Questions of the value of theological

---

[45] Of the flood of works on the relationship of biblical thought to Greek on the subject of time, cf. J. Guitton, *Le Temps et l'Eternité chez Platon et S. Augustin* (Paris, 1933).

[46] F. Nötscher, *Altorientalischer und alttestamentlicher Auferstehungsglaube* (Würzburg, 1926).

[47] J. Bonsirven, *Le Judaisme Palestinien au temps de Jesus Christ,* Vol. I (Paris, 1934); J. B. Frey," La vie de l'au-delà dans les conceptions juives au temps de Jesus Christ," *Biblica,* 13 (1932), pp. 129–168; Y. Trémel, "L'homme entre la mort et la resurrection d'après le Nouveau Testament," in *L'immortalité de l'âme,* special issue *of Lumière et Vie,* 24 (1955), pp. 729–754.

[48] This also clarifies the strange lack of a doctrine of an "intermediate state" in the New Testament as it has developed in contemporary Judaism (cf. Volz, *op. cit.*).

[49] *Der Glaube der Propheten,* Manesse (Zurich, 1950), esp. pp. 150, 299.

knowledge play decisive roles here. Not the least, though hardly acknowledged by anyone, is the problem of the theological meaning of Christian "mysticism." Basically, we are referring here to New Testament teaching on the charismas or gifts (cf. John and Paul) against the psychologico-ontological tradition of later mystical theology. It is only through a solution to this problem that we can bridge the gap between the mysticism of the Bible and the mysticism of the Church.[50] Mysticism displays here the eschatological function it enjoys in the Church, and we can see the logic in Albert Schweitzer's standing both for the radical eschatology of the Gospel and for the mysticism of the Apostle Paul.[51] Mere "literary forms" simply do not bring us to the genuine apocalyptic reality of the Bible.

The question of the relationship between the Judaic and the Hellenistic elements in the eschatology of St. Paul, and of the introduction of the presence of Alexandrian modes of thought in the eschatological passages of the Epistle to the Hebrews is also open.[52] So, too, is the whole history of the development of eschatological notions throughout the patristic age and later theology. If this extensive and fallow field is intelligently worked, it could prove to be one of the most fruitful in the history of theology. In any case, it can be given its full significance only when biblical eschatology has won some relatively clear contours for itself, so that it can then have some normative value for the theology that follows in the history of the Church.[53]

---

[50] Cf. my *Thomas und die Charismatik* (Latin-German edition of the works of St. Thomas, Vol. 23 [1954], pp. 251–464).

[51] Completely unappreciative, from the biblical point of view, is the alternative of Emil Brunner between Mysticism and the Word (cf. *Die Mystik und das Wort,* 1924); the same is true of Heiler's dichotomy between prophetism and mystical prayer (*Das Gebet,* 1918).

[52] F. J. Schierse, *Verheissung und Heilsvollendung,* in *Münchner Theologische Studien,* Vol. I, 1955.

[53] Nothing is of greater value in eschatology than what K. Rahner has said of dogmatic-historical monographs in general: "The majority of these works are absolutely retrospective. They derive from the past no power to push into the future. They show how it has happened that what is regarded as right today developed" (*Theological Investigations,* Vol. I, p. 15). How wearisome are such treatises as Niederhuber's 1907 study of *Die Eschatologie des hl. Ambrosius* or Eger's on the doctrine of Augustine (1933). The same is true of the eschatology developed by St. Thomas in his *Commentary on the Sentences,* despite its own value and the service it performed for his day.

2. The description of the presence of the Last Things in other theological areas is only beginning. We can mention several cases in point here. There is the confrontation of protology (predestination, doctrines of creation, paradise, etc.) with eschatology. Then there is the confrontation of the whole of salvation history with eschatology. There is the Church as the present and the future of the Last Things. There is the relationship between sacramental doctrine and eschatology.[54] Some foundation stones for a theology of history, still very disparate from one another, begin gathering. To Schmaus is due the credit for having brought the theology of history and apocalyptic reality back again into the broad stream of eschatology and thus for having restored a long-missed fullness and concreteness to the theological domain. Again it was Schmaus who recognized the necessity of giving, through the doctrine of the Last Things, a thoroughly new face to theology, without falling into any kind of "eschatologism." The character of history as expectation has been pointed up repeatedly by Jean Danielou both as a conscious response to the modern Protestant theology of history, and as an attempt toward regaining and building on the patristic theology of history.

3. Finally, the new meeting of theological and philosophical eschatology is, though it has already been consequential and fertilizing for both, more difficult than ever. Through the return of eschatology to the essentially theological realm, room is left for new quests in philosophy, which in turn work fruitfully upon theology. The philosophy of time and of history, of man and of his (natural) end, of death, of the finality of the universe in its totality is still a little explored territory.

If the risen Christ is at once the one who completes the Father's

---

[54] There are just a few of such studies. A few examine the teaching on baptism in Romans 6 (e.g., Dom O. Rousseau, "La descente aux enfers, fondement soteriologique du baptême chrétien," *Recherches de Science Religieuse, Mélanges Lebreton,* II 1952, pp. 273–297) and for the Eucharist as an eschatological mean (e.g., Pascher, *Eucharistia, Gestalt und Vollzug* [Münster, 1953]; O. Cullmann, *Urchristentum und Gottesdienst* [Basel, 1944]; M. Schmaus, *Letzte Dinge* [1948], p. 234 f; Daniélou *Mystère de l'histoire,* p. 211 ff.). But there is no study on the relationship of the sacrament of penance to the resurrection, of confirmation to the eschatological raising of the spirit on the last day, on the relations between the sacraments and the Last Things. A new version of the theology of dath has been proposed by K. Rahner.

intention for man, for history, and for the universe,[55] then the course of the creature's world can hardly be indifferent and foreign to this purpose. The thrust of the universe toward its fulfillment, encircled and permeated by a supernatural causality, must be integrated into the miracle of supernatural reality, grace, and redemption. It must be vested with the miracle of the resurrection of the flesh.[56] One should not overlook here the broad stream of cosmological thought which today, legitimately continuing the natural philosophy of High Scholasticism and Romantic Idealism (Baader, Görres), has a definitely anti-Platonic and antispiritualistic inclination toward the rehabilitation of the body[57] and of matter,[58] toward the idea of the embodiment of spirit,[59] toward sensitivity even in the act of religious knowledge of God.[60] H. E. Hengstenberg strives indefatigably in many of his works[61] to prove this tendency as that of a purification (enlightening) of matter through the spirit (transformation into organic-spiritual "corporality") and thus to propose the outline of a "natural eschatology."[62] All this tends toward a "natural transfiguration" of death (and after the Fall, death, in its decisiveness and purging power, assumes the sweeping role of master of the spirit), and pushes beyond the Platonic doctrine of perfection. As a result, Hengstenberg has been able to show the meaning of spirit for matter and to apply to the resurrection in a thoroughly positive way perhaps for the first time the law that grace supposes nature. Moreover, in doing so he does not distort theology by

---

[55] Fr. Meister, *Die Vollendung der Welt im Opfer des Gottmenschen* (Freiburg, 1938).

[56] This remains supernatural for the Scholastics (cf. N. Kübel, "Die Lehre von der Auferstehung der Toten nach Albertus Magnus," *Studia Albertina,* 1952, pp. 279–318). Cf. *Supplement* to *Summa Theologiae,* q. 74, a. 3.

[57] V. Poucel, S.J., *Mystique de la Terre,* 2 vols. (Paris, 1937, 1939).

[58] Gustav Siewerth, *Der Mensch und sein Leib* (Einsiedeln, 1953); *Wort und Bild* (1952); *Die Sinne und das Wort* (Schwann, 1956).

[59] K. Rahner, *Geist in Welt* (1939); Hans Andre, *Vom Sinnreich des Lebens. Eine Ontologie gläubiger Wurzelfassung* (Salzburg), and *Die Kirche als Keimzelle der Weltvergöttlichung. Ein Ordnungsbauriss im Lichte biologischer Betrachtung* (Leipzig, 1920). Cf. also the works of Hedwig Conrad-Martius and, on the question of history, of Friedrich Heer.

[60] Paul Claudel, "L'Art poétique. Sur la Présence de Dieu. La Sensation du Divin," in *Présence et Prophetie* (1942). Here we should also mention Johannes Pinsk, *Die sakramentale Welt* (Freiburg, 1941) and R. Guardini, *Die Sinne und die religiöse Erkenntnis* (Würzburg, 1950).

[61] His latest, *Der Lieb und die Letzten Dinge* (Regensburg, 1955).

[62] *Ibid.,* p. 18.

mingling with the fantasies of gnostic inspiration nor does he confuse it with natural mysticism.[63] Alois Dempf has brilliantly shown the pertinence of the anthropology and cosmology of German idealism (Schelling, Fr. Schlegel, Görres) for a Catholic metaphysics. A. Frank-Duquesne comes close to the Sophianism of the Orthodox (but this, we should note, runs the risk of uniting natural and supernatural eschatology into a universal religious metaphysics). The works of Teilhard de Chardin must still be examined to see whether or not his eschatological insights avoid the danger of attempting to erect the eschatological data of revelation into a system of cosmic universal evolution.

It should be the duty of Catholic thought to bring the themes of contemporary philosophy and theology, so profoundly affected by existentialism, into the framework of a healthy, meaningful, outgoing, and world-embracing eschatology of man, history, and the universe. We still have no complete philosophy of death.[64] The same must be said for a Catholic philosophy and theology of history[65] and of the universe, except for occasional essays, valuable as these may be.

Finally, we should point to the problem of the encounter between Christian and Jewish eschatology. This subject, though largely very hidden from view, is crucial today. The Jewish world, reflecting on its own meaning, has defined its own eschatology as an essentially earthbound, social messianism (Buber, Baeck, Rosenzweig, Achad Haam). It has stressed the typically "prophetic" bond between social reform (to the point of religious communism) and a "utopian" belonging to the God of the Covenant. The most dynamic force behind both capitalism and communism, both the radical West and the radical East is Jewish, and this is rooted in a tension between a cultural immanence and a Christian transcendence, a

---

[63] *Ibid.*, p. 156: "Consequently the supernatural transfiguration in some way encloses all the perfections of a natural transfiguration, without destroying the genuine character of the supernatural transfiguration by setting it on the level of the natural."

[64] Cf. the studies of Riesenfeld, "La descente dans la mort," *Mélanges Goguel* (1950).

[65] In addition to the works already mentioned by Pieper and Danielou there is that of Theodore Haecker, *Der Christ und die Geschichte* (1935), and that of Konrad Weiss, *Zum geschichtlichen Gethsemane* (1919); cf. also Peter Wust, *Dialektik des Geistes* (1938); J. Bernhart, *Der Sinn der Geschichte* (1931). Cf. Von Baltasar, *The Theology of History* (New York: 1963).

tension between a lust for the earth and things earthly and a longing for the divine. It is the dynamism of a rent world, open to a supracosmic and Christian reality, but defending itself against it just the same with every means at its disposal. But Christ, as man, is the one who completes the Jewish drive. In a final and fateful sense, Jewish and Christian eschatology belong together, regardless of how tragically they seem to contradict one another in the concrete forum of history. The transition from the Old to the New Covenant can never again mean indifference to the immense purpose of Israel in the midst of politics and society. Because Jesus is a man — and a Jew — the Kingdom of God comes not only from above and outside the world; it is also essentially the fruit of the earth. The fruit of Mary perhaps? Certainly. But in her the fruit also of the entire holy people, which has its true world mission.

SELECT BIBLIOGRAPHY

1. ON NATURE AND GRACE

by

William J. Weiler, S.J.

BOOKS

*Berkhouwer, G. C., *Man: The Image of God*, Grand Rapids, 1962.
———— *The Triumph of Grace in the Theology of Karl Barth*, tr. Harry R. Boer, Grand Rapids, 1956.
*Bishop, G. S., *Doctrines of Grace and Kindred Themes*, Grand Rapids, 1954.
Bocxe, Winfried, *Introduction to the Teaching of the Italian Augustinians of the 18th Century on the Nature of Actual Grace*, Hèveslé-Louvain, 1958.
Cuttaz, François J., *Our Life of Grace*, tr. Angeline Bouchard, Chicago, 1958.
*Daane, J., *Theology of Grace*, Grand Rapids, Mich., 1954.
Daujat, Jean, *The Theology of Grace*, New York, 1959.
Doolan, A., *Sanctifying Grace*, Cork, 1953.
Fairweather, A. M. (ed.), *Nature and Grace: Selections from the Summa Theologica of St. Thomas*, Philadelphia, 1954.
Fransen, Peter, *Divine Grace and Man*, New York, 1962.
Garrigou-Lagrange, Réginald, *Grace: Commentary on the Summa Theologica of St. Thomas, Ia IIae, q. 109–14*, St. Louis, 1952.
Gleason, Robert W., *Grace*, New York, 1962.
*Gray, Henry D., *The Christian Doctrine of Grace*, London, 1949.
Hamer, J., *Karl Barth: Essay on the Method of Dogma*, tr. D. M. Maruca, Westminster, Md., 1962.
Journet, Charles, *The Meaning of Grace*, New York, 1960.
Joyce, G. H., *Catholic Doctrine of Grace*, Westminster, Md., 1950.
Küng, Hans, *Justification: The Teaching of Karl Barth and a Catholic Reflection*, New York, 1964.
Le Troquer, René, *What Is Man?* tr. Eric E. Smith, New York, 1961.
McLaughlin, Barry S., *Nature, Grace, and Religious Development*, Westminster, Md., 1964.
*Mascall, E. L., *Grace and Glory*, New York, 1961.
———— *The Importance of Being Human: Some Aspects of the Christian Doctrine of Man*, London, 1959.
Matthews, John Vincent, *The Life That Is Grace*, Westminster, Md., 1953.
Moeller, Charles, *The Theology of Grace and the Oecumenical Movement*, tr. R. A. Wilson, London, 1961.
Morson, John, *The Gift of God: A Study of Sanctifying Grace in the New Testament*, Cork, 1952.

---

* Indicates author is not a Catholic.

Mouroux, Jean, *The Meaning of Man,* tr. A. H. G. Downes, New York, 1948.

Nicolas, Jean Hervé, *The Mystery of God's Grace,* Dubuque, 1960.

Rahner, Karl, *Nature and Grace and Other Essays,* tr. Dinah Wharton, London, 1963.

Scheeben, M. J., *Nature and Grace,* Westminster, Md., 1954.

*Smith, Charles Ryder, *The Bible Doctrine of Grace and Related Doctrines,* London, 1956.

Stevens, Gregory, *The Life of Grace,* Englewood Cliffs, N. J., 1963.

Watson, Philip S., *The Concept of Grace: Essays on the Way of Divine Love in Human Life,* London, 1959.

ARTICLES

Alfaro, J., "Supernatural: Immanent and Transcendent," *Theology Digest,* 8 (1960), 30–34.

Beck, G. A., "Living With God: The Meaning of Grace," *Clergy Review,* 42 (1957), 577–589.

Bourassa, F., "Adoptive Sonship: Our Union with the Divine Persons," *Theological Studies,* 13 (1952), 309–335.

Burch, R., "Problem of the Supernatural," *Theology Digest,* 8 (1960), 25–29.

Callahan, D. J. M., "Our Supernatural Organism," *Review for Religious,* 16 (1957), 293–299.

Coninck, L. de, "Holy Spirit and the Preaching of Grace," *Lumen Vitae,* 8 (1953), 73–76.

Cooke, B., "Relation of Supernatural to Natural," *Perspectives,* 4 (1959), 17–18.

Coyle, T. W., "Some Post-war Trends in *De Gratia,*" *Catholic Theological Society of America, Proceedings,* 16 (1961), 161–170.

Cunningham, F. L. B., "Spirituality for All: The Gift of God," *Cross and Crown,* 8 (1956), 451–471.

Cuskelly, E. J., "Actual Grace, Personal Attraction," *Australasian Catholic Record,* 38 (1961), 195–206.

———— "Grace and Person," *Australasian Catholic Record,* 38 (1961), 114–122.

De Letter, P., "The Catholic Doctrine of Grace," *Guide,* 177 (1963), 9 ff.

———— "Contemporary Theology of Grace," *Clergy Monthly,* 21 (1957), 326–336.

———— "Created Actuation by the Uncreated Act," *Theological Studies,* 18 (1957), 60–92.

———— "Created Actuation by the Uncreated Act," *Theological Studies,* 19 (1958), 1–31.

———— "Divine Quasi-Formal Causality," *Irish Theological Quarterly,* 27 (1960), 221–228.

———— "Gratiae Gratis Datae," *Clergy Monthly,* 19 (1955), 201–207, 294–300.

———— "Prayer for Grace (Three Ways to Attain Grace)," *Irish Ecclesiastical Record,* 93 (1960), 19–27.

———— "Pure or Quasi-Formal Causality," *Irish Theological Quarterly,* 30 (1963), 36–47.

———— "Sanctifying Grace and Our Union with the Holy Trinity," *Theological Studies,* 13 (1952), 33–58.

———— "Sanctifying Grace and the Divine Indwelling," *Theological Studies,* 14 (1953), 242–272.

———— "Sanctifying Grace and Divine Indwelling: Fr. de la Taille, and St. Thomas," *Gregorianum,* 41 (1960), 63–69.

Denis, Father, "Grace: The Christ-life in Us," *Spiritual Life,* 4 (1958), 331–336.

Dessain, C. S., "Cardinal Newman and the Doctrine of Uncreated Grace," *Clergy Review,* 47 (1962), 207–225.

Donnelly, M. J., "The Inhabitation of the Holy Spirit: A Solution according to de la Taille," *Theological Studies,* 8 (1947), 445–470.

———— "Sanctifying Grace and Our Union with the Holy Trinity: A Reply," *Theological Studies,* 13 (1952), 190–204.

———— 'The Supernatural Person," *Irish Theological Quarterly,* 30 (1963), 340–347.

———— "Two Works of Art: Natural Artistry; Supernatural Artistry," *Irish Theological Quarterly,* 24 (1957), 122–131.

Donnelly, P., "Gratuity of the Beatific Vision and the Possibiity of a Natural Destiny," *Theological Studies,* 11 (1950), 374–404.

Finili, A., "Nature and Supernature according to Cajetan and His Predecessors," *Dominican Studies,* 6 (1953), 153–166.

Fisher, J. P., "Nature and Grace," *Review for Religious,* 13 (1954), 142–148.

Forshaw, B., "The Doctrine of Grace Today," *Clergy Review,* 46 (1961), 449–462.

Foster, K., "Lines of Grace," *Blackfriars,* 42 (1961), 238–244.

Fraigneau-Julien, Bernard, "Grace and the Divine Indwelling," *Theology Digest,* 4 (1965), 79–85.

Gilby, T., "The Stuff of Grace," *Life of the Spirit,* 12 (1958), 393–401.

Greenstock, D. L., "Exemplar Causality and the Supernatural Order," *Thomist,* 16 (1953), 1–31.

Hill, W., "Uncreated Grace: A Critique of Karl Rahner," *Thomist,* 27 (1963), 333–356.

Kelly, B., "Divine Quasi-Formal Causality," *Irish Theological Quarterly,* 28 (1961), 16–28.

Kenny, J., "Deification of Man," *Sursum Corda,* 2 (1956), 715–772; 3 (1957), 25–33.

———— "Deification of Man: Healing Grace," *Sursum Corda,* 2 (1956), 366–375.

———— "Necessity of Deifying Grace," *Sursum Corda,* 2 (1956), 557–564.

———— "Reflections on Human Nature and the Supernatural," *Theological Studies,* 14 (1953), 280–287.

Kiesling, C., "Spirituality for All: Channels of Grace," *Cross and Crown,* 10 (1958), 87–107.

McNamara, K., "Scheeben's Doctrine of Grace and a Protestant Author," *Irish Theological Quarterly,* 21 (1954), 51–60.

Macomber, W., "De la Taille vs. Thomistic Tradition: A Reply," *Thomist,* 22 (1959), 233–354.

Meissner, W. W., "Prolegomena to a Psychology of Grace," *Journal of Religion and Health,* 3 (1964), 209–240.

Mitchell, J., "Nature and Supernature," *Downside Review,* 70 (1951), 23–66; (1952), 135–149.

Mullaney, T. U., "De la Taille and the Incarnation: A Rejoinder," *Thomist,* 22 (1959), 255–277.

Newman, M. R., "Spirituality for All: The Life of Grace Within," *Cross and Crown,* 12 (1960), 464–479.

O'Shea, Kevin F., "Pure Formal Actuation [A Reply to P. De Letter]," *Irish Theological Quarterly,* 28 (1961), 1–15.

——— "Pure Uncreated Unity [A Reply to P. De Letter]," *Irish Theological Quarterly,* 30 (1963), 347–353.

Trethowan, I., "The Union of Grace: a Suggestion," *Downside Review,* 81 (1963), 317–327.

Vasey, V., "Grace Perfects Nature," *Cross and Crown,* 12 (1960), 437–447.

Weigel, G., "Historical Background of the Encyclical *Humani generis,*" *Theological Studies,* 12 (1951), 520–549.

Wheeler, Mother M. C., "Actual Grace according to St. Thomas," *Thomist,* 16 (1953), 334–360.

2. MAN'S ORIGIN AND CONTEMPORARY ANTHROPOLOGY

by

Bruce Biever, S.J.

BOOKS

Anderson, James F., *The Cause of Being: The Philosophy of Creation in St. Thomas,* St. Louis, 1952.

Barnett, S. A., *A Century of Darwin,* London, 1958.

*Barzun, J., *Race, a Study in Modern Superstition,* New York, 1937.

*Berrbower, J. R., *Search for the Past,* Englewood Cliffs, N. J., 1960.

Bivort de la Saudée, Jacques de (ed.), *God, Man and the Universe,* New York, 1953.

*Boule, M., and Vallois, H. V., *Fossil Man,* New York, 1957.

*Bronowski, J., *Science and Human Values,* New York, 1956.

*Carstairs, G. M., *The Twice-Born,* Bloomington, Ind., 1958.

*Cassirer, E., *An Essay on Man,* New Haven, 1944.

*Childe, G. V., *Social Evolution,* New York, 1951.

*Coon, Carleton S., *The Story of Man,* New York, 1962.

——— *The Origin of Races,* New York, 1962.

Corte, Nicolas, *The Origin of Man,* tr. by Eric Smith, New York, 1958.

Count, E. W., *This Is Race,* New York, 1950.

*Darlington, C. D., *The Facts of Life,* London, 1953.

——— *Darwin's Place in History,* London, 1959.

*Dewar, Douglas, and Shelton, H. S., *Is Evolution Proved?* London, 1947.

*Diamond, S., *Culture in History,* New York, 1960.

*Dobzhansky, T., *Genetics and the Origin of the Species,* New York, 1951.

——— *Mankind Evolving,* New York, 1960.

*Dodson, E. O., *Evolution: Process and Product,* New York, 1960.

*Eiseley, L., *Darwin's Century*, New York, 1958.
———— *Fossil Man and Human Evolution. Yearbook of Anthropology, 1955*, New York, 1955.
*Fothergill, Philip G., *Evolution and Christians*, London, 1961.
———— *Historical Aspects of Organic Evolution*, New York, 1953.
Fraine, Jean de, *The Bible and the Origin of Man*, New York, 1962.
*Garn, S. M., *Human Races*, Springfield, Ill., 1961.
*Greene, J. C., *Darwin and the Modern World View*, Baton Rouge, 1961.
———— *The Death of Adam*, Ames, Iowa, 1959.
Haber, Francis C., *The Age of the World, Moses to Darwin*, Baltimore, 1959.
Hardin, G., *Nature and Man's Fate*, New York, 1959.
Harrison, R. J., *Man the Peculiar Animal*, Baltimore, 1957.
Hauret, Charles, *Beginnings: Genesis and Modern Science*, tr. by E. P. Emmaus, Dubuque, 1955.
Hayes, C., *The Ape in Our House*, New York, 1951.
*Hessler, B., *The Bible in the Light of Modern Science*, Chicago, 1960.
*Hoebel, E. Adamson, *Man in the Primitive World*, New York, 1958.
*Howells, William, *Mankind in the Making*, Garden City, N. Y., 1959.
Huizinga, J., *Homo Ludens*, Boston, 1955.
Jepsen, G. L. (ed.), *Genetics, Paleontology and Evolution*, Princeton, N. J., 1949.
*Johnson, H. J. T., *The Bible and the Early History of Mankind*, London, 1943.
*Jung, C. J., *Modern Man in Search of a Soul*, New York, 1955.
Keith, A., *A New Theory of Human Evolution*, New York, 1949.
*Klineberg, O., *Race Differences*, New York, 1955.
*Klotz, John W., *Genes, Genesis and Evolution*, St. Louis, 1955.
*Kluckhohn, C., *Mirror for Man*, New York, 1949.
*Koppers, Wilhelm, *Primitive Man and His World Picture*, London and New York, 1952.
*Kroeber, A., *Anthropology Today*, Chicago, 1953.
*Krutch, J. W., *The Great Crutch of Life*, Boston, 1957.
La Barre, W., *The Human Animal*, Chicago, 1954.
Lattey, C. (ed.), *Man and Eternity*, London, 1937.
*LeGros Clark, W. E., *History of the Primates*, Chicago, 1947.
———— *The Fossil Evidence of Human Evolution*, Chicago, 1955.
*Lerner, I. M., *The Genetic Basis of Selection*, New York, 1958.
*Lever, Jan, *Creation and Evolution*, Grand Rapids, Mich., 1958.
*Lovell, A. C. B., *The Individual and the Universe*, New York, 1958.
MacGillivray, G. J. (ed.), *Man*, London and New York, 1932.
*Mayr, E., *Systematics and the Origin of Species*, New York, 1942.
Messenger, Ernest C. (ed.), *Evolution and Theology*, New York, 1952.
Meyer-Abich, A., *The Historico-Philosophical Background of the Modern Evolution-Biology*, Leiden, 1964.
*Montagu, A., *The Direction of Human Development*, New York, 1955.
Moody, Paul A., *Introduction to Evolution*, New York, 1953.
*Murdock, G. P. (ed.), *Evolution and Anthropology: A Centennial Appraisal*, Washington, 1959.
Murray, Raymond W., *Man's Unknown Ancestors*, Milwaukee, 1943.
*Nesturkh, M. F., *The Origin of Man*, Moscow, 1958.
*Nogar, Raymond J., *The Wisdom of Evolution*, Garden City, 1963.

Ong, W. J., *Darwin's Vision and Christian Perspectives,* New York, 1961.
*Persons, S., *Evolutionary Thought in America,* New Haven, 1950.
Pontecorvo, G., *Trends in Genetic Analysis,* New York, 1958.
Rahner, K., "The Theological Concept of Concupiscentia," *Theological Investigations I: God, Christ, Mary and Grace* (tr. by Cornelius Ernst), Baltimore, 1961.
———— "Theological Reflections on Monogenism," *Theological Investigations I: God, Christ, Mary and Grace* (tr. by Cornelius Ernst), Baltimore, 1961.
Rensch, B., *Evolution above the Species Level,* New York, 1959.
*Rhodes, F. H. T., *The Evolution of Life,* Baltimore, 1962.
*Roe, A., and Simpson, G. G., *Behavior and Evolution,* New Haven, 1958.
*Ross, H. H., *A Synthesis of Evolutionary Theory,* Englewood Cliffs, N. J., 1962.
*Sahlins, M. D., *Evolution and Culture,* Ann Arbor, 1960.
Schmalhausen, I. I., *Factors of Evolution,* Philadelphia, 1949.
Senet, André, *Man in Search of His Ancestors,* New York, 1956.
*Shapiro, H. L. (ed.), *Man, Culture, and Society,* New York, 1960.
Shapley, H. (ed.), *Science Ponders Religion,* New York, 1960.
*Simpson, George G., *Tempo and Mode in Evolution,* New York, 1944.
———— *The Major Features of Evolution,* New York, 1953.
———— *The Meaning of Evolution,* New York, 1951.
*Stern, C., *Human Genetics,* San Francisco, 1960.
*Tax, Sol (ed.), *Evolution after Darwin* (3 vols.), Chicago, 1960.
Teilhard de Chardin, P., *The Phenomenon of Man,* New York, 1959.
Weidenreich, F., *Apes, Giants, and Man,* Chicago, 1946.
*White, L., *The Science of Culture,* New York, 1949.
*Zirkle, C., *Evolution, Marxian Biology, and the Social Scene,* Philadelphia, 1959.

ARTICLES

Alexander, Andrew, "Human Origins and Genetics," *The Clergy Review,* 49 (1964), 344–353.
Birdsell, J. B., "On Methods of Evolutionary Biology and Anthropology," *American Scientist,* 45 (1957), 393–400.
Bosio, G., "Reflections on Darwinism," *American Ecclesiastical Review,* 143 (1960), 1–17.
Breghby, Laurence, "Creation: A Philosophic Point of View," *Downside Review,* 26 (1958), 150–159.
Brennan, M., "Science and Ourselves — Evolution," *Irish Ecclesiastical Record,* 95 (1961), 396–402; 96 (1961), 43–49.
Brunner, August, "Pierre Teilhard de Chardin: A Critique," *Theology Digest,* 8 (1960), 143–147.
*Carre, Meyrick, "Doctrines of Creation and the Rise of Science," *London Quarterly* (1959), 54–59.
*Coblentz, S. A., "The Mystery of Evolution," *Personalist,* 44 (1963), 357–369.
Collins, J., "Darwin's Impact on Philosophy," *Thought,* 34 (1959), 185–248.

*Deevey, D. S., 'The Human Population," *Scientific American*, 203 (1960), 195–204.

*Dobzhansky, T., "Anthropology and the Natural Sciences: The Problem of Human Evolution," *Current Anthropology*, 4 (1963), 146–148.

——— "On Species and Races of Fossil and Living Man," *American Journal of Physical Anthropology*, 2 (1944), 251–265.

——— "Evolution at Work," *Science*, 127 (1958), 1091–1098.

*Dodson, E. O., "Some Problems of Evolution and Religion," *Review of the University of Ottawa*, 31 (1961), 380–395.

Dubarle, A. M., "History and Myth in Genesis," *Theology Digest*, 6 (1958), 95–99.

*Ellwood, R. S., "The Creation of Time," *Anglican Theological Review*, 41 (1959), 215–229.

Eslick, L. J., "The Thomistic Doctrine of the Unity of Creation," *New Scholasticism*, 13 (1954), 49–70.

*Fulton, J. S., "Philosophical Adventures of the Idea of Evolution," *Rice Institute Pamphlet*, No. 46 (1959), 1–31.

Gleason, R. W., "Theology and Evolution," *Thought*, 34 (1959), 249–257.

Goudge, T. A., "Is Evolution Finished?" *University of Toronto Quarterly*, 26 (1957), 430–442.

Johann, Robert, "The Logic of Evolution," *Thought*, 36 (1961), 537–554.

Hartman, L. F., "Sin in Paradise," *Catholic Biblical Quarterly*, 20 (1958), 26–40.

Lambert, G., "Creation in the Bible," *Nouvelle Revue Théologique*, 75 (1953), 252–281.

*Leakey, L. S. B., "Finding the World's Earliest Man," *National Geographic*, 118 (1960), 420–435.

——— "Exploring 1,750,000 Years into Man's Past," *National Geographic*, 120 (1961), 564–589.

Marcozzi, Vittorio, "The Origin of Man according to Science," *Theology Digest*, 2 (1954), 43–47.

Melendez, B., "Teleogenesis," *Theology Digest*, 1 (1953), 123–127.

Moore, J. J., "The Darwin Centenary and the Theologian," *Irish Theological Quarterly*, 26 (1959), 117–130.

O'Neill, J., "The Bible and Evolution," *Scripture*, 11 (1959), 6–22, 42–51.

Reilly, Conor, "Adam and Primitive Man," *Irish Theological Quarterly*, 26 (1958), 331–345.

Seiler, J., "The Origin of Living Things," *Cross Currents*, 9 (1959), 129–139.

*Straus, W. L., "The Riddle of Man's Ancestry," *Quarterly Review of Biology*, 24 (1949), 200–223.

*Tappen, N. C., "A Mechanistic Theory of Human Evolution," *American Anthropologist*, 55 (1953), 605–607.

Vollert, Cyril, "Evolution and the Bible," *Symposium on Evolution*, Pittsburgh, 1959.

3. THE FIGURE OF CHRIST IN CATHOLIC THEOLOGY TODAY

by

A. Ransom Marlow, S.J.

BOOKS

Adam, Karl, *The Christ of Faith*, New York, 1957.

——— *The Son of God*, New York, 1940.

*Anderson, H., *Jesus and Christian Origins*, New York, 1964.

*Beyer, M. W., *Christ*, Toronto, 1949.

Bichlmair, George, *The Man Jesus*, Westminster, Md., 1953.

Bourke, Myles M., *Passion, Death and Resurrection of Christ*, New York, 1963.

*Braaten, C. E., and Harrisville, R. A., *The Historical Jesus and the Kerygmatic Christ*, New York-Nashville, 1964.

*Bultmann, Rudolf, *Jesus and the Word*, New York, 1934.

*Cadbury, H. T., *Jesus, What Manner of Man?* Naperville, Ill., 1962.

Cerfaux, L., *Christ in the Theology of St. Paul*, New York, 1960.

*Cullmann, Oscar, *The Christology of the New Testament*, Philadelphia, 1959.

Daniélou, Jean, *Christ and Us*, New York, 1962.

*Davis, John Gordon, *He Ascended into Heaven*, London, 1958.

De La Taille, M., *The Hypostatic Union and Created Actuation by Uncreated Act*, West Baden Springs, Ind., 1952.

Dewan, Wilfred F., *The Person of Christ*, New York, 1962.

*Dillistone, F. W., *Jesus Christ and His Cross*, Philadelphia, 1953.

Durrwell, F. X., *The Resurrection: A Biblical Study*, New York, 1960.

*Erskine, John, *The Human Life of Jesus*, New York, 1945.

Fernan, J. J., *Christ as Prophet and King*, Syracuse, 1952.

——— *Christ Our High Priest*, Syracuse, 1953.

*Ferré, N. F. S., *Christ and the Christian*, New York, 1958.

*Filson, Floyd V., *Jesus Christ the Risen Lord*, New York, 1956.

*Forsyth, Peter Taylor, *The Person and the Place of Jesus Christ*, Naperville, Ill., 1948.

*Fuller, Reginald H., *The Mission and Achievement of Jesus: An Examination of the Presuppositions of New Testament Theology*, Naperville, Ill., 1954.

*Fuchs, E., *Studies of the Historical Jesus*, Naperville, Ill., 1964.

Galot, Jean, *The Heart of Christ*, Westminster, Md., 1955.

Garrigou-Lagrange, R., *Christ the Saviour*, St. Louis, 1950.

Gelin, A. (ed.), *Son and Saviour*, London, 1962.

Gleason, R. W., *Christ and the Christian*, New York, 1960.

Goppelt, L., Thielicke, H., and Müller-Schwefe, Hans-Rudolf, *The Easter Message Today: Three Essays*, New York, 1964.

Graham, A., *Christ of Catholicism*, New York, 1957.

Grillmeier, A., *Christ in Christian Tradition*, New York, 1965.

Guardini, Romano, *The Humanity of Christ*, New York, 1963.

——— *The Lord*, Chicago, 1954.

*Hanks, H. A., *Christ and the Church in the Old Testament*, Grand Rapids, Mich., 1957.

Heinisch, P., *Christ in Prophecy*, Collegeville, 1956.

*Herbert, A. G., *The Christ of Faith and the Jesus of History*, London, 1962.
Héris, C. V., *The Mystery of Christ*, Maryland, 1950.
*Jeremias, Joachim, *The Parables of Christ*, London, 1963.
*Johnson, F. A., *Christ and Catholicism*, New York, 1954.
*Knox, J., *Christ the Lord*, New York, 1958.
——— *Death of Christ*, New York, 1958.
*Komroff, Manuel, *Jesus Through the Centuries*, New York, 1953.
*Laymon, Charles M., *Christ in the New Testament*, New York, 1958.
Leclercq, J., *Christ and the Modern Conscience*, New York, 1961.
*Lowe, M. L., *Christ in All the Scriptures*, New York, 1954.
Lovasik, L. G., *My Beloved Son*, New York, 1963.
*Lövestan, E., *Son and Saviour*, Copenhagen, 1961.
Manson, T. W., *The Servant-Messiah*, New York, 1953.
*Mascall, E. L., *Christ, the Christian and the Church*, London, 1955.
Murray, J. Courtney, *The Problem of God*, New Haven, 1964.
Murray, Robert, *Behold the Lamb of God*, New York, 1963.
*Nash, C. H., *Christ Interpreted*, London, 1954.
*Niebuhr, H. R., *Christ and Culture*, New York, 1951.
*Ogden, S. M., *Christ without Myth*, New York, 1961.
Rahner, Karl, *Theological Investigations, I*, Chap. 5, 149–200, Baltimore, 1961.
*Redding, D. A., *The Miracles of Christ*, Westwood, N. J., 1964.
*Relton, H. M., *Studies in Christology*, London-New York, 1960.
Ricciotti, G., *The Life of Christ*, Milwaukee, 1945.
*Robinson, John, *Jesus and His Coming: The Emergence of a Doctrine*, New York, 1958.
Schillebeeckx, E., *Christ the Sacrament of the Encounter with God*, New York, 1963.
*Sidebottom, E., *The Christ of the Fourth Gospel in the Light of First-Century Thought*, London, 1961.
Sloyan, G. S., *Christ the Lord*, New York, 1962.
Stanley, David M., *Christ's Resurrection in Pauline Soteriology*, Rome, 1961.
Sullivan, F. A., *The Christology of Theodore of Mopsuestia*, Rome, 1956.
*Taylor, Vincent, *The Person of Christ in New Testament Teaching*, New York, 1958.
*Trueblood, E., *The Humor of Christ*, New York-London, 1964.
*Wilder, Amos N., *Eschatology and Ethics in the Teaching of Jesus*, New York, 1950.
The Word: Readings in Theology, New York, 1964.
*Zimmerli, W., and Jeremias, J., *The Servant of God*, Naperville, Ill., 1957.

ARTICLES

Benoit, Pierre, "The Ascension of Christ," *Theology Digest*, 8 (1960), 105–110.
Biser, Eugen, "He Descended into Hell," *Theology Digest*, 8 (1960), 111–114.
Bligh, J., "Jesus in Galilee," *Heythrop Journal*, 5 (1964), 3–26.
Ceroke, C. P., "The Divinity of Christ in the Gospels," *Catholic Biblical Quarterly*, 24 (1962), 125–139.
Congar, Yves, "Real Significance of the Incarnation," *Theology Digest*, 8 (1960), 74–75.

*Cullmann, Oscar, "Functional Christology: A Reply," *Theology Digest*, 10 (1962), 215–219.

Davis, Charles, "The Place of Christ," *The Clergy Review*, 45 (1960), 706–718.

De Letter, P., "The Theology of God's Self-Gift," *Theological Studies*, 24 (1963), 402–422.

Feuillet, André, "Incarnation: Mystery of Salvation," *Theology Digest*, 8 (1960), 76–79.

Fischer, Balthasar, "The Risen Christ and the Liturgy," *Theology Digest*, 8 (1960), 123–126.

Fraine, Jean de, "Adam and Christ as Corporate Personalities," *Theology Digest*, 10 (1962), 99–102.

Gaillard, Jean, "Mystery of Christ's Birth," *Theology Digest*, 10 (1962), 220–221.

Geiselmann, T. R., "Easter Mystery in the Light of Apostolic Preaching," *Theology Digest*, 1 (1953), 151–152.

*Gilmour, S. MacLean, "Jesus Christ," *Dictionary of the Bible*, New York, 1963, 477–496.

*Grant, F. C., "Jesus Christ," *Interpreter's Dictionary of the Bible*, New York, 1962, 869–896.

Grech, Prosper, "Protestant Theories Explaining the Redemption," *Theology Digest*, 5 (1957), 183–188.

Holtz, Ferdinand, "The Soteriological Value of the Resurrection of Christ," *Theology Digest*, 3 (1955), 101–106.

*Howton, J. F., " 'Son of God' in the Fourth Gospel," *New Testament Studies*, 10 (1964), 227–237.

*Johnson, S. E., "Christ," *Interpreter's Dictionary of the Bible*, New York, 1962, 563–571.

Leeming, Bernard, "The Human Knowledge of Christ," *The Irish Theological Quarterly*, 19 (1952), 234–253.

———— "Christ's Physical Appearance," *Theology Digest*, 1 (1953), 57–58.

Lyonnet, Stanislas, "Redemptive Value of the Resurrection," *Theology Digest*, 8 (1960), 89–93.

———— "St. Paul and a Mystical Redemption," *Theology Digest*, 8 (1960), 83–88.

———— "Scriptural Meaning of 'Expiation,' " *Theology Digest*, 10 (1962), 227–232.

Malevez, Léopold, "Functional Christology in the New Testament," *Theology Digest*, 10 (1962), 77–83.

Martto-Salin, "The Mystery of Christ's Suffering," *Theology Digest*, 2 (1954), 48.

Merton, Thomas, "The Name of the Lord," *Worship*, 38 (1964), 142–151.

Miquel, Pierre, "Christ's Ascension and Our Glorification," *Theology Digest*, 9 (1961), 67–73.

Moeller, Charles, "Jesus Christ in the Minds of Moderns," *Lumen Vitae*, 7 (1952), 509–527.

Nicolas, J.-H., "Controversy about the Psychological Unity of the Christ," *Theology Digest*, 2 (1954), 97–98.

O'Donnell, R. E., "The Servant Christology in the New Testament," *Dunwoodie Review*, 4 (1964), 177–195.

O'Shea, K. F., "The Human Activity of the Word," *The Thomist*, 22 (1959), 143–232.

Perego, Angelo, "The Psychological Unity of Christ," *Theology Digest*, 6 (1958), 58–62.

*Rowlingson, D. T., "The Theme of Promise and Fulfillment in Jesus' Thought," *Religious Life*, 33 (1963), 80–89.

Semmelroth, Otto, "Christ on the Cross," *Theology Digest*, 1 (1953), 131–133.

Stanley, D. M., "The Divinity of Christ in Hymns of the New Testament," *Proceedings of the Society of Catholic College Teachers of Sacred Doctrine*, 4 (1958), 12–29.

Stephenson, A. A., "Christ's Presence in the Church," *Theology Digest*, 8 (1960), 115–116.

*Streiker, L. D., "The Christological Hymn in Philippians II," *Lutheran Quarterly*, 16 (1964), 49–58.

Vawter, Bruce, "Resurrection and Redemption," *Theology Digest*, 1 (1953), 153.

Walvoord, J. F., "The Ascension of Christ," *Bibliotheca Sacra*, 121 (1964), 3–12.

Willaert, Benjamin, "Jesus as the 'Suffering Servant,'" *Theology Digest*, 10 (1962), 25–30.

4. CONTEMPORARY MARIOLOGY

by

Thomas J. Shanahan, S.J.

BOOKS

Alastruey, Sanchez G., *The Blessed Virgin Mary*, St. Louis, 1963.

Attwater, D., *Dictionary of Mary*, New York, 1956.

Bernard, R., *The Mystery of Mary*, St. Louis, 1960.

Bouyer, L., *The Seat of Wisdom*, New York, 1962.

Burghardt, W. J., *Testimony of the Patristic Age Concerning Mary's Death*, Westminster, 1957.

Burke, A. (ed.), *Mary, in History, in Faith, and in Devotion*, New York, 1954.

Burke, Thomas J. (ed.), *Mary and Modern Man*, New York, 1954.

———— *Mary and the Popes*, New York, 1954.

Carol, J. B., *Mariology*, Vol. I, Milwaukee, 1955; Vol. II, Milwaukee, 1957; Vol. III, Milwaukee, 1961.

Charmot, F., *Presence of Mary*, South Bend, Ind., 1948.

Congar, Yves M.-J., *Christ, Our Lady and the Church*, Westminster, 1957.

Cranny, T. F., *Our Lady and Reunion*, Garrison, N. Y., 1962.

Daniel-Rops, H., *The Book of Mary*, Garden City, 1963.

Dehau, P. T., *Eve and Mary*, St. Louis, 1958.

Dühr, Joseph, *The Glorious Assumption of the Mother of God*, New York, 1950.

Friethoff, C. X. J. M., *Complete Mariology*, Westminster, 1958.

Galot, Jean, *Mary in the Gospel*, Maryland, 1964.

Garofalo, S., *Mary in the Bible*, Milwaukee, 1961.

Garrigou-Lagrange, R., *Mother of the Savior and Our Interior Life*, St. Louis, 1949.

Graef, H. C., *Mary: A History of Doctrine and Devotion*, New York, 1963.

Guitton, Jean, *The Virgin Mary*, New York, 1952.

Hanke, H. A., *The Validity of the Virgin Birth*, Grand Rapids, Mich., 1963.

Kenney, F. J., *Mary's Spiritual Maternity According to Modern Writers*, Washington, 1957.

Laurentin, R., *Our Lady and the Mass*, New York, 1960.

———— *Queen of Heaven*, New York, 1957.

Le Frois, Bernard J., *The Woman Clothed with the Sun*, Rome, 1954.

Lubac, Henri de, *The Splendor of the Church*, New York, 1956. See chapter entitled "The Church and Our Lady."

McNamara, K. (ed.), *Mother of the Redeemer*, New York, 1960.

Marian Library Studies: published eight times a year, October to May, by the Marian Library of the University of Dayton, Dayton, Ohio, and specializing in mariological literature:

Neubert, E., "Development of Marian Doctrine," no. 77, pp. 1–13.

Flanagan, D., "Mary and the Church," no. 78.

Dillenschneider, C., "Mary, Prototype and Personification of the Church," no. 82.

Laurentin, R., "Mary and the Church," no. 86.

Nicolas, M. J., "Protestants, Catholics and Mary," no. 90.

Cole, W. J., "Mary at the Council and Reunion," nos. 101–102.

Bea, Cardinal, "Mary and the Protestants," no. 83.

Bouyer, L., "Devotion to Mary in the Church," no. 63.

Laurentin, R., "The Blessed Virgin at the Council," no. 109.

Marian Studies: the annual of the Mariological Society of America, containing the proceedings of the annual study conventions, available through the Circulation Dept., Montfort Fathers, Bay Shore, L. I., N. Y.:

Vol. 9 (1958) on Mary and the Church.

Vol. 11 (1960) on Our Lady in the New Testament.

Vol. 12 (1961) on Our Lady and the Old Testament.

Vol. 15 (1964) on Mary and Ecumenical Problems.

Vol. 16 (1965) on Our Lady and Salvation History.

*Mascall, E. L., and Box, H. S. (eds.), *The Blessed Virgin Mary: Essays by Anglican Writers*, London, 1963.

Mathews, S. G. (ed.), *Queen of the Universe*, St. Meinrad, 1957.

Most, W., *Mary in Our Life*, New York, 1954.

Neubert, E. N., *Mary in Doctrine*, Milwaukee, 1954.

Newman, John Henry (Cardinal), *The New Eve*, Westminster (England), 1952.

O'Carroll, M., *Mediatress of All Graces*, Westminster, 1958.

O'Connor, E. D. (ed.), *The Dogma of the Immaculate Conception*, Notre Dame, 1958.

———— (ed.), *Mystery of the Woman*, South Bend, 1956.

Palmer, P. F. (ed.), *Mary in the Documents of the Church*, Westminster, 1953.

Papal Teachings: Our Lady, Boston, 1961.

Papal Documents on Mary, compiled by William J. Doheny and Joseph P. Kelly, Milwaukee, 1954.

Patsch, J., *Our Lady in the Gospels,* London, 1958.
Philipon, M. M., *Mother of God,* Westminster, 1954.
Philippe, P., *Blessed Virgin and the Priesthood,* Chicago, 1955.
Rahner, H., *Our Lady and the Church,* New York, 1961.
Rahner, K., *Mary, Mother of the Lord,* New York, 1963.
Roschini, G. M., *Divine Masterpiece,* Cork, Ireland, 1955.
Schillebeeckx, Edward, *Mary, Mother of the Redemption,* New York, 1964.
Scheeben, M. J., *Mariology,* St. Louis, Vol. I, 1946; Vol. II, 1947.
Semmelroth, O., *Mary, Archetype of the Church,* New York, 1963.
Smith, G., *Mary's Part in Our Redemption* (2 ed.), New York, 1954.
Suarez, Federico, *Our Lady the Virgin,* Chicago, 1959.
Suenens, L. J., *Mary the Mother of God,* London, 1959.
—— *Theology of the Apostolate,* Techny, Ill., 1962.
*Thurian, M., *Mary, Mother of All Christians,* New York, 1964.
Voillaume, René, *Abodes of God: The Church — Our Lady,* London, 1959.
von Campenhausen, Hans J., *The Virgin Birth in the Theology of the Ancient Church,* Naperville, Ill., 1964.
Weiger, J., *Mary, Mother of the Faith,* London, 1960.

ARTICLES

Ahern, Barnabas, "Mary, Prototype of the Church," *New Horizons,* Notre Dame, 1963.
Burghardt, W. J., "Mary and Reunion," *Catholic Mind,* 60 (1962), 13–18.
—— "Mary, Obstacle to Reunion?" *Ecumenism and Vatican II,* Milwaukee, 1964.
Butler, C., "Marian Doctrine Seen as Uniting, Not Dividing Christians," *Unitas,* 15 (1963), 305–306.
Carol, J. B., "Dangerous Marian Year Reefs," *Homiletic and Pastoral Review,* 55 (1955), 698–702.
Carroll, E. A., "A Recommended Reading List in Mariology," *Marian Era,* 6 (1960), 94–99.
—— "English Marian Literature," *Marian Era,* 3 (1962), 123–128.
—— "Recommended Reading in Mariology 1962–1964," *Marian Era,* 5 (1964), 123–128.
—— "Ten Years of Mariology," *Marian Era,* 1 (1960), 74–85.
Davis, C., "The Starting Point of Mariology," *Catholic World,* 197 (1963), 15–20.
Davis, H. F., "Newman and Our Lady," *Clergy Review,* 34 (December, 1950), 369–379.
Diekmann, Godfrey, "Mary, Model of Our Worship," from *Come, Let Us Worship,* Baltimore, 1961.
Doyle, S. C., "The Fundamental Principle of Mariology," *Interest,* 1 (1961), 21–25.
Durrwell, F. X., "Mary Amongst Us," from *In the Redeeming Christ,* New York, 1963.
Ernst, C., "Starting Point of Marian Doctrine," *Blackfriars,* 40 (1959), 450–466.
Freithoff, C., "Dogmatic Definition of the Assumption," *Thomist,* 14 (January, 1951), 41–58.
Furrow, "Ecumenism and Mariology: The Contribution of Catholics," 14 (1963), 212–224; "Ecumenism and Mariology: The Contribution of Protestants," 14 (1963), 349–360.

Geenen, G., "Mother of the Mystical Body," *Cross and Crown*, 2 (1950), 385–402.

Hamer, J., "Mary and the Protestants," *Worship*, 37 (1963), 580–589.

―――― "Mariology and Protestant Theology," *Theology Digest*, 2 (1954), 67–70.

Hardon, J. A., "Mariology of Pope Pius XII," *Review for Religious*, 18 (1959), 205–213.

Heath, T. R., "Our Lady in Biblical and Speculative Theology," *Thomist Reader*, (1958), 106–120.

Jones, Alexander, "The Word Made Flesh" and "The Word in the Church," from *God's Living Word*, New York, 1961.

Le Frois, B. J., "Function of Mariology," *American Ecclesiastical Review*, 136 (1957), 242–245.

Mahoney, P., "Unitive Principle of Marian Theology," *Thomist*, 18 (1955), 443–479.

Mersch, Emile, "Mary, Mother of Jesus," from *The Theology of the Mystical Body*, St. Louis, 1951.

Moeller, C., "Doctrinal Aspects of Mariology," *Lumen Vitae*, 8 (1953), 226–251.

―――― "Virgin Mary in Contemporary Thought," *Lumen Vitae*, 8 (1953), 184–212.

Montague, G., "Concept of Mary and the Church in the Fathers," *American Ecclesiastical Review*, 123 (November, 1950), 331–337.

Most, W. G., "New Eve: Human Race Has Two Mothers," *Marianist*, 46 (1955), 13–14.

Müller, A., "Basic Principles of Mariology," *Theology Digest*, 1 (1953), 139–144.

Murphy, J. L., "The Development of Mariology," *American Ecclesiastical Review*, 138 (1958), 89–103 and 158–172.

Murray, C., "The Basic Principle of Mariology: K. Rahner and Duns Scotus," *Australasian Catholic Record*, 39 (1962), 68–74.

Norris, Frank, "The Fulness of Time," from *God's Own People*, Baltimore, 1962.

O'Connell, F. J., "Toward a Systematic Treatment of Mariology," *Marian Studies*, 1 (1950), 56–66.

O'Connor, E., "Theology of Mary and the Critical Spirit," *Marian Studies*, 15 (1964), 19–26.

O'Donoghue, N. D., "Mary and the Church," from *What Is the Church?* (ed. D. Flanagan), Glen Rock, N. J., 1962.

O'Meara, T., "Marian Theology and the Contemporary Problem of Myth," *Marian Studies*, 15 (1964), 127–156.

Palmer, P. F., "Mary in Protestant Theology and Worship," *Theological Studies*, 15 (1954), 519–540.

Philippe, T., "Our Lady and Our Times," *American Ecclesiastical Review*, 126 (February, 1952), 97–108.

Pius XII, "Inter complures" (radio message to the participants of the International Mariological Congress), *American Ecclesiastical Review*, 132 (1955), 64–67. In *The Pope Speaks* as "Mariology and the Standards Which Govern Its Study," 1 (1954), 343–346; available as a reprint from *The Pope Speaks*, Washington, D. C.

Pocock, Archbishop Philip F., "Mary in the Church," *The Ecumenist*, 2 (1964), 72–73.

Quinn, R., "Ecumenical Mariology," *At-One-Ment*, 5 (1963), 84–90.

Rahner, K., "The Fundamental Principle of Mariology," *Theology Digest*, 4 (1956), 72–78.

———— "The Immaculate Conception" and "The Interpretation of the Dogma of the Assumption," *Theological Investigations*, Vol. 1, Baltimore, 1961.

Sartory, Thomas, "Does Christ's Mother Divide Us?" *Theology Digest*, 12 (1964), 14–18.

St. John, H., "Authority of Doctrinal Development," *Blackfriars*, 36 (1955), 483–493.

Van Ackeren, G., "Mary's Place in Theology," *Perspectives*, 6 (1961), 16–21.

Vaughan, A., "The Development of Marian Doctrine as an Ecumenical Problem," *Marian Studies*, 15 (1964), 27–47.

Vincentine, Sr. M., "Controversial Issue of Mary's Merit," *Thomist*, 19 (1956), 415–445.

5. THE INTEGRAL IDEA OF THE CHURCH

by

Louis A. McKeown, S.J.

BOOKS

Adam, Karl, *One and Holy*, tr. by Cecily Hastings, New York, 1951.

———— *The Spirit of Catholicism*, tr. by Justin McCann, O.S.B., New York 1954.

*Bender, Harold Stauffer, *These Are My People*, Scottdale, Pa., 1962.

Berrigan, Daniel, *The Bride: Essays in the Church*, New York, 1959.

Bouyer, L., *The Word, Church, and Sacrament in Protestantism and Catholicism*, Tournai, Belgium, 1961.

Bovis, André de, *The Church: Christ's Mystery and Sacrament*, London, 1961.

———— *What Is the Church?* tr. by R. F. Trevett, New York, 1961.

*Brunner, Heinrich Emil, *The Misunderstanding of the Church*, tr. by Harold Knight, London, 1952.

Bullough, Sebastian, *The Church in the New Testament*, London, 1958.

Burghardt, W. J., and Lynch, W. F. (eds.), *The Idea of Catholicism*, New York, 1960.

Burns, Patrick J. (ed.), *Mission and Witness; the Life of the Church*, Westminster, Md., 1964.

Butler, Basil Christopher, *The Church and the Bible*, Baltimore, 1961.

———— *The Idea of the Church*, Baltimore, 1962.

Cerfaux, Lucien, *The Church in the Theology of St. Paul*, tr. by Geoffrey Webb and Adrian Walker, New York, 1959.

Colomer, Luis, *The Catholic Church, the Mystical Body of Christ*, tr. by Palmer L. Rockey, Paterson, N. J., 1952.

Congar, Yves M.-J., *Christ, Our Lady and the Church*, tr. by Henry St. John, Westminster, Md., 1957.
———— *Mystery of the Church*, tr. by A. V. Littledale, Baltimore, 1960.
———— *The Mystery of the Temple*, Westminster, Md., 1962.
*Cullmann, Oscar, *The Early Church*, ed. by A. J. B. Higgins, London, 1956.
———— *Peter: Disciple, Apostle, Martyr*, tr. by Floyd V. Filson, Philadelphia, 1953.
Fernan, J. J., *Christ in His Members*, Syracuse, 1955.
Finlay, Peter, *The Church of the Living God*, revised by Kevin Smyth, Dublin, 1957.
*Flew, Robert Newton, *Jesus and His Church*, London, 1951.
———— (ed.), *The Nature of the Church* (World Conference on Faith and Order), London, 1952.
*Gable, L. J., *Church and World Encounter*, Philadelphia, 1964.
Guitton, Jean, *The Church and Gospel*, tr. by Emma Cranfurd, Chicago, 1961.
Hamell, P. J., *Membership of the Mystical Body*, Dublin, 1958.
Hanssler, Bernhard, *The Church and God's People*, tr. by Gregory Roettger, Baltimore, 1964.
Hasseveldt, Roger, *The Church, a Divine Mystery*, tr. by William Storey, Chicago, 1954.
Hastings, Adrian, *One and Apostolic*, New York, 1964.
Journet, Charles, *The Church of the Word Incarnate* (2 vols.), tr. by A. H. C. Downes, New York, 1955.
Killgallon, J. J., *You Are the Church*, Westminster, 1961.
Knox, Ronald A., *Bridegroom and Bride*, New York, 1957.
Lubac, Henri de, *Catholicism*, tr. by Lancelot C. Sheppard, New York, 1950.
———— *The Splendour of the Church*, tr. by Michael Mason, London, 1956.
Mackey, J. P., *The Modern Theology of Tradition*, New York, 1963.
*Mascall, Eric Lionel, *Christ, the Christian, and the Church*, London, 1955.
———— *Corpus Christi*, London, 1953.
Mersch, Emile, *The Theology of the Mystical Body*, tr. by Cyril Vollert, St. Louis, 1951.
*Minear, P. S., *Images of the Church in the New Testament*, Philadelphia, 1960.
———— *Jesus and His People*, London, 1956.
Moran, Gabriel, *Scripture and Tradition*, New York, 1963.
Mura, Ernest, *The Nature of the Mystical Body*, tr. by M. Angeline Bouchard, St. Louis, 1963.
Murphy, John L., *The Living Christ*, Milwaukee, 1952.
Norris, F. B., *God's Own People*, Baltimore, 1962.
Novak, Michael, *The Open Church*, New York, 1964.
*Nygren, Andrés T. S., *Christ and the Church*, Philadelphia, 1956.
———— et al. (eds.), *This Is the Church*, tr. by Carl Rasmussen, Philadelphia, 1952.
*Otto, Rudolf, *The Kingdom of God and the Son of Man*, tr. by F. Filson and B. Lee-Woolf, Boston, 1957.
*Pelikan, Jaroslav, *The Riddle of Roman Catholicism*, New York, 1959.
Pius XII, *Mystici Corporis*, ed. by Joseph J. Bluett, New York, 1943.
Rahner, Hugo, *et al.*, *The Church*, New York, 1963.
Rahner, Karl, *The Church and the Sacraments*, New York, 1963.

—— *Theological Investigations,* Vol. II: *Man in the Church,* Baltimore, 1963.

—— *The Dynamic Element in the Church,* New York, 1964.

Rea, James Edward, *The Common Priesthood of the Members of the Mystical Body,* Washington, D. C., 1947.

Ripley, F. J., *One Christ, One Church,* Westminster, Md., 1960.

*Robinson, John A. T., *Essays on Being the Church in the World,* London, 1960.

St. Cyprian, *On the Unity of the Catholic Church,* tr. by O. R. Vassal-Phillips, St. Louis, 1924.

Schillebeeckx, Edouard Henricus, *Christ the Sacrament of the Encounter with God,* New York, 1963.

Schlitzer, Albert L., "The Church — Sacrament of Christ's Presence," in *Our Life in Christ: The Realization of Redemptive Incarnation,* U. of Notre Dame Press, 1962, I:10–26.

Schnackenburg, Rudolf, *God's Rule and Kingdom,* New York, 1963.

*Schweizer, E., *The Church as the Body of Christ,* Richmond, Va., 1964.

*Seitz, O. J. F., *One Body and One Spirit,* Greenwich, Conn., 1960.

*Skydsgaard, K. E., *et al., The Church as the Body of Christ,* Notre Dame, Ind., 1963.

Smedt, Emile-Joseph de, *The Priesthood of the Faithful,* tr. by Joseph F. M. Marique, New York, 1962.

Suhard, E. C., *Church Today — Growth or Decline?* Montreal, 1950.

Tromp, S., *Corpus Christi, Quod Est Ecclesia* (2 ed.), New York, 1960.

*Visser't Hooft, W. A., *Renewal of the Church,* Philadelphia, 1957.

Vonier, Anscar, *The Church and the Sacraments,* Westminster, Md., 1952.

ARTICLES

Ahern, Barnabas, "The Concept of the Church in Biblical Thought," *Proceedings of the Society of Catholic College Teachers of Sacred Doctrine,* 7 (1961), 32–61.

*Barth, K., "The Church between East and West," *Cross Currents,* 1 (1951), 64–77.

*Barth, M., "A Chapter on the Church, the Body of Christ," *Interpretation,* 12 (1958), 131–156.

Baum, G., "The Community of Believers," *Perspectives,* 8 (1963), 12–14.

Beck, Bishop G. A., "The Church on Earth: Her Purpose and Function," *The Tablet,* 206 (1955), 322–:323.

Becker, A., "God's Great Design: the Church," *Lumen Vitae,* 8 (1953), 448–466.

Berrigan, Daniel, "Reflections on the Church," *Today,* 18:16–20 (1963), 14 ff.

Beumer, J., "Identity of the Mystical Body and the Catholic Church," *Theology Digest,* 4 (1955), 55–58.

Bruns, J. E., "Our Changing Image of the Church," *Catholic World,* 192 (1961), 239–244.

*Bultmann, R., "The Transformation of the Idea of the Church in the History of Early Christianity," *Andover-Newton Quarterly,* 1 (1960), 6–16.

Burke, Eugene M., "What Is the Catholic Church?" *National Catholic Educational Association Bulletin,* 59 (1962), 363–370.

Butler, B. C., "St. Cyprian and the Church," *Downside Review,* 71 (1952–1953), 1–13, 119–134, 258–272.

Congar, Yves M.-J., "Holy Church," *Perspectives,* 7 (1962), 104–106.
──── "Reality of the Church," *Perspectives,* 5 (1960), 17–20.
Darby, J. H., "Psalm XLIV (XLV) The King and His Bride," *Irish Ecclesiastical Record,* 91 (1959), 248–255.
Davis, C., "The Mass as the Assembly of Christians," *Furrow,* 12 (1961), 549–563.
De Letter, P., "The Soul of the Mystical Body," *Sciences Ecclésiastiques,* 14 (1962), 213–234.
Dulles, Avery R. "Protestant Concept of the Church," *American Ecclesiastical Review,* 132 (1955), 330–335.
Fenton, J. C., "Father Journet's Concept of the Church," *American Ecclesiastical Review,* 127 (1952), 370–380.
Feuillet, A., "The Messia Born of the People of God," *Theology Digest,* 11 (1963), 10–11.
Fransen, Peter, "The Church and the Trinity," *Thought,* 38 (1963), 68–88.
Guillet, Jacques, "From Synagogue to Early Christian Assembly," *Life of the Spirit,* 12 (1957–1958), 22–29, 64–72.
Hambye, E. R., "Nature of the Church according to the Teaching of the Greek Dissidents," *Clergy Review,* 42 (1957), 140–151.
Holland, T., "The Church in the New Testament," *Furrow,* 9 (1958), 102–110.
*Horton, W. M., "The New Testament Doctrine of the Church," *Encounter,* 17 (1956), 99–132.
Howell, C., "The Church — A Community of Worship," *Furrow,* 9 (1958), 576–583.
──── "Life Together: the Mystical Body of Christ," *Orate Fratres,* 25 (1951), 104–112.
*Hurley, M., "The Nature of the Church," *Doctrine and Life,* 13 (1963), 15–25.
"Karl Rahner on the Nature of the Church," *The Tablet,* 217 (Oct. 12, 1963), 1102–1103.
Kearns, Conleth, "The Church, the Body of Christ according to St. Paul," *Irish Ecclesiastical Record,* 90–91 (1958–1959), 1–11, 145–157, 1–15, 313–327.
King, J., "Towards an Adequate Concept of the Church," *The Thomist,* 27 (1963), 11–29.
*Knox, J., "The Church Is Christ's Body," *Religion in Life,* 27 (1958), 515–526.
Leclercq, J., "The Catholic Church: A Mystery of Fellowship," *Worship,* 35 (1961), 470–485.
Lubac, Henri de, "The Church in Reality," *Social Order,* 3 (1953), 161–173.
MacRae, George W., "Building the House of the Lord," *American Ecclesiastical Review,* 140 (1959), 361–376.
McCabe, Herbert, "What Is the Church? The Eucharistic Community," *Life of the Spirit,* 17 (1962), 3–11.
──── "What Is the Church? The New Creation," *Life of the Spirit,* 16 (1961), 223–236.
──── "What Is the Church? The People of God," *Life of the Spirit,* 15 (1961), 529–540.
McEwan, H., "Monseigneur Journet's Study of the Church," *Unitas,* 8 (1956), 71–78.

*Middleton, N., "The Community of Christ," *Life of the Spirit*, 16 (1962), 359–370.

——— "The Mass and the Community of God," *Life of the Spirit*, 17 (1963), 483–489.

Mooney, Christopher F., "Paul's Vision of the Church in *Ephesians*," *Scripture*, 15 (1963), 33–43.

Murphy, John L., " 'Ekklesia' and the Septuagint," *American Ecclesiastical Review*, 6 (1958), 381–390.

——— "Use of 'Ekklesia' in the New Testament," *American Ecclesiastical Review*, 140 (1959), 250–259, 325–336.

Murray, C., "Body and Soul of the Church," *Sursum Corda*, 3 (1957), 405–411.

——— "Chosen People of God," *Sursum Corda*, 3 (1957), 346–351.

Noronha, S., "Nature of the Church according to the Teaching of the Greek Orthodox," *Eastern Churches Quarterly*, 12 (1957), 51–61.

O'Neill, C., "The Church: Mother of Christians," *Doctrine and Life*, 11 (1961), 13–23.

Palmer, Paul F., "The Sacramental Principle," in *Sacraments and Worship; Sources of Christian Theology*, Vol. I, Westminster, Md., 1955, I, 72–77.

——— "Church of Sinners," *Cross Currents*, 1 (1951), 64–74.

——— "Personal and Sacramental Sanctity," *Theology Digest*, 3 (1955), 93–98.

Riga, P., "Christ's Members and God's Holy People," *The Way*, 20 (1964), 14–20.

Roberts, R. P., "St. Augustine and the Church," *American Ecclesiastical Review*, 132 (1955), 373–377.

Ryan, W., "The Church as the Servant of God in Acts," *Scripture*, 15 (1963), 110–115.

Semmelroth, Otto, "Towards a Unified Concept of the Church," *Yearbook of Liturgical Studies*, 2 (1961), 85–102.

Snoeks, Remi, "The Two Bodies of Christ," digest of "De Relatione Inter Corpus Christi Eucharisticum et Corpus Christi Mysticum," *Theology Digest*, 6 (1958), 90.

Spiazzi, R., "Faithful of Christ," *Cross and Crown*, 6 (1954), 98–110.

Spicq, C., "The Pastoral Church in the New Testament," *The Thomist*, 27 (1963), 1–10.

Stanley, D. M., "Kingdom to Church: the Structural Development of Apostolic Christianity in the New Testament," *Theological Studies*, 16 (1955), 1–29.

——— "Reflections on the Church in the New Testament," *Catholic Biblical Quarterly*, 25 (1963), 387–400.

Stephenson, A. A., "Yesterday and Today: Christ's Presence in the Church," *Month*, 19 (1958), 23–32.

Stibbs, W. J., "Living in the Mystical Body of Christ," *Clergy Review*, 47 (1962), 16–24.

Suhard, Cardinal, "Immortal Youthfulness of the Church," *Spiritual Life*, 3 (1957), 189.

Tegel, A., "The Church: House of God's People," *Worship*, 35 (1961), 494–501.

*Torrance, T. F., "What Is the Church?" *Ecumenical Review*, 11 (1958), 6–21.

Van Roo, William, "Reflections on Karl Rahner's *Kirche und Sakramente,*"
    Gregorianum, 44 (1963), 465–500.
Vodopivec, John, "The Church — the Continuation of Christ," *Euntes Docete,*
    7 (1954), 312–325.
Vollert, Cyril, "The Church and the Sacraments," *Proceedings of Society of
    Catholic Teachers of Sacred Doctrine,* 8 (1962), 38–58.
Weigel, Gustave, "The Inwardness of the Living Body of Christ," *Catholic
    World,* 193 (1961), 352–359.
———— "Nature of the Church to Be Clarified," *Catholic Messenger,* 81
    (1963), 9.

6. THE CHURCH AND THE CHURCHES

by

Thomas A. Duggan, S.J.

BOOKS

Adam, Karl, *One and Holy,* New York, 1951.
Algermissen, Konrad, *Christian Denominations,* St. Louis, 1953.
———— *Christian Sects,* tr. by J. R. Foster, New York, 1962.
*Asmussen, Hans, *The Unfinished Reformation,* tr. by Robert J. Olsen,
    Montreal, 1961.
At-One-Ment: Studies in Christian Unity, Vol. IV, Washington, Atonement
    Seminary, 1961, VII–152, p. Doll. 1.
*Aulén, Gustaf E. H., *Reformation and Catholicity,* tr. by Eric Wahlstrom,
    Philadelphia, 1961.
*Bainton, R. H., *Christian Unity and Religion in New England,* Boston, 1964.
Baum, Gregory, *Progress and Perspectives: The Catholic Quest for Christian
    Unity,* New York, 1962.
———— *The Quest for Christian Unity,* London, 1963.
———— *That They May Be One,* Westminster, Md., 1958.
———— *The Jews and the Gospel,* Westminster, Md., 1961.
Bea, Augustin Cardinal, *The Unity of Christians,* ed. by Bernard Leeming,
    New York, 1963.
*Beaver, R. Pierce, *Ecumenical Beginnings in Protestant World Mission,* New
    York, 1962.
*Bell, G. K. A. (ed.), *Documents on Christian Unity,* Fair Lawn, N. J., 1958.
*Bevan, R. J. W. (ed.), *The Churches and Christian Unity,* Fair Lawn, N. J.,
    1963.
*Blakemore, W. B. (ed.), *The Challenge of Christian Unity,* St. Louis, 1963.
Bosc, J., Guitton, J., and Daniélou, J., *The Catholic-Protestant Dialogue,* tr.
    by R. J. Olsen, Baltimore, 1961.
Bouyer, Louis, *The Spirit and Forms of Protestantism,* tr. by A. V. Littledale,
    Westminster, Md., 1956.
———— *The Word, Church and Sacraments in Protestantism and Catholicism,*
    tr. by A. V. Littledale, New York, 1961.
Boyer, Charles, *Christian Unity,* tr. by Jill Dean, New York, 1962.
———— *One Shepherd; the Problem of Christian Reunion,* tr. by Angeline
    Bouchard, New York, 1952.

*Bridston, K. R., and Wagoner, W. D. (eds.), *Unity in Mid-Career*, New York, 1963.

*Brown, Robert McAfee, *The Spirit of Protestantism*, New York, 1961.

*Brown, R. M., and Scott, D. H. (eds.), *The Challenge to Reunion*, New York, 1963.

*Brown, R. M., and Weigel, G., *An American Dialogue. A Protestant Looks at Catholicism and a Catholic Looks at Protestantism*, New York, 1960.

Callahan, Daniel, and others (eds.), *Christianity Divided*, New York, 1961.

Congar, Yves, *The Mystery of the Church*, tr. by A. V. Littledale, Baltimore, 1960.

———— *The Wide World, My Parish*, tr. by Donald Attwater, Baltimore, 1961.

Cristiani, Leon, *Catholics and Protestants: Separated Brothers*, tr. by Joseph I. Holland and Gilbert V. Tutungi, Westminster, Md., 1960.

*Cullmann, Oscar, *Message to Catholics and Protestants*, Grand Rapids, Mich, 1959.

*Day, P., *Strangers No Longer*, New York, 1962.

*Doeswyck, P. J., *Ecumenicalism and Romanism, Their Origin and Development*, Long Beach, Calif., 1961.

Dumont, C. J., *Approaches to Christian Unity*, tr. by Henry St. John, Baltimore, 1959.

*Ehrenstrom, Nils, and Muelder, Walter G. (eds.), *Institutionalism and Church Unity*, New York, 1963.

*Gardner-Smith, P. (ed.), *The Roads Converge*, New York, 1964.

*Good, J., *The Church of England and the Ecumenical Movement*, Cork, Ireland, 1961.

*Goodall, Norman, *The Ecumenical Movement, What It Is and What It Does* (2 ed.), Fair Lawn, N. J., 1964.

Hanahoe, Edward Francis, *Catholic Ecumenism; the Reunion of Christendom in Contemporary Papal Pronouncements*, Washington, 1953.

Hardon, John, *Christianity in Conflict*, Westminster, Md., 1959.

Hastings, A., *One and Apostolic*, New York, 1964.

Heenan, J. C. (ed.), *Christian Unity: a Catholic View*, London, 1962.

Jaeger, L., *The Ecumenical Council, the Churches and Christendom*, New York, 1961.

*Käsemann, E., *Essays on New Testament Themes*, Naperville, Ill., 1964.

Knox, R. A., *Enthusiasm*, New York, 1950.

Küng, H., *The Council, Reform and Reunion*, New York, 1962.

*Lackmann, M., *The Augsburg Confession and Catholic Unity*, New York, 1963.

*Latourette, *Christianity in a Revolutionary Age: History of Christianity in the Nineteenth and Twentieth Centuries. V. 4. The Twentieth Century in Europe: The Roman Catholic, Protestant, and Eastern Churches*, New York, 1961.

*Lawrence, J., *The Hard Facts of Unity*, London, 1961.

Leeming, Bernard, *The Churches and the Church*, Westminster, Md., 1960.

*Lewis, Arthur J., *Zinzendorf the Ecumenical Pioneer*, Philadelphia, 1962.

*Lewis, G. F., *Toward Anglican-Roman Unity*, Toronto, 1962.

*McDonagh, E., *Roman Catholics and Unity*, New York, 1962.

McNamara, K. (ed.), *Christian Unity*, Dublin, 1962.

*Mascall, Eric Lionel, *Corpus Christi; Essays on the Church and the Eucharist*, New York, 1953.

————— *Recovery of Unity,* Toronto, 1958.

*Maximos IV, patriarch of Antioch (ed.), *The Eastern Churches and Catholic Unity,* New York, 1963.

*Miller, S. H., and Wright, G. E. (eds.), *Ecumenical Dialogue at Harvard,* Cambridge, Mass., 1964.

*Minear, Paul (ed.), *The Nature of the Unity We Seek,* St. Louis, 1958.

*Mudge, L. S., *One Church: Catholic and Reformed,* Philadelphia, 1963.

*Nelson, Claude D., *The Vatican Council and All Christians,* New York, 1962.

*Nelson, John Robert (ed.), *Christian Unity in North America,* St. Louis, 1958.

————— *One Lord, One Church,* New York, 1958.

————— *Overcoming Christian Divisions,* New York, 1962.

*Newbigin, J. E., *Is Christ Divided?* Grand Rapids, Mich., 1961.

————— *Reunion in the Church,* London, 1960.

*Nichols, J. H., *Evanston: An Interpretation,* New York, 1954.

*Nichols, W., *Ecumenism and Catholicity,* London, 1952.

*North American Conference on Faith and Order, *The Nature of the Unity We Seek,* St. Louis, 1963.

*Nygren, Andrés, *Christ and His Church,* Philadelphia, 1956.

O'Neill, Charles J., *Ecumenism and Vatican II,* Milwaukee, 1964.

*Paton, D. M., *Anglicans and Unity,* New York, 1963.

Pol, Willem Hendrik Van De, *The Christian Dilemma; Catholic Church — Reformation,* tr. by G. Van Hall, New York, 1952.

————— *World Protestantism,* New York, 1964.

*Rouse, R., and Neill, S. C. (eds.), *History of the Ecumenical Movement, 1517–1948,* London, 1954.

St. John, Henry, *Essays in Christian Unity,* Westmister, Md., 1955.

Sartory, T. A., *The Ecumenical Movement and the Unity of the Church,* Westminster, Md., 1963.

*Skydsgaard, K. E., *One in Christ,* tr. by Axel Kildegard, Philadelphia, 1957.

Swidler, L. (ed.), *Dialogue for Reunion,* New York, 1962.

Tavard, George, *Holy Writ or Holy Church,* New York, 1960.

————— *Protestantism,* tr. by Rachel Attwater, New York, 1959.

————— *The Catholic Approach to Protestantism,* New York, 1955.

————— *The Quest for Catholicity,* New York, 1964.

————— *Two Centuries of Ecumenism,* tr. by Royce W. Hughes, Notre Dame, Ind., 1960.

*Thurian, M., *Visible Unity and Tradition,* Baltimore, 1962.

*Tobias, R., *Preaching on Christian Unity,* St. Louis, 1958.

Todd, John M., *Catholicism and the Ecumenical Movement,* New York, 1956.

*Van Dusen, H. P., *One Great Ground of Hope,* Philadelphia, 1961.

————— *World Christianity: Yesterday, Today, and Tomorrow,* New York (no date given).

*Villan, M., *Unity: A History and Some Reflections,* Baltimore, 1963.

*Visser't Hooft, W. A. (ed.), *New Delhi Report,* New York, 1962.

————— *Pressure of Our Common Calling,* Toronto, 1959.

————— *The Renewal of the Church,* Philadelphia, 1956.

Weigel, Gustave, *A Catholic Primer on the Ecumenical Movement,* Westminster, 1957.

————— *Catholic Theology in Dialogue,* New York, 1961.

———— *Faith and Understanding in America,* New York, 1959.

———— *A Survey of Protestant Theology in Our Day,* Westminster, Md., 1954.

Weigel, Gustave, and Brown, R. McAfee, *An American Dialogue,* Garden City, N. Y., 1960.

Whalen, W. J., *Separated Brethren: A Study of Non-Catholic Christian Denominations,* Milwaukee, 1958.

*Willebrands, J. G. M. (and others), *Problems Before Unity,* Baltimore, 1962.

*World Council of Churches, Commission on Faith and Order, *The Old and the New Church,* Minneapolis, 1962.

———— Study Commission on Institutionalism, *Institutionalism and Church Unity,* New York, 1963.

———— *Faith and Order Findings,* Minneapolis, 1963.

ARTICLES

Abbott, W. M., "Cardinal of Unity"; Cardinal Bea at Harvard University's four-day Catholic-Protestant colloquium, *America,* 108 (1963), 484.

Ahern, S., "Where Protestant and Catholic Meet," *Friar,* 21 (1964), 56–62.

*Angell, P., "An Orthodox Bishop Speaks Out; Abp. Iakavos,'" *Lamp,* 62 (1964), 10–11.

*"Anglican in St. Peter's: Hopes for the Reunion of Christians," *Round Table,* 53 (1963), 111–117.

Bea, A., "The Council and Christian Unity," *Cross Currents,* 12 (1962), 255–268.

———— "The Ecumenical Movement in the U. S. A.," interview of Card. Bea by Abp. Hallinan, *Catholic Mind,* 62 (1964), 16–21.

———— "How the University Can Further Christian Unity," excerpt from *Unity of Christians, Catholic World,* 197 (1963), 8–14.

———— "Prejudice and Church Unity," excerpts from an address, *America,* 109 (1963), 444.

———— "Protestant Groups and the Nature of the True Church," *Unitas,* 15 (1963), 48–55.

Bellucci, D., "Unity of the Church and the World Council of Churches," *Unitas,* 14 (1962), 239–251.

*Bobrinskoy, B. A., "Orthodoxy in the Ecumenical Movement," *Ecumenical Review,* 14 (1962), 323–328.

*Borovoi, V., "Russian Observer Says Unity Is Work of the Holy Spirit," *Unitas,* 15 (1963), 306–307.

*Brown, R. M., "Emerging Ecumenical Complex," *Theology Today,* 20 (1964), 528–540.

———— "Monoliths, Existent and Non-existent," *Commonweal,* 77 (1963), 596–597.

Clark, F., "Trends in Ecumenical Ecclesiology," *The Heythrop Journal,* 4 (1963), 25–31, 264–272.

Congar, Y. M., "The Church, the Council, and 'The Others,'" *Cross Currents,* 12 (1962), 241 ff.

———— "Progress of the Ecumenical Dialogue," *Theology Digest,* 11 (1963), 67–71.

Corson, P. "Bridges to Unity," address at St. Joseph's College, Philadelphia, *Catholic Mind,* 62 (1964), 8–15.

Cowley, R., "The Causes of the World Ecumenical Movement," *Thomist*, 27 (1963), 551–569.

*Cullmann, O., "The Early Church and the Ecumenical Problem," *Anglican Theological Review*, 40 (1958), 181–188, 294–300.

Curren, F. X., "One Fold," from *Ecumenism and American Converts*, ed. by E. F. Hanahoe and T. F. Cranny, Graymoor, 1959.

Davis, C., "Past Trends and Present Tensions; Christian Unity, the New Conception of the Church, the Sacraments, Liturgical and Biblical Movements," *Clergy Review*, 48 (1963), 417–436. Reply by C. Ernst, 48 (1963), 590–591.

——— "Return or Reconciliation?" *America*, 109 (1963), 710.

"Ecumenics and Non-Christians; New Secretariat for Non-Christians," Bibliog., *America*, 110 (1964), 753.

*Ehrenstrom, N. "Seminar in Ecumenical Trialogue," Greater Boston Ecumenical Seminar, *Christian Century*, 81 (1964), 579–581.

*Faller, A., "An Evangelical Movement towards the Church of Rome," *Unitas*, 15 (1963), 287–292.

Granfield, P., "Reunion and Realism; Recognizing the Obstacles," *American Ecclesiastical Review*, 148 (1963), 207–208.

Guitton, J., "Interview with Jean Guitton, the Only Catholic Layman at the Council," ed. by J. Pelissier, *Catholic World*, 196 (1963), 279–284.

Hamell, P. J., "The Ecumenical Movement," *Irish Ecclesiastical Review*, 96 (1961), 356–374.

Hardon, J. A., "Plan for Christian Community," *Today*, 18 (1962), 20–23.

Heenan, J., "Christian Unity: the Need to End Confusion and Misunderstanding," *Tablet*, 218 (1964), 109–110.

——— "Our Separated Brethren; Rules for Fostering Christian Unity," *Catholic Mind*, 60 (1962), 62–63.

*Hodgson, L., "Faith and Order's Vision of Unity," *Ecumenical Review*, 12 (1960), 281–288.

*Hoefer, J., "The Word of God: Towards a Catholic-Lutheran Dialogue," from *Christian Unity*, Maynooth, 1962, 74–102.

Jedin, H., "The Council of Trent and Reunion. Historical Notes," *The Heythrop Journal*, 3 (1962), 3–14.

——— "Is the Council of Trent an Obstacle to Reunion?" tr. from *Ephemerides Theologicae Lovanienses*, O–D, 1962, in *Eastern Churches Quarterly*, 15 (1963), 209–224.

Küng, H., "Council, Reform and Reunion," review in *Christian Century*, 80 (1963), 709–710. A. J. Wolf, discussion, 80 (1963), 864–865.

*Lackman, M., "Evangelical Thoughts on the Reunion of Christians," *Unitas*, 15 (1963), 293–298.

Leeming, B., "Ecumenical Dialogue and Conversions," *Catholic World*, 198 (1964), 223–229.

Leger, P. E., "Reformation, Reaction and Christian Unity," *Catholic Messenger*, 80 (1962), 8.

McNamara, K., "Theology of Christian Unity," *Irish Theological Quarterly*, 28 (1961), 255–278.

*Meyendorff, J., "What Holds the Church Together?" *Ecumenical Review*, 12 (1960), 296–301.

*Nelson, J. R., "Theological Education and 'Homo Ecumenicus,'" *Ecumenical Review*, 15 (1963), 164–172.

*Nissiotis, N., "Witness and the Service of Eastern Orthodoxy to the One Undivided Church," *Ecumenical Review,* 14 (1962), 192–202.

O'Hanlon, D. J., "Grass-roots Ecumenism," *Catholic World,* 199 (1964), 8–15.

*"Patriarch Maximos IV and Vatican Council II," interview, ed. by E. Englessis, *Catholic World,* 198 (1964), 372–379.

Pol, W. H. Van De, "Problem of Unity," *Unitas,* 6 (1954), 91–95.

Putz, L. J., "Unfinished Reformation: a Catholic View," *Christian Century,* 81 (1964), 109–112.

*Ramsey, A., "The Archbishop of Canterbury Discusses Eventual Church Unity," *Unitas,* 15 (1963), 307–308.

*Richardson, H. N., reply in *Christian Century,* 81 (1964), 206–207, to "Do We Really Mean This Unity Talk?" *Christian Century,* 81 (1964), 38.

*Romanides, J. S., "Orthodox: Arrival and Dialogue," *Christian Century,* 80 (1963), 399–403.

Rousseau, O., "Dogmatic Integrity and Prayer for Unity," *Cross Currents,* 13 (1963), 77–85.

St. John, H., "After the Council, What?" *Lamp,* 62 (1964), 4–7.

———— "Approach to Unity through Scripture and Tradition," *Clergy Review,* 48 (1963), 75–90.

———— "Ecumenical Studies; Progress of Unity among Protestants," *Blackfriars,* 44 (1963), 196–204.

———— "Unity and Authority," *Blackfriars,* 34 (1953), 435–443.

Sartory, T., "Divided Christians and the Eucharist," *Theology Digest,* 11 (1963), 73–77.

Sherwood, P., "Understanding Rite — a Key to Christian Unity," *Theology Digest,* 7 (1959), 15–20.

*Sittler, J. A., "Called to Unity," *Ecumenical Review,* 14 (1962), 177–187.

Stephenson, A. A., "Ecumenical Question," *Clergy Review,* 46 (1961), 5–9.

Stirnimann, H., "A Collection for Unity: Cullmann's Proposal for Realizing Solidarity," *Blackfriars,* 42 (1961), 19–25.

*Thurian, M., "The Visible Unity of Christians," *Ecumenical Review,* 13 (1961), 313–334.

Todd, J. M., "The Church and the Ecumenical Movement," *Christus Rex,* 8 (1954), 261–264.

*Van Dusen, H. P., "Ecumenical Christianity Tomorrow," *Theology Today,* 18 (1961), 296–308.

*Visser't Hooft, W. A., "Calling of the World Council of Churches," *Ecumenical Review,* 14 (1962), 216–226.

———— "The Super-Church and the Ecumenical Movement," *Ecumenical Review,* 10 (1958), 409–419.

———— "Una Sancta and the Local Church," *Ecumenical Review,* 13 (1960), 2–13.

*Wagoner, W. D., Bridston, K., and Nicholls, W., "The Protestant Ecumenical Dilemma," *Christian Century,* 81 (1964), 329–332.

Ward, B., "Quest for Unity," *Way,* 19 (1963), 7–13.

Weigel, G., "Theological Reflections on Ecumenism," *Theology Digest,* 7 (1959), 312–317.

Wentz, F., "Ecumenism and the Reformation," *Theology Digest,* 11 (1963), 72.

*Wolf, H. H., "Towards an Ecumenical Theology," *Ecumenical Review,*
13 (1961), 215–227.
Wright, John J., "Reflections on the Current Ecumenism," *American Ecclesiastical Review,* 145 (1961), 220–232.

7. THE SACRAMENTS: AN ENCOUNTER WITH GOD

by

John Wambach, S.J.

BOOKS

*Baillie, D. M., *Theology of the Sacraments, and Other Papers,* New York,
1957.
Bouyer, Louis, *Liturgical Piety,* Notre Dame, Ind., 1955.
——— *The Word, Church, and Sacraments in Protestantism and Cathol-
icism,* New York, 1961.
Burns, Patrick J. (ed.), *Mission and Witness: The Life of the Church,*
Westminster, Md., 1964.
Clark, N., *Approach to the Theology of the Sacraments,* Toronto, 1956.
*Cully, K. B., *Sacraments: A Language of Faith,* Philadelphia, 1961.
Daniélou, J., *Bible and the Liturgy,* Notre Dame, Ind., 1956.
*Davies, J. G., *Spirit, the Church and the Sacraments,* New York, 1954.
Davis, Charles, *Liturgy and Doctrine,* New York, 1960.
Didier, J. C., *Death and the Christian,* Englewood Cliffs, N. J., 1961.
*Dillistone, F. W., *Christianity and Symbolism,* Toronto, 1955.
Ellard, G., *Christian Life and Worship* (9 ed.), Milwaukee, 1950.
Garland, P. B., *Definition of Sacraments according to St. Thomas,* Ottawa,
1959.
Goldbrunner, J., *Teaching the Sacraments,* New York, 1961.
Grente, G., *Power of the Sacraments,* New York, 1951.
Hastings, C., *The Sacraments,* New York, 1961.
Howell, C., *Of Sacraments and Sacrifice,* Collegeville, Minn., 1953.
Jungmann, J. A., *The Eucharistic Prayer,* tr. by R. L. Batley, Chicago, 1956.
——— *Public Worship: A Survey,* tr. by C. Howell, Collegeville, Minn.,
1957.
——— *The Sacrifice of the Church: The Meaning of the Mass,* tr. by C.
Howell, Collegeville, Minn., 1956.
Krueger, A. F., *Synthesis of Sacrifice according to Saint Augustine,* Munde-
lein, Ill., 1950.
Leeming, B., *Principles of Sacramental Theology,* London, 1960.
Louvel, F., and Putz, L., *Signs of Life,* Notre Dame, Ind., 1956.
McAuliffe, C. R., *Sacramental Theology,* St. Louis, 1958.
McCarthy, J., *Sacraments,* Westminster, Md., 1959.
Miller, J. H., *Signs of Transformation in Christ,* Englewood Cliffs, N. J.,
1963.
O'Neill, Colman E., *Meeting Christ in the Sacraments,* Staten Island, N. Y.,
1964.
Palmer, P. F. (ed.), *Sacraments and Worship,* Westminster, Md., 1957.
——— (ed.), *Sacraments and Forgiveness,* Westminster, Md., 1960.

—————— (ed.), *Sacraments of Healing and Vocation,* Englewood Cliffs, N. J., 1963.
Phillipon, M. M., *Sacraments in the Christian Life,* Westminster, Md., 1954.
Piault, B., *What Is a Sacrament?* Englewood Cliffs, N. J., 1964.
Rahner, Karl, *The Church and the Sacraments,* New York, 1963.
Roguet, A. M., *Christ Acts through the Sacraments,* Collegeville, Minn., 1953.
Schillebeeckx, E., *Christ the Sacrament of the Encounter with God,* New York, 1963.
Schnackenburg, R., *Baptism in the Thought of St. Paul: a Study in Pauline Theology,* New York, 1964.
Taymans, d'Eypernon, *The Blessed Trinity and the Sacraments,* Westminster, Md., 1961.

ARTICLES

Andrews, P., "Pagan Mysteries and Christian Sacraments," *Studies,* 47 (1958), 54–65.
Bernardin, A., "The Sacraments: Symbols of Life," *Dominicana,* 46 (1961), 5–10.
Bouyer, L., Cunnane, A., McNamara, S., and Grace, K., "A Conversation on the Sacraments," *Furrow,* 14 (1963), 479–489.
Burkhardt, E., "Sacraments as Acts of Christ," *National Catholic Educational Association Bulletin,* 60 (1963), 297–302.
—————— "Teaching the Sacraments in the Setting of Salvation History," *Catholic School Journal,* 63 (1963), 31–34.
Clarkson, J., "The Sacrament of Sacraments; Eucharist as the Center of the Sacramental System and of Christian Life," *Way,* 3 (1963), 115–123.
Cooke, B., "Christ Acts through the Sacraments," with comments by R. Aiken and C. Michael, *North American Liturgical Weekly,* 21 (1960), 14–22.
—————— "Personal Development through Sacramental Life," *Catholic World,* 194 (1961), 157–162.
Davis, C., "Past Trends and Present Tensions: Christian Unity, the New Conception of the Church, the Sacraments, Liturgical and Biblical Movements," *Clergy Review,* 48 (1963), 417–436.
Delcuve, G., "Is Confirmation the Sacrament of the Apostolate? The Theological and Pastoral Meaning of Confirmation," *Lumen Vitae,* 17 (1962), 609 ff.
Diekmann, G., "Two Approaches to Understanding the Sacraments," *North American Liturgical Weekly,* 18 (1957), 12–27.
—————— "Two Approaches to Understanding the Sacraments: Sign and Cause," *Worship,* 31 (1957), 504–520.
—————— "The Theology of Worship," *Theology Digest,* 10 (1962), 131–141.
Egan, A. M., "The Worship of the Church," *Dominicana,* 45 (1960), 29–35.
Fransen, P., "Sacraments, Signs of Faith," *Worship,* 37 (1962), 31–50.
Gerken, J. D., "Dialogue between God and Man," *North American Liturgical Weekly,* 22 (1961), 34–42.
Godin, A., and Sister Marthe, "Magical Mentality and Sacramental Life in Children of 8 to 14 Years," *Lumen Vitae,* 15 (1960), 277–296.
Gunthor, A., "Christian Morality: Life Flowing from the Sacraments," *Sponsa Regis,* 34 (1963), 291–301.

Häring, B., "God in Your Marriage, Your Marriage and the Sacraments,"
    Marriage, 46 (1964), 6–9.
——— "Liturgical Piety and Christian Perfection," *Worship*, 34 (1960),
    523–535.
Kiesling, C., "Faith, Sacraments, and Calvary," *Cross and Crown*, 8 (1956),
    430–451.
——— "Spirituality for All: Channels of Grace," *Cross and Crown*, 8
    (1956), 430–441.
Leeming, B., "Recent Trends in Sacramental Theology," *Irish Theological
    Quarterly*, 23 (1956), 195–207.
McDonough, W. K., "The Sacramental Approach to the Liturgy," *Pastoral
    Life*, 9 (1961), 15–21.
McGowan, F. A., "Liturgy of the Sacraments," *Life of the Spirit*, 10 (1956),
    499–503.
McShane, P., "On the Causality of the Sacraments," *Theological Studies*,
    24 (1963), 423–436.
Norris, F. B., "The Response of Faith in the Sacraments," *North American
    Liturgical Weekly*, 21 (1960), 23–27.
O'Brien, I., "Role of the Sacraments in Relation to the Mysteries of Christ,"
    Irish Theological Quarterly, 27 (1960), 152–160.
O'Connell, M. J., "The Sacraments in Theology Today," *Thought*, 36 (1961),
    40–58.
O'Neill, C., "The Mysteries of Christ and the Sacraments," *Doctrine and
    Life*, 12 (1962), 118–128.
——— "Sacraments: Worship of the Whole Christ," *Irish Ecclesiastical
    Record*, 96 (1961), 193–206.
Rahner, K., "Personal and Sacramental Sanctity," *Theology Digest*, 3 (1955),
    93–98.
Ranwez, P., "The Sacrament of Confirmation, Builder of the Personality for
    Service in the Mystical Body of Christ; a Doctrinal and Pastoral Study,"
    Lumen Vitae, 9 (1954), 17–34.
Rideau, E., "Technique and Eucharist," *Lumen Vitae*, 13 (1958), 655–670.
Schillebeeckx, E. H., "The Sacraments, Encounter with God," *Theology
    Digest*, 8 (1960), 117–121.
Schoonenberg, Piet, "The Sign: Introduction to the Catechesis of the Word
    and of Sacred Signs," *Lumen Vitae*, 14 (1959), 9–18.
Seaver, P., "The Sacraments: A Bridge or Barrier to Reunion?" *Dominicana*,
    48 (1963), 93–107.
Stuhmueller, C., "Teaching the Sacraments from 'Scripture,'" *Perspectives*, 5
    (1960), 17–24.
Sullivan, F. J., "How Well Do I Use the Sacraments?" *Sponsa Regis*, 27
    (1956), 320–323.
Tierney, C. F., "Sacraments — Signs of Glory," *Australasian Catholic Record*,
    33 (1955), 123–127.
Toland, T., "Christian Sacrament: Sign and Experience," *North American
    Liturgical Weekly*, 20 (1959), 247–253.
Twomey, J., "Sacraments in General: What They Mean in Our Lives," *Irish
    Ecclesiastical Record*, 101 (1964), 1–11; 101 (1964), 73–86.
VanCaster, M., "Selfsurrender to God at Mass. Some Psychological Problems
    Set by the Different Aspects of the Doctrine," *Lumen Vitae*, 9 (1954),
    35–45.

Van Roo, W., "Reflections on Karl Rahner's *Kirche und Sakramente,*" *Gregorianum,* 44 (1963), 465–500.

Vollert, C., "The Church and the Sacraments," *Proceedings of Catholic College Teachers of Sacred Doctrine,* 8 (1962), 38–58.

8. ON ESCHATOLOGY

by

Michael J. Garland, S.J.

BOOKS

*Abram, V. P., *The Restoration of All Things,* Amherst, N. H., 1962.

*Altizer, T. J. J., *Oriental Mysticism and Biblical Eschatology,* London, 1961.

Arendzen, J. P., *What Becomes of the Dead,* New York, 1952.

von Balthasar, Hans Ur, *A Theology of History,* New York, 1963.

*Barth, Karl, *The Resurrection of the Dead,* London, 1933.

*Bartsch, H. W. (ed.), *Kerygma and Myth,* New York, 1961.

*Beasley Murray, G. R., *Jesus and the Future,* London, 1954.

Beaucamp, Évode, *The Bible and the Universe,* Westminster, 1963.

Becqué, Maurice, and Becqué, Louis, *Life After Death,* New York, 1960.

*Berdiaev, N. A., *The Beginning and the End,* London, 1961.

———— *Destiny of Man,* New York, 1960.

*Bloch, J., *On the Apocalyptic in Judaism,* Philadelphia, 1952.

Bonsirven, J., *Palestinian Judaism at the Time of Christ,* New York, 1964.

*Braaten, C. E., and Harrisville, R. A., *The Historical Jesus and the Kerygmatic Christ,* New York, 1964.

———— (eds.), *Kerygma and History,* Nashville, Tenn., 1962.

*Bright, J., *The Kingdom of God in Bible and Church,* New York, 1953.

*Brunner, H. E., *The Christian Doctrine of the Church, Faith, and the Consummation,* London, 1962.

———— *Eternal Hope,* Philadelphia, 1954.

*Bultmann, R. K., *Jesus Christ and Mythology,* New York, 1962.

———— *History and Eschatology,* Edinburgh, 1957.

———— *Theology of the New Testament,* Vol. I, 1955.

*Bush, M., *Adventure Called Death,* New York, 1950.

*Cullman, O., *Immortality of the Soul or Resurrection of the Dead?* New York, 1958.

———— *Christ and Time,* Philadelphia, 1962.

Daniélou, J., *The Lord of History,* Chicago, 1958.

D'Arcy, M. C., *The Meaning and Matter of History,* New York, 1959.

*Davies, W. D., and Danbe, D. (eds.), *Background of the New Testament and Its Eschatology,* London, 1956.

*Dodd, C. H., *The Interpretation of the Fourth Gospel,* Cambridge, 1953.

———— *The Parables of the Kingdom,* London, 1935.

———— *The Parables of the Kingdom,* 2 rev. ed., New York, 1961.

Dyer, George J., *Limbo, Unsettled Question,* New York, 1964.

*Erb, P., *Alpha and the Omega,* Scottdale, Pa., 1955.

*Fuller, R. H., *The Mission and Achievement of Jesus,* London, 1954.

———— *The Mission and Achievement of Jesus,* London, 1954.

Garrigou-Lagrange, Reginald, *Life Everlasting,* St. Louis, 1952.

*Glasson, T. Francis, *Greek Influence in Jewish Eschatology,* London, 1961.

———— *His Appearance and His Kingdom,* London, 1953.

———— *Moses in the Fourth Gospel,* Naperville, Ill., 1963.

Gleason, R. W., *The World to Come,* New York, 1958.

*Graham, Neville, *The Advent Hope,* London, 1961.

Guardini, Romano, *The Last Things,* New York, 1954.

*Guy, Harold A., *The New Testament Doctrine of the 'Last Things,'* New York, 1948.

*Hamilton, Neill Q., *The Holy Spirit and Eschatology in Paul,* Edinburgh, 1957.

*Haynes, C. B., *Life, Death, and Immortality,* Nashville, Tenn., 1952.

*Heidel, A., *Gilgamesh Epic and Old Testament Parallels,* Chicago, 1949.

*Hendricksen, W., *Lectures on the Last Things,* Grand Rapids, Mich., 1951

Henry, A. M., *The Triumph of Christ,* Notre Dame, Ind., 1962.

*Hodgson, Leonard, *The Bible and the Training of the Clergy,* London, 1963.

*Jaspers, K., and Bultmann, R. K., *Myth and Christianity,* New York, 1958.

*Jeremias, J., *Jesus' Promise to the Nations,* Naperville, Ill., 1958.

———— *The Parables of Jesus,* London, 1954.

*Kantonen, T. A., *Christian Hope,* Philadelphia, 1954.

*Kümmel, W. G., *Promise and Fulfillment,* Naperville, Ill., 1957.

Ladd, G. E., *The Eschatology of the Didache,* dissertation at Harvard, 1948.

*Lündstrom, G., *The Kingdom of God in the Teaching of Jesus,* Richmond, Va., 1963.

*MacQuarrie, J., *Scope of Demythologizing,* London, 1960.

*Maeterlinck, M., *Great Beyond,* London, 1951.

Malevez, L., *Christian Message and Myth,* Westminster, Md., 1960.

*Martin, J. P., *The Last Judgement in Protestant Theology from Orthodoxy to Ritschl,* Grand Rapids, Mich., 1963.

*Miegge, G., *Gospel and Myth in the Thought of Rudolf Bultmann,* London, 1960.

*Minear, P. S., *Christian Hope and the Second Coming,* Philadelphia, 1954.

*Mowinckel, S., *He That Cometh,* Oxford, 1956.

*Norman, Perrin, *The Kingdom of God in the Teaching of Jesus,* 1963.

O'Connell, John P., *The Eschatology of St. Jerome,* Mundelein, Ill., 1948.

*Ogden, S. M., *Christ without Myth,* New York, 1961.

*Otto, Rudolf, *The Kingdom of God and the Son of Man,* Boston, 1957.

*Pelikan, J., *The Shape of Death,* London, 1962.

*Petry, R. C., *Christian Eschatology and Social Thought,* Nashville, 1956.

Piolanti, A. (ed.), *Problems of the Future Life,* London, 1962.

*Quistorp, H., *Calvin's Doctrine of the Last Things,* London, 1955.

Rahner, H., *Greek Myths and Christian Mystery,* London, 1963.

Rahner, Karl, *On the Theology of Death,* New York, 1961.

*Robinson, J. A. T., *Jesus and His Coming: The Emergence of a Doctrine,* London, 1957.

*Robinson, J. M., *A New Quest of the Historical Jesus,* 1959.

*Rust, E. C., *Salvation History,* Richmond, Va., 1962.

*Rutledge, D., *Cosmic Theology,* London, 1964.

Schnackenburg, R., *God's Rule and His Kingdom,* New York, 1964.

*Schweitzer, Albert, *The Mystery of the Kingdom of God,* New York, 1957.

*Smith, C. R., *Bible Doctrine of the Hereafter,* London, 1958.

*Smith, R. C., *Theory of Eternal Life,* Capetown, South Africa, 1950.
Josef Staudinger, *Life Hereafter,* Westminster, Md., 1964.
*Summers, R., *Life Beyond,* Nashville, Tenn., 1959.
Troisfontaines, Roger, *I Do Not Die,* New York, 1963.
*Vos, G., *Pauline Eschatology* (reprint), Grand Rapids, Mich., 1952.
*Werner, M., *The Formation of Christian Dogma,* New York, 1957.
Wicklow, W. C. J. H. (ed.), *Life after Death,* Westminster, Md., 1959.
*Wilder, A. N., *Eschatology and Ethics in the Teaching of Jesus* (rev. ed.), New York, 1950.
Winklhofer, A., *The Coming of His Kingdom,* New York, 1963.

ARTICLES

Ahern, B. M., "Concept of Union with Christ after Death," *Catholic Theological Society of America Proceedings,* 16 (1961), 3–21.
Allagree, H., "A New Heaven and A New Earth," *Nuntius,* 45 (1963), 211–224.
Biser, E., "He Descended into Hell," *Theology Digest,* 8 (1960), 111–114.
Boissard, E., "Many Are Called, Few Are Chosen," *Theology Digest,* 3 (1955), 46–50.
Brown, R. E., "The Pater Noster as an Eschatological Prayer," *Theological Studies,* 22 (1961), 175–208.
Brunner, August, "Pierre Teilhard de Chardin: A Critique," *Theology Digest,* 8 (1960), 143–147.
*Burrows, M., "Thy Kingdom Come," *Journal of Biblical Literature,* 74 (1955), 1–8.
Cornelis, H., "Et Vitam Aeternam, Amen," *Lumen Vitae,* 9 (1954), 415–424.
*Cullmann, O., "Immortality and Resurrection," *Theology Digest,* 5 (1957), 86–87.
———— "Rudolf Bultmann's Conception of Myth and the Old Testament," *Theology Digest,* 4 (1956), 136–139.
Daniélou, J., "First Thing and the Last," *Month,* 2 (1949), 329–333.
*Davies, G. H., "The Clues of the Kingdom in the Bible," *Interpretation,* 14 (1960), 155–160.
*Davies, J. G., "The Genesis of Belief in an Imminent Parousia," *Journal of Theological Studies,* 14 (1963), 104–107.
Davis, C., "End of the World: The Second Coming," *Worship,* 34 (1960), 128–131.
———— "Resurrection of the Body," *Theology Digest,* 8 (1960), 99–103.
Equiliz, A., "Father Gonzalo Tenorio, O.F.M., and His Providentialist Eschatological Theories on the Spanish Indies," *The Americas,* 16 (1960), 329–356.
Ernst, C., "The Theology of Death," *The Clergy Review,* 44 (1959).
Fransen, P., "The Doctrine of Purgatory," *Eastern Churches Quarterly,* 13 (1959), 99–112; *Theology Digest,* 10 (1962), 38–39.
Garcia-Cordero, M., "Corporal Resurrection in the Book of Job," *Theology Digest,* 2 (1954), 90–93.
Gelin, A., "To See God," *Theology Digest,* 7 (1959), 171–174.
Gleason, R. W., "Hell: An Apology," *Theology Digest,* 7 (1959), 97–98.

—— "Toward a Theology of Death," *Thought,* 32 (1957), 39–68.

Glorieux, P., "Moment of Death," *Theology Digest,* 10 (1962), 94–95.

Graystone, G., "Dead Sea Scrolls and the New Testament," *Irish Theological Quarterly,* 23 (1956), 25–48.

Héris, C.-V., "Theology of Suffrages for the Dead," *Theology Digest,* 5 (1957), 172–175.

*Hunter, A. M., "Interpreting the Parables," *Interpretation,* 14 (1960), Part I, 70–84; Part II, 167–185; Part III, 315–332; Part IV, 440–454.

Kenny, A. J., "Eschatology and the Eucharist," *Clergy Review,* 41 (1956), 514–526.

—— "Until He Comes," *Theology Digest,* 6 (1958), 183–184.

Knox, R. A., "Eschatology: A Guess," *The Month,* 3 (1950), 341–383.

*Ladd, G. E., "The Kingdom of God in the Jewish Apocryphal Literature," *Bibliotheca Sacra,* 109 (1952).

Le Frois, B. J., "Eschatological Interpretation of the Apocalypse," *Catholic Biblical Quarterly,* 13 (1951), 17–20.

Letter, P. de, "The Judgment after Death," *Clergy Monthly,* 27 (1963), 365–374.

Lussier, E., "Universal Conflagration of the Parousia," *Catholic Biblical Quarterly,* 12 (1950), 243–247.

*MacQuarrie, J., "Demonology and Atonement," *Theology Digest,* 6 (1958), 106–108.

Malevez, Léopold, "Method of Teilhard and Methodology," *Theology Digest,* 8 (1960), 137–142.

McCabe, H., "What Is the Church," Pt. VIII: "The Place of Death and Judgment," *Life of the Spirit,* 18 (1964), 308–321.

Melendez, B., *"Teleogenesis:* A New Finalistic Theory of Evolution," *Theology Digest,* 1 (1953), 123–127.

*Obrenstein, Edward W., "Immortality in the New Testament," *Encounter,* 22 (1961), 28–36.

*Otwell, John H., "Immortality in the Old Testament," *Encounter,* 22 (1961), 15–27.

*Pentecost, D., "The Godly Remnant of the Tribulation Period," *Bibliotheca Sacra,* 117 (1960).

Pieper, J., "Indestructibility of the Soul," *Theology Digest,* 10 (1962), 97–98.

Rumble, L., "The Second Coming of Christ," *Homiletic and Pastoral Review,* 61 (1960), 67–69.

Schillebeeckx, E. H., "Death of the Christian," *Life of the Spirit,* 16 (1962).

Schuler, B., "Problem of Hell," *Theology Digest,* 5 (1957), 117–119.

Thompson, R., "Resurrection of the Body and Life Everlasting as Portrayed in the Pauline Epistles," *Australasian Catholic Record,* 40 (1963), 19–34.

Toland, T., "The Risen Body in the Next Life," *North American Liturgical Week,* 23 (1962), 274–283.

Tremel, Y. B., "Man Between Death and Resurrection," *Theology Digest,* 5 (1957), 151–156.

Troisfontaines, R., "Death: A Test for Love, a Condition of Freedom," *Cross Currents,* 7 (1957).

Vollert, C., "Toward Omega: The Vision of Man," *Theology Digest,* 8 (1960), 133–136.

Worden, T., "Christ Jesus Who Died or Rather Who Has Been Raised Up," *Scripture,* 10 (1958).

INDEX OF PERSONAL NAMES

SUBJECT INDEX